Praise for *Mystery Stories: A Jo...* W9-APR-381

Come to the Waters
by Sister Mary Jean Dorcy, O.P.

MYSTERY STORIES

A Journey Through the Rosary

by James L. Carney

Madison, WI

| *Nihil Obstat:* | Reverend John G. Stillmank, S.T.L. |
| | *Censor Librorum* |

Imprimatur:	✠ Most Reverend William H. Bullock, ED.S.
	Bishop of Madison
	January 2, 2000

Cover design by Ian Chalgren

Publisher's Cataloging-in-Publication
(Provided by Quality Books, Inc.)

      Carney, James L.
         Mystery stories : a journey through the rosary
      / by James L. Carney. -- 1st ed.
         p. cm.
         Includes bibliographical references.
         LCCN: 99-64130
         ISBN: 0-9673328-0-X

         1. Bible stories, English--N.T. 2. Mysteries
      of the Rosary--Meditations. 3. Rosary.
      I. Title.

      BS2400.C37 1999   225.9'505
                    QBI99-1268

Crown of Mary Publishing Company
P.O. Box 259237
Madison, WI 53725-9237

Printed and bound in the United States of America

Dedication

This book is dedicated to Our Lady of the Rosary, a name which the Holy Mother of God has used to identify herself,[1] and is offered in reparation for offenses committed against her Immaculate Heart.

---

[1]At Fatima, Portugal, on October 13, 1917.

The Blessed Virgin Mary to the Children of Fatima:[2]

May 13, 1917: "Pray the Rosary every day, in order to obtain peace for the world, and the end of the war."

June 13, 1917: "I wish you to come here on the 13th of next month, to pray the Rosary every day, and to learn to read."

July 13, 1917: "I want you to come here on the 13th of next month, to continue to pray the Rosary every day in honor of Our Lady of the Rosary, in order to obtain peace for the world and the end of the war, because only she can help you."

Lucia: "What I do remember is that Our Lady said it was necessary for such people to pray the Rosary in order to obtain these graces during the year." [Lucia had conveyed to the Blessed Virgin Mary some prayer requests that she had received from other people.]

"When you pray the Rosary, say after each mystery, 'O my Jesus, forgive us, save us from the fire of hell. Lead all souls to heaven, especially those who are most in need.'"

August 13, 1917: "I want you to continue going to the Cova da Iria on the 13th, and to continue praying the Rosary every day. In the last month, I will perform a miracle so that all may believe."

September 13, 1917: "Continue to pray the Rosary in order to obtain the end of the war."

October 13, 1917: "I am the Lady of the Rosary. Continue always to pray the Rosary every day."

December 17, 1927: "I promise to assist at the hour of death, with the graces necessary for salvation, all those who, on the first Saturday of five consecutive months, shall confess, receive Holy Communion, recite five decades of the Rosary, and keep me company for fifteen minutes while meditating on the fifteen mysteries of the Rosary, with the intention of making reparation to me."

---

[2]Sr. Mary Lucia of the Immaculate Heart, *Fatima in Lucia's Own Words*, ed. Fr. Louis Kondor, SVD. (Fatima, Portugal: Postulation Centre, 1976), 160, 161, 162, 166, 168 and 195, respectively.

MYSTERY STORIES
A Journey Through the Rosary

TABLE OF CONTENTS

JOYFUL MYSTERIES

SORROWFUL MYSTERIES

GLORIOUS MYSTERIES

NOTES AND APPENDICES

Illustrations

ACKNOWLEDGMENTS

Many people helped in the writing of this book. I am deeply grateful to them all. Their deep faith in Our Lord Jesus Christ and devotion to the Holy Mother of God were both an inspiration and a challenge. An inspiration because their longing for a closer relationship with God was a constant reminder that this project was worthwhile. A challenge because their goodness demanded a work in which they might find some inspiration and insights.

First and foremost, I thank my wife, Pinkey, whose great heart and deep love for the Blessed Virgin Mary provided the first litmus test for this book.

Numerous people reviewed parts of the manuscript. I am especially grateful to Father Tom Prior, C.M., who read the entire manuscript plus several revisions and offered numerous suggestions and criticisms, all of which greatly improved this work. This book would not exist without his encouragement, patience and knowledge. Any errors or excesses that remain in the book are entirely my own fault and should not be imputed in any way to Father Prior.

Kathy Braga, Marileen Maher and Ty Cullen provided invaluable comments, suggestions, criticisms, and copy editing assistance. They are living proof that the Lord sends help when it is truly needed.

Also contributing encouragement and/or their talents and insights to improve this work were Father James Bruse; Father Paul Duffner, O.P.; Father Charles Hagan; Father Stan Krempa; Father Tom Pontolillo, O.F.M. (Cap.); Father George Pucciarelli; Deanna Andrew; my brother, Dick Carney; Gene Epperly; Mary Flanagan; Johanna Gregory; Christine Haapala; Nancy Hall; Pam Hood; Marie Irmen; Miss Ronnie Lauderdale; Jacquelyn Lindsey; Eileen Needham; Louise Rochette; Elizabeth Spoth; and many others.

Ian Chalgren brought his high professional graphic artistry not only to the cover but to much of the artwork throughout the book. Brian Varrieur and Rita Purtell contributed their exceptional artistic talents in several places.

Thanks, too, to Brother William M. Fackovec, S.M., Librarian at the Marian Library, University of Dayton, who was kind and helpful beyond all my expectations, and to Ann Spinnato and her late husband, Joe, for their generous hospitality during that week of concluding research.

My son, Jay, and my daughter, Jenny, provided very positive and helpful suggestions for improving the manuscript. To both of these special young people, gifts to Pinkey and me from an unimaginably generous God, I say thanks for not only making this work better than it would have been, but for transforming my very life by the love, affection and good humor which the four of us have shared in such great abundance in our family.

Acknowledgments for a book about the rosary must include my mother, whose entire life has been a witness to her strong faith and deep love for Our Lord and His Blessed Mother.

Thanks to the Marian Foundation which generously funded much of the research for this book.

The beautiful scissor-cuttings by internationally-known artist, Dan Paulos, which introduce each mystery story, and the frontispiece by the late Sr. Mary Jean Dorcy, O.P., are used by permission.

The cover features illustrations based on Fontanini Nativity figures © 1999 Roman, Inc. Fontanini® is imported from Italy exclusively by Roman, Inc. Permission granted.

Pictures of Herod's Temple, the Fortress Antonia, Herod's Palace and other scenes of Ancient Jerusalem are drawn from or based upon the Model of the City of Jerusalem at the time of the Second Temple, located on the grounds of the Holyland Hotel in Jerusalem, and are used by permission of the Hotel.

The illustration of pilgrims approaching Jerusalem for the Passover celebration (p. 22) is reproduced from *JESUS AND HIS TIMES*, copyright © 1987 by The Reader's Digest Association, Inc. Used by permission of The Reader's Digest Association, Inc., Pleasantville, NY, www.readersdigest.com. Illustration by Dennis Lyall.

Temple Mount illustration (p. 84) by J.-B. Heron is reprinted with permission from the March-April issue of *The World of the Bible* published by Bayard Press USA (P.O. Box 180, Mystic, CT 06355) © 1999.

The prayer/poem by Caryll Houselander, presented following the fourth glorious mystery, is taken from *The Essential Rosary*, Copyright © 1996 Sophia Institute Press, used by permission.

The prayer, "*Come, Holy Spirit*," presented following the third glorious mystery, is taken from *Handbook of Prayer*, Copyright © 1995, Scepter Publishers, Princeton, NJ, used by permission.

Excerpts from the Blessed Virgin Mary's locutions to Father Stefano Gobbi, quoted in Appendix III, are taken from *To the Priests, Our Lady's Beloved Sons*, 14th ed., Marian Movement of Priests, Copyright © 1993, used by permission.

About This Book

This is a book about truth and historical reality. It concerns Jesus Christ, his family, his followers and his enemies. It is solidly anchored in the revealed truth of the Bible, especially the New Testament. But it adds detail, color, dialogue and a few minor characters to achieve its purpose of helping you to see these events as real human drama involving a direct interaction with God in the unfolding of His plan of salvation for mankind.

The purpose of the book is to facilitate your meditative prayer by reflecting upon the events from Scripture and Church teaching that comprise the 15 mysteries of the Catholic rosary. The *Catechism of the Catholic Church* recognizes the importance of meditative prayer:

> Meditation engages thought, imagination, emotion, and desire. This mobilization of faculties is necessary in order to deepen our convictions of faith, prompt the conversion of our heart, and strengthen our will to follow Christ. Christian prayer tries above all to meditate on the mysteries of Christ, as in *lectio divina* or the rosary. This form of prayerful reflection is of great value.[1]

If you question whether such an historical fiction, or "docudrama," approach to rosary meditations is appropriate, consider this: *all* of the great religious art of the Middle Ages was fictionalized. New Testament scenes were almost always presented in medieval settings, which varied with the artist. The Sistine Chapel presents a picture of creation and the Last Judgment that are Michelangelo's imaginative vision. Zeffirelli's magnificent miniseries, *Jesus of Nazareth*, contains fictional characters, dialogue and interpretations that are not found in Scripture, yet this video program has its own teacher's guide for religious instruction. Charles Tazewell's *The Littlest Angel* is entirely fictional, yet we have no difficulty seeing the great and deeply moving truth of God's love represented in this simple story of a child's innocence and generosity. If you are unable to find spiritual inspiration in these works and the countless others like them, you will not find it in the pages of this book, either. But if the conceptual elements selected by the artist help rather than hinder your ability to see the core truths and to relate to

---

[1]*Catechism of the Catholic Church* (Libreria Editrice Vaticana: St. Paul Books & Media, 1994), §2708.

them more easily, then you should find this book a great help for your own rosary reflections.

When we reflect on our own lives, we don't see them in abstract principles. We see them in the events and experiences of which they are made. We see them as relationships with other people, institutions, our environment, nature, animals, and, of course, spiritual beings. Our emotions provide the color for these relationships and give them their drama and often their value. From these experiences and their consequences, we draw conclusions about our life and its meaning, its successes and failures, its regrets and consolations.

Since this is the way we evaluate our own lives and those of other human beings, it seems to me that the mysteries of the rosary are most effectively considered in the same way.

I am in good company in this approach. His Holiness, Pope Leo XIII (1878-1903), was a Pontiff with such an extraordinary devotion to the rosary that he was called the "Rosary Pope." He issued nine encyclicals between 1883 and 1898 on the benefits and merits of this method of praying. Here is what the Rosary Pope said about the best way to consider the mysteries of the rosary:

> It is not dogmas nor articles of faith that the rosary proposes for our meditation, but rather events to be contemplated with our eyes and to recall to mind, and these events presented in their circumstances of place, time and persons are impressed all the more so on the soul and move it more advantageously.[2]

But how can we do this when we have no contemporary biographies to give us the necessary details, much less the thoughts and feelings of these holy figures? Well, we have holy Scripture, which, on one level, gives us four versions of the life of Christ. These divinely-inspired texts must be the bedrock of our reflections about Jesus and his accomplishments because they are the fundamental means by which God intended us to contemplate the significance of His Son's life. This book attempts to incorporate most of the relevant Scriptural passages. More than this, the reader should consider what is offered here as an invitation to pick up the Bible and read for oneself. There is no better way to find the inspiration and the truths that will unlock the mysteries of our relationship with our Creator.

But the books of the New Testament were not written as biographies. They are very sketchy in that regard. There is very little detail about Joseph and Mary, for example, and the hidden life of the Holy Family is called "hidden" precisely because there is only a single event described (Jesus left behind in Jerusalem at the

---

[2]Pope Leo XIII, Encyclical *Jucunda Semper* (Mary Mediatrix), ¶151, September 8, 1894, reported in *The Holy Rosary, Papal Teachings* (Boston: Daughters of St. Paul, 1980), 109.

age of 12) from the time they return from Egypt until Jesus is ready to begin his public ministry.

We do have, of course, the visions of certain mystics who claimed to have revealed to them by Our Blessed Mother herself many of these details of her life. However, these holy ladies (the Venerable Anne Catherine Emmerich, the Venerable Mother Mary of Jesus of Agreda, St. Bridget of Sweden and St. Elizabeth of Schoenau) often do not agree with one another on the details. Some of the "facts" they include are obviously not true; e.g., Mother Mary of Agreda asserts the radius of the earth to be 1,251 miles, when it is actually nearly 4,000 miles, and Anne Catherine Emmerich has Jesus saying that the world was created just under 4,000 years before he was born. As Raphael Brown, who synthesized these visions in a single text, *The Life of Mary as Seen by the Mystics*, put it:

> We may therefore concede with the learned Father Herbert Thurston, S.J., that "it seems impossible to treat the visions of Anne Catherine [Emmerich]—or, indeed, any other similar visions—as sources which can contribute reliably to our knowledge of past history."[3]

Nonetheless, there are great spiritual insights in these works and some people may prefer their depiction of the life of Mary and Jesus to the way it is presented in this book. The holiness and extraordinary mysticism of these visionaries cannot be denied.[4]

But for me, the portrait of Mary in these mystical visions is so supernatural as to remove her from any apparent connection with human beings as we know them, and, indeed, as they appear in the pages of Scripture. The Church teaches us that Jesus came to earth to be like us in all ways except sin. It was the will of God that His Son be of mankind, so that all mankind could see their hope and their future in him. If Our Lord, his Blessed Mother and Joseph did not experience

---

[3]Raphael Brown, *The Life of Mary as Seen by the Mystics* (Rockford, IL: TAN Books, 1991), 4, quoting Father Thurston in *The Month*, Dec. 1921, 19.

[4]Anne Catherine Emmerich, for example, bore the stigmata of Christ, including the crown of thorns and a cross over her heart, from 1812 until her death in 1824. During this time, she subsisted for long periods almost entirely on water and the Holy Eucharist and repeatedly experienced the Passion of Our Lord as a true "victim soul." *The Life of Jesus Christ and Biblical Revelations. From the Visions of the Venerable Anne Catherine Emmerich. Recorded by Clemens Brentano*, ed. Very Rev. Carl E. Schmöger, C.SS.R. (Rockford, IL: TAN Books, 1979), v. 4, Biographical Note. Her visions led to excavations at Ephesus, now in modern Turkey, that uncovered what is believed to be Mary's home after she left Jerusalem following the early period of the new Church. Ibid., 475-476.

The Venerable Mary of Agreda's body was incorrupt after her death and there are reliable reports that she bilocated more than 500 times from Spain to the southwestern United States between 1620-1631. Joan Carroll Cruz, *Relics* (Huntington, IN: Our Sunday Visitor, 1984), 274-276.

happiness, laughter, tears, excitement, anxiety, joy, fear, sadness, humility, anger and all the other emotions that are common to human beings everywhere, how could we find inspiration in them? But we know from Scripture that they learned. They grew in knowledge.[5] They thought, spoke, understood and acted as other Jews of their economic and social class did in Palestine. Their humanness enables us to draw strength and hope in our own often difficult lives from these stories of people who once were very much like we are today.

There is another reason for preferring a more down-to-earth view of the rosary mysteries. We live in a time when many of the New Testament details are challenged for their historicity and Christ's miracles are dismissed as simply literary devices by the Gospel writers to convey their notion of his importance. If we are to recapture a sense of their literal truth and the awe and excitement that filled his witnesses, we need to place these events in their real historical context. That is the only way to make them come alive for us. This is not the time to tell of trees bending over to offer the Holy Family their fruit, or of garments that magically grow with the body of the Lord.

Although these stories are anchored securely in the narratives of the New Testament and in the disclosures of history and archaeology, I have also included several elements that are entirely imaginative. In some cases, such as the last two glorious mysteries, there is no alternative. These imaginative elements are designed to stimulate reflection upon the personalities and situations involved in the events contemplated in the rosary, to expand the scope of reflection to include peripheral activities, and to provide context for consideration of the theological truths of our faith.

The encounters with Roman soldiers in the fourth and fifth joyful mysteries call to mind the fact that Mary, Joseph and Jesus lived in a country occupied by a foreign military power.

The experiences of Benjamin and Natali in the fourth and fifth glorious mysteries are intended to convey a sense that heaven is joyful and lighthearted and to provide a subplot that might be helpful for children to consider as they reflect on these last two mysteries of the rosary.

Since the purpose of this book is to facilitate personal reflection, the imaginative elements selected are those to which the modern reader can easily relate. Thus, placing Mary as a young girl in a normal home environment for her time and place, rather than portraying her as a resident of the Temple of

---

[5]Luke 2:52 tells us that even Jesus, the Son of God, in his humanity *"progressed steadily in wisdom and age and grace before God and men."* In verse 33 we see Joseph and Mary marvelling at what Simeon says to them when he recognizes the Infant Jesus as the Anointed of the Lord. In verse 50, Mary and Joseph fail to understand that their 12-year old son knows that God is his Father and salvation is his work. Mary treasures the birth events and reflects upon them in her heart (Lk 2:19). All of these passages describe people who learn from their experiences, just as we do.

Jerusalem, or an orphan, or living in other, possibly harsh, circumstances is not intended to suggest that she grew up placidly in Nazareth. She may have. No one knows what Mary's historical circumstances were. But placing her in a regular family environment makes it easier for most of us to empathize—to place ourselves in her position, or the position of her parents—when the Angel Gabriel extended his startling invitation to her to become the mother of the Messiah.

In these pages I have tried to relate these great mysteries, including the imaginative additions, as plausible human experiences. I have taken sketchy Gospel accounts and attempted to reconcile their narratives in certain respects and to suggest transitional details and motivations that may help explain what at first glance appears to be odd, if not inexplicable, human behavior. The time sequence may vary in some instances. However, it is an obvious fact that the Gospel authors were very casual about chronological sequence.[6] Their aim was to report *selected* important events in their approximate time frames. Mine has been the same. The liberties I have taken are in this spirit of reporting *what* happened in a plausible sequential narrative.

After each rosary mystery, a prayer, hymn or Bible passage has been selected that seems particularly appropriate for the content of that mystery. In addition, there is a series of questions that address various aspects of the mystery story. All of these are a reminder to the reader that the rosary mysteries are, at heart, reflective prayers intended to draw us deeper into the mystical relationship of God with His people.

The author's commentaries discuss some of the theological, historical and archaeological issues presented explicitly or implicitly by the New Testament narratives. They explain, in part, some of the stories' imagery.

The appendices are for those who want to know as much as possible about the rosary. I encourage you to read them. You will find them informative and even inspiring in places.

Where words are used that are found in the Bible, they are quoted verbatim from the *New American Bible* (1970), the 1986 edition of which is the basis for the Catholic lectionary readings every Sunday. **In addition, these quotes are emphasized in bold type in the text of the stories.**

In summary, this book is an antidote for those who complain that rosary meditations are boring, or dry, or too limited to sustain daily repetition. There is enough Scriptural, historical, archaeological, medical, and imaginative material in these pages to occupy your mind for many years—hopefully your lifetime. But it is all just seed for your soul, to assist you in growing your own understanding and love for Jesus Christ into a magnificent Tree of Life, nurtured and watered by God's infinite mercy, graces and love.

---

[6]See J.R. Porter, *Jesus Christ: the Jesus of History, the Christ of Faith* (New York: Oxford University Press, 1999), 60.

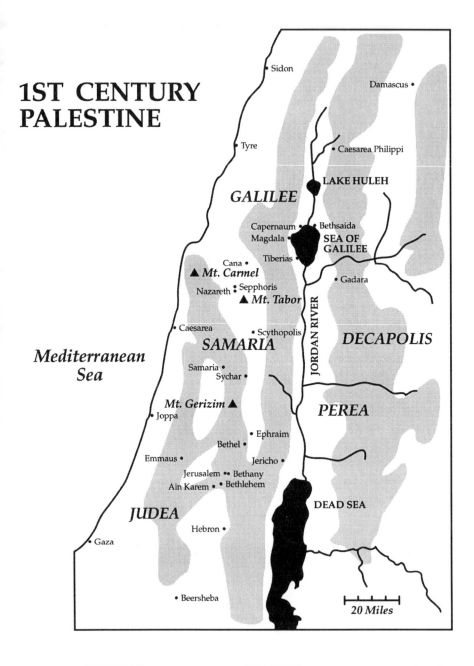

1ST CENTURY PALESTINE

Sidon

Damascus

Tyre

Caesarea Philippi

LAKE HULEH

GALILEE

Capernaum • Bethsaida
Magdala •
SEA OF GALILEE
Tiberias •

Cana •
▲ *Mt. Carmel*
Nazareth : Sepphoris
▲ *Mt. Tabor*

Gadara

Caesarea •
Scythopolis •

SAMARIA

JORDAN RIVER

DECAPOLIS

Mediterranean Sea

Samaria •
Sychar •

Mt. Gerizim ▲
• Joppa

PEREA

• Ephraim
Bethel •
Emmaus •
Jericho •
Jerusalem •• Bethany
Ain Karem • • Bethlehem

DEAD SEA

JUDEA

Hebron •

• Gaza

• Beersheba

20 Miles

■ Water   ▨ Mountainous/Hilly

I am the servant of the Lord. Let it be done to me as you say.
Lk 1:38

FIRST JOYFUL MYSTERY

The Annunciation

That morning in late March was one of those magnificent early Spring days when nature paints her hues from a pallette so brilliant that even the great artists are humbled. Life in Nazareth, already awakened from its winter slumber and renewed by the Spring rains, rejoiced in the luminous lime green of new leaves waving at the deep blue sky. The world sparkled. The small, gray limestone houses of the little village[1] nestled closely together, clinging to one of the steep slopes of the Galilean hills that stood sentinel over the vast plain and marshes to the south. This great "bread basket" of Palestine, a superhighway for ancient armies moving east and west to and from the *"Via Maris,"* or Road by the Sea, sang its own song of rebirth. Great stretches of wildflowers[2] in hues of crimson, white, yellow and purple splashed themselves joyously across the landscape. A few weeks earlier, the flax farms, for which Galilee was known, had announced their impending harvest with fields of sky blue flowers.

Mary stood in the open doorway of the small courtyard at the front of her parents' home, dreamily absorbing the warm sunshine, exchanging pleasantries with some of the village women passing by on their way to the well or to their vegetable gardens. She was a favorite of the small children, who often darted over to show her some new "treasure" they had found before hurrying

---

[1]Nazareth was home to a carpentry center, small flax and wheat farms and flocks of sheep with their owner-shepherds. Here and there the houses were joined in clusters sharing a common courtyard, often a central kitchen.

[2]The "lilies of the field" at the time of Christ would have included the brilliant crimson crown anemones, poppies, mountain tulips, white lilies and varieties of daisies. Bougainvillea and oleander thrive there today and likely had their ancient counterparts as well.

back to rejoin their mothers. A gentle breeze danced along the front of the house, lovingly caressing Mary's long, dark brown hair beneath her sky blue shawl. She was fourteen, about five feet in height, on the thin side. She gazed at the world through widely-spaced, deep blue eyes beneath dark, arched eyebrows. In repose, her mouth turned down slightly, toward a delicate, pointed chin, which gave her a serious, reflective mien. This only accentuated her smile, however, behind even white teeth and full lips which transformed her face much the same way that the sun, emerging from behind a cloud, transforms a day. She was strikingly pretty, but there was about her a seriousness of purpose, a depth, which tended to intimidate her young contemporaries.

Mary's mother, Anne, called her out of her reverie and she turned quickly and went inside. Stepping over the raised threshold, she entered a room only moderately lit by the light from the doorway, three small windows set high in adjoining walls, and an olive oil lamp sitting on a table near the center of the room. In the rear was the sleeping area, elevated and separated from the front portion of the living room by a blue and white striped curtain hung from the ceiling. The curtain was drawn back, revealing the pallet where Anne and Joachim slept. Near the front of the room, along one side, was the hearth. Anne was bent over it, attempting to restart the fire made the night before from the root of the white broom plant (juniper tree), valued for its ability to retain heat for long periods of time.

"Mary, in a little while I will need you to go to the village well and get a jar of water for our meal tonight. In the meantime, please see if you can finish weaving the new cloak for your father. He will be home soon and it would be wonderful if we could surprise him with it."

"Of course, Mother," replied Mary cheerfully. She enjoyed creating intricate designs as she moved the shuttle back and forth, pulling the horizontal *woof* threads through the hanging, vertical *warp* threads. This project was a striped cloak which her father, Joachim, would wear proudly for the next year or two, depending upon how many lost sheep he had to chase out of the brambles! With the light hop-step of youth gifted with an unquenchable joyousness, Mary disappeared into a small room off the main, two-tiered living room where most of the family activities took place.

* * * * * * *

Anne had been in her thirties and Joachim had just turned forty when Mary was born. Now Anne could scarcely believe that she had already celebrated her 49th birthday and Joachim, why, was it possible that he was 54 already? A handsome man with a full head of hair, its black not yet fully gray, she still felt a thrill when he came in from the fields with their flocks of sheep and goats.

Theirs had been a gloriously happy marriage, blessed by Almighty God in every way except one: they had had no children. How she had prayed and prayed and prayed! All to no avail. Together they had searched their consciences, wondering if they might have done something, or failed in some important way, to offend the Lord. But there was never anything that they could identify.

Joachim and Anne, like their contemporaries, expected God to intervene in their lives. "I AM," the God of their fathers, of Abraham, Isaac, Jacob and Moses, rewarded virtue in this life with prosperity. And He punished sin with hardship. This was believed by all, despite the lesson of the Book of Job, which was seen as a way of "explaining" occasional anomalies. Inconsistencies were attributed to the sins of fathers or being caught up in Israel's collective guilt when the nation as a whole strayed too far from the commands of the Lord.

But Anne and Joachim's prosperity did not console them. And Joachim could barely tolerate the whispers and gibes of his friends and acquaintances, who, like the misguided friends of Job, attempted to help him by suggesting his fault lay in his stubborn unwillingness to examine his life closely enough to find the way in which he must have offended the Lord.

Still, Joachim had been unable to resign himself to the will of the Lord. Neither had she, for that matter. Joachim's anguish besieged heaven like the rain of a summer storm on the Sea of Galilee, bursting forth in protests and supplications, subsiding in tears and frustration. He was not a particularly patient man, but his anxiety was driven by an unshakable conviction that a child of his would have an important role to play in the liberation of Israel. He didn't know how he knew this but the certainty filled his soul and drove him wild with impatience as the years passed without fruit from their union. To Joachim's credit, he never once blamed Anne for her childlessness. Nor did he ever complain about the difficulties he had in taking care of his flocks and fields without any sons to help him.

Anne remembered the terrible afternoon when Jephthah, a village elder, had reported his wife was pregnant with their seventh child. "Joachim," he had asked, "have you learned why God has punished you with barrenness? Perhaps your heart is too hard!"

Jephthah was not prepared for Joachim's reaction. Always before he had simply turned his head, teeth and jaws clenched, and strode angrily away from such questions. This time the question seemed to pierce his very breast as he collapsed to his knees, ripping at his cloak and casting handfuls of dirt into the air above his head. Alarmed, several of the townspeople began to gather around, attempting to calm Joachim. But he would have none of it. His wails and shrieks cascaded off the walls of the houses and synagogue nearby and echoed out through the city gate into the hills beyond.

As suddenly as the outburst began, it ended. Joachim lay face-down on the hot, dry ground for nearly an hour, not moving, not speaking, not responding to anything around him. Then, slowly, he rose to his feet and asked for two goatskin water bags. These were brought to him and Joachim said: "I am going into the desert to pray, for forty days if necessary, until the Lord removes this reproach from me!" The villagers watched him until he was out of sight, then two of the women hurried to inform Anne.

Joachim's cries had been as nothing compared to Anne's tears and sobs. To her guilt and anxiety over her inability to conceive a child was now added terror for her husband's safety and an overwhelming loneliness. She herself began a nine-day fasting and mourning novena of constant prayer, followed immediately by another similar period.[3]

Early one morning, when she was halfway through the second novena and kneeling on the floor with her face pressed into her hands, her head resting on them against the cold, rough tiles, her eyes now dry after days of crying, she had prayed with total resignation. *Oh, Lord God of Israel, God of Abraham, Jacob and Moses, of David and the prophets, of all your chosen people. Forgive my failings and my wilfulness. I accept your will for me and praise you, beloved Lord! I ask only that you return Joachim to me that we may continue to serve you and the people you have chosen to proclaim your greatness! No other request do I make of you, Lord, than to serve you as your humble handmaiden. But I cannot do this without your servant and my husband, Joachim, without whose love I shall be as barren of heart and soul as I have been of body!*

At once, Anne felt a peace come upon her like no joy she had ever known before. In that radiance which now filled her being and seemed to physically lift her up, she sensed she was not alone. Slowly, she dropped her hands from her face and rose to an upright kneeling position. There before her stood the most beautiful man she had ever seen. He wore a white robe which shone as though lit from within. The light enveloped him, even beneath his bare feet which seemed, impossibly, not to be touching the floor.

With a gentle smile and eyes so kind that Anne's momentary fright dissipated like the pre-dawn fog on a summer morning, he spoke. "Anne, be at peace. The Lord has heard your prayer. Joachim is returning to you now. I have visited him at his place of fast in the desert beyond the Jordan to tell him what I am about to tell you. You shall conceive and bear a child who will bring glory to Israel and to all the nations. Her name will be revered for all generations and her place in the Kingdom of God second to none for through her will come the salvation promised to Israel from the days of Abraham. Go now to the Eastern Gate. Your husband nears."

For a moment, Anne could not move. She stared at the spot where the angel had been just a moment before, now empty and still, its normalcy already making her wonder if she had really seen what still seemed so vivid in her memory. No! It WAS real! No experience in her life could have conjured up an imagination of what she had just experienced. And the angel's promise. A child to bring glory to Israel. To her and Joachim! Warm tears streamed down Anne's cheeks as she

---

[3]The nine-day *devotional* novena began in the early Middle Ages as a preparation for Christmas. The nine days each represented one month of Mary's pregnancy. But the *mourning* novena, or *novendialia*, dates to the Greeks and Romans. It was a nine-day period of mourning following a death or burial. The Pope's Novena is still used for this purpose whenever a supreme pontiff dies. Anne's two mourning periods are for her barrenness and the temporary loss of her husband. They are mentioned in the legend concerning the birth of Mary.

turned her face upward and thanked God with a depth of gratitude, praise and astonishment that only totally unexpected miracles can produce. Suddenly, she remembered Joachim.

The angel had said that Joachim was returning. Even if the angel had not told her of his visit to her husband, she would have known that Joachim knew they were going to have a child. He was a strong, determined man who would never have returned prematurely from his petitionary fast. She leaped to her feet, seemingly on wings herself, and flew toward the Eastern Gate of the city, crying and laughing and begging people's pardon as she jostled them in her race to embrace her husband.

As soon as he saw her, Joachim realized that Anne, too, knew she was to have a child. He had been a little worried about telling her about the angel's visit to him in the desert, fearing that she would think he was simply suffering from the ordeal of his fast. It was obvious that was not going to be a problem when Anne threw herself into Joachim's arms, laughing, crying and kissing him, saying over and over: "God has heard us! He has had mercy on us. Praised be His name!"

Mary had been born within the year. The birth had not been easy, but never before, and perhaps since, was any new mother less complaining of the hardships of childbirth. From Mary's first moments in the world, when she greeted her arrival like any new baby, protesting the forceful eviction from a life of security and peace into a strange new world filled with bright light and unfathomable sensations, Mary was an extraordinarily happy child. Yes, she cried when she was hungry, or needed her diaper changed, or hurt herself. But there was a great peace about her, a quiet kind of joyfulness that seemed to emanate from her to anyone around her. It was almost impossible to remain angry about anything once Mary fixed her lovely blue eyes on you with their look of compassion and concern. Animals flocked to her side and a mere touch and a whisper calmed even beasts which moments before had seemed fierce and threatening.

She had been a gifted child, quick to learn, curious about everything. Anne and Joachim doted on her, but their lavish love and attention produced none of the usual symptoms of the spoiled, self-centered child. Instead, Mary seemed to grow in love itself, blossoming imperceptibly from each stage, when her goodness already seemed perfect, to the next. Then those who knew her discovered to their constant amazement that perfection could actually become more perfect in this child. Of course, there were those who were jealous and spiteful. But even they were curiously muted in her presence, seemingly finding it impossible to utter the petty insults they had been planning to express before she greeted them with her smile.

Traditionally, Jewish women in that time were not taught to read. There was no need for such an extravagance. The demands of daily living and domesticity, not to mention the scarcity of reading materials and poor lighting conditions, made the effort seem like an obvious waste of time. But Mary had a strong interest in the traditions of Israel, told to her every night from the age of two by one or both of her parents. And, as he had often done with Anne, Joachim cheerfully acceded to

Mary's wish to be able to see for herself and to understand the scriptural sources of Israel's sacred relationship with the One God. So Joachim brought home fragments of the Torah whenever he could, sometimes even getting permission to borrow an entire scroll. With these, Anne taught Mary how to read, as she herself had been taught by her mother years before.

Throughout the land, people were filled with anxious longing for the arrival of the Messiah. He had long been promised by God to restore Israel to its glorious destiny of leading the world as His chosen nation. Mary loved to read the prophecies which the elders and priests had marked as pointing to the Messiah. She imagined the New David, incredibly strong, yet gentle, brilliant in song, verse and battle, although she did not like to think about the struggles of warfare. She preferred to imagine that the Messiah would be so powerful and impressive that his enemies would plead for peace without even lifting a sword.

In this manner, Mary's childhood years passed in contentment and quiet happiness until that day a few months past her fourteenth birthday. Her parents had stopped her as she rose to clean the dishes used for their evening meal.

"Mary," began her father. "You are now a young woman of marriageable age. Although you are the joy of our lives and the special blessing of God, it is time to consider your future, to ensure that you will have a good home with a loving husband after your mother and I are gone. Of course, it may also be necessary for you and your husband to take care of us if God wills that we should live so long. Either way, we know that He has a special destiny for you. We learned that before you were born. We are convinced that you are to be the mother to sons who will bring honor and glory to His Name and to His people. For that you must have a husband."

Mary sat quietly, looking at her father as he spoke these words. It was clear that his love for his daughter made the task difficult. Although he understood the need to arrange a marriage for Mary, his heart wanted nothing more than to live out his life in the daily company of this child. She was music for the heart, a perfect antidote to anger or depression, even when he had plenty of cause to be upset from some unpleasant encounter with his fellow Jews, or the Roman soldiers, or just the arbitrary experience of nature. She always knew the exact thing to say to make him smile, to lift his spirits, to restore his faith in the goodness of humanity. Joy bubbled out of her very pores. If it is possible to conceive of a person smiling with her entire being, that is the feeling Mary conveyed to those who loved her.

Anne reached out and took Mary's hand in hers. "Dear, your father is right. It is time that you have your own family. We have in mind young Joseph. He has sent his brother, Clopus Alphaeus, to inquire about the possibility of a marriage to you."

Mary looked from one parent to the other, smiled slightly, and sighed. She knew this day must come, but she had been so happy living with her parents in this home suffused with the love of God that she had tended to push the thought out of her mind. Now she considered Joseph, her proposed suitor. He was, to all appearances, a fine person, perhaps ten or fifteen years older than she. He was a carpenter by trade, and from a good family. In fact, his family was descended from King David himself, as was her own family through Joachim. She did not know Joseph well, but she had liked him instantly the first time they had met.

That had been during the week-long Festival of Tabernacles, or Booths, held in the month of *Tishri*, which ran from about mid-September to mid-October in the modern calendar. This was perhaps the most joyous feast of the year as the last of the major crop harvests, olives, coincided with the first tasting of the summer wine harvest. It was customary to travel to Jerusalem for the celebration if circumstances permitted. But whether in Jerusalem or at home in Nazareth and the many other small villages throughout Galilee and Judea, families slept for a week in small huts, built from date palm branches, mats and willow and myrtle greenery, commonly constructed on the tops of their houses. Part feast of thanksgiving, part New Year's celebration, the festival also commemorated the forty-year sojourn of Israel in the desert under the care and tutelage of God who, through Moses, led His people to the Promised Land.

Joseph's quick wit and kindness had been apparent immediately. She had been twelve, high-spirited, and excited about the adventure of camping out for a week. She had been describing to some of her friends the passage through the Red Sea, waving her arms around and picturing in vivid terms the shouts, trumpets and crashing hooves of Pharaoh's army in pursuit. She had turned suddenly in these gyrations and nearly struck Joseph as he was passing by. Only a quick duck by the agile young man had spared him. All the girls froze, fearing some chastisement from the handsome, powerfully-built man with the thick dark beard. But Joseph had merely smiled at them, his dark eyes shining, as he looked especially at Mary and said: "Child, if you had led our people, Israel, instead of Moses, it would have taken only twenty years to get through the wilderness as they raced to keep up with you!"

Mary had giggled in spite of herself, then blushed as her original embarrassment was compounded. "I am terribly sorry, sir! It is entirely my fault. Please forgive us."

Joseph smiled again and said: "No need to apologize . . ." He hesitated.

Sensing his question, Mary answered before he finished: "I am Mary, daughter of Joachim and Anne."

"Mary," repeated Joseph. He looked at her quizzically, entranced not only by the child's great beauty, but by a look of such innocence and honesty that it almost took his breath away. "Perhaps I can have the opportunity some day to hear directly from your lips exactly how our people escaped the clutches of the Egyptians. It is clear that you have a much more vivid understanding of it than do the fussy old priests in the synagogue!" Joseph laughed. He paused a moment longer, looking at Mary, sensing . . . what? He shrugged it off and walked away.

"Joseph is a fine man," said Mary now to her parents. "I would be pleased, Father, to have you arrange the betrothal on terms agreeable to you."

The amount of the dowry to be paid by Joseph to Joachim was fixed and, in addition, the *mohar*, or compensation for the loss of Mary's services, was decided. The dowry would be held in trust for Mary by her father, as was the custom, as a kind of insurance policy against being left unsupported in her old age. The wedding was set for a year hence in *Iyyar*, the month of flowering (May). The engagement became official the day Joseph brought to Mary a beautiful ivory comb as his betrothal gift to her, presenting it formally in a simple ceremony with the two families, a rabbi, and close friends, saying, "By this, thou art set apart for me according to the laws of Moses and of Israel."

And so it was done, a mere two weeks before this day which was about to mark the most dramatic turning point in human history.

* * * * * * *

Mary sat down at the loom and began to pass the shuttle back and forth through the woolen threads. The pattern she was developing in her father's new cloak was not complicated and she could have woven it in her sleep, so she released her mind to follow where her heart was always beckoning, to thoughts of I AM, the one true God, the God of her fathers and of all the earth, the God who would soon send the Messiah, she prayed passionately, to lead Israel out of its bondage and restore the greatness of King David's people. At these moments, Mary often found herself drawn into a state of prayer so deep that she lost all sense of time and space. Like the solar winds which blow from the sun outward to the planets, Mary felt her soul lifted gently from the bonds of earth and carried ever so lovingly into, not exactly "somewhere" but, rather, more a wholly different state of existence, one of indescribable peace and joy. In these raptures, Mary knew she was in the presence of God.

But now Mary was not drawn into such a mystical experience. Rather, her mind wandered in pleasant reveries about the wonderful things which would happen when the Messiah came. She wondered if he might come during her lifetime and whether she could possibly have the chance to meet him if he did. She knew that Nazareth was not held in high repute in Judea, where Jerusalem, God's special city and the capital of Israel, was located. Nor, for that matter, was it esteemed in Galilee, its own province. And her parents, while comfortable and respected members of the community, were not of the priestly class. True, her father was a descendant of David, but after a thousand years there were innumerable people who claimed descent from the royal house of David. Besides, it was well accepted in Israel that the Messiah would come from Bethlehem, for had not the prophet Micah written:

> **But you, Bethlehem-Ephrathah,**
> **too small to be among the clans of Judah,**
> **From you shall come forth for me**
> **one who is to be ruler in Israel;**

**Whose origin is from of old,
from ancient times.**[4]

No, Mary was fully convinced that the Messiah's path and hers were extremely unlikely to cross even if by some gracious miracle of God he were to come during her lifetime. Still, the realization did not dampen her spirits and she turned her attention back to the loom, considering whether she might add a little variation in the cloak's pattern to delight her father.

Intent in her study of the pattern's development and how it might be varied at this point, Mary did not notice that someone had entered the room and stood now not more than an arm's length away just behind her right shoulder.

"Mary." The voice enveloped her, soft and melodious, male but gentle as a caress of breeze at dusk on a balmy summer evening. She was startled, nonetheless, and her alarm grew when she whirled around and confronted a young man gazing at her with eyes filled with love. **"Rejoice, O highly favored daughter! The Lord is with you. Blessed are you among women."**[5]

Mary stared at the angel, noting that although he looked like a young man, he was extraordinarily . . . well, beautiful! He shone like the purest crystal, wrapped in a brilliant white light that was not in the least dazzling to her eyes. His attention was fixed entirely on her face, as if he expected her to say something! What was it he had said to her, she tried to recall, as her mind swirled with both confusion and awe? **"Blessed . . . among women."** And **"favored daughter!"** What could such words possibly mean for her, a simple child of the hill country of Galilee? Her heart pounding, Mary started to rise from her seat.

"Do not fear, Mary. You have found favor with God. You shall conceive and bear a son and give him the name Jesus. Great will be his dignity and he will be called Son of the Most High. The Lord God will give him the throne of David his father. He will rule over the house of Jacob forever and his reign will be without end,"[6] said the angel, still gazing intently at Mary's face.

Now Mary was truly alarmed. She understood that the angel meant an immediate conception.[7] She looked away, staring briefly out the window that her

---

[4]Mi 5:1

[5]Lk 1:28

[6]Lk 1:30

[7]Although the angel's statement to Mary, "*shall conceive and bear a son*," is, in English at least, ambiguous as to timing, we know that God's intention was that conception take place immediately. Surely the angel sent on this most important of all missions would have been able to communicate his message accurately, even without using words (by the well-recognized means of locution, for example). I assume, therefore, that Mary understood that

father had put about eight feet up the limestone wall in the small room. Through the narrow opening Mary watched a dove circling in the calm blue sky. *How can I bear a child when I am only betrothed and shall not be wedded until more than a year from now?* she said to herself. *Surely the Lord God would not intend such a scandal.*

Mary said to the angel, **"How can this be since I do not know man?"**[8]

The angel answered her: **"The Holy Spirit will come upon you and the power of the Most High will overshadow you; hence, the holy offspring to be born will be called Son of God. Know that Elizabeth your kinswoman has conceived a son in her old age; she who was thought to be sterile is now in her sixth month, for nothing is impossible with God."**[9]

Mary's mind swirled under the staggering implications of these words. A baby created directly by God in her womb! It was . . . impossible! It was . . . already prophesied! She gasped as she suddenly recalled the ancient prophecy of the Messiah's birth:

> **Therefore the Lord himself will**
> **give you this sign:**
> **the virgin shall be with child,**
> **and bear a son,**
> **and shall name him, Immanuel.**[10]

She was to be the mother of the Messiah! God had chosen her, his most humble servant in all Israel, to be the instrument for the salvation of His people. *O gracious and almighty Lord, from age to age your works announce the glory of your Name. Praised be the goodness and the wisdom of the Lord who accomplishes His mighty deeds through the weakest and least likely of His people.* Mary prayed silently in thanks to her God, not realizing that of all God's creation, not since Eve had there been such a perfect soul created without the stain of original sin. With tears of gratitude and joy overflowing her eyes and down her cheeks, Mary turned to the angel and said: **"I am the servant of the Lord. Let it be done to me as you say."**[11]

---

conception was to take place before her wedding to Joseph and so she would have been very concerned about how that could occur without engaging in conduct she certainly would have considered improper and possibly even in violation of a vow of virginity she might have made. Children born of parents who were betrothed but not yet married were considered legitimate in the Jewish culture. However, there was still the taint of scandal associated with such pregnancies, especially in the province of Galilee.

[8]Lk 1:34

[9]Lk 1:35-37

[10]Is 7:14

[11]Lk 1:38

As Mary spoke these words, the angel knelt before her, understanding fully, as Mary did not quite yet, that he kneeled before the Son of God, now growing in the womb of the woman who would one day reign in heaven as Queen of all the angels and saints. A moment later, he vanished, leaving Mary sitting at the loom in stunned silence. After a few minutes, she rose and went into the main room of the house, there to see her mother, Anne, just starting toward the room where she had been weaving.

"Mother." Mary spoke softly before Anne, who was coming to ask her daughter to go to the village well and get a jar of water for their evening meal, could say anything. There was something in Mary's tone that caught Anne's attention, an undercurrent of great excitement but the voice had been restrained. Anne paused and waited for her daughter to continue.

"The Messiah is coming to Israel. I have been chosen to be his mother. I know this because an angel just visited me and told me that I am to bear a son and name him Jesus," Mary told her mother.

Anne gasped. She knew that her daughter did not lie. In fact, from her first words as an infant until those just spoken to her, Mary had never so much as shaded the truth, although she was gentle and kind and tried to avoid saying things that, while true, might be hurtful to her listener.

Anne reached for a reed chair and sat down, staring open-mouthed at Mary. "But . . . but I did not see anyone, Mary," stammered Anne. "Where is the angel now?"

Mary replied, "He has gone in the same way he came, appearing without warning to me while I was working on Father's cloak and disappearing after I agreed to be the mother of the Lord."

"But, Mary, can you be so sure that you saw a real angel, one actually sent from God? Couldn't it have been just your imagination, dear? After all, we know that your heart is very close to God and that your thoughts often dwell in His company. Perhaps you fell asleep and simply dreamt what you now recall as a visit by an angel?" Anne wrung her hands anxiously, struck suddenly by an even more troubling thought.

"Mother," said Mary, looking at her mother steadily with that incongruous look of wise innocence which so often marked her expression. "Never in my life have I experienced anything more real than the heavenly creature who bore me the incredible news that I have just shared with you. And that's not all!" Mary's voice rose as she recalled excitedly the angel's words about Elizabeth, who was her kinswoman, a second cousin. "Your cousin, Elizabeth, is going to have a baby . . . . a son!"

Anne gasped again, reflexively putting her hand over her heart, her other hand on her forehead. "Mary, Elizabeth is older than I am! Her mother was my mother's oldest sister and gave birth to her five years before I was born. She has been barren all her life and is certainly much too old to be even possibly having a child now. Only God could work such a miracle!" Even as she spoke these words, Anne remembered her own visit from the angel and the birth of her daughter,

Mary, who had been God's miraculous answer to her own prayers. Elizabeth's miracle would be even more remarkable. And announced in conjunction with the coming of the Messiah. *Surely, the destiny of these two sons will be linked in a special way,* thought Anne.

Mary interrupted her thoughts. "It will not be long before Elizabeth has her baby, Mother. The angel told me that she is in her sixth month. I ask your permission to go to her. She is our kinswoman and we should provide her as much help as we can. She will not have many young friends at her age and I can be of great assistance in her final, most difficult months. I will do all the heavy work and make sure she has nothing to do but rest!"

Anne smiled at her daughter's enthusiasm and generosity. Then she frowned, remembering the troubling thought she had before Mary mentioned Elizabeth. "Mary, may I assume your baby, the Messiah, will not come until the normal time after your wedding to Joseph?" Anne asked nervously, afraid of what the answer might be. She had heard the priests in the synagogue debating the prophesied origin of the Messiah and knew of the prediction that he would be born of a virgin. But there was much dispute as to exactly what that meant. Some of the teachers argued that it only meant the Messiah would be the first-born of his mother and would be conceived on the wedding night. Others said the term "virgin" applied to the birth as well, meaning that the mother would have to have conceived without losing her virginity. As she looked upon her daughter's radiant face, Anne knew what Mary's answer would be before she even uttered a word.

"Mother, I have been with child since the angel left me a few minutes ago. He has been conceived by the Spirit of God Himself in my womb and no man may ever claim to be the father of the Son of the Most High," said Mary, confirming both lesson and conviction in Anne.

At that moment, Joachim entered the house. His cloak was caked with dust and torn in three places from brambles, a few of which yet dangled from the sides and rear of the once ivory-colored, now mud-brown, garment.

"I never saw such wild and unruly sheep!" exclaimed Joachim, collapsing on a wooden bench as the fatigue of the day settled around him like the dust he had trailed into the room. Anne and Mary had been so involved in their conversation that they had not heard his approach. Now Joachim looked around for the jar of fresh water that he would use to wash his face, hands and feet before changing into a clean linen tunic, woolen cloak and cloth slippers.

Seeing his glance, Mary remembered that in the excitement of the day's events, she had not gotten around to making the trip to the village well. She took a quick step in the direction of the empty jar by the door. Her mouth opened to tell her father that she was sorry but she would run down to the well as quickly as she could. Anne's grasp of her arm brought all these activities to a halt, as Mary turned to see why she had been stopped in mid-flight.

"Mary, wait. Your father will want to hear the news we have for him even before he has washed himself. This is the most important news ever conveyed from God to man and it must not be kept from him a single moment longer," Anne said to Mary while looking at Joachim.

Joachim, hot and tired as he was, was a man of enormous good humor and enjoyed the company of these two lovely women in his life more than he had ever thought possible. The joy shared in this family had almost made him forget that God had not chosen to bless him with any sons. So he looked indulgently at Anne and waited for the momentous news, assuming that her terminology was just female hyperbole (admittedly extreme!) to describe some exciting plan for Mary's wedding feast with Joseph. Later, when Joachim tried to recall exactly how he had felt when the two women related the news of the angel's visit and his announcement that Mary was to be the mother of the Messiah, making him the Messiah's grandfather, he would be unable to remember anything but words which were so vivid they crowded out all memory of his surroundings at the time. He would not remember even that he had been exhausted, dirty and hungry. Only the joyful smile of his daughter, Mary, and the beaming, expectant expression of his wife would remain as a vivid frame for his discovery that God had finally implemented his long-promised plan for the salvation of mankind.

Mary and Anne, however, saw a face flushed with fatigue and perspiration suddenly drain of color and remain staring, open-mouthed, at the two of them as they explained all that had transpired less than an hour ago.

When he had recovered from his shock, Joachim could postpone his ablutions no longer, so Mary dashed off to fill a water jar and Anne laid out his fresh clothes. After he had changed, and the news had settled into his consciousness with all of its worldly ramifications, Joachim emerged from the sleeping area. Small whispers of doubt had begun to play at the corners of his mind. He wondered about the prudence of God in choosing an unmarried woman to be the mother of His son in a society where adultery was punishable by death. *Surely*, he thought to himself, *if this were really from God He would wait until Mary was married to Joseph. But, then, how would the prophecy of the virgin birth be fulfilled?* It was now obvious to Joachim that the virginity prophesied by Isaiah meant that it would continue until the Messiah's birth and not merely refer to a woman who was a virgin prior to marriage. He thought, *Even if Joseph knew of God's plan and did not consummate the marriage, it would be much more difficult to believe that the child had not simply been conceived by Joseph on his wedding night. No, God would, in fact, want this point to be crystal clear.*

Joachim paced as his thoughts continued: *Was it possible, then, that Mary, whose unique goodness was recognized and admired throughout Nazareth, could have fantasized the whole episode? What about Joseph? Would he believe them? If they told him, and it turned out to be just Mary's imagination, then he would certainly question the wisdom of marrying such a girl. On the other hand, if they did not tell him and Mary truly was with child, he would learn it soon enough and might well report her to the authorities to be stoned as an adulteress!*[12] Joachim prayed earnestly to God for enlightenment, half expecting the angel to reappear and tell him what to do. But only silence greeted his fervent petitions for guidance.

It was Anne whose good sense first saw how God had already arranged to resolve their dilemma. The angel had told Mary about Elizabeth's miraculous pregnancy. They had not known of this and, since they had not been to Jerusalem in more than six months, had no way of learning it other than by a communication directly from God. The two families were not close and did not visit often, but there was nonetheless an obligation to provide to Elizabeth whatever assistance they could. Besides, Mary was very anxious to go, feeling impelled by something more profound than mere familial obligation and empathetic excitement. The visit, Anne pointed out to Joachim, would provide confirmation of the angel and the message he brought. After that, no one could doubt the truth of what Mary had reported. Even Joseph would have to acknowledge that Mary's pregnancy must be of divine origin. Joachim nodded, letting his need for reassurance overcome his critical judgment.

In any event, there could be no immediate disclosure to Joseph because he was away from Nazareth for at least a month on a building project in Bethsaida, nearly two days' journey from there. They also agreed that Joseph must hear the news directly from them. It was going to be difficult enough without him learning of it through gossip and rumor. Besides, the story was so incredible on its face that they were reluctant to expose Mary and themselves to ridicule. If they told what had happened and were not believed, Mary would literally be at risk for her life. Even their unaccountable knowledge of the miraculous pregnancy of Elizabeth might not be enough to deflect the judgment of the elders. So, although they were bursting with excitement and the desire to share the greatest news since the dawn of mankind, they kept the story to themselves.

Since Anne and Joachim would not travel with her, it was imperative that Mary be sent with friends and relatives to look after her. A caravan was being prepared for the annual trip from Nazareth to Jerusalem to attend the Passover celebration. From there, she could make arrangements to travel into the hill country of Judah where Elizabeth and Zechariah lived. But Passover was early this year, less than a week away, and the Nazareth caravan was departing the next morning.

"Joachim, Mary wishes to leave immediately to visit Elizabeth," said Anne. "I, too, think she should go at once. The Passover caravan leaves tomorrow morning. Run and see if Clopas can take Mary with his family while I help her get some things together."

Mary, whose faith in God was absolute, entertained no doubts about Joseph's reaction when he learned of her miraculous pregnancy. She hardly gave

---

[12]In Jewish law, betrothal had the same legal effect as marriage. Infidelity during that time was considered to be adultery and exposed women to the same penalties.

it a thought, assuming that he would be as thrilled as she to be the "host family" for the divinely conceived Messiah. But she was very excited about visiting Elizabeth and quickly packed her few garments and the foodstuffs that she would need for the journey. Then she waited impatiently for the dawn when the caravan would leave on its five-day journey to Jerusalem.

The next morning, just before the caravan departed, Anne pressed a papyrus scroll, sealed with wax, into her daughter's hands. "Mary," she explained, looking directly at her face and very serious in demeanor. "Be sure to give this letter to Elizabeth as soon as you see her. It is very important." Anne gave no other explanation, and Mary accepted her silence and did not inquire further.

In the weeks to come, Anne and Joachim spent many hours in excited speculation about the nature and mission of the Messiah, fundamentally astonished that the child had been conceived directly by God in their daughter, but assuming that all their other expectations of the earthly might and splendor of the Chosen One would be realized. Their role model for these ruminations was King David, whose own beginnings were humble but whose career was spectacular in its multifaceted achievements (warrior, poet, musician, statesman, philosopher, prophet). Surely the Messiah would surpass David by as much as God surpassed mankind. It really seemed that the Day of the Lord was at hand when all the earth would be restored to the righteous and the just. They dreamed that in their own lifetime, the words of Isaiah might be fulfilled:

**Then the wolf shall be a guest
of the lamb,
and the leopard shall lie
down with the kid;
The calf and the young lion
shall browse together,
with a little child to guide them.
The cow and the bear shall be
neighbors,
together their young shall rest;
the lion shall eat hay like the ox.
The baby shall play by the
cobra's den,
and the child lay his hand on
the adder's lair.
There shall be no harm or ruin
on all my holy mountain;
for the earth shall be filled
with knowledge of the LORD,
as water covers the sea.**

THE ANGELUS

The angel of the Lord declared unto Mary.
And she conceived of the Holy Spirit. (Hail Mary)

Behold the handmaid of the Lord.
May it be done unto me according to your word. (Hail Mary)

And the Word was made flesh.
And dwelt among us. (Hail Mary)

Pray for us, O holy Mother of God.
That we may be made worthy of the promises of Christ.

Let us pray.
Pour forth we beseech you, O Lord, your grace into our hearts;
that we to whom the incarnation of Christ, your Son,
was made known by the message of an angel,
may by his passion and cross
be brought to the glory of his resurrection.
Through the same Christ our Lord.

Amen

QUESTIONS FOR REFLECTION

1) What kind of personality do you think a person would have who was born without original sin and, therefore, without any concupiscence, or propensity to sin?

2) Do you think that Mary would have had a relatively normal childhood as a young Jewish girl, or do you think her Immaculate Conception and calling to be the Mother of God would have made her, as the mystics tend to see her, the world's first Catholic nun?

3) How do you think Mary's parents, Anne and Joachim, would have reacted to Mary's report of the Angel Gabriel's visit and his announcement of the forthcoming virginal birth of the Messiah? How would you react in the same situation? Do you think Mary would even have told them? In her place, would you have?

4) Do you imagine that you could have been friends with Mary and Joseph when they lived on earth? How do you see their personalities? Would they have been fun to have over for dinner, do you think?

5) Do you think Mary had a duty to tell Joseph about the impending birth of the Messiah since they were engaged to be married? How would you do it? Would you expect him to believe you?

6) If you had been Anne or Joachim, would you have been concerned about Joseph's reaction? What would you have done?

7) Would you be willing to be put in an embarrassing, even dangerous, position to be the parent of someone like Abraham Lincoln, who would be of great historical importance to your country?

8) If an angel appeared to you and asked you to undertake some important but risky mission for God, would you assume that the Lord would take care of everything for you? Or would you seek reassurances and guarantees?

9) How would you apply Mary's example of trust in God to your own life?

10) Does the fact that in the Gospel of Luke Mary apparently went alone to visit Elizabeth suggest to you that she might have been an orphan by this time? Or that she did not tell her mother (or father, if still living) about the angel's visit?

Blest is she who trusted that the Lord's words to her would be fulfilled.
Lk 1:45

SECOND JOYFUL MYSTERY

The Visitation

Normally, Joachim, Anne and Mary would travel as a family to Jerusalem for the annual Passover celebration. It was a time when Jews from all over the civilized world assembled together in the city which they believed had been chosen by God for special eminence among men. They came to commemorate the great and terrible event that had finally precipitated the release of the Israelites from the bondage of the Egyptians some 1,200 years earlier: the death of all the first-born in Egypt, both man and animal. The Israelites had been protected from the scourge by sprinkling the blood of a newly killed sacrificial lamb upon their doorposts and lintels. This great intervention by God in the affairs of His chosen people would be commemorated ever after as the most important of all festivals for the Jewish nation. This year, however, Joachim and Anne were unable to go to Jerusalem and would join the other residents of Nazareth at appropriate ceremonies in their local synagogue. But the great ceremonial sacrifice of the Passover lambs was reserved to the Jerusalem Temple, the dwelling place of Yahweh.

Among those who were making the trip from Nazareth to Jerusalem were Joseph's brother, Clopas (also called Alphaeus), and his wife, Mary, and their two young sons, James and Joseph. Mary of Clopas was a few years older than Mary. They had been friendly while growing up in Nazareth, although not close until their families were united by Joseph's betrothal to Mary. The family relationship was ideal for Mary's protection during her trip to see Elizabeth. Clopas would ensure that she had safe travel arrangements for the half-day leg of the journey from Jerusalem to Ain Karem in the hill country of Judea, where Elizabeth and Zechariah lived.

With the sun barely clear of the horizon, shining cheerfully in the newness of the day, the Nazareth caravan set out amid the bleating, braying and clatter of sheep and goats and donkeys bearing baggage and household utensils for the two-week round trip journey. A few of the villagers had camels, who loped along genially wearing their odd *"What, me worry?"* camel smiles. The men and women walked in two separate groups, the men leading, while the children bounced between the two, distracted variously by games, sights and competitions. As the day wore on, the excited chatter and high spirits surrendered a little to fatigue. The girls and the younger boys fell in with the women. The older boys preferred to walk with the men, although even some of them tended to fall back with their mothers, or perhaps simply to be near some comely girl who had caught their fancy.

Clopas's wife, Mary, kept a careful eye on Mary. Not merely out of concern for her welfare, but as much from fascination with this beautiful young girl just blossoming into her full womanhood. Mary was well known in Nazareth. It was difficult to find anything negative to say about her. She was kind and generous to all, even the despised Samaritans and Romans. This inspired some persons to reflect upon their own tendency to judge without knowing, but most just thought her lacking in discernment. Through it all, Mary walked serenely, always smiling, always with a helpful or encouraging word, never with even a hint of insincerity or condescension. *Where did she come from?* Mary of Clopas wondered. She was so *good* that it was sometimes difficult to recall whether her stunning beauty was actually physical or simply Mary's internal radiance transplanting itself into the eye of every beholder. Whatever the source, Mary Clopas thought to herself, she was thrilled to have this most special person become a member of their family. The grace of God was palpably upon her, a grace that reflected upon everyone in her presence as if Mary herself were a little sun, banishing shadows wherever she went.

Mary was oblivious to Mary Clopas' oft-repeated stares as she walked along beside her in the noisy caravan. Her feet, delicate and sure, glided over the stony ground propelled by a mind alternately lost in reveries about the Angel Gabriel's visit and then so excited that she wanted to shout to the entire caravan to stop while she disclosed to them the most momentous news in the history of mankind. A few times she had to consciously bite her tongue to keep from exclaiming to Mary Clopas that the Messiah was on his way to Israel and she was to be his mother! But each time she remembered that Joseph must be told before anyone else in Nazareth.

And, then, as she thought about how she would tell him, she began to realize that this was a story not easily believed. Mary was a perfect innocent, but there was nothing naive about her. Never in the history of the human race had there been a child born without participation by both a man and a woman. Who would believe such a story? Who *could* believe such a story? This realization dampened Mary's enthusiasm and helped to control her excitement. But her thoughts still roamed the known universe, projecting the coming triumph of the Messiah, the triumph of *her* Son, whose Father was the Creator of all that existed. Surely the world was on the verge of its total transformation. Mary imagined a return of the Garden of Eden, with all peoples subjected to the gentle but firm and always just guidance of the new King. From time to time, Mary could contain her excitement no longer and would throw her arms up to the sky, pirouetting with joyful smile and closed eyes, as Mary Clopas stared at her half amused, half alarmed.

The caravan, numbering about forty persons and nearly as many pack animals, wound its way down out of the hills where Nazareth perched and into the Valley of the Esdraelon, the great plain which swept from Mount Carmel in the northwest to Mount Gilboa in the southeast. The travelers headed down this valley toward the Jordan River. There they would join one of the primary caravan routes of the ancient world, moving south toward the Dead Sea. Near Jericho, the highway turned west southwest toward Jerusalem, a distance of nearly 20 miles. This final day's journey into the Holy City was arduous, requiring the travelers to climb from the Jordan River valley almost continuously up through the barren, khaki-colored hills of the Judean Wilderness. The road followed the general path of an aqueduct, built by Herod the Great to bring water from a spring on Mount Scopus, the highest hill overlooking Jerusalem, to his lavish palace at Jericho. Already the precious water was transforming the arid land into a fertile oasis, making Jericho a popular overnight stay for travelers. But the road through the Wilderness was often harrowing, skirting along the edge of ravines and ancient wadis that plunged hundreds of feet below. It was not without reason that this forbidding terrain was called the "Valley of the Shadow of Death" and the inspiration for Psalm 23.

The Nazarene group would arrive at Jerusalem through the pass between the Mount of Offence on the south and the double-humped Mount of Olives, so-named because of the extensive groves of olive trees which grew there, to the north. This route was a little longer than the direct route through the heart of Samaria, but, except for the last leg, it was generally easier going and avoided the always-real possibility of rude encounters with the Samaritans.

As the Nazarenes passed Bethany, a little village nestled in the foothills just beyond the harsh Wilderness, they found themselves often jostling with other pilgrims and traders who were also going to the city for the great feast. The population of the city increased two- or three-fold during the two-week period before and after Passover. With such numbers, not to mention knots of Roman soldiers occasionally sweeping by, bandits and thieves were not the concern they usually were. Nonetheless, the group drew closer together, compelled by congestion and fear of being separated.

When the group rounded the Mount of Olives, Jerusalem lay before them in a breath-taking panorama of history, culture, religion and architecture. As always, Mary felt her heart skip a beat in the excitement of gazing upon the City of David. The huge Herodian Temple complex, under construction by King Herod the Great for the past thirty years, dominated the scene and seemed clearly to validate Jewish beliefs that God Himself lived here.

The Temple itself was built in the shape of a "T." The truncated crosspiece of the "T" was an imposing porch with a towering three-story rectangular

Pilgrims approaching the City of Jerusalem for the annual Passover Celebration.

doorway yawning in its center. The Holy Place and Holy of Holies, flanked with small rooms and vaults along the side, formed the leg of the "T." Architecturally, the building's broad front and narrower body replicated the broad shoulders and narrow haunches of the Lion of Judah. Flanking the entrance like mighty sentinels were two great, red-veined marble columns with golden Corinthian capitals that sent sun rays sparkling in all directions.

Like all Jews who came to Jerusalem, Mary was thrilled by the glistening white marble walls of the central structure, surmounted by an inlaid gold band just below the triangular shaped cornices, also overlaid with gold, which crowned the whole edifice as a statement of I AM's rule in Israel. What a special kinship she felt with the LORD, who was honored there in the Holy of Holies, a place where neither she nor any other woman could ever gaze, much less enter. How ironic that in her womb lay the Son of God in a real, physical way vastly beyond the special presence with which God had blessed the Israelites in their Temple!

As Mary gazed joyfully toward the Jewish House of God, her sight fell upon the north wall of the Temple enclosure. She shuddered involuntarily when she saw the squat, menacing facade of the Antonia Fortress with its narrow windows and crenellated battlements crowning the four corner towers. Perhaps it was a premonition of the suffering she would endure 34 years hence through her Son as he struggled to carry his cross from this intimidating home of the Roman garrison in Jerusalem.

The Temple of Herod (Second Temple), front view from inside the Court of Women.
(Temple faces east)

It was late afternoon before the Nazarene party had wound its way through the olive groves and past the garden of Gethsemane, location of the olive press (*gethsemane* in Aramaic) which supplied much of Jerusalem's need for the valuable oil. After years and years of attending the high festivals, the logistics of the visits had become routine. The Galileans and other geographical entities were accustomed to making their camps in specific areas. Leaving the women to set up camp, the men headed down the hill and across the Kidron Valley to pay their respects to Yahweh. They entered the Temple Mount through the Susa Gate,[1] then up a series of ramps into Solomon's Portico, a colonnaded porch running the entire length of the Temple area on the eastern side. Here the moneylenders and the sacrificial animal stalls and cages were operating at their usual fever pitch.

---

[1]Later rebuilt as the double-arched Golden Gate, which can be seen today. It was sealed over, however, and a cemetery created in front of it by the Arabs in an effort to defeat an ancient Jewish prophecy that the Messiah would enter Jerusalem through this gate. Jewish customs did not permit a member of the priestly class, which the Messiah was expected to be, to ride through a cemetery.

The Fortress Antonia, adjacent to the Temple Mount.

Clopas arranged for his family and Mary to stay overnight with friends who lived in the city. Through their contacts, he was also able to find a small merchants' caravan heading up into the Judean hills southwest of Jerusalem toward Ain Karem, home to Elizabeth and Zechariah. It was an affluent village located about seven miles from the city, and set in a beautiful valley.

Just after dawn the next morning, the party set out. Mary's bags were carried on one of the camels that loped along beside her. The merchants all rode their own camels. Mary, some servants, and a couple of other guest travelers walked. Descending from the hills surrounding Jerusalem on its high mountain plateau, the caravan found level ground for awhile but soon began to ascend again into even more spectacular scenery, winding through steep, terraced hills clumped with towering cypress trees.

The caravan dropped Mary and her things at the entrance to the village and then proceeded on its way. She hefted the small goatskin bag of water she had brought from Nazareth and a wicker basket with clothing, some food items and gifts, and headed briskly up the road toward the village spring located approximately in the center of the town. It had been several years since her family had visited here and she was not certain where Elizabeth's residence was located. She remembered that it was quite large. Zechariah was an important priest of the class of Abijah. He, like the other priests when selected by lot, burned incense at the altar of the Lord in the Holy Place in the Temple in Jerusalem.

Two women and a young girl were drawing water from the spring[2] when Mary approached. "I am Mary of Nazareth, of the house of Joachim and Anne, descendants of God's holy servant, King David. My kinswoman is Elizabeth, of the house of Zechariah, who lives in this village. Could you tell me where she lives?" asked Mary.

The women regarded her for a moment, questioning any stranger. But the young girl, still innocent, still open to the impulses of her heart, immediately responded: "I know where she lives! She lives in that house up there." The girl pointed toward an imposing home perched near the top of a steep hill overlooking the village. There was a very long line of steps, broken up periodically with landings and benches, leading up to the house. Mary took a deep breath, but before she could take a step the young girl continued: "She has been blessed by God with a miracle! She's very, very old . . . maybe even older than my grandmother . . . and she's going to have a baby! Everyone says this baby will be a great prophet. Some say he might be the Messiah himself!"

"Shush, Rachel!" One of the women stepped forward and grabbed the girl by her upper arm, pulling her away from Mary. "It is not necessary to share such matters with strangers. Besides, if this visitor really is Elizabeth's kin, she will find out soon enough what wonders God can do when He chooses."

Mary smiled at the girl and thanked her with a voice that would forever ring in the child's memory as the sound of silver chimes tinkling in a gentle wind. Now, as she turned and climbed the stone steps to Elizabeth's house, stopping occasionally to admire the sweeping vistas of terraced fields and vineyards stretching off toward Jerusalem, she began to run over in her mind what she would say to Elizabeth about her own miraculous pregnancy. She considered various approaches, but all of them seemed simply incredible. It was astonishing enough that God would permit His Son to be born of a woman. And to her! That made it even more unbelievable, Mary thought, because she was so insignificant. At least Elizabeth was married to an important priest, who ministered on behalf of the whole people of Israel in the most sacred place on earth. *I, on the other hand,* thought Mary, *am truly one of God's least notable persons, daughter of simple people in a small, poor village in Galilee.* Mary blushed as she imagined Elizabeth's reaction when she told her of the angel's visit to her in Nazareth. *I'll sound like some foolish child trying to top someone else's wonderful news,* she sighed.

Mary paused to lift her thoughts and heart to God. Whenever she did that, all heaven stopped to listen. Before she could even formulate the words of her prayer, a great calm settled over her, evaporating her fears, replacing her anxiety of the moment before with a joy that practically carried her to Elizabeth's and Zechariah's threshold. She knocked at the imposing wooden door, too caught up in the excitement of the moment to notice the intricate, raised design on the rich

---

[2]Today this spring is known as "Mary's Spring" and is an abundant source of water for the local area.

cedar surface. A minute passed and Mary was about to knock again, when she heard the slow shuffle of feet on the other side.

The door opened. Standing before Mary was a woman in her mid-fifties, obviously pregnant. Her face showed the strain of bearing a child long after her body had lost the resiliency and strength that God gave to women for just this purpose. But the radiance of her happiness was unmistakable. It thrilled Mary for she saw in Elizabeth's face exactly the joy which overwhelmed her own being.

"Elizabeth, it's true!" exclaimed Mary. "Oh, blessed and merciful Lord, gracious and kind beyond all understanding, thank you, thank you!" Mary started to identify herself, but before she could say more than, "I am Mary . . ." Elizabeth clasped her in her arms and pulled her inside the house.

"I know who you are, child. You are the mother of the Messiah!" Elizabeth stepped back then a couple of steps, as if to take in the whole of Mary's appearance. She stared at the young teenager, her face registering both awe and rapture. Mary herself was speechless with astonishment that Elizabeth already knew what she had been so concerned about explaining.

At that moment, Zechariah appeared on the landing of the staircase leading from the main floor to the upper level where the couple had their bedroom, a guest room and rooms for sewing and study or prayer. Seeing Elizabeth standing near the front door with a young woman, but not yet having recovered his powers of speech,[3] he started to descend the steps to welcome their guest. She looked familiar but he could not place her.

Elizabeth heard her husband on the stairway but could not pull her gaze away from Mary. So she cried out in a voice loud enough to be heard by Zechariah, in fact throughout the house, as the Holy Spirit prompted her:

> **"Blest are you among women and blest is the fruit of your womb. But who am I that the mother of my Lord should come to me? The moment your greeting sounded in my ears, the baby leapt in my womb for joy. Blest is she who trusted that the Lord's words to her would be fulfilled."[4]**

Zechariah stopped in mid-step. Elizabeth's last words stung a bit as he remembered his own disbelief in the Temple and the Angel Gabriel's punishment for his skepticism about the impending birth of his son, who was to be a great instrument of God's plan for Israel. But the phrase that echoed in his mind was *"mother of my Lord."* The announcement itself was stunning beyond any other words which an Israelite could ever hope to hear. But there was more here . . . much more.

---

[3]He was reduced to this state of silence after doubting the word of the Angel Gabriel that Elizabeth would bear him a son. See Lk 1:18-20.

[4]Lk 1:42-45

Elizabeth still stood before Mary, now with her hands clasped together at her bosom, then clutching her abdomen with wide eyes and open mouth, obviously attuned to the activities of her unborn son. She grinned and laughed, then hugged Mary again and began to dance around and around the room with her until her frail body reminded her that such exertions were not a good idea.

Zechariah, much wiser now to the mysterious ways of God and His messengers, understood that Elizabeth had learned the momentous news not from this child's lips but by a direct revelation from God. The Messiah was coming to save His people! *My God!* he realized. *My son is to be His messenger!*

Then Mary spoke:

> **"My being proclaims the greatness of the Lord,**
> > **my spirit finds joy in God my savior,**
> **For he has looked upon his servant**
> > **in her lowliness;**
> > **all ages to come shall call me blessed.**
> **God who is mighty has done great things for me,**
> > **holy is his name;**
> **His mercy is from age to age**
> > **on those who fear him.**
>
> **"He has shown might with his arm;**
> > **he has confused the proud in their inmost thoughts.**
> **He has deposed the mighty from their thrones**
> > **and raised the lowly to high places.**
> **The hungry he has given every good thing,**
> > **while the rich he has sent empty away.**
> **He has upheld Israel his servant,**
> > **ever mindful of his mercy;**
> **Even as he promised our fathers,**
> > **promised Abraham and his descendants**
> > **forever."**[5]

"Mary, your song is beautiful!" Elizabeth exclaimed. "Truly you will be called 'blessed' by all future generations, and by all those past, too! But do you think that the Messiah has come to disturb the social order, perhaps to turn out those now in power and to install those who will be His followers? Will He be the new King of Israel, like David before Him?"

Mary answered, "By choosing me, His most insignificant and unimportant child, God has already turned the social order upside down! In selecting the least of His servants to be the instrument of salvation, He has magnified His own greatness to the highest heavens! His mission of deliverance

---

[5]Lk 1:46-55

is to the poor and to those who suffer. To those who have nothing, He brings everything, for in God is all that there is or can be. But they who have much, and who scheme and oppress in the name of power and privilege, will be cast aside by our Lord who will make a kingdom out of the hearts that love Him. I hope He will restore His people Israel to the favor of His Father, and that all peoples of the earth shall acknowledge Him and serve Him and live in harmony as He guides us. But God's ways are most mysterious. Already He has put to flight all the confident predictions and expectations of our priests and elders, who have long foretold of a great king who would appear one day, drive out all foreigners, and install Israel as the ruler of the earth under His divine tutelage. They look for their messiah in the halls of royalty and power. They will never find Him there. I am so excited, Cousin Elizabeth, because now I understand that the promise of the Lord to Israel is to be fulfilled through mercy, goodness and love. The kingdom where these reign is, indeed, as far above our earthly kingdoms as is the sky above the earth!"

Zechariah was humbled by the wisdom which tumbled from this mere child's lips. As Mary spoke, he felt the truth and power of what she said as though it were conviction carried in him from his birth. Overwhelmed by the realization that he stood in a room next to the Son of God and His mother, and that he himself had been honored beyond all comprehension by the son to be born soon to Elizabeth, Zechariah began to weep. His tears filled his eyes, then rolled slowly down his pale cheeks, dripping onto his costly brocaded cloak. *What a fool I have been, confident of my understanding and filled with my own self-righteousness because I adhered to the commands of the Lord,* he thought. *The wisdom of God stands here before me in the form of this uneducated girl. Truly His judgment was just when he reduced my babbling to silence! May my tongue not be loosed again until I shall be taught by the Holy Spirit how to speak His truth!*

With his tears flowing freely, Zechariah turned to leave. Elizabeth attempted to console him with a hug, sensing the thoughts and emotions he was experiencing. But Zechariah held up his hand, entreating her with his eyes to excuse him, and retired to his prayer room upstairs.

Elizabeth, now quite tired herself, invited Mary to follow her upstairs to her guest room. When they arrived, Mary began to unpack her few things and discovered there the papyrus scroll that Anne had given her before she started out on the journey. "Oh, Elizabeth. I nearly forgot. Mother sent this letter for you. I was to give it to you as soon as I saw you but I am afraid the excitement and relief of the Lord's revelation to you pushed aside all other thoughts."

Elizabeth broke the seal and opened the letter. She smiled as she read a mother's love and concern for her daughter's welfare:

> *My dearest Elizabeth,*
> *I am writing this letter to you because Mary will soon tell you about the most wonderful news since God chose our ancestor Abraham to establish a people for him on earth. The Lord is sending the Messiah! He is on his way now. Mary is to*

be his mother. This may be hard for you to believe, but an angel appeared to Mary and told her of this great event. What may be even more difficult for you to accept is that Mary's child was conceived in her womb directly by the power of God. There is no earthly father!

The angel also told Mary that you are with child, in fact in your sixth month. Praised be God for His mercy and His kindness! I know how you have suffered from your barrenness for nearly forty years but also how graciously you had accepted His will for you and Zechariah.

As you may recall, Mary, too, was born late in my child-bearing years. From her birth she has walked in the grace of God so palpable that sometimes I think I can actually hear the voices of angels surrounding her. Not one time in her entire life has Mary so much as shaded the truth, much less told an outright lie. If God has not worked this miracle in her, it can only mean that Mary is not well. But if you are, indeed, with child as the angel foretold, then all that was revealed to Mary must be true for we had no other way of learning about your wonderful news.

May God bless you and Zechariah and your house. Surely the son to be born to you will be great in the sight of both God and men!

Your loving cousin,
Anne

Elizabeth put the letter down and smiled at Mary, her fatigue momentarily forgotten. "Child, tell me about the angel's visit to you! I want to hear every wonderful detail! And then I will tell you about the angel's visit to Zechariah to announce the child who already from my very womb lives to serve the Son of God. No doubt it was the same angel. He said his name was Gabriel. Poor Zechariah cannot speak now, but he has written of what happened to him in the Temple in Jerusalem." The two women shared their stories and their joy for hours that night.

For the next several weeks, Mary helped Elizabeth in all the myriad tasks that were the responsibility of a homemaker in Israel 2,000 years ago. Elizabeth's large house was demanding and she had domestic help. She also had many friends and family members who visited often. In fact, there were people coming and going almost constantly, at least until nightfall. But she was a woman in her mid-fifties about to deliver her first child. She tired easily and sometimes every bone and muscle in her body ached. Mary quickly learned the routine of the household and intuitively sensed when Elizabeth needed her personal attention. The two women spent every moment they could in excited and joyful speculation about what God had in store for Israel, and through it, all the nations of the earth now that the Messiah was on His way. They wondered about the exact role that Elizabeth's son[6] would play.

The angel had told Zechariah:

"God himself will go before him, in the spirit and power of Elijah, to turn the hearts of fathers to their children and the rebellious to the wisdom of the just, and to prepare for the Lord a people well-disposed."[7]

"Do you think that God will send Elijah back to earth to help my son, John?" Elizabeth asked Mary.

"I don't know, Elizabeth," Mary replied. "The Scribes teach that Elijah must return to the earth before God will restore His kingdom here. But the hand of the Lord is clearly already upon your son. It may be that the Holy Spirit will convey the spirit and power of Elijah *through* him to call our people back to the faith of our fathers."

And so the two women passed three months together. One day, when Elizabeth was nearly at term, she paused to watch Mary as she passed by on her way to help with the cleaning. It was early yet, but Mary's own pregnancy was approaching four months and the changes in her body were becoming more noticeable.

"Mary," Elizabeth said to her. "Does Joseph know that you are with child?"

"No," replied Mary. "At the time of the angel's visit to me, he was away from the village. I had to leave Nazareth to visit you before he returned. So I have not yet had an opportunity to tell him. I'm sure he will rejoice as we have at this wonderful, wonderful news!"

Elizabeth frowned and was pensive for a few moments. "Mary, I think you must return at once to Nazareth and tell Joseph about the impending birth of the Messiah. If he learns that you are with child before he understands the miraculous circumstances of this conception, he may think the worst. As you know, he could even expose you to the law, which requires stoning in such cases."

Mary's face grew troubled for a moment but then brightened again. "Elizabeth, surely God will not leave this detail unaddressed. He may already have sent His angel to tell Joseph as he told me. And, if I leave now before your baby is birthed, who will help you care for him and look after you better than I?"

"My child, there will be so many relatives and neighbors in here to help me and to see this child about whom everyone is curious that we'll all be standing shoulder to shoulder!" laughed Elizabeth. "No, you must return to Nazareth. It is time to share this great news with the man who has been chosen to be the foster father of the Son of God. This is a great responsibility and he will need time to reflect on what God has called him to do."

---

[6]He was to be named, "John," according to the order of the Angel Gabriel. Lk 1:13.

[7]Lk 1:17

And so Mary made preparations to leave. Two weeks later, she arrived at her home in Nazareth. In her maternity she grew more lovely every day. But the reason for her radiance had also become more apparent.

———

THE CANTICLE OF ZECHARIAH

Blessed be the Lord, the God of Israel,
because he has visited and
ransomed his people.

He has raised a horn of saving strength for us
in the house of David, his servant,
As he promised through the mouths of his holy ones,
the prophets of ancient times:
Salvation from our enemies
and from the hands of all our foes.

He has dealt mercifully with our fathers
and remembered the holy covenant he made,
The oath he swore to Abraham our father
he would grant us:
that, rid of fear and delivered from the enemy,
We should serve him devoutly
and through all our days
be holy in his sight.

And you, O child, shall be called
prophet of the Most High;
For you shall go before the Lord
to prepare straight paths for him,
Giving his people a knowledge of salvation
in freedom from their sins.

All this is the work of the kindness of our God;
he, the Dayspring, shall visit
us in his mercy
To shine on those who sit in darkness
and in the shadow of death,
to guide our feet into the way of peace.[8]

---

[8]Lk 1:68-79

QUESTIONS FOR REFLECTION

1) If you had been Mary's mother, would you have sent a note to Elizabeth (assuming you knew how to write and could find something to write on)? Would you have done something else?

2) How did Elizabeth know that Mary was to be the mother of the Messiah?

3) Why did the Angel Gabriel take away Zechariah's ability to speak when he questioned the prophecy of John's birth but not Mary's when she questioned how she was to conceive?

4) Why do you think Mary "left in haste" to visit Elizabeth after learning of Elizabeth's pregnancy?

5) Why does Luke tell this story? Is it to show the connection between Jesus and John the Baptist? Or might he have been accounting for Mary's absence during the first part of her pregnancy? Can you think of another reason?

6) When Elizabeth was "moved by the Holy Spirit" she recognized that Mary was the mother of the Messiah, even though she didn't know before then that Mary was even pregnant. Have there been any moments in your life when you have suddenly seen a spiritual dimension in an everyday scene?

7) In Mary's Canticle (p. 27 above), she states, "My being proclaims the greatness of the Lord . . ." In other translations, this poem/song/prayer of Mary's has been translated, "My soul does magnify the Lord . . ." What do you think Mary means here?

8) Mary goes on to say about God: "The hungry he has given every good thing, while the rich he has sent empty away." Is she saying that only the poor and hungry will find God and that all those who are rich in worldly goods are doomed? Or is she referring not to material wealth but rather to spiritual hunger (the hungry), for whom God gives Himself (every good thing), while the rich (the self-righteous) will never find God because they are content with themselves?

9) In Mary's visit to Elizabeth, what parallels do you see with your own life? Do you reach out quickly to help those in need? When you receive honors, do you bask in your own glory or are you more concerned that others also be appreciated, for their own achievements, or perhaps for the assistance they gave to you in achieving your successes?

10) Mary's visit to Elizabeth has been characterized as "faith in action." In what ways might you put your faith into action?

Let this be a sign to you: in a manger you will find an infant wrapped in swaddling clothes. Lk 1:12

THIRD JOYFUL MYSTERY

The Nativity

It was late in July when Mary trudged up the steep streets of Nazareth toward her parents' home. The caravan which had brought her to Nazareth from Jerusalem had stopped in the village center to replenish its water supply before proceeding on to Sepphoris, a thriving city with a Roman garrison and a predominantly Greek culture, located about three miles from Nazareth.

Despite her youth, the demands upon her physical resources of the baby growing in her womb and the hot summer sun had taken their toll. She wiped the perspiration from her brow, frowning to see the dirt streaks left on the linen cloth from the omnipresent dust. She passed through the courtyard and stepped over the low threshold of Anne and Joachim's home, entering the shady, relatively cool area of the family's main living area. Mary called to her mother, announcing her return.

Anne emerged from the small room which she and Mary used as a place for sewing and reading. Located on the south side of their house, with two windows, it received the best light. It also served as Mary's bedroom. "Mary! Welcome home, my dear, dear child! Your father and I have missed you terribly. How was your journey? Are you feeling all right? Did Elizabeth have her baby? What did Elizabeth and Zechariah say to you when you told them about the Messiah?" There were more questions in the queue of Anne's excitement, but they were temporarily sidetracked as she embraced and kissed her daughter, not noticing and not caring whether she was dusty.

She stepped back and, holding Mary at arm's length, appraised her figure. "You are positively glowing, child! Have you been well? Any morning sickness? Poor dear, you must be exhausted from such a journey."

Mary smiled and then, touched by her mother's solicitude, began to weep silently. But tears of love and happiness feel incongruous, which made Mary laugh as she wiped them away. The effect was not unlike seeing rain fall while the sun remains shining. Anne hugged her again and began to cry herself.

After a few moments, when the two women had composed themselves, Mary said: "I had a little sickness at Elizabeth's, not much. But as you can see, Mother, my feelings do seem to be a little closer to the surface now! Anyway, I am fine and very happy to be home. The visit was wonderful, for the Lord preceded me everywhere I went. Even the camel drivers, and you know how difficult they can be, went out of their way to be pleasant. I cannot describe to you the joy that has filled my soul these past four months. Let me freshen up just a bit and then I will tell you all the amazing things which God has accomplished already for Israel and for us."

That evening's meal would feature day-old bread because no housework or cooking was accomplished that particular afternoon. Mary told her mother about all the things she had experienced since leaving home four months earlier. She tried to remember every detail of the visit, including Elizabeth's recognition of her as the mother of the Messiah before she had barely had time to say her name. Anne listened rapturously, sometimes asking her to repeat segments for the sheer joy of hearing them again. It was thus that Joachim found them when he returned home that evening. Then, of course, the stories had to be told all over again, much to Anne's delight, who enjoyed sharing the great news almost as much as hearing it the first time.

The family's excitement was dampened only slightly by the realization that Joseph still did not know anything about what was taking place. He had to be told at once, of course. The fact of Mary's pregnancy was not obvious yet, but the discerning eyes of the village women would quickly note the changes in Mary's body and deduce the likely explanation. Then the rumors would fly and Joseph would be deeply hurt if he found out that way. Worse, he might be so offended that he would refuse to believe Mary's story. His reputation as a gentle and kind man was well known. But so was his absolute integrity. Even if his love for Mary kept him from reporting her to the elders, it was highly unlikely that he could be persuaded to accept responsibility for the child unless he knew the circumstances of Jesus' conception. This thought so troubled Joachim that he leaped to his feet and said, "We must tell Joseph tonight! It's not too late. I'll go and bring him back here. He'll be very anxious to see Mary, anyway."

"No," Anne said. "Mary has not even had a chance to recover from her journey, which has certainly been difficult for her. Tomorrow will be soon enough to meet with Joseph. He will understand when we explain all the circumstances. After all, if the Holy Spirit told Elizabeth, surely He will do the same for Joseph. For now, we all need a good night's rest, although I am so excited myself that I may not be able to sleep!"

The next day, Joachim went in search of Joseph. He found him working on the very small house that he and Mary would share after their wedding. It was only about one hundred yards from Anne and Joachim's home, but then, everything in Nazareth was close to everything else. Although he had little money, Joseph's skill as a carpenter would be put to good use in making a door and furniture for the new home. He had already moved his shop to the side of the little limestone cottage.

Joseph saw Joachim walking up the street and called out to him. "Good morning, Joachim! Come and see how the place I am preparing for Mary is coming along. Tell me if you think it will be adequate for one of God's most wonderful creations! It's not much yet, but by the time we are married next year it will be quite comfortable, I think."

Joachim was cheered to see how deeply Joseph loved his daughter. He knew she would be in the best possible care. He trembled a little now as he considered the purpose of his visit. "Good morning, Joseph! You are, indeed, a genius with tools and wood. Yes, Mary is a very special child. But it is clear to me that you, too, have been chosen by God Himself to be Mary's husband. Together, you will have the most important mission of any family since God created Adam."

Joseph paused in mid-hammer stroke at this last comment. What on earth was Joachim talking about? He was merely a simple carpenter; talented, yes, but no one who could hope to be more than moderately prosperous and then only if Herod the Great's extensive building program continued. The nation had definitely prospered since she made her uneasy peace with Rome. Many Jews, however, viewed Roman peace and commercial union as coming at the cost of their identity as God's chosen people. In other words, at the cost of their souls. Joseph sympathized with this point of view, advocated most stridently by the Zealots, but saw clearly the folly in violent resistance. He was firmly convinced that only a more rigorous and faithful adherence to God's commandments to Israel, as given through Moses, could protect her people from the malign influences of the Roman culture.

Now Joseph reflected on Joachim's extravagant phrases. *Most important mission . . . since Adam! The old man has been spending too much time in the hot sun,* thought Joseph. He decided to ignore the comment.

"Have you heard from Mary, by the way?" Joseph asked. "I have missed her since she's been away visiting her cousin. My brother Clopas' wife, Mary, told me about the trip to Jerusalem at Passover. I've also heard the amazing rumors about this woman's pregnancy, long after her child-bearing years should be over. The story was all over Jerusalem about an angel telling the woman's husband, a Temple priest, that his wife would conceive. For some reason, the man was unable to speak after that. Zechariah is his name, isn't it? Anyway, there's been a lot of excited talk about this child maybe being the Messiah himself. I'd like to hear what Mary thinks when she gets back."

Joachim turned pale at Joseph's words, but answered his question in what he thought was an even voice. "Mary is back, Joseph. She returned yesterday afternoon. It is very important that you meet as soon as possible. Could you join us for supper tonight?"

Joseph noted the underlying urgency in Joachim's voice but his excitement at seeing Mary again overwhelmed the warning signal. "Of course I will come! Thank you for inviting me. Please tell Mary that I look forward with all the joy of my heart to seeing her again!"

Late in the afternoon, Joseph arrived at the house of Joachim, Anne and Mary. Passing through the small courtyard in front, he knocked at the door and was greeted by Anne. He presented her with a bundle of pomegranates and figs, wrapped in a small linen cloth that could be used later as a handkerchief or for any number of other household purposes. Galilee was known for its linen industry, produced from flax, and Sepphoris was one of the principal trade centers for the cloth. Joseph apologized for the figs, noting that while they were edible, it was still a few weeks before the fig season would reach its prime. He also carried a small bouquet of rockrose.[1] The plant was highly regarded, not only for the beauty of its flowers and fragrance, but also for its medicinal qualities. Shyly, he offered the flowers to Mary, who stood near the back of the room, a few steps away from Anne.

"Joseph, how very kind of you!" said Mary with a smile that vanquished every shadow in the room. "Thank you very much!"

Joseph felt his head swirl with the joy of being in the presence of this beautiful young woman, giddy with the realization that she had consented to be his wife. Not a day had passed since then that he had not thanked God from morning till night for what he considered to be the greatest of all possible blessings. He had been kidded by some of his friends and relatives about marrying such a beautiful girl. What he had not been able to explain was that there was an inner beauty in her which so enveloped him when they were together that it was almost as if she had swallowed the sun and the moon and now they shone forth from her face to light the world.

The meal was served on wooden dishes atop a low, square table. The participants sat on rush mats and ate most of the food with their fingers. Normally, the women would serve while the men ate, but this was treated as a family occasion and Mary and Anne joined Joseph and Joachim after serving the table. The variety and portions of food were generous, consisting of fish, nuts, eggs, vegetables, cheese, bread and honey, accompanied by goat's milk and wine. After eating, the family relaxed in conversation. Mary told about Elizabeth's pregnancy and details of the visit of the angel to Zechariah, but left out any reference to her own angelic visit and the ensuing conception of the Messiah. She looked to Joachim to broach the subject, although she was not anxious about it. Since that was one of the principal purposes of this evening's occasion, she knew it would be brought up soon.

Joachim, on the other hand, had been tense throughout the meal. Reports of the astonishing, if not downright miraculous, pregnancy of Elizabeth and the angel's visit to Zechariah had floated around Nazareth since shortly after the Passover excursion had returned more than three months ago. It was a desperate hope, but one that Joachim couldn't resist clinging to, to think that Joseph would not also have heard the same rumors. After all, Clopas was his brother. This meant their most convincing argument for the truth of Mary's own angelic appearance was essentially worthless. The fact that he, Anne and Mary had not known of the pregnancy then did not mean that news of it could not have been brought up earlier from Jerusalem by one of the numerous caravans which passed regularly

---

[1]The rockrose is a fragrant flower with large white petals, each of which is marked at its base with a glowing scarlet-rose splotch deepening to black, surrounding a golden center of stamens and pistil. The flower grows on an evergreen shrub, three to five feet high, and was common in Palestine.

very near to Nazareth. Others might very easily choose to believe the family had learned of it this way, rather than through a direct report from a heavenly messenger. Besides, it was old news by now.

Joachim had also noticed an occasional quizzical expression on Joseph's face when Mary had moved in such a way as to reveal her swelling abdomen. He prayed now more fervently than he had ever prayed in his life, even when he had been so distraught over the barrenness of Anne, for help in convincing Joseph that what was about to happen was a miracle and not a scandal.

"Joseph," Joachim began. "We invited you here tonight for several reasons. Certainly, you were anxious to see your betrothed after these several months, as she has been to see you. Anne and I also enjoy your company very much. You are a fine man and we are proud that we are soon to become kin to one another. But there is one reason which overshadows all of these and dwarfs them in importance, as well." Joachim paused, took a deep breath, and continued: "Before Mary left to visit her cousin Elizabeth, she was visited by an angel."

Joseph had been listening with the kind of mellow attention one gives to after-dinner toasts until Joachim mentioned the angel. At that, he sat bolt upright and stared intently at Joachim, wondering if he had misunderstood, or if perhaps Joachim had drunk too much wine and simply slurred his words. But there was no mistake. Joachim went on talking about a real angel, a messenger from God, someone who had actually visited Mary in this house a mere four months ago.

"The message which the angel brought is what we must discuss, Joseph," said Joachim. He hesitated, trying to decide how to put it, then just plunged ahead. "God is sending the Messiah; in fact, has already sent Him. He is to be born of a woman. Mary is to be His mother."

Joseph was thunderstruck. He looked at Mary, who at first returned his gaze, but then blushed and turned away. Now he stared at Joachim and Anne, who were studying him carefully, with some alarm. He looked back at Mary and said, "You *are* pregnant! I thought I noticed some of the village women pointing and snickering as I walked over here tonight. Now I understand why! Do you expect me to believe that an angel is the father of Mary's baby?"

Anne spoke up now. "No, Joseph, we do not expect you to believe an angel is the father because that would not be true. Mary's baby has been conceived by the power of God without the normal interaction of man and woman. The child to be born will be literally the Son of God. Israel has long dreamed of and prayed for fulfillment of the Lord's promise to send a savior for His people. Few, however, considered that the Messiah might be from God Himself. As always, God's actions and goodness overwhelm the understanding and expectations of His people."

The color rose in Joseph's cheeks. This was too much. *But, Mary . . .* He stared at her while his thoughts tumbled confusedly through his mind. *Mary, unfaithful! No, it was not possible!* Even now, he felt her goodness and the peace and joy which always surrounded him in her presence. But this story was too hard! No one would believe it . . . because it was unbelievable!! Joseph stood and Joachim rose with him.

"Joseph, listen, please! When the angel appeared to Mary, he told her that her kinswoman Elizabeth, who is long past her childbearing years, was also pregnant with a son who would play a great role for the Messiah in the deliverance of Israel. We had no knowledge whatsoever of this until Mary learned it from the angel. But, as you know yourself, the story is true. Elizabeth was pregnant. By now, she will have had her baby and news of his birth will probably arrive from Jerusalem before long. Does this not offer confirmation of what we have told you?" Joachim spoke hopefully to Joseph.

"That story was all over Nazareth since Clopas and the other Passover pilgrims returned three months ago!" replied Joseph. "Your knowing it proves nothing."

"Joseph, we are honest people and have never deliberately deceived anyone," said Anne with a hint of indignation in her voice. "And we are not deceiving you now."

Joachim tried another tack. "Joseph, have you not read in the Prophet Isaiah that the Messiah is to be born of a virgin?"

Joseph replied, "Many of our teachers say the passage refers only to the birth of Hezekiah, son of King Ahaz, before the time of troubles. Even those who find in the words a reference to the Savior of Israel generally claim simply that the Messiah will be a first-born son and that His mother will have been a virgin prior to His conception. Only the most radical think otherwise, and even they have not suggested that God Himself would be the father. Admittedly, if the birth itself is to be from a virgin, the method of conception would be a great mystery, but then what man could put limits upon the power of God?" Joseph's voice trailed off as he uttered this last thought. He shook his head. "I'm sorry. I want to believe you because otherwise I shall never feel joy again. But the story is just too fantastic and Mary's sudden absence too convenient. Even if we marry quickly, people will count the months and make jokes about us behind our backs."

As he finished speaking, Joseph looked again at Mary. She was looking at him with an expression of such sadness that he nearly burst into angry tears. There was no shame in her face. Only pity, and innocence, and great, great love. Joseph felt himself losing control and, mumbling an apology and a promise to talk more about it later, he rushed out the door. Once outside, he could hold back his tears no longer and he wept with great wracking sobs.

For the next two days, Joseph was in torment. Actually, "torment" is too gentle a word for the agony that assailed Joseph's soul. He simply was not convinced of the truth of what he had been told. On the other hand, he could not quite bring himself to believe that Mary had been unfaithful to him. It was like trying to imagine Israel without her special relationship with God. His heart and mind were locked in ferocious argument with each other. Finally, he resolved he would divorce her but do everything in his power to see that she was taken care of and that her baby was well provided for. He knew that there was no way he could expose her to the law, which would mean her being stoned to death. He would help her resettle someplace far away from Nazareth and he, himself, would refuse all further comment on the matter. If he had to suffer some ridicule and even contempt for this, so be it. Having made the decision, and a generous, humane one at that, Joseph assumed he would feel better. However, his heart gave him no rest. Something still felt terribly, terribly wrong to him. Although his sense of justice was satisfied, he went to bed that night, still at war with himself, and still in the deepest despair he had ever felt.

Since his dinner at Mary's, Joseph had been tossing and turning into the wee hours of each morning. He had recurrent nightmares, dreaming of Mary fleeing an angry mob, carrying her baby, as they gathered up stones to cast at her. He dreamed of himself, angrily pointing at Mary, who cowered before him, as the elders of the village demanded the punishment of the law. He saw himself accused by God for rejecting the Messiah, then being flung from the top of the Temple because he had blocked Israel's salvation. Joseph woke from each nightmare, drenched with sweat, often crying out before he realized he had only been dreaming, then falling back onto his straw mattress and beginning the cycle all over again. Just before dawn on the third day, he fell into a deep, dreamless sleep, exhausted from the emotional turmoil of this third wretched night in a row.

The voice was clear and commanding. It pierced Joseph's deep fatigue and snapped him awake as if he had been merely napping.

"Joseph, son of David, have no fear about taking Mary as your wife. It is by the Holy Spirit that she has conceived this child. She is to have a son and you are to name him Jesus because he will save his people from their sins."[2]

Joseph bolted to an upright sitting position. Standing before him was a man, with the face of youth but a look of ancient wisdom, dressed in a brilliant white tunic with a gold sash. Although it was still night and there was no light from fire or moon, the man was perfectly illuminated. He looked at Joseph with such kindness and love that Joseph was immediately put at ease.

Joseph exclaimed, "It's true, then!" This realization and its import for Mary, Israel and for him sent his mind whirling and he turned away for a moment, while the implications settled in. When he looked back a few moments later, the angel was gone. Yet Joseph had not been aware of any diminution of light, although he sat now in total darkness. Had he dreamed it? He thought about this possibility for a moment then shook his head. *If that was a dream,* he said to himself, *then I can no longer tell reality from fantasy. No,* thought Joseph, *that was a messenger from God, sent to help a stubborn fool see the truth which his heart has been screaming at him for days!*

Joseph leaped from his bed, all thought of further sleep now impossible. He longed to fly to the house of Joachim and Anne and throw himself at Mary's feet, begging her forgiveness for his stubbornness and pride. But, clearly, that would not do. So he dressed himself and went outside in the cool, predawn

---

[2]Mt 1:20-21

darkness. Soon enough, the sun would rise and bestow another scorching summer day on Galilee. Joseph pondered the enormous significance of the angel's message. "Conceived by the Holy Spirit," the angel had said! The child was conceived by direct action of God, who would, therefore, be his Father. What kind of child would he be? Would angels attend to his every need? *Why would God pick me?* wondered Joseph. *I am only a simple carpenter. Not a very prosperous one, at that. It seems that God is coming to save Israel, not on the clouds of Heaven amid trumpets and lightning, but quietly and unobtrusively. Why?* Joseph mulled the questions over and over in his mind, sensing that God's plan, and probably His purpose also, was dramatically different from anything he or anyone else in Israel had expected.

About an hour after dawn, when Joseph was sure that Mary and her family would have arisen and completed their morning prayers, he knocked on their door. Joachim answered the knock. He was surprised, and a little wary, too, to see Joseph standing there after not hearing from him for nearly three days.

"Joachim, forgive me for this early, unannounced visit," said Joseph. "But I must speak to Mary now."

Joachim admitted Joseph but not without glancing around a bit to be sure he had not come accompanied by villagers with stones for his daughter.

Mary had been helping her mother at the hearth, but both women had stopped in curiosity to watch Joachim in conversation with the unseen visitor. Now, as Joseph entered the room, Anne's heart skipped a beat, fearing that his previous unbelief had hardened into anger. But Joseph's demeanor was humble and apologetic. He had been anxious to see Mary, to tell her he was sorry and to offer amends; he had been at once excited, scared and joyful. But now, seeing the trust and innocence in Mary's eyes, shame fell upon him and scattered his thoughts as she gazed expectantly at him. He started to speak, stammered, and stopped altogether when tears rushed down his cheeks and drowned his words in a torrent of emotion. Mary hurried to him and silenced his anguish by placing her hands gently upon his two rough, carpenter's hands and gracing him with the most loving smile and a simple statement: "I knew God would show you the truth, Joseph. You will be a wonderful father to the Messiah."

Mary asked him about the angel, wondering if it was the same one who had appeared to her. Joseph attempted to describe the angel, but was a little vague about his facial features.

"I was in a deep sleep when the angel appeared to me," he explained. "He told me how your baby was conceived, instructed me to name him Jesus, and then vanished. It lasted only a few moments." Because of the circumstances of the apparition, when the story was retold later, it would be described as a dream that Joseph had. But there was no comparison between this vividly real experience and the strange, shadowy images of normal dreams. Certainly, Joseph never had any doubts.

The wedding was quickly arranged. Neither family attempted any explanation. Gossip was rampant throughout the village that Mary and Joseph had to advance their wedding date prematurely because they had been unable to wait.

A few particularly malicious persons hinted that perhaps Joseph was not even the father since Mary had been gone so long. But anyone who knew Mary at all found this suggestion as incomprehensible as they would have found the truth, if they had known it. Mary and Joseph bore the gibes and looks stoically, saying simply that it was God's will that they begin their life together immediately if anyone was bold enough to ask why they did not wait the customary year between betrothal and wedding celebration, especially since the wedding date had previously been announced as taking place the following Spring.

The accelerated ceremony was a hardship on all concerned. The small house with the attached carpenter's shed, which Joseph had planned to improve considerably before Mary moved in, was still in a rough, unfinished condition. He had not had time to accumulate the money he planned to have for his new life. Anne, working with her kin and Joseph's kin, did not have time to make all the arrangements she would have liked. She also understood that Mary's pregnancy changed the tone of the wedding since everyone would naturally assume Mary was no longer a virgin. So, rather than the normal festive occasion when the bride and groom dressed as nearly like queen and king as they could afford or borrow, and the feasting and dancing would go on for days, Mary and Joseph were quietly wed in a ceremony with only family members and a few close friends present. Mary of Clopas acted as Mary's Matron of Honor.

The day-long celebration, however, was anything but melancholy. Mary and Joseph's happiness was so complete and so contagious that everyone was practically giddy with the sense that never had there been a more perfectly matched couple. The usual boisterousness was replaced with a total sense of ease and contentment. Laughter was replaced with smiles and loving hugs. This occasion was a wedding fashioned in heaven and the unseen myriad of angels who graced the company brought with them the absolute peace and joy of their heavenly realm. During this part of the ceremony, Mary wore a thin veil covering her face from just below her eyes. Her dress was a white silk gown elaborately embroidered with gold thread depicting lilies in full bloom, tied in the middle with a blue silk sash matching the color of her deep blue eyes. Although the wedding was accomplished by the signing of a legal contract, the traditional blessing was pronounced by a rabbi who was a friend of both families: "Our sister," he intoned, "may you increase to thousands upon thousands; may your offspring possess the gates of your enemies."

At the end of the day, Joseph returned to the limestone bungalow that he and Mary would share. Later that evening, he walked back to Joachim and Anne's home, accompanied by his male family members and friends with lighted torches. They passed the bride's attendants, spread out like mobile lamp posts, each holding a small clay oil lamp with flickering flame. Extra vials of oil dangled from cords attached to their fingers.[3]

When he arrived at the door of Joachim and Anne, Joseph followed the wedding ritual and asked to see his bride. Mary stepped forward and Joseph lifted her veil in preparation for uttering the prescribed expression of joy at the treasure he had found. But words failed Joseph as he looked into the wide, gentle eyes of Mary gazing at him with perfect trust and gratitude. His own sense of unworthiness overwhelmed him. He tried to speak but no sound emerged. He swallowed hard, struggling to maintain his composure. But all he could manage was to stare silently as a solitary tear crept quietly from one deep brown eye, falling softly down his cheek and into his dark beard. His brother, Clopas, saved the moment from embarrassment by taking up the cry of Mary as treasure. The whole wedding party followed suit. Then the party wound its way back along the hilly path to Joseph's house, where the celebration continued amid toasts and blessings from the new couple's family and friends.

Inside their little cottage, Joseph turned to Mary and said, "Mary, we both understand that the Savior is to be born of a virgin. It is clearly God's will that your virginity continue until His Son has come into the world for there must never be any doubt about this Child's origin and uniqueness.

"But I have also come to realize that in a very real way you are espoused to another, to the Spirit of God who has begotten the Child you bear. You are thus the wife of another and it is not my place to be a husband to you in that way which is reserved for spouses.

"I want you to know that I accept this role which the Lord has assigned me with joy and gratitude for the great honor He has bestowed upon me. I am overcome by my own unworthiness to be the guardian of the Son of God and the companion of a woman elevated above all others since the beginning of time. My heart bursts with happiness. Willingly and joyfully do I dedicate my life to this task. Please never feel that you have failed any wifely duty toward me because we both well know that what I have spoken is the will of God for us."

As Mary listened to Joseph, her heart began to sing. His words fit perfectly the divine music that was playing there. She threw her arms around Joseph's neck and, with tears flowing down her cheeks, exclaimed: "Joseph of the House of David, you are, indeed, our Lord's manifest blessing to me and to Israel! Since the angel's visit to me, I have known that my life and my very being have been consecrated to God from the moment of my conception. I knew, too, that in choosing you to be His Son's father in the eyes of men that you would understand and accept this special consecration.

"But, dear, dear Joseph! Do you not see that you, too, have been called to serve God with all your being? No prophet, not even our patriarch, Abraham, ever

---

[3]Years later, Jesus would use similar wedding imagery in warning how the kingdom of heaven can arrive unexpectedly when we are not prepared because we have not remained vigilant and faithful and kept "our oil lamps burning." Mt 25:1-13.

had a more important role to play in the service of the Lord. We belong to God, Joseph, body and soul! As unworthy as we are, and truly He has chosen the most special man in all Israel to be my companion and His Son's guardian, God's love will lift us above all our trials and all our burdens.

"In this house, the flame of divine grace will light the very walls with joy and gladness. The Holy Spirit shall live with us as surely as if He were visible to all who shall visit the home of the Savior of Israel!"

After the wedding, Mary and Joseph settled into their new life together as much as Mary's advancing pregnancy and their unfinished house permitted. Nazareth was a carpentry center for the region and Joseph's house served as both residence and shop. It was located at the end of a row of similar house/shops. Joseph worked at the side of his house, under an awning for protection against the harsh Middle Eastern sun or the periodic seasonal rains. He had plans to construct a regular addition to the house there, complete with doors and windows so that he would not have to move his tools and materials in and out of his living quarters each day. As a skilled carpenter, Joseph was much in demand for construction of farm tools; wooden dishware and utensils, mostly made from the fine-grained amber-colored hardwood of the olive tree; furniture, and housing construction materials, such as posts, beams, doors, and door and window frames.

Mary busied herself with the normal domestic chores of preparing meals, washing and drying their clothing, feeding a few chickens and a couple of goats given to the new couple by Joachim and Anne, and weaving cloth to be made into the tunics, mantles, cloaks, robes, girdles and headpieces worn by first century Palestinians. Bread making began with grinding wheat or barley into flour and used a bit of fermented dough from the previous day's baking as a leavening agent. Besides being a primary mealtime beverage, goat's milk was also used by Mary to make cheese and curds. Her day began around daybreak and did not end until the supper dishes had been cleaned that evening. Ordinarily, she would also manage a small garden plot, raising such crops as cucumbers, melons, leeks, onions, garlic, peas and beans. This task required that a lot of water be carted from the village well and cisterns to keep the plants growing in the dry season. These gardens were commonly located in a few central locations where the soil and topography were best suited for their growth. Planting normally occurred after the first Fall rains in September/October. This year, however, Mary did not plant her own garden but continued to help her mother in the garden they had been tending together for many years, practically since Mary was a toddler.

The weeks passed rapidly and Mary's projected delivery date marched inexorably toward them. Joseph, well aware of the ancient prophecy that the Messiah would be born in Bethlehem,[4] grew increasingly concerned as the baby's birth drew nearer.

---

[4]Mi 5:1: "But you, Bethlehem-Ephrathah/ too small to be among the clans of Judah,/ From you shall come forth for me/ one who is to be ruler in Israel;/ whose origin is from of old,/ from ancient times."

Joseph broached the subject to Mary after supper one evening in mid-November. "Mary, you know about the prophecy that the Messiah will be born in Bethlehem. Do you think we should move there now? Already you are near the end of your eighth month and travel is going to be a great hardship for you. Soon we will not dare make such a journey. What do you think we should do?"

Mary replied, "I, too, have wondered whether we should move to Bethlehem. I have prayed frequently for guidance, but the Lord has chosen not to reply in any way that I can understand. But my heart is at peace for certainly this child and his destiny have been planned by his Father from the beginning of the world. If it is His will that Jesus be born in Bethlehem, that will happen. Perhaps the prophecy does not mean birth but, rather, refers to an event to occur later in our son's life. We must wait and trust in the Lord. He will guide us at the appropriate time."

Joseph saw the wisdom in what Mary said. But he could not help being anxious as the days passed and he watched his beautiful young bride struggle bravely to cope with her long days and many household chores. Anne came over to assist as often as she could, and Mary of Clopas and other relatives also pitched in. Mary never complained and her delight in her baby's movements within the womb was infectious. Even during the winter rains which began that year in late November, her smile and friendliness to all she encountered belied the dark days and brought visitors to her house who sought her presence simply for the joy they found there.

About a week into December, their questioning was answered. Quirinius, governor of Syria, posted a decree issued by Caesar Augustus, directing a census of the entire Roman Empire. Within Israel, every male head of household was required to return to his ancient tribal home to register himself and his family members. For Joseph, this was Bethlehem, where King David was born and raised, because Joseph was a member of the House of David. The census required that he be in Bethlehem no later than the end of the month. The purpose of the census was to update Rome's taxation records and only the male head of household, not family members, was required to appear. Joseph felt that Mary was simply too close to term to travel safely and planned to go by himself, though he was deeply distressed by the thought that he might not be present when Jesus was born. But Mary insisted on making the journey, believing this sudden census to be a clear statement of God's intention for them and the Savior about to arrive. Whatever the hardships, she understood there was a higher purpose behind it all.[5] Better than anyone before or since, Mary accepted without question or doubt the dictates of God and hastily prepared for their departure from Nazareth.

---

[5]At the time, Mary could not foresee how the difficulties of this journey and the humbleness of Jesus' birth would inspire humanity for thousands of years. Past the lavish winter palace of Herod at Jericho. Past the glittering gold and marble of the great Temple in Jerusalem. The God-Man took upon himself and his family the most arduous and humble circumstances so that no person might ever feel too insignificant or too rejected to be loved by God.

Several Nazarenes were required to make the trip. Many family members went along voluntarily, too. Joseph's brother, Clopas, had to delay his departure by a week because of work commitments. Joachim would normally have been required to go, also, but he had contracted a serious illness and was too weak to travel. He obtained a certification of his condition and the number of persons in his family (two), sealed by the local tax collector for Nazareth, and sent it with Joseph to present to the census takers.

The caravan with Mary and Joseph was quickly organized and outfitted and set out from Nazareth, again following the valley route down the Great Plain south of Mount Tabor to the southeast, headed for the Valley of Jezreel and Scythopolis where they would pick up the primary north-south route along the Jordan River.

All the travelers from small villages such as Nazareth usually walked wherever they were going. Only the wealthy could afford litters and horses and camels with saddles. The poor, which included the vast majority of the Israelites, rode "Shank's Mare" on their journeys.

But Mary was nearly nine months pregnant with delivery imminent. Walking to Bethlehem was out of the question. Further, they planned to stay there awhile, so they packed most of their belongings in two bundles. A third bundle contained foodstuffs and two goatskins filled with water. Joseph acquired a donkey and fastened the bundles with cords on either side and at the rear of the animal. He made a makeshift saddle for Mary out of a spare cloak. She sat side-saddle on this, her feet tucked tightly against the animal's side, between its shoulder and the bulging bundle. Joseph walked beside the donkey, guiding it to as gentle a trail as he could find. Mary never complained, but Joseph noticed how she grimaced and blinked back tears of pain whenever the donkey lurched or jostled her as the little animal stepped over rough spots on the trail, especially coming down and going up the hills which filled the countryside of Galilee and Judea. Joseph stopped frequently to let Mary rest and soon they had fallen behind the rest of the caravan.

The first night they were able to catch up to the caravan and spend it in the tents and shelters which the Nazarene group had brought with them. But after that, they were simply too far behind and spent each night alone in one of the many caves which dotted the barren hills along the Jericho route. The road was generally flat and tracked the Jordan River, staying about a quarter mile from the green vegetation which marked the limits of the precious water's influence. From time to time they passed small flocks of sheep and goats, scavenging for food among the scrub plants and sparse grass of the hills. They were traveling at the height of the winter rainy season, but in this regard, God took pity on these most special of all travelers. No rain fell on them throughout the journey.

As they walked along, Joseph pondered how differently God conducted human affairs. The children of the royal families of men lived plush, pampered lives, objects of privilege and ease.[6] The Lord God, on the other hand, Creator of the universe and all that is in it, author of life and sustainer of all that is or ever will be, sent His Son to earth to be born of a simple village girl in an obscure corner of the world. If Joseph had ever entertained fantasies of Jesus' birth by and in the company of angels, surrounded by the splendor of heaven, adored visibly by Israel's great patriarchs, those notions were banished forever by this rough, exhausting journey to Bethlehem. Every step of the way, Joseph prayed that Mary's delivery would not be hastened by the jogging and bumping of the donkey. His prayers and his efforts to stabilize Mary's ride intensified as the little animal made its way up the treacherous rocky paths and steep slopes rising through the arid, intimidating cliffs of the Judean Wilderness east of Jerusalem. For her part, Mary whispered thanks to both God and Joseph for his great devotion to her and often encouraged the little donkey with words of affection and gratitude for its steadiness.

Mary and Joseph spent the fifth night of their journey outside Bethany, a small town about a mile and a half east of the great city. As they had for the previous portion of the trip, they avoided the crowded, noisy inns, called *caravansaries*, filled to capacity and beyond with traders, Jews responding to the census call, merchants, soldiers, camel drivers, muleteers, slaves, servants and pilgrims, not to mention camels, horses, donkeys, mules and an occasional goat or two. They found an olive grove where other families had also put up for the night, erecting makeshift lean-to's out of mats, branches and leaves, or simply rolling up in their cloaks under the starry sky.

The women clucked and fussed over Mary's condition, chiding Joseph for letting his young wife travel in such a condition, and bringing them food, for which they were extremely grateful. After dinner, Mary and Joseph both fell exhausted into a deep sleep, so tired from the exertions and strain of their five days' trip from Nazareth that they overslept, not stirring even in the commotion of the dawn departure of the other travelers.

It was nearly nine a.m. before Joseph awoke with a start. He scrambled up, awoke Mary, joined her in their morning prayers, loaded up the donkey and

---

[6]The children of Israel saw such favored treatment as a right conferred by God. Wealth and status were deemed signs of God's favor, although abuse of such privilege was also considered sinful and worthy of condemnation by God and men. Then, as now, real human events tended to reinforce these notions of God punishing those who proved themselves unworthy of His favor because those who held power were almost always corrupted by it. Of course, the Romans and other Gentile conquerors were considered to be outside the realm of God's favor since they were not only not members of His Chosen People but actively interfered with what they saw as their God-ordained destiny: to be free peoples fully in charge of their own lives, accountable only to I AM, the One God.

The suffering poor, who strove to honor their God despite His apparent punishment of them, perhaps, they thought, for sins committed by their ancestors, were a much thornier theological conundrum, finally answered by the Book of Job's conclusion that God's ways are sometimes impossible for us to fully understand. Jesus' life and teachings put an end, once and for all, to the notion that there is a connection between worldly success and favor in God's eyes. He warned us that material prosperity is a *hindrance* to the holiness to which God calls everyone.

Rocky hills and pasture on the outskirts of Bethlehem.

headed down the road toward Jerusalem. Their route took them around the city on the south side, past the Pool of Siloam and Mount Zion with its Tomb of King David, onto the principal trade route known as the Way of the Patriarchs. They trudged the remaining five miles wearily but with mounting excitement and anxiety until Bethlehem, clustered on the slopes of limestone hills decorated with caves and flocks of sheep, lay before them. The town swarmed with travelers reporting for the census.

"Joseph," Mary whispered with just a hint of anxiousness in her voice. "I am afraid we must hurry. The baby had been very active but now he's dropped. I think he plans to make his appearance in the world very soon."

Joseph stared in alarm at Mary, then urged the donkey forward to cover the remaining half mile or so. As they entered the village, Joseph felt a growing sense of panic. People were everywhere! He had seen the campsites outside the town. But Mary was about to have her baby, the Son of God! She needed better accommodations than a grassy spot under a tree somewhere. She needed privacy and a place to lay the new baby after he was born. Already she was grimacing periodically. They both realized that her labor pains had begun.

Joseph hurried to the main caravansary just outside the north entrance to the town. He helped Mary down from the donkey and arranged a place for her to sit on the ground in a quiet place around the corner from the busy entrance. Inside, the hubbub was deafening as travelers sought accommodations for themselves and their animals. Many sat at tables to one side eating while others scurried along the second floor walkway overlooking the central courtyard.

Joseph identified the innkeeper but could see that several other travelers were already arguing with him and waving their coin purses in apparently vain attempts to acquire a place to stay. The innkeeper merely shrugged and gestured toward the crowds of people milling everywhere inside the packed inn. With his spirits shrinking inside him, Joseph pushed through the mob to reach the innkeeper. When he was nearly able to grasp his sleeve, the innkeeper glanced at him but quickly turned away. It was obvious that Joseph would not have a lot of money to tempt him to squeeze yet one more person into some obscure corner of the inn. "My wife is going to have a baby!" Joseph shouted at the innkeeper. "The baby is coming. I must have a place tonight! One with some privacy. Please!" He considered telling the innkeeper that the Messiah was about to be born, but thought better of it when he realized that such a claim would not only not be believed but would probably get him tossed out of the inn on his ear.

Instead, Joseph told the innkeeper a more ambivalent but no lesser truth: "This child is favored by God. If you help us, your name will be revered in history and God Himself will bless you for it!"

The innkeeper laughed at Joseph and shoved him away, saying, "Every parent thinks their child is the next prophet! What I revere is cash, cold hard coins with the emperor's face on them! If you've got a bag full of that kind of history, then maybe we could talk. But, to be honest with you, friend, I probably couldn't find a private place for your wife and her baby if I wanted to. You see what the situation is here, don't you? And let me tell you, no one else in this town has any room either!"

Joseph felt the tears well up in his eyes. He clasped his hands and prayed from the depth of his soul: "Dear God, forgive me! I have brought the mother of Your Son to this city without a proper place for him to be born. Please help us!"

Joseph was still standing where the innkeeper had left him, praying fervently with his eyes closed, when he felt a tap on his chest and a gentle voice say: "Young man, I overheard your plea to the innkeeper. Where is your wife? Take me to her."

Joseph opened his eyes and saw a middle-aged woman peering intently up at him. She was wearing an apron, but Joseph did not inquire who she was. He simply grasped her hand and pulled her after him as he pushed back through the crowd still milling around the courtyard and doorway. Outside, he led the woman around the corner to where Mary lay quietly praying and gasping as the increasingly strong labor pains continued their rhythmic preparation for the birth of the Savior. Their donkey was tethered nearby.

"Oh, dear!" exclaimed the lady when she saw Mary. "You are so young, child!" Turning to Joseph she said, "I know a place where you will have privacy and some warmth. It is a stable in a cave just down the hill from here. Follow the trail which you will find just over the crest there." She pointed past the caravansary to a rocky slope angling sharply downward into a grassy valley.

"When you get to the bottom, turn right and continue along the trail for about two hundred yards. On your right you will see a cave with a manger and straw in it. There may also be oxen and a sheep or two. I know the farmers who use this stable and I will send word to them that you will be sharing it for awhile. They are good people and will not object. When I get a chance, I will send food down for you and your wife. Hurry now! You are going to be a father very soon, judging by the frequency of those labor pains!"

Joseph helped Mary to her feet and onto the donkey. Then he guided them carefully down the hill and along the trail to the cave. By now, the sky was darkening as the early winter sun set. He led Mary into the cave, which was surprisingly spacious. There were, indeed, as the lady in the apron had said, a couple of oxen resting near the back left of the cave inside a rough stall created by the farmers who owned these beasts. On the right side near the back there was a manger which had been constructed to hold the animals' barley feed. Here Joseph was able to create a small enclosure by extending a cord from the oxen stall to the rock wall and hanging up the extra cloaks they had brought. He brushed the floor of the enclosure as clean as he could and spread fresh straw around from a pile which he found beneath a kind of tarpaulin made of goatskins. He took off his own cloak and spread that over the straw, settling Mary in the middle as best he could.

"Thank you, dear Joseph," Mary said to her harried husband. "This is wonderful. Now I want you to leave me in privacy for awhile. I will be fine. There are angels here with us, although I know you cannot see them. I know what to do when the baby comes and I will call you then. Please give thanks to our Father in heaven for His goodness and His providence."

Joseph started to protest, but seeing the firmness in Mary's eyes, he nodded and assured her he would be right outside the enclosure if she needed him. Using a flint, he lit an oil lamp, being careful to place it well away from anything flammable. And then he prayed.

With his eyes tightly closed and his heart pounding in his chest, hands clenched so tightly his knuckles had turned white, Joseph did not see the resplendent light that filled the cave and spilled into the outside darkness.

Inside the little enclosure her husband had made, Mary also prayed for the strength to deliver her baby alone and to do all the things her mother had taught her would be needed to protect the health of the newborn infant as well as herself. Her contractions were very strong now and she breathed deeply both to ease the pain and manage her anxiety. She briefly considered calling Joseph to come and help her, but decided against it. Not for a moment, however, did she question the wisdom and fairness of God in requiring her to deliver her baby, the Son of the Most High Himself, on the ground inside a dark and dirty stable. She felt the presence of the divine all around her and knew God's angels hovered nearby. Thus, the normal apprehension and fears of a first-time mother were all but smothered by her excited anticipation of seeing the world's Savior, her baby! Like Joseph, Mary, too, had her eyes tightly closed when the dazzling light burst forth around her. She vanished inside its brilliance, swept away in exultation and transcendence.

As Joseph knelt in prayer, he heard the heavy breathing of someone who had apparently been hurrying some distance. Suddenly, the woman from the inn, who had directed him to this cave, rushed in. She was carrying a large pottery jar, containers of salt and olive oil, a knife and several linen cloths. She spoke quickly to Joseph: "My name is Esther. I have helped to birth many, many Bethlehem babies, although few in conditions like these. I can stay only a little while, but I will help your wife deliver her baby. Stay nearby in case we need something!"

But when Esther pulled back the curtain to Mary's enclosure, she saw that her midwife services would not be needed. Mother and child were resting peacefully, Mary propped against the wall next to the manger, Jesus wrapped in her arms against the chill of the night, held tightly against her breast. Esther and Joseph stared at Mary, then at the cloak upon which she sat, which remained as clean as it had been when Joseph spread it over the straw beneath.

"Joseph," came the soft, tired but exhilarated voice of Mary. "Come and behold the King whom God has sent His people."

Joseph took a tentative step and then stopped, staring in astonishment and awe at the tiny baby, perhaps eight pounds, sleeping contentedly in his mother's arms. Mary, with her dark hair framing her radiant face, smiled at Joseph and gestured for him to sit beside her.

Esther was confused but realized that something incomprehensible had occurred here this night. There was none of the usual messy evidence of birth, the afterbirth and blood. It was not until that moment that she suddenly realized she should not be able to see so well in this dark cave, presumably lit only by a single oil lamp burning where Joseph had left it a few feet from Mary. Yet the entire scene was suffused with a soft light that enfolded them all in its gentle embrace, the visible manifestation of an overwhelming feeling of happiness. Peace and her soul mate, joy, sparkled and danced throughout the humble stable.

Like Joseph, Esther stared open-mouthed at the infant Jesus, finally breaking her reverie when she realized that although the baby was clean and beautiful, he was still unclothed. She hurried over to complete this part of the birthing process. She started to bathe the baby with the water she had brought, but saw that was pointless. She then took a handful of salt and rubbed it gently all over his body as a protection against infection. Next she gently spread olive oil over him and helped Mary to swaddle him in the strips of linen cloth which both women had brought. Jesus was now bound from feet to neck.[7]

As the baby slept on, Mary's own need for rest overtook her. She nodded to Esther, who handed the child to Joseph, who, looking around, saw that the manger next to Mary would make a perfect crib, especially cushioned with the barley feed. Wrapping the baby loosely in a small blanket, he laid him down. The baby Jesus murmured but did not wake up. Joseph, suddenly exhausted himself,

---

[7]This was standard postnatal care for the time, reflecting the belief that this practice would ensure the growth of limbs straight and strong.

lowered himself slowly, back against the manger, to sit quietly beside Mary. She herself had fallen into a deep sleep. Esther watched them for awhile, trying to comprehend what had taken place here. Then she motioned Joseph to follow her outside the enclosure.

"Who are you?" asked Esther.

"Just a simple carpenter," said Joseph. "But the child you see is not my son. He is far more than I or even the great King David himself could ever hope to be. He is the fulfillment of Isaiah's prophecy that the Messiah would be sent from God to be born of a virgin. He is the Son of God," said Joseph simply.

Esther gasped and pulled back the curtain to gaze once more on the sleeping mother and child. Then, realizing she was overdue back at the inn, she hurried out, taking with her the various items that she had brought.

Meanwhile, out on the hillside where several shepherds were minding their flocks on this cool but unusually warm night in December, a remarkable drama unfolded. Nearly a dozen men and boys were grazing their flocks of sheep and goats. The night sky glimmered with the twinkle of thousands of stars shining brightly in the cloudless, clear air. The waning moon contributed some light but on this evening played second fiddle to the sparkling firmament. Most of the shepherds were in or near their caves, sleeping until their turn to take the watch would come up. Four were awake on duty in pairs, keeping an eye on the goats and sheep, who were generally resting themselves. Only a few of the animals could not resist the opportunity for an evening snack of grass clumps.

Without warning, light burst all around them, bathing the four shepherds in its brilliance and piercing even into the darkness of the caves. Those who had fallen asleep were startled awake by the inexplicable light and the shouts of the shepherds on duty. With eyes adjusted to the dark, they stumbled outside, blinking furiously in an effort to see where the light was coming from and what kind of danger it presented. But, strangely enough, the flocks of sheep and goats barely stirred. They were untroubled by this particular light.

As the shepherds congregated together near where the four had been keeping watch, a man appeared to them out of the center of the glowing light. The man was dressed in a white tunic that reached to his wrists and hung below his feet, or at least where his feet should have been because they themselves ended about a foot above the ground. He extended his hands toward them in a gesture of openness and said:

"You have nothing to fear! I come to proclaim good news to you—tidings of great joy to be shared by the whole people. This day in David's city a savior has been born to you, the Messiah and Lord. Let this be a sign to you: in a manger you will find an infant wrapped in swaddling clothes."[8]

---

[8]Lk 2:10-12

The shepherds felt their fear leave them, blown away like loose leaves before the beauty and peace conveyed by this heavenly messenger.

Then, wonder upon wonder, there appeared a great crowd of similar creatures behind him, hundreds of them, singing the praises of God in indescribably magnificent voices. The entire valley was filled with the light of their radiance. Later the shepherds would remember one phrase in particular:

> **"Glory to God in high heaven,**
> **peace on earth to those on**
> **whom his favor rests."[9]**

As suddenly as they had appeared, the angels vanished. The night was once again dark and still. The shepherds remained in stunned silence for a moment, then began to speak all at once. They confirmed that each had seen and heard the same things. Recalling the reference to a manger, which could only refer to a stable somewhere, one of them said: **"Let us go over to Bethlehem and see this event which the Lord has made known to us."[10]**

The shepherds turned as one and began to hurry in the direction of the city where lamps still cast light from many of the windows. A few hundred yards along their journey, they noticed a dim light flickering from the hillside cave where Joseph, Mary and Jesus were resting. This was the oil lamp which Joseph had lit earlier. The shepherds turned and ran toward the light, their head cloths flapping in the wind behind them. Arriving breathless, they crowded into the cave. Joseph was startled awake at once and he gently roused Mary. The shepherds stared at the baby. They seemed to see something which Joseph and Mary did not, because all of them fell to their knees before the sleeping child.

"See the glory of the Chosen of the Lord!" one whispered in hushed tones. "Praised be the great kindness and judgment of the God of Israel, Who sends His Savior to be adored first by the lowliest of His people!" exclaimed another.

"What is his name?" asked yet a third shepherd.

"Jesus," replied Mary.

"Did the angel tell you to name him that?" the shepherd asked.

Mary was startled by the question. "Yes, but how did you know about the angel?"

"This night we have seen the glory of the Lord shine upon us. He sent angels beyond counting to tell us things that our people have longed to hear for thousands of years. Now that we have seen for ourselves, we understand that God has poured out His love upon all mankind. Blessed are you who bore him and blessed are we who celebrate the birth of the Prince of Peace!"

Joseph watched the shepherds as they gazed rapturously upon the sleeping infant. "What do you see when you look at him?" he asked the shepherd nearest him.

---

[9]Lk 2:14

[10]Lk 2:15

The shepherd replied: "A new-born baby sleeping peacefully. But it is not what I see that is important. Rather, I am nearly fainting with the sense of joy and love that envelops me in this child's presence. All heaven must be here with us!"

The shepherds remained perhaps an hour longer and then, seeing Mary's obvious fatigue, departed as a group. The news of what they had seen spread rapidly among the other shepherds and their families. Most of these were open to belief and came to see for themselves, bringing food and simple gifts. But shepherds were near the bottom of the social and economic scale in ancient Palestine. The merchants, landowners and religious elders scoffed at their claims that the Messiah had been born in a cave in Bethlehem and chased them away with threats and ridicule. Soon they realized that this news could not be shared readily and so they kept it to themselves. Some tried for years afterward to find out what had happened to the Messiah, whose birth had been announced with such heavenly fanfare, but the sudden departure of the Holy Family for Egypt and their quiet return after Herod the Great's death to Nazareth in Galilee frustrated these efforts. Further, the universal paranoia among rulers about threats to their throne made such inquiries dangerous. So for many years the story of the miraculous visit of the angels to announce the birth of the Messiah remained a secret shared only among the shepherds, a kindly midwife, and the baby's parents.

* * * * * * *

Meanwhile, far off to the east in the lands of Arabia, Parthia and Persia, a bright new star was seen to burst forth in the night sky, coinciding with the moment of the Christ Child's birth. Many people noted the new star's appearance. There were various astrological theories associated with it, from the rise or fall of some local potentate to wishful thinking about the collapse of Roman rule. But most of it was idle speculation. The star glistened in the sky night after night, outshining any other single object except the moon. Three men, however, saw in it a uniquely special significance which transcended earthly kingdoms. These three were priests of Zoroastrianism, a Persian religion founded by Zoroaster,[11] a man who lived several centuries before Christ was born and taught that there is only one God. They shared with most of the Mediterranean intelligentsia of the time a belief in astrology as a reliable science for predicting the affairs and future of mankind.[12]

These *Magi*, or Wise Men, were also students of other religions, particularly Judaism with its great emphasis on monotheism. Jewish prophetic writings were known to them, and they followed the concept of a Messiah for the Jewish nation with great interest. When the Star of Bethlehem burst forth high in

---

[11]Also known as Zarathushtra.

[12]The three men, wealthy and prominent in their communities, have come down to us in tradition as Gaspar, Balthasar and Melchior.

the western sky, therefore, they were among a small handful of ancient philosopher/priests prepared to deduce its meaning, or at least to respond to its invitation to come and see.

The three Wise Men first observed the star from their own countries, studying it and researching it for a few weeks in the context of ancient writings and prophecies known to them. Then each decided to travel to Babylon, one of the principal centers of learning in the Middle East, where they hoped to discuss the star's significance and their own research with other priest/scholars.

The three men met when they were introduced to one another by Arioch, perhaps the city's most prominent astrologer/philosopher. When he learned what had brought each of them to Babylon, it was obvious that they shared a common mission. Together, they spent months researching all of the pertinent ancient writings and planning their caravan to Israel. Meanwhile, the bright new star blazed patiently among the constellations.

It was Melchior who first called their attention to another celestial event which reinforced their opinion that something very significant had happened in Israel. "Have you observed, my friends, the conjunction of the planets, Jupiter and Saturn?"

"Yes, Melchior, we saw that conjunction three times last year, in May, again in September and, finally, in December. In fact, the third appearance of the two planets passing each other coincided with the appearance of the new star we are following," answered Balthasar.

"We shall not see a triple conjunction like that again in our lifetimes," Gaspar added.

"You are certainly right about that, Gaspar," responded Melchior. "Our children's children's children, down to the fortieth generation, shall not see such a conjunction because this one involved *three* planets!"

"That's true, Melchior!" added Balthasar excitedly. "Mars passed shortly after the third conjunction. And the whole affair took place in the constellation Pisces!"

"But what connection does this have with a possible new king of the Jews?" asked Gaspar, the youngest and least scholarly of the three.

"The constellation Pisces signifies the end times for mankind," explained Melchior. "It has also been associated with great events involving the Hebrew nation."

Balthasar was on his feet now, pacing and waving his arms around. "Not only that, but Jupiter is the planetary sign of a world ruler and Saturn is the star of the Amorites, who lived in the Palestine-Syria region! Put those together with Mars, the planet of upheaval, and we have the very heavens themselves announcing the birth of a new Jewish ruler who will shake the foundations of the world!"

Gaspar was thoroughly caught up in the excitement of the moment now. "Well, what are we waiting for?" he demanded. "Let's get going! I am anxious to pay homage to this great new king."

"Precisely right, Gaspar!" said Melchior. "But to do that, we need gifts, gifts which are appropriate for history's greatest king, one greater even than the incomparable Alexander."

"I will bring frankincense, a rare and precious incense made from resin from the Boswellia tree,"[13] responded Gaspar. "It is the finest burning incense in the world and is used before the altars of all mankind's deities. It will be my honor to present it to the new king who has been sent from the One God."

"And I, Balthasar of Arabia, will give myrrh, for this week I have had a premonition that the new king's mission is not to conquer but to save, a salvation which will come through his own death."[14] Balthasar's dour prediction startled Melchior and Gaspar but they did not question it since such divine insights can only be tested by the passage of time.

"And you, Melchior. What will be your gift for the child?" asked Gaspar.

Melchior explained, "I considered many things: robes and fine clothing for the child and his family, jewels, even lands from my own kingdom, flocks of sheep and goats. But then I asked myself: whom do we go to honor? It is a king to whom we pay our homage. And no gift surpasses gold, the most precious of all metals, as the gift to honor him who is to be king of all kings. I have had fashioned a golden scepter as well as coins. I shall lay these at the child's feet."

A little more than five months after the star first appeared, the caravan of the Three Wise Men set out from Babylon on their long journey to Jerusalem. They assumed that is where the new king would be found by now. Traveling through Palmyra, Damascus and then Tyre along the Mediterranean coast, it would be just under two months before they arrived at the grand palace of Herod in the City of David.

* * * * * * *

In Bethlehem, the Holy Family remained in the cave for a few days following Jesus' birth. Then Joseph found work as a carpenter working on, of all things, a new inn being built at the southern end of the town. This enabled the family to move out of the cave and into a small house located on the southeastern side, not far from the shepherds' fields.

When the eighth day after Jesus' birth arrived, Joseph arranged with the local synagogue to have Jesus circumcised. This, of course, was required of all Jewish males. God had imposed the requirement as a sign of the covenant between Him and Abraham.[15] At this ceremony, the name of Jesus was formally proclaimed, just as Zechariah had written (because he was still unable to speak)

---

[13]The Boswellia tree is found in Africa, the Himalayas and northern Arabia.

[14]Myrrh is an aromatic gum resin which was used in the holy anointing oil in the Jerusalem Temple and in embalming rites for the dead.

[15]Gn 17:9-14

the name of his own son, John, when John had been circumcised. In Hebrew, Jesus' name was *"Yeshua,"* meaning *"the Lord saves."*

For the next four weeks, Mary and Joseph debated whether to remain in Bethlehem to live. There was plenty of work for Joseph, especially so close to Jerusalem, and already his reputation as a skilled carpenter was gaining him more requests than he could satisfy. The prophecy concerning the Messiah's birth made them think that perhaps God desired His Son to be not only born in the town of David, but raised there as well. On the other hand, their families lived in Nazareth. They had a house there—unfinished, true, but still theirs. They missed the tree-covered hills and fertile vistas of the Galilean countryside and the opportunity to visit the beautiful Sea of Galilee for holiday outings. They prayed for guidance, but heaven was silent. They decided to postpone a decision until after Jesus had been presented in the Temple on the fortieth day following his birth. Perhaps there, they reasoned, God would send them a sign. In any case, they would return to Nazareth after Jesus' presentation in the Temple because Anne and Joachim were dying to see their new grandson, a child unique in human history. Before leaving on their journey to Bethlehem, Mary had promised them that she and Joseph would bring Jesus home after he had been presented to his Father in the Temple.

A few days later, Mary, Joseph and Jesus departed Bethlehem for Nazareth, with an interim stop at Jerusalem for his presentation and his mother's ritual purification. Although by this time Jews did not routinely travel to the great Temple to present their first-born male children to God, this particular child was uniquely appropriate for such a presentation. Following that remarkable event,[16] the family returned to Nazareth, this time taking the shorter ridge route through Samaria.

The Holy Family remained in Nazareth only about four months. Joseph's work as a carpenter was adequate for the family's needs but there were difficulties. Many of the building projects were distant from Nazareth. Others involved work distasteful to a faithful Jew, such as projects in the Romanized city of Sepphoris. And, certainly, the level of building activity was less in Galilee than it had been in Judea under the ambitious and insecure Herod. From time to time, Joseph received news of a great demand for skilled carpenters and other craftsmen in Judea. While in Bethlehem, he had developed an excellent reputation in a short period of time and he was confident that he would have no trouble quickly finding employment there. Each time these "employment reports" came through, Joseph discussed with Mary whether they should relocate. After the third one, they decided to go. She and Joseph still wondered whether it was not God's plan for His Son to have them raise him in Bethlehem, as King David had been. They decided the repeated reports of employment opportunity, besides holding out the promise of a better living, might be signs from God that they should return to

---

[16]See the Fourth Mystery, *"The Presentation in the Temple,"* following the story of *"The Nativity."*

Bethlehem. And so they went when Jesus was not quite six months old. If the truth be told, it was also a relief to get away from the gossip of some of the women in the village who made catty remarks about the "premature" birth of Mary and Joseph's baby.

They found a small house on "Carpenters' Row" not far from where they had lived before and settled down to life in Bethlehem. How little they suspected that their tenure there would be short-lived! It was not long before Esther, the midwife from the inn, and some of the shepherds learned they had returned. These provided a steady and enjoyable source of company and support for Mary and Joseph, who also developed friendships with some of the other carpenters and their families. If they had any doubts when leaving Nazareth, they were now quite convinced that they were exactly where God wished His Son to be. They looked forward to many years of happy and relatively prosperous living in this city so near to the great capital.

About a month later, the caravan of the Wise Men arrived in Jerusalem. Coming from Tyre in the north, they had journeyed down the coastal route past the Roman port of Caesarea, on past Apollonia, turning east southeast at Joppa for the remaining thirty-five mile leg into Jerusalem. They traveled in a party of eleven camels and twice as many servants, camel drivers and attendants. Just outside the Damascus Gate in the northwest corner of the city wall, the caravan found quarters for their stay. Leaving the servants to settle the pack animals and set up their tents, the Wise Men and one retainer each rode into the city to find out what they could about the newborn king. Their inquiries produced only puzzled shrugs and quizzical stares. Those who were willing to respond at all indicated that anything to do with royalty in Jerusalem would be found with Herod in his grand palace along the western wall in the wealthy upper city. The Wise Men, lavish in dress and stately in bearing, turned their camels in that direction.

By this time, word had reached Herod that three royal-looking personages were in the city, asking about a new king for Israel. Herod suffered from numerous infirmities in his old age, not the least of which was a recurrent ulcer and other gastro-intestinal ailments.[17] Three strangers asking about his successor did nothing to relieve his pain or improve his normally surly disposition. He sent a party of his personal guards out to find the Wise Men and lead them back to his palace.

They passed with their camels through the narrow streets to the arched entryway in the eastern inner wall which protected the palace from any attack from the city side. Leaving their camels outside, the Wise Men followed their guide through the long, stately portico curved on opposite sides to frame a lavish central garden with twin circular reflecting pools. They were ushered into a spacious, sparsely-furnished reception room with patterned mosaic floors and

---

[17]One theory holds that he died from advanced syphilis.

ornate tapestries hanging on the walls. "Wait here," said Eleazar, Herod's chief steward. "The king will send for you."

They did not have long to wait. Another servant returned and escorted them down another long open corridor into a room richly-appointed with thickly-upholstered furniture, woolen carpets, and glistening white marble walls. The elegance and harmony of the room was accented by the soft tinkle of water cascading down a small fountain. Herod sat at the opposite end of the room with perhaps three dozen other middle-aged and elderly men lining the walls to his left and right. They were all well-dressed in expensive, brocaded cloaks over fine linen tunics, wearing soft camels' hide sandals.

One wore the ephod, a kind of vest embroidered with bands of gold, purple, scarlet and blue. On his chest, this imperious-looking individual wore a purse decorated with 12 gemstones, each a different color, each representing one of the twelve tribes of Israel. The current High Priest was present.

With a wave of his hand, Herod invited the Wise Men forward, standing to greet them as they neared his throne. "Noble visitors, welcome to Jerusalem! We are honored to have such distinguished guests. What is it that you seek?" Herod asked unctuously. He was anxious to learn as much as he could about a possible pretender to his crown.

Melchior replied. **"Where is the newborn king of the Jews? We observed his star at its rising and have come to pay him homage."**[18] Melchior went on to describe the great three-planet conjunction and the strange, brilliant star which had actually changed its position in the heavens as their journey had progressed from Babylon to Jerusalem.

Herod was startled and not a little agitated by the forthrightness of the answer. The visitors were respectful, but clearly they perceived that the king they sought was superior to anyone present. Herod's paranoia blossomed into panic. He struggled to get his feelings under control. "I am the only king in Palestine. However, it has long been foretold that a great Messiah would be sent from God to restore Israel to its favored place as His chosen people, as in the time of David. Such signs as you have described can only herald the imminent arrival of this king of all kings. However, we have heard nothing of his birth before word of your inquiries reached us. Nor did our own astrologers see the star which you have told us about. Perhaps you could point it out to them tonight?"

Balthasar spoke up now. "We would be most pleased to do that, your majesty, except that the star disappeared from the heavens two nights before we arrived in Jerusalem. We took that as a sign that our journey had reached its destination. We can explain to them where in the firmament it was located, of course."

---

[18]Mt 2:1-2

Herod frowned. Turning to the elders and scribes clustered on both sides of the room, Herod asked: "Where do the prophets say that the Messiah shall be born?"

This was a question well known to all of the Jewish religious leaders. And the answer was well known, too. The high priest stepped forward and gave it: **"In Bethlehem of Judea . . . Here is what the prophet has written:**

> **'And you, Bethlehem, land of Judah,**
> **are by no means least among the**
> **princes of Judah,**
> **since from you shall come a ruler**
> **who is to shepherd my people Israel.'"**[19]

Herod sat pensively, stroking his beard, lost in thought. After a few minutes, he beckoned to his trusted advisor, perhaps his only real friend at court, Nicolaus of Damascus. They conferred in low voices, unintelligible to anyone else in the room. Finally, Nicolaus turned to the Jewish elders and scribes and said: "You may go now." They bowed and filed quickly out.

Only the Wise Men were left in the room with Herod and Nicolaus. The king forced a smile and said to them: "Well, you see where you must go. Bethlehem is but a few miles south of here, little more than an hour by camel. It will be our pleasure to replenish your supplies and to assist you in any other way that we can. I am as anxious as you are to find and honor this great new king! I would go with you myself but I have other pressing business here and I will need a few days anyway to arrange proper ceremonies."

"Thank you, your majesty. With your leave, we will be on our way," replied Melchior. "By now our camels will have been refreshed and our caravan refitted. Our journey has been long and our visit overdue. Although it grows late, we will depart this evening."

"Of course, of course!" said Herod. "But tell me a little more about the child first. When exactly did his star first appear?"

"It was late in the month of Chislev last year, the 25th as I recall. A child born on that date would now be seven months old." Balthasar, who had spoken, looked to the other two Wise Men for confirmation. They nodded in agreement.

Herod quizzed them further until he was satisfied they had no more specific information to share that would assist in the identification of the child. So he sent them on their way with the directive: **"Go and get detailed information about the child. When you have found him, report it to me so that I may go and offer him homage, too."**[20]

When the Wise Men had left the palace, Herod once again conferred with Nicolaus. "Does your majesty wish that I should have them followed to Bethlehem?"

---

[19]Mt 2:5-6

[20]Mt 2:8

"No, it would be difficult to do without being detected. If that happened, they might become suspicious and not return to us. Even worse, they might cause this pretender to my throne to hide and escape my grasp. Now they trust us. It seems that God Himself is leading them. So let God show them the rest of what we need to know and then we'll deal with this new 'king' in our own way."

Outside, the three Wise Men hastened away from Herod's palace, back to the Damascus Gate. "Strike the tents! Get the camels up! We are leaving tonight!" shouted Gaspar.

The servants and camel drivers scrambled to respond. Once assembled, they rode south around the western wall of the city, past the barren and forbidding hillock/quarry called Golgotha, turning south onto the Way of the Patriarchs toward Bethlehem.

"Melchior, Balthasar, look!" shouted Gaspar, pointing at a spot low in the sky ahead of them. "It is the star!" The brilliant star sparkled in the darkening void, beckoning them onward.

Their excitement mounted as they entered Bethlehem, passing the north side caravansary and processing through the center of the city toward the southern end. The star, inexplicably, amazingly, had descended from the sky above them, shrinking as it did so, and now stood approximately 10 meters above a small house clustered with several others not far from the grassy fields sloping away from the town. It was after dark, albeit early in the evening, and most of Bethlehem's residents were indoors. The caravan of the Wise Men passed relatively unnoticed. There was no mistaking which house to enter since only one stood bathed in the light that streamed down from the star.

As the Wise Men dismounted from their camels, the door to the house opened slowly. Joseph stood there, staring at the richly-dressed Wise Men and their caravan of camels and servants. "What is it that you seek?" he asked.

"We come to pay homage to him who is born king of the Jews, a king destined to be king of all kings," replied Melchior.

Joseph swallowed his astonishment and held the rough olive-wood door open for them to enter. Inside the small, one-room cottage, Mary sat on a low wooden stool holding the baby in her arms. The baby, with uncut dark brown hair, slightly curly, dressed in a white woolen gown, had been engrossed in investigating his toes before Joseph had opened the door. Now he, too, stared at the strangers who gazed back at him. Mary looked quizzically at Joseph who shrugged his shoulders.

"I am Melchior, of the House of Darius in Persepolis. My companions are Balthasar, of the House of Salazar in Arabia and Gaspar, of the House of Bin-Salaam in India. We have seen the star of a child born to be the salvation of men, the Lord of all, the promise of God to mankind. This star, which now rests nearly upon the brow of your home, has led us here. Joyfully do we acknowledge this child as our Lord." With that the Wise Men prostrated themselves on the floor of the house and pledged themselves, their descendants and all their possessions to the service of the child Jesus.

After a few minutes, Melchior whispered something to Gaspar, who left the house. He returned shortly, leading three servants, each bearing a carved wooden chest with a family crest on it. Melchior opened his first, setting the box with its treasure of gold coins and golden scepter on the floor before the baby. "I present gold to honor the kingship of this child," he said bowing low.

"And I present frankincense to honor him who is sent from the One God," said Gaspar, also bowing.

Balthasar opened his chest last. As he did so, most solemnly, the fragrance of the myrrh filled the room. "I bring myrrh to honor him who will lead his people through the valley of death and into the life of our Creator." Balthasar bowed deeply, hiding a great sadness which filled his heart.

The Wise Men stayed perhaps an hour longer, talking with Mary and Joseph and staring at the child who smiled and burbled unintelligibly as babies do.

Yet there was something more here. Not seen by the eye, but felt by the heart. With an effort, the Wise Men turned to go. "Our mission is accomplished. We must return to our own countries. Your King Herod has also expressed a desire to pay homage to this child and so we shall report to him on our way home," said Melchior.

Mary and Joseph exchanged startled, anxious glances. Herod, that wily and brutal old fox, willing to acknowledge their son as his king? That seemed highly unlikely. They pressed the Wise Men for details of their visit with Herod. Melchior explained that the king had seemed genuinely interested and willing to acknowledge that this new king was the Messiah long promised for the salvation of Israel. They had detected no harmful intent in Herod, but they were not naive about the ways of royalty in their time. Still, there had been numerous miraculous events already associated with the birth of Jesus, so perhaps the stony heart of a killer like Herod the Great could also be softened. Mary and Joseph put their anxieties away, trusting in the providence of the Child's Father.

When the Wise Men and Mary and Joseph were finished conversing, the entire caravan party was invited in to see the child they had traveled so far to see. Personal retainers, other servants and the camel drivers all crowded into the small room as best they could with only a few lingering just outside the doorway, waiting for someone ahead to leave. Each bowed or knelt to acknowledge the kingship of this baby to whom homage had been paid by their masters. They stared at the baby, who smiled back and periodically waved a chubby hand at them. Just a baby, and yet . . . once in the presence of this child, no one wanted to leave. There was such peace here. And holiness. The young mother and her husband were kind and gracious to all, offering to share the bread, cheese, nuts, fruit and goat's milk which they had on hand for their own needs.

After everyone had seen the Holy Family, Melchior called them to assemble and prepare to depart. The star continued to shine down on the house where the Christ Child now slept. A few of the neighbors had heard the commotion and peered through their windows and doorways to see what was happening. They were astonished to see the well-equipped, rich-looking caravan parked in front of the house of the humble carpenter and his young wife and baby. These co-workers and friends of Joseph could hardly wait until morning to find out what in the world was going on.

The caravan of the Magi moved slowly away, heading for an encampment just outside the southern limits of the city. The three Wise Men left last, turning around as they rode to gaze one last time on the little house where the Savior of mankind had welcomed them in innocence and joy. The star was gone. The little house rested in darkness now, a harbinger of the obscurity that would soon swallow up the very Creator of the world for nearly thirty years.

The Wise Men intended to rise early and return to Jerusalem for several days, reporting to Herod and consulting with some of the Jewish scribes and teachers before heading back to Babylon and thence to their own homes. They retired for the night, weary but exhilarated, each in his own tent with his personal retainer nearby.

In the morning, the three Wise Men looked anything but refreshed and eager to confront the day. Their appearances were haggard with dark shadows under their eyes and their hair wildly askew upon their heads as if they had tossed and turned violently most of the night. Which indeed they had.

"Brothers, I have had a most terrible dream!" exclaimed Melchior. "In this dream, I saw Herod holding in one hand a great sword dripping with blood, while with the other hand he reached for the Child whom we have seen to be the great King sent from God Himself. As he brought the sword down to strike the baby, I heard a voice command me to return immediately to my own country without the knowledge of Herod. The baby was snatched away from the king's blow but the sword's arc carried it through other babies who were clutched in the arms of their weeping mothers.

"I awoke from this nightmare drenched in my body's own sweat, wondering what had caused such a terrible dream. When I dozed again, the dream recurred! This must have happened three or four times at least! May God spare me another such night!"

Balthasar and Gaspar stared open-mouthed at Melchior. "I had exactly the same dream!" gasped Balthasar.

"And I!" exclaimed Gaspar. The three men looked at each other, each knowing the other's thoughts.

Then Gaspar called to the chief camel driver and told him to make preparations to leave Bethlehem as soon as the men and animals had been fed. "We shall not be returning to Jerusalem, Agonides," Gaspar told him. "Rather, chart our route south through Hebron where we will turn west and pick up the coastal trade route at Azotus."

Melchior called his man-servant to him. "Go back to the house of Joseph and tell him of our dream. I believe his child, and perhaps he and his wife as well, are in great danger!"

The man found another servant and together they returned to the house where they had visited the Christ Child the night before. But the house was now empty, its occupants gone.

After the Wise Men had left, Mary and Joseph had gone to bed, filled with excitement and joy that God had sent these important people, Gentiles no less, from the great lands in the East to acknowledge the divine kingship of Jesus. Clearly, the Messiah's mission was to the whole world and not merely to the children of Israel. Sleep had come slowly but inevitably.

As Joseph lay deep in slumber, a great light burst forth in the room. Inside the light, a gloriously beautiful young man spoke urgently to him: **"Get up, take the child and his mother, and flee to Egypt. Stay there until I tell you otherwise. Herod is searching for the child to destroy him."**[21]

Joseph was on his feet almost before the light faded from the room. He had no doubts about this vision, whether it was dream or not. The angel was the same one who had reassured him about Mary's conception of Jesus.

"Mary, get up quickly!" said Joseph, shaking her to help wake her. "We must gather our things and leave immediately. An angel has appeared to me and warned that Herod intends to kill the baby!"

Mary had not seen the dream, but she did not for a moment doubt the truth of Joseph's statements. She had been sound asleep, too, but fear for her child quickly drove away her grogginess and fatigue. "Where are we to go, Joseph? Back to Nazareth?"

"No, Mary. The angel told me to flee with you and Jesus to Egypt. Hurry now! The message was urgent."

They quickly pulled on cloaks and head covers over the tunics in which they slept, packed their belongings, including food and water for the journey, and gathered up Jesus, still sleeping peacefully. Mary held him while Joseph fetched their donkey from the community stable nearby. Carefully, quietly, he arranged the baggage on the donkey and helped Mary and the baby to a sitting position on the patient little animal's back. Then, taking his staff, he led them away down the same street the caravan of the Wise Men had followed. Not long after, the Holy Family quietly passed the encampment where the Wise Men were tossing and turning from the same warning, not so personally delivered, that sent all of them fleeing from King Herod's evil wrath.

In Jerusalem, the day passed slowly in the great palace of Herod. He paced back and forth, periodically demanding of Nicolaus whether the Magi had returned yet from Bethlehem. When they still had not appeared by the next morning, Herod sent two soldiers down to find out what was going on. They were back by noon, informing Herod that the caravan of the Wise Men had been seen heading south the day before. No one in the town was willing to acknowledge the presence of any rival to Herod's throne. The soldiers had made only cursory

---

[21]Mt 2:13

inquiries, however, deciding to return quickly to Jerusalem with news of the Wise Men's change in plans.

Herod was enraged. He shrieked and cursed. No pottery or small furniture escaped his fury. The servants quailed as far away from him as they could cower, while still being near enough to respond if summoned. They knew well that failure to come when called by the king in this mood would mean an instant death sentence, although the death itself might not be so quick. Only Nicolaus felt close enough to the king and was trusted enough to attempt to calm him.

"The Wise Men have only just departed, your majesty. Obviously, they found the child whom they were seeking. Bethlehem is a small town. There cannot be more than 20 or 30 such male babies in the whole community. Why don't we just identify them all and investigate the circumstances of their births? We are bound to find this child among them," advised Nicolaus.

Herod stopped ranting and listened to Nicolaus' words. He said nothing for a long time, just looked at him until Nicolaus began to feel quite uncomfortable. Then in a voice which chilled even Nicolaus, Herod said: "You are quite right. But we need not 'investigate' these children. The astrologers said the star first appeared on the 25th of Chislev last year. This pretender to my throne, therefore, is barely half a year old. Send Hyraclon, the captain of my guard, to me."

Hyraclon responded quickly to Herod's summons. "Your majesty," he said bowing.

"Take fifty soldiers, Hyraclon, to Bethlehem and there slay every male child two years old and under. Include all those born in the town, found there or located in the surrounding area. No one is to be spared! If even one escapes, you and your whole family will be boiled in pig's grease!"

Hyraclon swallowed any revulsion he felt for the task given him and ran off to do Herod's monstrous bidding. He and his soldiers performed their grisly duty quickly and efficiently.

> **A cry was heard at Ramah,**
> **sobbing and loud lamentation:**
> **Rachel bewailing her children;**
> **no comfort for her, since they**
> **are no more.**[22]

Nearly two dozen infant boys were slaughtered by sword and spear. The soldiers went from house to house, tent to tent, encampment to encampment to ensure that all of the two-and-under male children were found. A few of the families affected had been aware of the family from Nazareth and later learned that they had apparently escaped. But no inquiry was made and none of the embittered parents sought to inform Herod of the escape of one small child. Their

---

[22]Mt 2:18

inconsolable grief and hatred for the brutal Herod took comfort in the knowledge that his plan had been foiled in some small degree. A few shepherds and a midwife understood that his plan had been history's absolutely greatest failure. As for the children themselves, their lives were cruelly terminated but their honor and joy in heaven are great for they were the very first Christian martyrs.

The day before these Bethlehem Innocents lost their lives, the one whom Herod really sought had reached Hebron, high in the Judean Mountains about 14 miles south of Bethlehem. They passed the Cave of Machpelah, revered as the burial site for Abraham, Isaac and Jacob and their wives. Some traditions held that Adam and Eve, and Moses and his wife, were buried there as well.

At Hebron, the family turned west, following a curving road through the difficult terrain to Gaza on the Mediterranean coast. From there, they continued on down the Sinai Peninsula, finally entering Egypt. They would remain in Egypt for two years, living in several predominantly Jewish communities before settling near Alexandria. Between the gifts the Magi had brought for Jesus and Joseph's skills as a carpenter, the family had no problems making ends meet.

Meanwhile, in Jerusalem, Herod the Great's court seethed with intrigues and malice. Herod himself, in his seventies and ill health, was obsessed with his power and paranoid to the point of insanity. So dangerous was it to be an heir apparent to the king that Caesar Augustus is said to have remarked after Herod had his son, Antipater, executed in 4 B.C., only days before his own death, "I would rather be Herod's pig than his son."[23] Herod's sixth, and last, will named Herod Archelaus, a vicious killer[24] in the mold of his father, to be King of Judea (later downgraded by the Romans to *ethnarch*). Another son, Herod Antipas, was named *tetrarch* of Galilee and Perea.

A few weeks after Herod the Great's death, Mary, Joseph and the almost three-year old Jesus were sound asleep in their simple lodgings in Egypt. Once again, as it had on two occasions before, a brilliant white light filled the room. From the light came the Angel Gabriel's voice, powerful yet gentle like distant, rolling thunder: **"Get up, take the child and his mother, and set out for the land of Israel. Those who had designs on the life of the child are dead."[25]**

Joseph shook Mary from her slumber. "Yes, Joseph, what is it? Is it dawn already?" She sat upright and realized it was still the middle of the night. "Is everything all right?" Mary glanced with concern over at Jesus, but he was still sleeping soundly on his own pallet.

---

[23]*Who's Who in the Bible* (Pleasantville, NY: Reader's Digest Association, 1994), 144. As a Jew, of course, Herod did not eat pork.

[24]At the very beginning of his reign in 4 B.C., he suppressed an incipient rebellion at the cost of 3,000 lives. Nine years later his own subjects successfully petitioned Rome to have him banished to Europe. Ibid.,148.

[25]Mt 2:20

"Mary, Herod is dead. The angel has visited me again in my sleep. We are to arise now and depart for our homeland."

"Of course, dear husband. We shall certainly do as the messenger of God commands us. Let us begin packing and let Jesus sleep awhile longer. We will need to acquire supplies and a donkey for our journey."

"We can use the last of the Persian Wise Man's gold coins for that, Mary. With that and what we have saved, we should be able to reach Bethlehem in just a few weeks."

"Will we be able to find a northbound caravan so quickly, Joseph?"

"The angel's command seemed quite imperative, Mary," responded Joseph. "I believe it is the will of God that we set out immediately even if we must travel alone. I am certain no harm will come to us."

And so the Holy Family left Egypt two years and a couple of months after they had arrived. They found boat transportation up the River Nile and down its easternmost tributary, disembarking at a primary assembly point for the principal trade route, the Via Maris, which would take them back through the Sinai and on into Israel. When they reached Gaza, however, from where they had been planning to head east toward Hebron, and from there north to Bethlehem, they learned that only five days before his death, Herod had executed his eldest son, Antipater, and that his kingdom had been divided between Archelaus, Antipas and Philip. This was a chilling report because Judea had gone to Archelaus.

Joseph was torn with indecision. "Mary, I know it was our plan to return to Bethlehem to raise Jesus there in the House of David. Yet I feel this great fear. We are not likely to come to the notice of anyone in the royal house of Herod, but surely the danger remains real."

"I, too, am disquieted, Joseph. Let us pray to the Lord to show us the way."

That night Joseph's sleep was fitful. He dreamed that a dark cloud rested over Bethlehem. From the cloud he heard the pounding of horses' hooves and then wailing and cries of anguish. As his mind recoiled from this image, he heard another voice, gentle and kind, saying: **"He shall be called a Nazorean."**[26] When Joseph awoke, he explained his dream to Mary. It was with glad hearts that they continued north on the coastal trade route to Caesarea, turning east across northern Samaria, heading for home in Nazareth.

––––––––––

[26]Mt 2:23

AVE MARIS STELLA

Hail, bright star of ocean
God's own Mother blest,
Ever sinless Virgin,
Gate of heavenly rest.

Taking that sweet Ave
Which from Gabriel came,
Peace confirm within us,
Changing Eva's name.

Break the captives' fetters,
Light on blindness pour,
All our ills expelling,
Every bliss implore.

Show thyself a Mother;
May the Word Divine,
Born for us thy Infant,
Hear our prayers through thine.

Virgin all excelling,
Mildest of the mild,
Freed from guilt, preserve us,
Pure and undefiled.

Keep our life all spotless,
Make our way secure,
Till we find in Jesus
Joy forevermore.

Through the highest heaven
To the Almighty Three
Father, Son and Spirit,
One same glory be.

Amen

QUESTIONS FOR REFLECTION

1) Why do you think God sent an angel to tell Joseph about the miraculous origin of Mary's conception? Why not reveal it to him in the same way that He did to Elizabeth?

2) Do you think God was testing Joseph? Is there a message here for us? What is it? Have you jumped to conclusions about someone because of circumstantial evidence, only to find out later that your conclusions were wrong? How did that make you feel? How, then, do you imagine Joseph felt after being told by the Angel Gabriel that Mary's conception was from God?

3) If you had been Mary's mother or father, what arguments would you have used to convince Joseph that Mary's baby had been conceived by the power of the Holy Spirit? Or do you think it was a "mission impossible" from the beginning?

4) After Joseph's rejection of the explanation for Mary's pregnancy, do you think her parents would have been fearful for her safety? Would you have been in their place? Would you have wondered what God was doing and perhaps begun to have some doubts about it all? Do you think Mary was upset to discover that God had not told Joseph about Jesus' unique conception? Would you have been?

5) Do you think Joseph would have told his family or anyone else about the miraculous circumstances of Jesus' conception? Would you have? How would you have explained it?

6) If you had been Mary and Joseph traveling to Bethlehem late in Mary's pregnancy and being unable to find decent lodgings, would you have wondered why God was not providing better for the mother and foster father of His Son? Have there been times in your life when God's demands have seemed unfair and harsh? Can you see Mary and Joseph as role models for you in dealing with the trials and tribulations of life? Explain.

7) Why does Matthew tell us about the three Magi from the East? Why doesn't Luke? What do they represent? Wisdom? Gentiles who would recognize Jesus before His own people would? People who are rich but who place God first in their lives? Science in the service of faith? All of the above? Other?

8) Do you think the Magi are symbolic figures in the Gospel? Does this mean they were not also real? What other examples in the Bible can you find where God uses real things in a symbolic way to teach His people?

9) God sent an angel to warn Joseph and Mary to get out of town to save Jesus from Herod. Why didn't He warn all the other parents of the infant boys who would be killed by the soldiers looking for Jesus? Does this suggest that God plays favorites? Why do you suppose God did not simply take Herod's life and save everyone, not to mention sparing Mary and Joseph from a very arduous trip all the way to Egypt? Do you see any parallels here with the story of Job? What are the lessons for your life?

10) Luke tells us, "Mary treasured all these things and reflected on them in her heart."[27] Why does Luke mention this since it is obvious Mary would remember the circumstances of Jesus' birth? Is Mary through Luke telling us something profound about prayer and our relationship with God? Is Mary's reflection more than mere memory but, rather, a way of discovering the many layers of God's truth? Is Mary giving us advice here about how to pray the rosary?

---

[27]Lk 2:19

A revealing light to the Gentiles, the glory of your people Israel.
Lk 2:32

FOURTH JOYFUL MYSTERY

The Presentation in the Temple

As the fortieth day following Jesus' birth approached, Mary and Joseph prepared to visit the Temple at Jerusalem. From there they would continue on their journey back to Nazareth. Mary's presentation in the ritual of purification was required on the fortieth day following the birth of her son. They were excited that this would be done at Judaism's most sacred shrine, the Jerusalem Temple. They trembled a little, too, wondering if the Father might acknowledge His Son in some spectacular fashion as He had sent angels to announce Jesus' birth.

This was also the time for redeeming a first-born son from God in accordance with the command given to Moses.[1] Of course, this particular Son would not, in fact, be redeemed from his Father's service. On the contrary, he came into the world from Him for the sole and exclusive purpose of fulfilling His will. But the requirement of the law referred to service in the Temple, a function institutionalized by this time in the tribe of Levi.[2] All other first-born males had to be "bought back" from God at a cost of five shekels, or twenty denarii, paid in Tyrian silver coins. Tyrian silver was the most reliable currency in the ancient world. By necessity, it became the standard of exchange for the multitude of currencies minted by the various empires, kingdoms, provinces and governors that crowded the political landscape. The business of money changing was a major revenue producer for the Temple treasury.[3] Thus, the graven images on these coins, although objectionable to the Jewish religion, had to be tolerated.

Now Joseph packed their belongings on their faithful donkey. He had settled affairs with their Bethlehem landlord earlier that morning. One of the

---

[1] Ex 13:1: "The LORD spoke to Moses and said, 'Consecrate to me every first-born that opens the womb among the Israelites, both of man and beast, for it belongs to me.'"
Ex 13:11ff: "When the LORD, your God, has brought you into the land of the Canaanites, which he swore to you and your fathers he would give you, you shall dedicate to the LORD every son that opens the womb . . . "

[2] See Num 8:18: "But in place of all the first-born Israelites I have taken the Levites."

[3] As an adult, Jesus probably sealed his date with Golgotha by his attack during Holy Week on the money changers and the sellers of sacrificial animals. Nothing is quite so inciteful as a threat to the Establishment's economic well-being nor so readily used as an excuse for violence.

neighbors held Jesus while Joseph helped Mary onto the small animal before placing the baby in her arms. They said their goodbyes and headed north through the town of Bethlehem toward Jerusalem, some five miles up the road that wound along the spine of the ridge of hills reaching all the way through Samaria to southern Galilee. It was a beautiful day, crisp and clear with a cheerful blue sky. Mary felt her heart lighten with anticipation at seeing her mother and father again.

But there was another reason for excitement, too, because now Mary was going to present her son, *His Son*, to God in the one place on earth where He seemed to be uniquely present.

"Joseph, Jesus seems to be particularly happy today. Do you see how he smiles and pats my cheek? Do you suppose he knows he is going to be presented to his Father?"

Joseph looked back at Mary cooing at her baby. "Everything about Jesus is fascinating and mysterious to me, Mary. On the one hand, he seems like any other baby. But, then, strange and wondrous things have a way of happening around him. All I know is that I ask his Father every day to help me to do the right thing for this Child. I feel terribly unworthy of the task the Lord has given me."

Mary smiled at Joseph. "Dear husband, God does not make mistakes. In your care, Jesus and I are in the best possible hands. Thank you for your love and your unfailing kindness in all that you do for us."

Joseph beamed and blushed at the same time. Mary laughed, charmed by the innocence in this strong and gentle man.

As Mary and Joseph made their way up the caravan route, paved with stone blocks near Jerusalem by the Romans and marked with their stone mile markers, they passed four Roman soldiers arguing with four Jewish men. The soldiers had been headed north toward Jerusalem, probably assigned to the Fortress Antonia, while the four Israelites had been walking toward Bethlehem. Voices rose and the soldiers grasped the hafts of their short swords. Phinehas, one of the four civilians, spoke urgently to his friend, as he himself hefted a Roman pack: "Pick it up, Jashub! It is the law![4] Or would you rather be picking lice out of your hair in the dungeons at Antonia?"

"But they're making us go back where we just came from! I was expected in Bethlehem an hour ago!" grumbled Jashub.

Joseph halted the donkey on which Mary and Jesus rode. "Soldiers, my family and I are going to Jerusalem. Perhaps we could help you? I would be pleased to carry one of your packs, and I believe we could squeeze another one on the donkey here. Let this gentleman go on his way. He is needed elsewhere."

---

[4]Roman law permitted Roman soldiers to compel civilians to carry their packs from one marker to the next, a duty much resented by Jewish men. You can imagine the astonishment, even outrage, of Jesus' listeners when he advised them: "Should anyone press you into service for one mile, go with him two miles." Mt 5:41. It was a long time before his followers began to understand this teaching. Most still are unwilling to apply it.

One of the soldiers, Gaius by name, turned and stared at Joseph, astonished that any Jew would actually volunteer to carry a Roman soldier's pack. They were more accustomed to having rocks thrown at them than being offered a helping hand from this unruly population. Most of the soldiers in the Roman garrison hated assignment to Judea. This strange people seethed with religious fanaticism, viewing the Romans as not only unwelcome conquerors, but unclean in the sight of their God as well. They wouldn't step foot inside a Roman dwelling for fear they would be contaminated by it! Gaius thought them insane. He much preferred the ineffectual Roman gods, in whom he didn't believe anyway, to the great Terror which the Jews were always trying to call down upon their enemies, especially the Roman soldiers. And Jerusalem was the place where this unnamed God of theirs apparently lived! Gaius, then, was highly skeptical of Joseph's unsolicited offer.

"What are you waiting for, Gaius?" laughed his more easygoing buddy, Marcellinus. "Give the man your pack!" Marcellinus removed his own pack and helped Joseph secure it on the back of the donkey, which shuffled its feet in mild complaint but was still far from overloaded.

Phinehas and another friend, Silas, took the other two Roman packs while Jashub, astounded at this unexpected reprieve, muttered his thanks to Joseph and hurried off toward Bethlehem before Joseph could reconsider. The rest of the travelers set out again for Jerusalem, approximately two Roman miles distant.[5] The soldiers stayed in a group about ten meters behind the Holy Family and the two Jewish men carrying their packs. At the first mile marker they reached, Phinehas and Silas dumped the packs and turned back around for Bethlehem. The soldiers glared at them, but said nothing since the law compelled civilian assistance for only one Roman mile. "All right, Jew. You did your duty. Give me the packs so I can find another couple of 'volunteers,'" grumbled Gaius to Joseph.

Joseph merely smiled and said, "Friend, my family and I are continuing your way and would be happy to help you farther. There is no need to find anyone else for these two packs."

Gaius' jaw fell open once again. He looked at Marcellinus questioningly. Marcellinus just shrugged and said, "Thank you, sir. Your hospitality does credit to you and your country. We don't meet many Jews like you. We've been walking since before dawn and appreciate the break."

As the group headed off again, the two Roman soldiers moved up to walk beside Mary and Joseph, put at ease by their extraordinary, almost unheard of, kindness. "Where are you and your family headed?" asked Marcellinus, making conversation.

"To the Temple of I AM to present . . ." Joseph hesitated for a moment then continued: "my son as first-born and my wife for purification in accordance with the law of Moses."

---

[5] A Roman mile, the distance between their mile markers, was 4,850 feet, as opposed to the modern mile of 5,280 feet.

"Congratulations on such a handsome son!" Marcellinus offered to Mary. She smiled and turned Jesus so the Roman could see him better. Jesus stared at the soldier in that unselfconscious, disconcerting way that babies have. Marcellinus felt his heart stir, felt the pull of this tiny baby who seemed to be looking directly into his soul.

Mary, swaying gently to the donkey's gait, asked in return, "And you, sir? Have you been assigned to Palestine?" Marcellinus had not stopped looking at Jesus but now glanced up into Mary's gentle smile and deep blue eyes, a strikingly pretty girl with thick, dark brown hair mostly hidden by a light blue scarf that covered her head and fell halfway down her back.

"Yes. We'll probably be here for a long time, unless the Zealots kill us." The thought of the ongoing terrorist war between the Jewish Zealots and the occupying Roman soldiers dispelled the pleasant reverie that had enfolded Marcellinus as he chatted with Mary. Nonetheless, he reached over and took his pack off the rump of the donkey. "I'm feeling a lot better now. Rested. Thank you for your help. We'll be turning off soon to rendezvous with some of our other troops. Tell me your name, please, and remember me to your God."

"My name is Mary of the house of Joseph of Nazareth. My husband carries your companion's pack." Joseph turned halfway around without breaking his stride and acknowledged Mary's introduction of him. "And this is my son, Jesus. I thinks he finds you to be a good man, Marcellinus. I will certainly remember you to our Father in heaven."

The four soldiers turned off. Even Gaius grumbled thanks to Joseph, who had carried his pack nearly two miles. Both men watched the Holy Family as they moved away to the north. Both would remember this encounter for the rest of their lives. Gaius because never again would he be treated kindly by a Jewish family. Marcellinus because he would eventually realize just who this baby was who somehow spoke directly to his heart long before he could speak with his mouth.

"Mary," said Joseph thoughtfully as they followed the road toward the Jaffa Gate.

"Yes, Joseph?"

"Something is very odd about our conversation with the soldiers. They spoke only in Latin, which I learned along with Greek as a young man. But I thought you spoke only Aramaic and Hebrew?"

"That is right, Joseph. I have not learned Latin or Greek," agreed Mary.

"Then how were you able to converse with the soldiers?"

"I don't know. I just understood what they were saying and they seemed to understand me."

Joseph shook his head. "As I said, wondrous things tend to happen around Jesus!"[6]

---

[6]This incident, of course, is fictional. However, it seems quite likely that Mary and Joseph would have encountered similar situations when they traveled. If so, it is equally likely they would have responded in a kind and charitable way. The purpose of

In the Court of the Women within the precincts of the Temple of Jerusalem, near the Chamber of the Nazirites, two elderly Jewish people, a man and a woman, were engaged in a very intense discussion.

"Anna, the Messiah is coming today!" said Simeon, a long-time Temple priest in his early 80s. "When I went home this morning I was feeling very discouraged. I even began to doubt my own self. It's been nearly fifty years since God revealed to me that I would not die until I had seen the Anointed One with my own eyes. Fifty years of looking at thousands and thousands of Israelite babies! I thought perhaps I AM had forgotten His promise to me."

Anna was a holy woman, a prophetess from the house of Asher, daughter of Phanuel. She was 84 years old and had spent nearly all her life in the Temple. Widowed after only seven years of marriage, she had devoted the rest of her days and a good part of her nights to constant worship of God, praying and fasting for Israel. Like Simeon, she longed with all her heart to see the Messiah, the Salvation of God's people, before she died.

"Why do you think this day will be any different than all the days in the past forty-nine years, Simeon?" Anna spoke skeptically, unable to suppress a little flame of hope that flared up in her heart but also mindful of the thousands of times before when Simeon was optimistic. This time he seemed different, however, more assured.

"Anna, listen to this! I was at home very early, not even planning to come to the Temple today because my joints, indeed my whole body, ached as if they would no longer bend willingly. Then a feeling came over me, like someone was pulling me toward the door. I ignored it at first, since I felt wobbly anyway, but the urge gave me no peace. I tried to lie down and the restlessness grew worse. Only when I gave up and decided to come to the Temple did the 'pulling' cease. Never have I felt such a force, gentle but overpowering, too!"

"Have you forgotten, Simeon, that just last week you said you had a feeling that the Messiah was coming that day? And the month before that? And seventy times seven times in the years before that?"

"I know, Anna. You are right. When I am filled with the joy of our Lord, everything looks so bright that I expect great things to happen all around me. Sometimes they do! But this feeling was very different. It came from outside me. Besides, I was feeling discouraged this morning, not optimistic."

Anna regarded Simeon carefully. He was dressed in his Temple priest clothing: ankle-length white linen tunic, seamless, bound at the waist with a long girdle fashioned of a multi-colored cord with tassels on its ends. On his head he wore a matching white linen cap, resembling a modern baker's cap except it was

---

contemplating the rosary mysteries is to reflect upon not only the events included therein but also the character and actions of the holy persons involved. Since the Holy Spirit brought the gift of tongues to Pentecost, it also seems probable that Mary, whose baby, Jesus, was conceived by the Holy Spirit, would already have had this gift for her use whenever it might be useful for God's plan.

narrower at the top. Like all priests in the Temple, he was barefoot. His hair and full beard were mostly white, his beard trimmed at about six inches. He was a big man, large of frame, but not overweight. He used his hands a lot when he spoke. His principal priestly function was to accept the redemption of first-born males and the offerings for ritual purification and to convey, in return, God's blessing upon these persons.

Anna herself was somewhat stooped. She wore the usual long linen tunic as an undergarment, but over that she wore a black mantle and covered her head with a black scarf that draped around her shoulders and hung nearly to her waist. Still in mourning dress. No longer merely for her deceased husband, whom she had dearly loved, but now mainly for the sins of Israel. She had outlived all of her immediate and extended family and was supported by the Temple treasury—unofficially, of course. As a woman, she was not allowed into the altar area of the Temple, much less into the Sanctuary or the Holy of Holies. But her years of inspiring prayer and sacrifice had convinced the Temple authorities that she had found favor with God and so they were glad to finance her continuing prayers and petitions. She was a special favorite with Simeon, who also enjoyed a reputation as a genuinely holy person. Mostly, Anna slept in the Temple, curling up with her cloak in a corner of the Court of Women.

"Well, I will try to keep an eye on you, Simeon, just in case you are right this time. It is exciting, though, isn't it?! Ooooh, the Messiah here today . . . maybe! Please God, let it be so!"

Meanwhile, outside the Jaffa Gate near the Hippicus Tower and Herod's palace, Mary and Joseph made arrangements to stable their donkey and safeguard their possessions. With Mary carrying Jesus tightly in her arms, against both the cold and the throngs of people trodding the cobbled stone streets, they headed for the great Temple Mount. There was an imposing viaduct with adjoining walkway, built by Herod, that led up from the street they walked upon into the Temple's vast Court of the Gentiles, large enough to hold several football fields. But Mary, Joseph and Jesus turned off to the south before mounting the viaduct. At the southern end of the Temple Mount were the entrances to the *mikveh*, or ritual baths. There Mary would need to bathe as part of the ritual purification ceremony. She arranged to meet Joseph and Jesus again in the Court of the Women, the usual meeting place for Jewish families and pilgrims in the huge Temple complex.

While Mary bathed, Joseph took Jesus to Solomon's Portico. There, for two denarii, he purchased two white turtledoves for Mary's offering. The area was crowded with vendors selling doves, pigeons, lambs, sheep, rams, goats, even some young bulls. Numerous others hawked their services as money changers. Between the shouted invitations to purchase, gesticulating and loud arguments over price and quality, competing enticements for currency exchange, and the bellowing, bleating, and chirping of the animals, it was difficult to even think, much less reflect upon matters divine. Joseph was relieved when he received his two doves in a small wooden cage and could escape back to the Temple enclosure.

Temple Mount viewed from southwest end of Lower City in Jerusalem.

"Joseph, I'm over here!"

Joseph spied Mary standing near the bottom of the steps leading up to the Nicanor Gate, which separated the Court of the Women from the narrow Court of the Israelites where only Jewish men could go. Beyond the Court of the Israelites was the Court of the Priests, which contained the altar of sacrifice. It was made of whitewashed stones untouched by iron and was ascended by a ramp without steps. Opposite the altar were the marble tables, posts and hooks of the Place of Slaughtering. A huge laver filled with water for the ceremonial ablutions stood close to the altar near the front corner of the Temple.

The Nicanor Gate was named after the wealthy Alexandrian Jew who donated the massive doors. The double gates were made of copper and left ungilded to commemorate their legendary miraculous rescue during a storm while being transported by sea. There were two smaller doors on either side of the main gate which replicated its style and materials. All the doors opened inward from a large, semi-circular landing that capped a flight of fifteen curved stairs leading up from the stone floor of the Court of Women. Offerings were accepted by Temple priests who stood on the landing and passed the animals and monetary contributions into the Court of the Priests for disposition.

Joseph waved back to acknowledge Mary's call and hurried over to join her. She welcomed Jesus back to her arms with a hug and a kiss on his rosy cheek, which produced a toothless smile and a gurgle of delight. Together, the Holy Family ascended the steps toward Simeon, who waited on the landing.

Temple of Jerusalem viewed from the Court of women, Nicanor Gate in the center.

Earlier, Simeon had had to struggle to even be on the landing to receive the day's offerings. "Abihar, I want to receive the public offerings today. In fact, I must receive them!"

Abihar, another Temple priest and Levite, snorted. "It is my turn, Simeon, and I prefer this duty to assisting at the altar of sacrifice. You are not even supposed to be here today. Go home. Enjoy your day off."

"No, I must be here today! The Messiah is coming!" spoke Simeon rapturously.

"In that case, I definitely want to receive the offerings!" said Abihar. But he was just being difficult because all the Temple priests had long ago decided that Simeon's expectation of seeing the Messiah was just the delusion of wishful thinking.

"Abihar, you will not know him when you see him. Has God promised to show him to you as He has to me?"

Abihar, tiring of the argument and seeing that Simeon would not be put off, surrendered. "Fine, Simeon. Take the offerings today. But you owe me for this. The next time you have the duty I will replace you. Is that agreed? As for the Messiah, I am certain that everyone will know of his arrival. Would God send the Savior of Israel with less splendor than that of King David? I think not. He will need to come in power and might to throw off the accursed Roman yoke."

"Thank you, Abihar! Of course we will switch whenever you wish. As for the Messiah's appearance, was not David a mere shepherd boy, almost overlooked in the company of his seven brothers when God named him to be king?[7] And did not God show Himself to Elijah not in power and majesty but in tiny whispering sounds?[8] I think we may be surprised once again by the way in which God redeems His people."

Abihar rolled his eyes and walked away. Simeon headed for the Nicanor Gate and his date with destiny, the fulfillment of God's promise to one who had the patience and the faith to wait upon the schedule of the Lord.

Simeon did not see the Holy Family until they were almost at the landing. They had been obscured by clumps of Jewish men passing through the Nicanor Gate into the Court reserved for them, from where the men could observe the activities in the Court of the Priests.

Simeon scanned the crowd anxiously, growing increasingly excited for no evident reason. Then they were there. Joseph, unaware that anything unusual was about to occur, extended the cage with the two turtledoves, explaining these were the sacrificial offering for Mary's ritual purification after childbirth. A Levite boy, in training for the priesthood, stood beside Simeon to receive the offerings and carry them back into the inner Temple precincts. He received the cage now and disappeared through one of the small side doors. Simeon had not even looked at Joseph as he spoke. He just stared at Jesus, resting in the arms of Mary.

Next, Joseph emptied into his open hand a small purse with five shekels in it, the price of redemption of Jesus as a first-born Jewish son, explaining his purpose as he did so. Another boy stepped up and received the shekels, then disappeared along the path of the earlier boy. Simeon never removed his eyes from the face of Jesus. Without a word, he extended his arms for the baby and Mary handed him over. Raising his eyes to heaven, Simeon declared:

"Now, Master, you can dismiss
your servant in peace;
you have fulfilled your word.
For my eyes have witnessed your
saving deed

---

[7] 1 Sm 16:1-13

[8] 1 Kgs 19:11-13

displayed for all the peoples to see:
A revealing light to the Gentiles,
the glory of your people
Israel."[9]

Mary and Joseph were taken aback by Simeon's words. "Joseph, he knows!" whispered Mary.

"Yes, like the shepherds the night Jesus was born," Joseph acknowledged. "But what does he mean about the Gentiles? Isn't the mission of the Messiah only to the people of Israel, God's chosen, to restore their greatness and faithfulness as in the time of King David and his son, Solomon?"

"I believe his mission is *through* Israel to the whole world, Joseph," Mary whispered back.

Simeon interrupted their discussion: "You are blessed above all the parents of Israel since before the time of our father, Abraham. From you has come the Anointed One, the Holy One of God. For all generations, our people and, indeed, all mankind shall give praise and thanks to I AM that two such persons came forth to be father and mother to this child. Blessed be the home you provide and all those who enter therein!"

Simeon looked once again upon the face of Jesus, smiling in his snug embrace. Simeon's expression grew grave. To Mary now, he spoke:

"This child is destined to be the downfall and the rise of many in Israel, a sign that will be opposed—and you yourself shall be pierced with a sword—so that the thoughts of many hearts may be laid bare."[10]

Joseph was stunned by Simeon's words and glanced quickly at Mary to see her reaction. She had placed one hand at her mouth and seemed disconcerted but remained focused upon Simeon. The old priest himself seemed not to notice nor to have considered what effect his words might have had. In fact, he seemed unaware that he had spoken as he carefully handed Jesus back to Mary. Pausing for one last look at the Holy Family, he extended his hand above them and prayed for God's blessing for their travels.

As Simeon finished his blessing, Anna dashed around a cluster of Jewish men who had been strolling leisurely up the steps toward the gate. She had been trying all morning to keep an eye on Simeon because of his premonition that he would see the Messiah that day. There had been false alarms before, but this time he did seem different. In any case, Anna believed his revelation from God was real and she was taking no chances. She would never forgive herself if the Messiah came and left without her seeing him. Out of the corner of her eye, she had noticed Simeon pause and pay special attention to one couple, a strong, handsome, black-haired man and a lovely young girl holding a newborn baby. Obviously, they were

---

[9]Lk 2:29-32

[10]Lk 2:34-35

here for the ritual purification of the mother and the customary redemption of the child, who would therefore be a first-born male. Anna had never seen Simeon look like he looked now—his face shining with joy. It must be the Messiah! She leaped up from where she had been sitting and ran, as best her eighty-four years would permit, toward the landing where Simeon and the young family stood.

"Is it . . . ?" Anna left the question unfinished but Simeon knew what she asked. He nodded. Simultaneously, Anna experienced what the shepherds had felt. The presence of the Holy Spirit cascaded through her like a waterfall of love.

Mary and Joseph were now staring at Anna, first surprised by the intrusion, then astonished to see tears flowing down the old woman's face. Mary offered Jesus to Anna, who reverently took the infant and carefully, ever so lovingly, stroked his cheeks. Some of her tears fell upon the baby but Jesus did not seem to mind. After a few minutes, Anna gave the child back to his mother, using a linen cloth to wipe away the tears she had shed, still glistening on the baby's cheeks.

Anna accompanied the Holy Family all the way to the gate in the outer Temple wall which led onto the viaduct that would take them down to the street and back to the stable where their donkey and possessions waited. On the way, she learned the baby's name and where he had been born. She found out the family was from Nazareth and was returning there now. She told them about herself and Simeon, explaining how he had received a revelation from God many years before that he would not die until he had seen the Anointed of the Lord.

When Anna had bid them goodbye and wished them the blessings of God upon all the days of their lives, she retraced her steps. She paused frequently to praise God and give Him thanks for this great privilege for her and blessing for His people. She tried to tell anyone who would listen that the Messiah had been sent, was here in Jerusalem at this very moment! But most simply sidestepped her, exchanging glances as if to say, "Another crazy person claiming to have inside knowledge of the Messiah." In fairness to them, the country was filled with persons claiming to have seen the Messiah, to know the Messiah, to *be* the Messiah. A few, however, did listen to her. They even got caught up in her excitement and tried to find the Holy Family themselves. But to no avail. Jerusalem was too crowded and the Holy Family too indistinguishable to be found. A few of the Temple priests were intrigued enough by Simeon's enthusiastic claims to wonder, but no more than that. It was a time when there were no news media and communications were slow and cumbersome. Further revelation of the Messiah would have to await God's own good time.

Only one young Temple scribe was open-minded enough to pursue the matter with Simeon and Anna. He was a Pharisee named Nicodemus, who, after seeing the conviction in the faces of the two old people, actually went in search of the baby Jesus. Not that he would admit it, of course, for that would have subjected him to considerable ridicule from his eminent peers. Later he would remember the all-important Bethlehem connection while forgetting any reference to the obscure village of Nazareth.

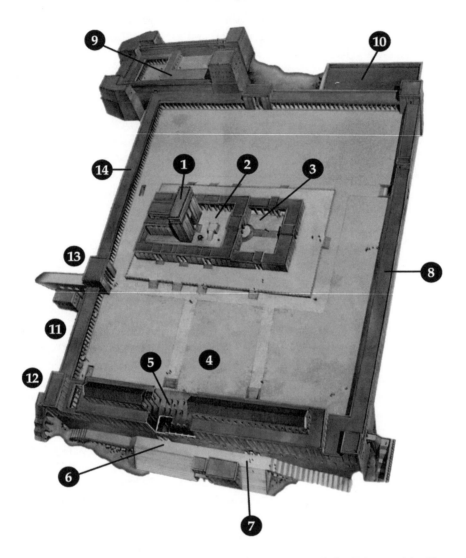

The Temple Mount. *(1) Temple of Herod. (2) Court of the Priests with Altar of Holocausts. (3) Court of the Women. (4) Court of the Gentiles. (5) Royal Portico. (6) Double Gate. (7) Triple Gate. (8) Solomon's Portico. (9) Fortress Antonia. (10) Pool of Israel. (11) Western Wall and Barclay's Gate. (12) Robinson's Arch. (13) Wilson's Arch. (14) Warren's Gate.*

Illustration by J.-B. Héron Le Monde de la Bible 1998

As Mary and Joseph walked back through the streets of Jerusalem, they discussed the prophecy of Simeon. Joseph was very agitated. "Mary, I don't understand the mission of Jesus. Can it be that he will not be welcomed in Israel? That is unthinkable! The Messiah awaited for centuries, two thousand years in fact, rejected by his own people. Please God, let that not be so! And you, his mother—pierced by a sword! Surely God can protect the mother of His own Son? Could we have misunderstood?"

Mary did not answer for a few moments, seemingly lost in her thoughts. "Dear husband, my own understanding of the mission of the Messiah is also changing . . . and growing. No longer do I believe he will be a new David, sent to re-establish the kingdom of Israel as a power on earth. But I do not know, either, what God has in mind for us. I am certain, however, that Jesus has come for all mankind, and not merely for the Israelites. If I am called to sacrifice my life in his struggle, I will do so willingly, joyfully!"

Joseph shook his head. "Well, the old priest had nothing to say to me. But if God will permit it, I promise that I will let no harm come to you so long as I am able to defend you!" he vowed.

"It seems that God has sent His Son to open our hearts, Joseph. There have always been struggles and violence for the prophets before him. Perhaps we should see in this a foretelling of the struggle that may ensue when God tries to draw sinful man closer to Himself. Certainly, it is our hearts which reveal our character. Somehow, Jesus will break open those hearts to reveal what is now often hidden behind fine clothes, smooth words, wealth and power. I pray only that my sufferings may lessen my son's, if such is God's plan."

By this time, they had arrived at the city gate where they had entered. Just outside was the stable where they had left their donkey and baggage. Joseph paid the stablemaster for the care of his animal and the safeguarding of his goods. He helped Mary and Jesus back onto the little donkey and they set off, once again, for Nazareth. It was just past noon and they would still have time to reach Bethel, a little over ten miles north along the ridge route.

———————

PROPHECIES OF ISAIAH

Then the glory of the LORD
shall be revealed,
and all mankind shall see it together.[11]
I formed you, and set you
as a covenant for the people,
a light for the nations.[12]
I will put salvation within Zion,
and give to Israel my glory.[13]
It is too little, he says, for you
to be my servant,
to raise up the tribes of Jacob,
and restore the survivors of Israel;
I will make you a light to the nations,
that my salvation may reach
to the ends of the earth.[14]
For the Lord comforts his people,
he redeems Jerusalem.
The LORD has bared his holy arm
in the sight of all the nations;
All the ends of the earth will behold
the salvation of our God.[15]

---

[11]Is 40:5

[12]Is 42:6

[13]Is 46:13

[14]Is 49:6

[15]Is 52:9-10

QUESTIONS FOR REFLECTION

1) A strong case can be made that Mary and Jesus need not have complied with Mosaic laws requiring her ritual purification or Jesus' redemption from service to God. They were a poor family and the payment of five shekels would have been a financial strain. Yet in this and in all other respects they adhered to the requirements of Judaism all their lives. What is the message for us in their obedience to the law? Is Mary telling us something important here about obedience to Church teachings as opposed to following our own wills?

2) Can you find explicit support for this view in the words of Jesus? [Hint: read the "keys of the kingdom" passage in Matthew at 16:19.]

3) Can you see a relationship between obedience and faith? Can you see that obedience is faith lived? That it rests upon trust that all things will work out for the best because God loves us?

4) What is the opposite of obedience? Disobedience? Is this not the very definition of sin; i.e., disobedience of God's commandments? Would Mary have sinned if she had refused God's invitation to be the mother of the Messiah? Explain.

5) We know from Scripture that the Holy Spirit sometimes gives the gift of tongues to the followers of Christ. Given Mary's relationship with the Holy Spirit in a unique way, do you think it likely or unlikely that she also received the gift of speaking and understanding foreign languages?

6) Why did God have Simeon say the things he did? Why has Luke reported them to us? What is the message for us?

7) If you had been Mary, how would you have reacted to Simeon's prediction that you would be pierced by a sword? How would you have reacted if you had been Joseph?

8) If you met an old woman today claiming to have seen Jesus, Mary, an angel or some other supernatural personage, how would you react? How do you react to reports of miraculous occurrences in the world today? How should one react?

9) How long are you willing to wait for God to fulfill His promises? In your mind, is there a point of diminishing returns?

10) In what ways, if any, are the Infancy Narratives of Luke and Matthew inconsistent? Contradictory? Why the differences, do you think?

On the third day they came upon him in the temple sitting in the midst of the teachers,
listening to them and asking them questions. Lk 2:46

FIFTH JOYFUL MYSTERY

The Finding in the Temple

Jesus was excited. He loved to visit the huge Temple of Jerusalem every year at Passover. The journey itself, in the company of aunts, uncles, cousins and friends was always fun, involving as it did a four-day journey down through Galilee, Samaria and northern Judea. This time of year, the fields and green hillsides would be carpeted in brilliant swaths of wild flowers, an image that Jesus would use in his ministry to contrast the glory of God's creation with the pale imitations of man.[1] Sometimes they traveled the mountain route through the middle of Samaria; at other times, they followed the Jordan River route. For this trip, they would make the more scenic journey down the ridge line of the central mountains, stopping for the first night a few miles past Ginae, just inside the Samaritan border, about twenty miles south of Nazareth.

As a twelve-year-old, Jesus was just a year shy of full Jewish manhood. He was now enrolled in the *bet talmud*, or "house of learning," conducted in the synagogue at Nazareth under the tutelage of a rabbi who was also a scribe. Formal sessions were held in the mornings and evenings, five days a week. The course of study focused on the *mishnah*, the body of rules and guidelines for interpreting the *Torah* (first five books of the Bible), attributed to the authorship of Moses. Centuries later, this body of interpretative law would be written down as the *Talmud*.

Little or no attention was paid in these schools to the Hellenistic subjects, such as physical training, mathematics, music, art, rhetoric and philosophy. Education for Jewish children began with their religion, examining and memorizing the verses of the *Torah*, and ended with their religion, expanding their understanding of the *Torah* by learning how its rules and requirements had been imposed and modified down through the centuries. Students learned orally by rote memorization, recitation and the use of parables to illustrate various points.

---

[1]"Learn a lesson from the way the wild flowers grow. They do not work; they do not spin. Yet I assure you, not even Solomon in all his splendor was arrayed like one of these." Mt 6:28-29

Most students (all male, by the way) would conclude their studies at age thirteen after which they would concentrate their learning on the trade, craft or activity that was to become their livelihood.

A few students would go on to study in the *bet midrash*, or "house of study." These boys would be on the path to becoming scribes, the ancient world's equivalent of a Ph.D., and would spend more time learning to write well.

Although girls received no formal schooling, they learned from their mothers and female relatives everything they needed to know to function as Jewish wives and mothers. This included knowledge of the strict dietary laws of the *Torah*, the various religious observance customs, the heritage of the Jewish people, and all of their homemaker tasks. Girls might also learn to sing and dance and to play such musical instruments as the flute, harp or timbrel. Musical displays, however, always had a religious purpose.

Jesus was an extraordinary student. He was quiet in his classes, rarely volunteering an answer unless called upon. But his powers of memory and reasoning were impressive, indeed. His teachers had been encouraging Joseph to send his son on to advanced study with a prominent scholar, to become a scribe who could return to Nazareth and become a teacher himself. Jesus, however, had expressed no interest in doing this, saying that he preferred to remain in Nazareth and become an excellent carpenter like his father. And so his formal education would end the following year.

The Nazarene party set out in high spirits in balmy, springtime weather. Their caravan fell in before and behind other groups from Sepphoris, Japhia, Asochis, Cana, Gabara, Exaloth and other villages north and south of Nazareth. Jesus walked with the men for awhile, and then walked with his mother in the women's group for awhile. He was a reserved child, friendly but not outgoing. He was tall for his age, slender, and he moved with the easy grace of a natural athlete. His shoulder-length hair was dark brown, like his mother's, and framed a symmetrical face with a long, narrow nose and even white teeth that lit up his countenance when he smiled or laughed. His eyes were brown, the color of polished maple, similar to those of his presumed father, Joseph. Like most 12-year olds, his energy level could not be suppressed and Jesus spent his share of the trip running and climbing nearby rock outcrops with his cousins and friends.

The group entered into Samaritan territory just north of the village of Ginae. Relationships with the Samaritans were never warm and cordial, but in this year, 7 A.D., Herod Archelaus had succeeded in uniting everyone in his three provinces of Samaria, Judea and Idumea against him. His rule since the death of his father, Herod the Great, had been so brutal and harsh that many of his countrymen were in open revolt. There had even been petitions to Rome for his removal. Recently, Augustus had complied and sent the tyrannical king into permanent exile in what would later become Vienna, Austria. For the next 35 years, Judea, Samaria and Idumea would be ruled by Roman governors, or procurators, the most famous of whom would be Pontius Pilate.

Despite the lessening of tensions between the inhabitants of Samaria and Galilee, the Nazarene group tended out of force of habit to tighten up its loose formation. They camped out in clearings which had become campgrounds for them by dint of regular usage over many years. In the evenings, the various families reunited for prayer and mealtime. Thereafter, there were community songs and dancing, sometimes shared with other villages, and trained storytellers dramatically recalling some of the great events in Israeli history. These usually related to the passage of the Israelites out of the bondage of Egypt since the purpose of this trip was to attend the great Passover celebration in Jerusalem. These were fun-filled occasions and the Holy Family looked forward eagerly to them each year.

Mary's parents, Joachim and Anne, had passed away within a few months of each other a few years earlier. Before that, they had usually traveled as part of the extended family to the great Jerusalem Passover celebration. Mary missed her mother. They had been good friends and Anne loved to look after Jesus when he was a young child following his return from Egypt at nearly the age of three. This was especially helpful during the jam-packed, noisy and festive celebrations accompanying the Passover pilgrimage. But "family" in ancient times meant much more than it does today. Joseph's family had welcomed Mary warmly and she had found a good friend in Mary, her sister-in-law with the same name ("Miriam" in Aramaic) . Their oldest son, James, was betrothed and soon to be married.

James was almost ten years older than Jesus, so they weren't close friends, but James was very fond of the boy. He tried to look out for him whenever he could. He found Jesus to be utterly fascinating, normal in so many respects, but possessing a depth that seemed other-worldly to James. Even as a child, Jesus understood human beings and their relationship with God better than anyone he had ever heard, including any of the learned rabbis and scribes who taught in Nazareth . . . or Jerusalem, for that matter.

James knew nothing of Jesus' miraculous background. Mary and Joseph had decided not to mention the divine origin of Jesus, and the events surrounding his birth, even to their family and close friends. It was clear to them by now that God was approaching the salvation of Israel in a way not anticipated by popular expectations. Nothing in Jesus' outward appearance suggested he was more than a normal Jewish child. Although an extremely apt pupil, he grew in human knowledge like all other people: by study and observation. He seemed content to blend into the quiet life of Nazareth. His parents concurred that Jesus and his Heavenly Father most certainly had a plan for fulfillment of his mission. They would let God develop it accordingly. After their experience with Herod the Great in Bethlehem, they were also much more cautious about letting such claims come to the attention of anyone in authority.

But James was an intelligent, observant man. He had long ago realized that Jesus was no ordinary person. He had been astonished when Jesus declined to pursue his education. James had been certain that Jesus was destined to become one of Israel's great teachers, maybe even a prophet of God. He had tried to suggest that himself to Jesus, but Jesus had only smiled, thanked him, and said he would try hard to become an equally great carpenter.

On the second day of the journey, the pilgrims traveled down the ridge which forms the backbone of Samaria. That evening they camped in the shadow of the craggy heights of Mt. Gerizim, a few miles from the village of Sychar, near the ruins of ancient Shechem. The village, located at the crossroads of two important trade routes, nestled at the northeastern corner of the mountain. Water was obtained from the famous Jacob's Well, where, during his public ministry some twenty years from now, Jesus would challenge the oft-married Samaritan woman to seek the "living waters" of eternal life.[2]

On the morning of the third day, the travelers continued south toward the Ascent of Lebonah, from where they would descend briefly before heading back up to cross over a series of hills, past Bethel and Ramah and through the pass between Mount Scopus and the Mount of Olives into Jerusalem.

At last, in the afternoon of the fourth day, the great walled city of Jerusalem shimmered into view. The white marble walls of the Temple Sanctuary glistened in the rays of the descending sun.[3] It was two days before Passover and the road was choked with religious pilgrims and the animals they brought for travel and sacrifice. Off to the right, just inside the western outer wall of the fashionable Upper City, crowded with the mansions of the rich, Herod's sumptuous palace stood in quiet splendor. Its principal occupant, the former ethnarch Herod Archelaus, was permanently gone. For the most part, the palace went unused. Romans ruled in Jerusalem now and their soldiers were everywhere, a threatening presence easily antagonized by even a hint of resistance. Despite a strictly enforced nighttime curfew within the city walls, the soldiers were extremely anxious about being in the midst of a city population swollen to three times its normal size and focused upon celebrating Israel's liberation from foreign domination.

As the Nazarenes neared the northeast corner of the massive wall surrounding Jerusalem, they turned off onto the Jericho Road, moving south down the Kidron Valley before turning east and heading up toward their traditional camping area on the Mount of Olives. The hillside was alive with similar groups mixing in a tumultuous riot of colorful garments and tents, children scampering, animal cries, and adults shouting commands, directions and queries. Jesus helped his family set up their tent and secure the donkey which had carried their provisions. When they had finished, they retraced their steps toward the Susa Gate and a late afternoon visit to the Temple complex. This would be the last normal

---

[2]He would startle his disciples by engaging in such discussions with a woman, and a Samaritan one at that! Jn 4:4-42.

[3]When the Talmud, the book of Jewish regulations and commentary, was finally compiled, it would pronounce: "He who has not seen the Temple of Herod has never in his life seen a beautiful building."

day of operations before the seven days of special sacrificial and celebratory procedures of Passover and the Feast of Unleavened Bread.

Well before they reached the gate, the Holy Family was submerged in the raucous chatter of vendors hawking all manner of goods, both edible and exotic. The din of enticement and bargaining was magnified by the plaintive cries and outstretched hands of beggars who lined the road practically shoulder-to-shoulder. The family stayed close together, holding hands, and pushed through the crowds. They separated briefly to immerse themselves in the male and female ritual baths (*mikveh*), agreeing to meet at a predetermined point on the outer edge of the Court of Gentiles. In this huge open area surrounding the Temple proper, Jews and Gentiles from all over the known world were gathered. Speaking in raised voices to surmount the general racket, the languages of Aramaic, Hebrew, Greek, Latin, Persia, Arabia and Egypt, to name but a few, all competed in a cacophony best described as a "Tower of Babble."

Joseph, Mary and Jesus slowly made their way toward the *Soreg*, a low stone balustrade that surrounded the inner courts of the Temple. This stone wall, about three feet high, was inscribed at intervals in bold Hebrew, Latin and Greek letters that announced the death penalty for any foreigner (Gentile) found inside the balustrade. This provision was enforced by the Roman authorities, even against Roman citizens.

Once past the wall, the crowds thinned and the Holy Family proceeded relatively unencumbered up a flight of fourteen steps onto a flat rampart (*Hel*) that surrounded the inner Temple wall. There were three gates into the Court of the Women, one on each open side. This court was the central meeting place for Jews visiting the Temple. Preachers and self-proclaimed prophets called out to all who would listen. Scribes and teachers gathered in groups around the perimeter to discuss and debate various issues pertaining to the Law and its practices, or the words of the prophets and their implications for Israel. The nature and imminence of the Messiah, plus the expected results of his arrival, were a frequent topic of discussion. With the nervous Roman guards safely posted outside the *Soreg*, the Jews felt comfortable in describing how the Messiah would cast off the yoke of Roman imperialism.

Joseph and Jesus left Mary with friends inside the Court of the Women while they passed through the Nicanor Gate into the Court of the Israelites. This long, narrow court permitted them to observe the sacrificial activities and even to see briefly into the Temple Sanctuary when a priest entered or left through the gilded, three-story outer doors, decorated with golden vines and clusters of golden grapes several feet tall. But no one except the high priest was able to see into or enter the Holy of Holies, an exact 30-foot cube perpetually isolated from natural light by a thick, overlapping double veil. According to tradition, the rock upon which Abraham was to sacrifice his son, Isaac, lay beneath this room.

As dusk approached, the Temple Mount cleared of visitors. Joseph, Mary and Jesus also left and returned to their campsite. The following morning, Passover week would begin. Instead of the usual slaughter of a single lamb at dawn to inaugurate a day of numerous private animal sacrifices (private intentions, personally paid for, not privately performed), Passover would begin with the slaughter of seven lambs plus two young bulls, a ram and a goat. The same number would be sacrificed each day of the week-long festival.[4]

In early afternoon, Joseph and Jesus returned to the Court of the Gentiles. There they joined thousands of other Jewish men, most of whom held a single, unblemished lamb. This was the paschal lamb, the lamb to be slaughtered not by the Temple priests, but by the man who brought it to the Temple. The lamb would then become the food for all those who would share the Passover meal, or *Seder*, that evening. In Joseph's case, that would be him, Mary, Jesus, Clopas Alphaeus and his wife, Mary, their children, James and Joses, Leah, Judith and Naomi—ten in all.

The huge crowd of Jewish men, holding their lambs in the Court of the Gentiles, were admitted by thirds to the Temple's inner precincts through the three gates opening into the Court of the Women. With a harsh and piercing cry from the *shofar*, or ram's horn trumpet, the gates would be closed behind the first group. Inside they would meet several long lines of priests holding gold and silver bowls into which the blood of each lamb would be poured after the man who brought it had cut its carotid artery. The bowls of blood would be passed back down the line to priests near the altar who would dash the blood against the base and return the bowls to the front of the lines. When all the lambs had been killed and flayed, the men in the first third returned to their family celebrations with their lambs, to be roasted and eaten that evening with unleavened bread and bitter herbs.

After the first third had left, another third was admitted. Finally, everyone remaining was admitted to complete the slaughter of the Passover lambs.

The remaining days of the Feast of Unleavened Bread were devoted to other aspects of the story of Exodus as well as to religious rituals to mark the beginning of the annual grain harvest. No leavened bread or anything else that contained yeast could be eaten during this week. This commemorated the rapidity of the Israelites' evacuation from Egypt when the women had not had time to wait for their bread to rise.

As the week drew to a close, Mary, Joseph and Jesus prepared to join the others in their party for the journey home to Nazareth. Jesus seemed distracted as the day for departure neared. He spent as much time as he could in the Temple enclosure, not in the Court of the Israelites, but in the Court of the Women, listening to the learned discussions and arguments among the scribes and teachers. On the morning of their departure, he rose early.

"Mother, I would like to visit the Temple a final time this morning before we depart. Is that all right?" Jesus asked Mary just after dawn.

"Yes, Jesus, but don't linger. We'll be leaving very soon."

---

[4]These numbers, however, were slight compared to the numbers slaughtered for the Feast of Booths, or *Succoth*, in September-October. During that eight-day festival, 71 young bulls, 15 rams, 8 goats, and 105 lambs were sacrificed upon the altar.

"Don't worry, mother. I'm going to find James and go with him. He told me yesterday that he wanted to visit the Temple one last time before we went home," replied Jesus as he dashed off in the direction of the Clopas family, who were busy gathering their things, packing, and tending their donkeys. When he arrived, he learned that James had left for the Temple a few minutes before. Mary of Clopas told Jesus that he could probably catch up to him before he reached the bottom of the hill, if he hurried. Jesus thanked her and ran off toward the city. In the meantime, however, James had second thoughts about visiting the Temple and had decided, instead, to go and help his betrothed and her family.

Jesus pushed his way through the crowds of people moving in clusters toward the roads that would take them back toward the four corners of the empire. Passing through the Susa Gate, he hurried toward the Court of the Women. Over the past few days, he had spent considerable time listening to one of the groups of scribe-scholars debating the mission of the Messiah. Now he burned with an irresistible desire to join that discussion.

When he arrived at the group, seated in semi-circle fashion near the Beautiful Gate at the east end of the Court of the Women, eight teachers were once again discussing the longed-for Messiah, the hope and salvation of Israel. They were led in this effort by a rabbi named Hanania. Also in the group was a Pharisee named Nicodemus. Several other men and boys sat at their feet, listening to them. Jesus joined them.

"Gershon," said Hanania to one of his fellow teachers. "When will the Messiah come to rescue Israel?"

"I believe his time may be soon, Hanania," replied Gershon. "For it is written by the holy prophet Daniel that the Anointed of the Lord shall come to restore dominion to the people of the Most High after the fourth 'beast' has been destroyed. This beast shall be a great kingdom, more powerful and terrible than the other three, and shall devour the whole earth. Surely, this kingdom must be that which rules from Rome, for its forces oppress our people more and insult the God of Israel more terribly than any kingdom before it!"[5]

Another teacher spoke up. "And has not Isaiah written that after the fall of Jerusalem and the destruction of her enemies that a Savior would be sent? Jerusalem has fallen before Assyria and Babylon and Rome. Before them, the Philistines and the Canaanites oppressed our people. Only Rome's boot remains planted on her neck. Surely there could be no better time to send the One who will finally and permanently restore Israel to the glory intended by the Lord?"

"Yet Roman power seems undiminished, growing even," said yet another teacher. "Doesn't this suggest that the time for the Messiah is not ripe?"

"But, surely, the Messiah shall be the instrument for the liberation of Israel for otherwise his role would be greatly diminished," responded Gershon.

---

[5]See Dn 7:13-27.

"And what shall be the nature of the Messiah's mission?" Hanania asked, changing tack slightly.

"David, whose House has been promised by God Himself to rule Israel forever, has called upon the Lord to cast down his enemies, to rescue him by the sword of God's wrath,"[6] said a teacher. "So, too, has Isaiah said:

> **'I will make your oppressors eat their own flesh,**
> **and they shall be drunk with their own blood**
> **as with the juice of the grape.**
> **All mankind shall know**
> **that I, the LORD, am your savior,**
> **your redeemer, the Mighty One of Jacob.'**[7]

Clearly, God will send His Anointed One in power and might."

Jesus followed this and the ensuing discussion intently, not saying anything but shaking his head slightly from time to time. Hanania had noticed the boy's body language responses to the discussions during the previous days. Now, seeing Jesus stand up as he started to leave to return to the Nazarene party that would be on the verge of its departure for Galilee, Hanania directed a question to him: "And you, young man; I see you do not agree with everything being said here. How do you think the Messiah will come to save Israel?"

Jesus hesitated. He knew he had little time to spare and would be scolded if he disrupted the family's schedule. But here was a rare opportunity to teach the teachers, and so he responded: "The Messiah shall come as a child, as foretold by Isaiah. He shall establish the Kingdom of God upon earth, a kingdom of love and peace. Has the prophet not written:

> **'For a child is born to us, a son is given us;**
> **upon his shoulder dominion rests.**
> **They name him Wonder-Counselor, God-Hero,**
> **Father-Forever, Prince of Peace.**
> **His dominion is vast**
> **and forever peaceful,**
> **From David's throne, and over his kingdom,**
> **which he confirms and sustains**
> **By judgment and justice,**
> **both now and forever.'?"**[8]

The quality and promptness of this reply from a twelve-year old boy immediately captured the interest and attention of the teachers. They began to ask Jesus other questions, and then to engage in spirited debates among themselves over various issues raised by his responses. Jesus, himself, ventured occasionally

---

[6]See Ps 17:13.

[7]Is 49:26

[8]Is 9:5-6

to ask a question, to probe an assertion. He was thoroughly fascinating to these teachers of the Jewish law.

For his part, Jesus decided that he would remain until someone from his family came to get him. When he explained the reason for his delay, he was certain they would understand.

Meanwhile, Jesus' parents had concluded their preparations for departure back to Nazareth. Mary knew that Jesus had gone up to the Temple, but she was traveling with the women and expected Jesus to walk with Joseph and the other men. When Mary saw James in the group of men, she relaxed, remembering that Jesus had said he was going to the Temple Mount with James. If James was back, then Jesus obviously was, too. Although she did not see him, the group was large, the commotion great, and the proclivity of adolescent boys to be elusive well known to her.

Joseph was unaware of Jesus' last minute visit, so he simply assumed that the boy was with his mother. The two of them were exceptionally close, joined by a bond of love and understanding that bypassed normal human communication. Joseph chuckled to himself as he recalled the many times when he and Jesus had been working on a carpenter's project away from home and Jesus would calmly announce that his mother needed assistance with some household task. Off he would run, with Joseph's permission, to help her.

One thing sure, the boy had no interest in the martial arts. Oh, he was well-coordinated and could outrun most of the other boys his age. But he was never involved in the kinds of contests and challenges whereby males attempt to assert their dominance over other males. *Then again,* thought Joseph to himself, *I rarely saw anyone else, even the older boys, attempt to bully him.* There was something about Jesus that drew most people to him. Those who did not wish to be his friend still tended to treat him with dignity and respect. Only occasionally did he confront an openly antagonistic person. *Strange how those situations always managed to defuse themselves,* Joseph mused. If physical conflict had seemed inevitable, then Jesus just . . . was suddenly elsewhere. It was never obvious, like vanishing into thin air when someone has his arms around you. There would always be some distraction, maybe someone defending Jesus or threatening his assailant, and in the commotion Jesus simply was no longer present. Those involved would assume he had run away without being noticed. But they were uneasy about it. By the time Jesus was twelve, no one attempted to pick on him anymore. Besides, he had a disconcerting way of immediately befriending whomever had been unpleasant to him. Joseph loved the boy fiercely. At the same time, he was awestruck by him.

The Nazarene group headed north, toward home. Their first night on the road would be spent at the Ascent of Lebonah in Samaria, about twenty miles from Jerusalem. Mary walked with her sisters-in-law and the other women from the village. As she rounded the base of Mount Scopus, the last point from which Jerusalem would be visible, she looked back at the City of David sitting high and confident among its phalanx of hills. She could see the shining Temple standing proudly just beyond the brooding Fortress Antonia. They made an odd couple, like the good and evil which seem to co-exist in people's souls. For a moment, she felt anxious for her son, uncomfortable that she had left without seeing him. "Mary, did you see Jesus this morning?" she asked her sister-in-law.

"Yes, I did. He came looking for James to go to the Temple. Actually, I haven't seen James either since we left," Mary Clopas replied.

"No need to worry," said Mary. "I saw James with the men as we were leaving. But I didn't see Jesus. I just assumed he was with him. I would feel better if I were sure we didn't somehow leave him behind. Would you help me keep an eye out for him?"

"Of course, dear. I'm sure he will turn up around lunchtime. You know boys—all limbs and stomach!"

The travelers did not stop for lunch. They just took out pieces of cheese and bread, nuts and fruit, and ate them as they walked. Raisin cakes were a favorite, made especially for the trip. Mary's anxiety continued to mount as the day passed into early afternoon. When Jesus failed to appear for lunch, she sent word by one of his friends up to Joseph, inquiring if he had seen Jesus since they left Jerusalem. The boy, however, got caught up in a game with some of the other boys and forgot his messenger role for nearly an hour. Remembering, he raced ahead to where the men were walking with the pack animals. He found Joseph with his brother, Clopas, and two other carpenters. They were discussing a building project in Sepphoris, the Hellenistic city just north of Nazareth.

"Sir, your wife is looking for Jesus and wonders if you have seen him?" the boy asked Joseph.

Joseph was surprised by the question. "I thought he was with her. Go back and tell my wife that I have not seen him, but I will check with the other families. He's probably just running with the boys."

Once again, however, the little "messenger" became distracted and forgot all about his task. After all, both parents were now aware of the problem and there seemed to be nothing else important for him to do.

The Nazarene party was strung out along the road. The young boys liked to play games among the rock outcrops and patches of forest along the way. As a result, it was late afternoon before Joseph had tracked down all of the likely companions of Jesus. None of them remembered seeing him since they had left Jerusalem. A chill ran through Joseph. He asked Clopas to keep an eye on his donkey and headed back hurriedly to see his wife.

With mounting anxiety, Mary had also been searching for Jesus among her friends and relatives. She wondered why she had not heard back from Joseph. The rational part of her decided that was good news, that Joseph probably had Jesus with him and so had felt no urgency about responding to her inquiry. But the mother in her felt only disquiet. Something was wrong. She knew it. When she saw Joseph hurrying back down the road toward her, alone, panic spread its paralyzing fingers into all her joints until she felt she could barely stand. By now they were over sixteen miles from Jerusalem, nearly a full day's walk.

"Husband, where is Jesus?" she said, fighting to keep her voice under control.

"I don't know. I thought he was with you until the boy brought your message. I have searched diligently but no one reports having seen him. Is it possible that he is with one of my sisters or your friends?"

"Oh, my dear Lord," said Mary. She burst into tears. Joseph hugged her but he felt like crying himself. "We left him in Jerusalem," Mary sobbed. "We must go back right now!"

Joseph's head pounded with the awful realization that Mary was right. Right about leaving Jesus, but not right about turning around. "Dearest Mary, we cannot go back now. We are nearly at our first night's campsite. It would be foolhardy to attempt the journey at night. Not only are there bandits and wild animals preying on lone travelers, but it would be very easy to lose our way or be injured. That would do Jesus no good at all.

"The boy will be safe during the day, especially in the Temple area where I am sure he will stay. He will certainly go to the house of our friends, Zairus and Joanna, tonight and they will keep him until we arrive tomorrow. It will be all right. And let us not forget whose Son he is. God will let no harm come to him." Joseph sounded more confident than he felt, but his words were balm for Mary's fears.

She clung to Joseph awhile longer, then wiped her eyes, sniffled a bit, and said, "Of course you are right, husband. But we must leave tomorrow at first light."

The night was long for both of them. At the campsite, they had confirmed what they already knew: that Jesus was not in the party. James explained that he had changed his mind about going to the Temple and had not seen Jesus at all that morning. Word of the missing boy spread among the Nazarenes. The frightened looks of concern and occasional thoughtless remark ("How could you leave the city without making sure he was with you?" "You must hurry because so-and-so had a child stolen by the slave traders." "I hope he remembers the curfew. The Roman soldiers won't ask questions.") aroused Mary and Joseph's fears all over again. They intensified as the dark night settled heavily around them. Mary spent the entire night in prayer. Joseph joined her for most of it but tried to get some sleep at intervals. He may have slept but he did not rest for his sleep was marred by recurrent dreams of God demanding of him what he had done with His Son.

Jesus spent the day engrossed with the teachers in the Temple. As the day wore on, other teachers, hearing the discussion and seeing a mere child holding his own with some of the most renowned scholars in Israel, joined the group. Each of them felt he had something vital to say, or to offer in rebuttal, so Jesus actually had little opportunity to speak. However, his questions regularly challenged their expectations regarding the Messiah and Israel's future, which always set off a new round of heated debate among them. Hanania understood the dynamic perfectly and his respect for this slip of a boy sitting in their midst grew by the hour.

Nicodemus found himself often staring at Jesus. There was something about him that was stirring a memory in him, a memory he could not quite bring to the surface of his mind. Finally, with great relief he remembered. *Simeon!* Simeon, the old priest in the Temple, who had waited almost fifty years to see the Messiah, claiming that God had told him personally that he would not die until he had done so. It had been nearly twelve years now since Simeon had died. Nicodemus thought back to that day when Simeon, his face shining with gratitude and joy, had told him that the Messiah had come to the Temple that very morning. He had been a first-born son from Bethlehem, brought to the Temple by his parents for the customary redemption offering. *And Anna! She, too, had insisted that she had seen the Messiah that day,* thought Nicodemus. He himself had gone in search of the child, but without success.

Twelve years ago. That infant would be about this boy's age today, Nicodemus mused. Finally, he asked Jesus: "Where are you from, young man?"

Jesus looked at him with an enigmatic smile, as if the question were more complex than Nicodemus realized. "I am from Nazareth. I live with Joseph the carpenter and my mother."

Nazareth! There was nothing in the prophets or Israel's long expectant traditions to suggest that the Messiah would come from Galilee, much less an insignificant village on the doorstep of Sepphoris, one of the most Gentile cities in all of Israel. Nicodemus sighed. *Well, he may not be the Messiah, but this child's knowledge of Scripture is remarkable!*

As evening drew near, the teachers began to disperse to their homes. Jesus, however, made no move to leave. Hanania had already noted that the boy's parents should have long since come looking for him. He had been with them since just after dawn. "What is your name?" he asked. He had not inquired before because to be concerned about a boy's name would accord him more respect and dignity than he merited. Only the teachers had names—officially.

"Jesus." It was not an unusual name in Israel at this time.

"Where are your parents? It is getting late and we violate the Roman curfew at our peril."

"I am afraid they have already left to return home to Nazareth," said Jesus. "They did not realize that I was remaining behind in the Temple. But they will come back for me soon."

"Well, you will need a place to sleep. Would you like to stay with me and my family?" Jesus accepted the offer graciously and went home with Hanania. In the course of the evening's small talk, the teacher learned that Jesus had been born in Bethlehem, had lived in Egypt for awhile as a baby, and now was learning to be a carpenter like his father. None of this raised any Messiah connection in his mind, because he had not been aware of Simeon's and Anna's claims. He wouldn't have been interested if he had known because he, like nearly all of Israel, wanted the Messiah to come in strength and glory to throw off the Roman yoke. There was almost no concept of a spiritual salvation of men's souls that would not be accompanied by a simultaneous restoration of glory to the Jewish body politic.

The next day, Mary and Joseph quietly left their camp just as the first rays of dawnlight stretched tentative fingers over the horizon. Leading their donkey, they made their way carefully down the hilly path until the sun was high enough in the sky to illuminate the obstacles clearly. Then Mary wanted to run all the way back to Jerusalem. But twenty miles are a long way, and both she and Joseph were already fatigued and emotionally exhausted from the night's sleeplessness. Their progress was slowed, too, by the crowds of pilgrims who had left Jerusalem a day after them and were now clogging the road as the Nazarene party had occupied it the day before.

Finally, in late afternoon, the city lay before them. They quickened their pace and hurried toward the Damascus Gate. The weary donkey brayed mildly in protest but was soon pacified at a small stable outside the gate. Joseph gave the stable master a denarii to feed and keep the donkey, telling him they would be back the following day.

Inside the gate, they paused. "I think we should go straight to the Temple. That is where Jesus said he was going yesterday morning and he may be there still," said Mary.

But Joseph disagreed. "It seems to me that he is more likely to be with Zairus and Joanna. After all, he had to have a place to sleep last night and that is almost certainly where he would have gone. Once arrived, I'm sure they would have kept the boy there to await our return for him."

This advice made sense to Mary and so they headed for their friends' home in a residential section of Jerusalem. The house was located southwest of the Temple Mount on the other side of the little Tyropoeon Valley, the "Valley of the Cheese Makers," which divided the city inside its walls. As is so often the case, however, they would have been more successful if they had followed Mary's maternal intuition.

In the Court of the Women, inside the Temple precincts, the teachers and listeners were concluding another day. Hanania turned to Jesus and noted, "Your parents may be back in the city by now. But I suggest you spend another night at my house rather than trying to find them. It is getting late and the Roman curfew will be in effect soon."

"Thank you, rabbi. I would be pleased to stay with you and your family another night. I would like to listen once again tomorrow to you and the other teachers."

Jesus and Hanania left the Court of the Women and passed through the Court of the Gentiles. It was nearly deserted now as the hour was late and the sun nearly sitting on the horizon. The two of them hurried across the large viaduct built by Herod the Great toward the elderly scribe's comfortable home in the Upper City. Half an hour earlier, Mary and Joseph had crossed this road at the point where it completed its descent from the Temple Mount, rushing anxiously to their friends' home on the slopes above the Lower City. Above them stood the mansions of the wealthy (including Hanania's spacious residence). Their position overlooking the less fortunate was a visible reassurance to those who wore fine robes and lived comfortable, prestigious lives that they were, indeed, the chosen of God. Jesus' suggestion twenty years hence that their prosperity might be more of a barrier to heaven than a sign of God's favor would enkindle both consternation and indignation among the smug and self-righteous.

Joseph pulled the rope that emerged from the wall enclosing the courtyard of their friends' home. A few minutes passed. Just as Joseph reached for the rope to tug it again, the door cracked open and then was flung wide by Zairus.

"Joseph and Mary! What has happened? You look exhausted." Zairus extended his hand and helped Mary step over the raised threshold. Joseph followed closely behind. As they crossed the courtyard, Joanna emerged from their living quarters. When Mary saw Joanna she could hold back her tears of frustration and anxiety no longer. She covered her face and sobbed. Joanna rushed to her and put her arms around her, and began to weep herself. The two women stood there for several minutes, holding each other, Mary crying from the depths of her soul, Joanna crying the sympathetic tears of a loving friend.

Zairus looked quizzically at Joseph and mouthed the words, "Where's Jesus?"

Joseph said nothing but signaled that he heard the question. He waited for the women to regain their composure. Then he explained:

"We have lost Jesus. Somehow, when we left Jerusalem yesterday morning, he was left behind. Mary is frantic with worry. I, too, have barely slept since night before last. We hoped that Jesus, who was going to the Temple yesterday morning, might have come here last night and that we would find him here today. But I see that is not to be."

Zairus tried to sound confident, but he was frightened for them and for Jesus. He had heard numerous rumors over the years of slave traders working the streets of Jerusalem during the major festivals, hoping to snare strong, attractive boys and girls for sale in the slave auctions in Rome, Athens, Alexandria, Babylon and elsewhere in the empire. He knew from Mary's muffled sobs and Joseph's pale, worried expression that this thought had already occurred to them. "There are numerous places to sleep in Jerusalem, dear friends. All of them perfectly safe. I'm sure Jesus is fine. He may even have slept in the Temple last night. It has been done many times by others."

Mary let go of Joanna and turned toward Joseph, her face brightening perceptibly even as her tears ceased their sad cascade. "Joseph, Zairus is right! Jesus said he was going to the Temple yesterday morning. He probably did just sleep there, awaiting our return. We must go there now."

Joanna was alarmed. "It is almost time for the Roman curfew. They have been very strict with this since the riots and rebellions against Herod Archelaus. If you are caught violating the curfew, you yourselves could be sent to Rome. Please stay with us tonight and tomorrow we will search all of Jerusalem, if necessary!"

Mary heard not a word. She was halfway to the outer door before Joanna finished speaking.

"We must go to the Temple tonight, friends. Mary is worried sick, as you can see, and neither of us can well endure another night of such torment. We will hurry. We'll be back before the curfew goes into effect." Joseph gave both Zairus and Joanna a quick hug and hurried after Mary, who was already in the street and practically running toward the Temple.

The streets were nearly empty as the residents of Jerusalem were mostly indoors already and the Roman soldiers had not yet turned out in force for their nighttime patrols. They followed a narrow, winding street toward the gate that would let them out onto the viaduct, a distance of less than half a mile. Knowing that running feet would attract unwelcome attention, Mary and Joseph walked as quickly as they could. It was growing dark.

As they hurried up the viaduct, past startled Jewish guards, and onto the Court of the Gentiles, they abandoned all pretense of restraint and broke into a run toward the Temple enclosure. All was quiet there but the gates were still open. They rushed into the Court of the Women. There were, in fact, many people, mostly elderly, resting on their cloaks or on thin mats along the walls. But Jesus was not among them. Nor did anyone remember seeing a twelve-year old boy. More correctly, as one irritable old fellow put it: "What's the matter with you? We get dozens, if not hundreds of boys that age in here on a daily basis. They are students and visitors and priest or Levite apprentices. Do you think we could remember one such boy out of all of those? Go away!"

"I think you would remember this one, friend," said Joseph wryly. "The boy is tall for his age, dark hair. He was wearing a white tunic with a gray linen sash and cowhide sandals. He has a way of looking so intently at people that they feel their souls exposed. I am pretty sure you would remember this child if he spoke to you."

It was no use. No one remembered seeing Jesus and no one could help them find him. Mary was inclined to spend the entire night there in the Temple. This was the revered place of central worship for the God of Israel, of I AM, and Mary felt His comfort. She would gladly have spent the night in prayer, kneeling on the marble steps leading to the closed Nicanor Gate. But Joseph saw the deep fatigue etched in her face and knew she needed to get at least some sleep that night. So he gently took her arm and led her back onto the Court of the Gentiles, back toward the silent viaduct. They hurried through the gate, past the Jewish Temple guards, who watched them suspiciously. Down the viaduct, once again rushing through the narrow, cobbled streets, past the grim slits of dark, recessed doorways, barred against the dangers of the night. But it was too late. The curfew was in effect.

Mary and Joseph slowed their pace as they walked between the houses packed tightly together on both sides of the passageways. There were no street lamps to light their way and the darkness was unfriendly. In the silence, every footstep and whisper shouted among the impassive walls. Joseph, holding Mary's hand, squeezed it to reassure her. Both of them stared intently ahead, dreading a wrong turn which would cast them into the bowels of the city and almost certainly into Roman custody.

As they rounded a corner, a mere two blocks from safety in the home of Zairus and Joanna, they heard the tramp of leather-soled feet and the clank and banging of swords and armor. Torch light pushed haphazardly at the darkness. The patrol was approaching from a side street to their left. Joseph and Mary froze, uncertain whether to flee or to try to hide. Surely they would be heard if they ran . . . not to mention the suggestion of guilt to men searching for just such evidence. On the other hand, no door opened to let them in, either. There was nothing to do, so they waited, holding hands, hearts pounding, praying silently, listening to death approach.

Joseph remembered the old priest Simeon's prophecy about Mary being pierced by a sword and half decided, as people so often do prematurely, that he now understood the meaning of the terrible prophecy. He vowed that he would give his life first to protect his wife if he could, and tensed his muscles to leap in front of her if necessary.

Was it a miracle, or just a blessing of dancing shadows? Whatever the cause, the soldiers swung sharply to their left, heading into a narrow street mere feet in front of the doorway where Mary and Joseph held their breath. After the tramp of the patrol had faded into the night, they ran the remaining distance to their friends' home, heedless now of the attention such motion might attract. Zairus must have been waiting by the door because it opened before they even had a chance to pull the knocker.

After many tears and prayers of relief and gratitude, everyone retired for the night, emotionally spent. Despite their anxiety for the missing Jesus, exhaustion overtook them and even Mary and Joseph slept soundly until the dawn. They would spend the following morning checking with other friends and acquaintances, visiting the carpenters' quarters in the Lower City to make inquiries, and canvassing as many of the stables and travelers' inns as they could visit. About mid-afternoon of this third day since Jesus was lost to them, anxiety was threatening to turn to despair, and so Mary and Joseph decided to go back to the Temple to ask again for Yahweh's help.

In the Temple since just after dawn, Jesus continued to challenge the teachers on their notions of the Messiah and his mission.

"How shall we know the Messiah when he comes?" Jesus asked to no one in particular.

Hanania chose to reply himself. "David has described the Kingdom of the Messiah in Psalm 72:

'He shall govern your people with justice
and your afflicted ones with judgment.
The mountains shall yield peace
for the people,
and the hills justice.
He shall defend the afflicted

among the people,
save the children of the poor,
and crush the oppressor . . . .
His foes shall bow before him,
and his enemies shall lick the dust . . . .
All kings shall pay him homage,
all nations shall serve him."[9]

Does this not tell us that the Messiah will come in power and strength to assume the throne of David, his father, and to govern Israel in the sight of all the world?"

Nicodemus chimed in: "Psalm 110 describes the Messiah as King, Priest and Conqueror. Thus,

'The scepter of your power the LORD
will stretch forth from Zion:
"Rule in the midst of your enemies.
Yours is princely power in the day of your birth
in holy splendor; . . . ."'
'The LORD is at your right hand;
he will crush kings on the day of his wrath.
He will do judgment on the nations,
heaping up corpses;
he will crush heads over the wide earth.'"[10]

Yet another teacher could not resist offering his opinion, citing the Prophet Isaiah:

"Who has stirred up from the East
the champion of justice,
and summoned him to be his attendant?
To him he delivers the nations
and subdues the kings;
With his sword he reduces them to dust,
with his bow, to driven straw . . . .
Fear not, O worm Jacob,
O maggot Israel;
I will help you, says the LORD;
your redeemer is the Holy One of Israel.
I will make of you a threshing sledge,
sharp, new, and double-edged,
To thresh the mountains and crush them,
to make the hills like chaff . . . .

---

[9] Ps 72:2-4, 9, 11

[10] Ps 110:2-3, 5-6

> **But you shall rejoice in the LORD,**
> **and glory in the Holy One of Israel."[11]**

"Clearly," summarized this teacher, "the God of Israel will send His Messiah to crush the enemies of His people and restore their greatness before all the nations."

Jesus looked thoughtful. "So you say the Messiah shall be a king on earth, a son of David, mightier than any other ruler before, now or to come?"

Several of the teachers, looking quite self-satisfied that they had helped this young boy to better understand God's plan for Israel, smiled complacently and uttered a brief affirmative.

Jesus continued. "And yet David calls him 'Lord'[12] and says of him that before the daystar [sun] he has been begotten of God. The Lord also calls him a priest forever, according to the order of Melchizedek.[13] Doesn't this suggest that the Messiah will be much more than an earthly king, that his reign will involve the function of a priest? What is it that the priests of Israel do?"

Nicodemus was astonished. This boy was challenging the best teachers in Israel! He was tempted to suggest to Hanania that it was beneath their dignity to engage in this debate with a child in a public forum. But the intellectual challenge got the better of him and he responded to Jesus' question: "Since the time of Moses, the priests of Israel have offered sacrifice to I AM. They are the means by which Israel offers sacrifice for her sins and reconciles herself to the Lord."

"Then the mission of the Messiah must include a redemption element, as well," said Jesus. "Consider, further, the words of King David in Psalm 22:

> **'I am like water poured out;**
> **all my bones are racked.**
> **My heart has become like wax**
> **melting away within my bosom.**
> **My throat is dried up like baked clay,**
> **my tongue cleaves to my jaws;**
> **to the dust of death you have**
> **brought me down.**
>
> **Indeed, many dogs surround me,**
> **a pack of evildoers closes in upon me;**
> **They have pierced my hands and my feet;**
> **I can count all my bones.**
> **They look on and gloat over me;**

---

[11] Is 41:2, 14-16

[12] Ps 110:1

[13] Ps 110:4

they divide my garments among them,
and for my vesture they cast lots.'"[14]

"But in Psalm 22 David is speaking of the nation of Israel and the many sufferings she has endured at the hands of hostile nations," protested yet another of the teachers. "This cannot be a prophecy for the Messiah. Indeed, if it were, it would suggest that he will be rejected by his own people, for the Psalmist says:

'But I am a worm,
not a man;
the scorn of men,
despised by the people.
All who see me scoff at me;
they mock me with parted lips,
they wag their heads:
"He relied on the LORD,
let him deliver him,
let him rescue him,
if he loves him."'"[15]

Jesus did not reply. He merely looked at the teacher who spoke, as if he were waiting for a child to grasp the point of a lesson.

"I think you are right, Elihu," said one of the teachers. "But the prophecy is very specific, not the kind of generalized suffering description we might expect. And it must be admitted that many of the prophets of old were mistreated by the authorities of Israel, who objected to their warnings."

"Who can remove the sins of all the people except the Lord?" asked Jesus.

The teachers looked at one another but no one attempted to answer Jesus' question. It was a knotty theological issue. What man, indeed, could offer recompense for the sins of all mankind? Especially since all men themselves were sinful in some degree.

Jesus continued. "And would it not be appropriate for Him to send His Son to be the Sacrifice for the people, to reconcile them once and for all, as the priests of Israel attempt but cannot do? Have you not read in Isaiah:

'Who would believe what we have heard?
To whom has the arm of the LORD been revealed?
He grew up like a sapling before him,
like a shoot from the parched earth;
There was in him no stately bearing
to make us look at him,
nor appearance that would attract us to him.
He was spurned and avoided by men,

---

[14] Ps 22:15-19

[15] Ps 22:7-9

a man of suffering, accustomed to infirmity,
One of those from whom men hide their faces,
spurned, and we held him in no esteem.

Yet it was our infirmities that he bore,
our sufferings that he endured,
While we thought of him as stricken,
as one smitten by God and afflicted.
But he was pierced for our offenses,
crushed for our sins;
Upon him was the chastisement
that makes us whole,
by his stripes we were healed.
We had all gone astray like sheep,
each following his own way;
But the LORD laid upon him
the guilt of us all.

Though he was harshly treated,
he submitted
and opened not his mouth;
Like a lamb led to the slaughter
or a sheep before the shearers,
he was silent and opened not his mouth.
Oppressed and condemned,
he was taken away,
and who would have thought
any more of his destiny?
When he was cut off from the land of the living,
and smitten for the sin of his people,
A grave was assigned him among the wicked
and a burial place with evildoers,
Though he had done no wrong
nor spoken any falsehood.
[But the LORD was pleased
to crush him in infirmity.]

If he gives his life as an offering for sin,
he shall see his descendants in a long life,
and the will of the LORD shall be
accomplished through him.
Because of his affliction
he shall see the light in fullness of days;
Through his suffering,

> my servant shall justify many,
> and their guilt he shall bear.

> Therefore I will give him his portion among the great,
> and he shall divide the spoils with the mighty,
> Because he surrendered himself to death
> and was counted among the wicked;

> And he shall take away the sins of many,
> and win pardon for their offenses.'?"[16]

Now it was time for several of the teachers to shake their heads. They were impressed with Jesus' analysis and argument, but the implications of his words were simply unacceptable. The authorities in Israel expected God to send a Messiah to restore Israel's power on earth. They had little notion of a greater spiritual world, or at least not one with which they should concern themselves. They understood their sphere to be the world, and understood the prophecies of the Messiah to apply to that sphere as well. They were important persons already. Like most authority figures throughout history, they were confident that God would explicitly endorse their right to power. A Messiah who came in humility and suffering was simply incomprehensible to this way of thinking.

Jesus pressed the point further, trying to get these learned scholars to look past the world of their senses. "Can you not see that the children of Israel, indeed all mankind, have been separated from God by their sins?

Nicodemus responded, a little offended: "We understand that we bear a great burden of sin . . . less, perhaps, than the Gentiles who refuse even to acknowledge the One God. It is for this reason that the nation offers constant sacrifice here in this sacred Temple, home to the God of Israel, to make atonement for such sins and to acknowledge the Lord as our God."

"But are not these things which you sacrifice also the gift of God? When you sacrifice, do you not merely return to Him what was His to begin with? How is that a sacrifice which can atone for the sins of men?"

No one said anything, so Jesus went on. "Have not the sins of men offended the divine justice of God who is infinite? Did not the sin of our ancestor, Adam, establish a gulf between man and God which only God Himself can bridge? How, then, can anyone but God make atonement for mankind? Who among all peoples from the beginning of time until now and forever shall possess such standing with God as to be able to purchase their freedom from God's just punishment?"

Hanania himself pounced on these questions. "Your argument proves too much, young man! Your suggestion is that only God can atone for the sins of men. But God is the offended party, so by definition He cannot make atonement to

---

[16]Is 53

Himself. The atonement must come from outside to offer reparation to the infinite majesty of Yahweh. Man is limited by his nature and cannot offer more than he has and is. God understands this and accepts our offerings as the best that we can do, just as we accept the limitations in the apologies of children." Hanania looked triumphantly at the other teachers, who nodded approvingly.

"But, rabbi," persisted Jesus. "The offenses of children match their limited capacity. And those offended are of the same nature. God, on the other hand, is Creator and man is creature. God surpasses mankind by an infinite degree. Have you not read in the Prophet Daniel of one like a son of man, who shall come on the clouds of heaven and receive dominion and kingship over all the earth?[17] Could not this one from God be also 'of God' and therefore able to take upon himself the sins of mankind so that God and man might be reconciled? Wouldn't such a one be able to satisfy the requirements of divine justice as well as demonstrate the unfathomable capacity of divine love?"

There was much sputtering and protesting among the lesser intellects of the listening elders. Others sat silently, considering the theological implications of Jesus' questions. But even the most brilliant among them did not begin to comprehend the mystery of the Holy Trinity which Jesus was cracking open ever so slightly for them. Their thoughts were focused exclusively on finding convincing rebuttals to Jesus' provocative challenges. None was immediately forthcoming.

Jesus addressed a last question to them: "You have said that the Messiah will be sent from God to restore glory to His people, Israel, as if all other nations would be of no interest to the Lord. But have you not read these words in Isaiah:

'It is too little, he says,
for you to be my servant,
to raise up the tribes of Jacob,
and restore the survivors of Israel;
I will make you a light to the nations,
that my salvation may reach
to the ends of the earth.'?[18]

A fairly large crowd had gathered by now to hear the exchange between Jesus and the teachers. At this last point, there was a murmur of appreciation from the attentive listeners. The teachers and scribes were simply amazed . . . and ready to call it a day.

The discussion had taken place in an area along the east wall of the Court of the Women in the Temple enclosure. About the time Jesus was asking his last question, Mary and Joseph entered the Court from the south side. They started to turn left toward the Nicanor Gate, through which Joseph would have continued on into the Court of the Israelites, but were distracted by a couple walking by,

---

[17]Dn 7:13-14

[18]Is 49:6

talking about an incredibly precocious boy who was actually instructing the teachers of Israel. Joseph and Mary looked at each other, sharing the same thought. Joseph grasped the sleeve of the man before he merged into the streams of people passing in all directions. "Excuse me, sir. Where is this boy of whom you speak?"

The man smiled at Joseph and pointed toward the east end of the Court. "Over there. You better hurry though. That boy has those teachers so befuddled they may just grab him and lock him away with the Essenes for about twenty years!"[19] Joseph thanked the man for his information and turned to Mary. She was already five yards ahead of him, rushing toward the Beautiful Gate where she could see a significant crowd of people standing in a cluster, facing one of the areas where the teachers gathered for discussions.

"Excuse me. Please excuse me. I'm sorry. Please let me through. Excuse me." Mary was polite, but there was no mistaking her goal. The crowd parted reluctantly and let the highly agitated woman pass. As the front row separated, Mary saw him. Jesus sitting calmly in the midst of the teachers, they looking at him in utter fascination. At the sound of the commotion caused by Mary's pell-mell push to reach the front, Jesus had turned around. His face lit up when he saw his mother, and Joseph a few steps behind her. Relief poured over them like high tide in a storm. But the waves of relief crashed upon rocks of bewilderment and hurt for the suffering they had endured the past forty-eight hours.

More wounded than angry and most of all perplexed, Mary asked: "**Son, why have you done this to us? You see that your father and I have been searching for you in sorrow.**"[20]

Back came the gentle and surprised response from Jesus that, given his mission on earth, his parents should have known where to look for him: "**Why did you search for me? Did you not know I had to be in my Father's house?**"[21]

Jesus' words swept away any remaining tension. Mary and Joseph looked ruefully at each other and laughed with relief. Mary's first instinct had been to look in the Temple. When they did look there, the timing was obviously compromised by the curfew. Then they had not come back for the better part of a day. Where else, indeed, would the Son go but to His Father's house? The Holy Family reunited in love, delighting once again in one another's company.

Jesus, of course, meant something far deeper by his response than merely pointing out that Mary and Joseph had mostly ignored the most obvious place to find him. Further, their question to him had been directed not merely to his location in Jerusalem but why he had missed the caravan departure for home in

---

[19]The Essenes were an ascetic sect of Jews who lived in desert communities and practiced celibacy, physical mortification and constant prayer. They basically constituted a strict Jewish monastery. They appear to have been the authors and custodians of the Dead Sea Scrolls.

[20]Lk 2:48

[21]Lk 2:49

the first place. It would be much later in his life before Mary would realize the full significance of this incident. After Jesus' resurrection, she would understand that this absence as a boy prefigured the time when he would appear to many of his followers as lost forever. But even though Mary and Joseph did not fully understand what Jesus was trying to tell them, they did realize one basic fact immediately: their son might live unobtrusively for years, but when the time came for him to perform his real Father's will, they would have always to defer to his judgment.

On the way home to Nazareth, Mary and Joseph talked about what had happened.

"I'm puzzled, Mary."

"Well, to some extent, I am, too, Joseph. But what do you mean exactly?"

"Jesus has been living quietly in Nazareth all these years, not attracting any particular attention, then suddenly he practically announces that he is the Messiah and that his mission has begun. I would not have been a bit surprised if he had refused to come home with us. Nor, of course, would I have questioned it, other than to be sure that he would be protected and provided for. Yet, he did not wish to stay. In fact, I think he was very happy to see us. Look at him now, like any other high-energy twelve-year old, bouncing around, hardly able to sit still."

Mary laughed as they watched Jesus clambering over some rocks with a new friend he had made. "I, too, was taken aback by Jesus' interaction with the scribes and teachers in the Temple. The old priest, Hanania, was almost reverential in his compliments of Jesus' intellectual prowess. He would have been delighted if Jesus had been willing to remain with him for advanced studies. I wondered myself if he might have decided to become a priest or a teacher in the Temple. But on further reflection, especially since he has shown no interest in following that path, I believe that Jesus was making a point and perhaps planting some seeds that will bear fruit in ways that we cannot foresee."

Joseph replied, "Maybe he just wanted to let us and the world know that he is aware at this young age of who he is, where he comes from, and why he is here. I think we lost sight of that in all our anxiety these past few days. If he were to disappear again, I would still search for him. But now I know that his Father has him well in hand. His mission will not be diverted by accident or the designs of evil men."

"Yes, but as his mother, I am not sure I could be quite so calm anyway. I love him so dearly I cannot bear the thought of him being hurt or suffering in any way. No matter how well I may understand his Father's plan for Jesus, my heart wants only to protect him and love him and see him happy as God intended all His people to be.

"But perhaps I was becoming a little too possessive. Maybe Jesus wanted to give us a little shock, a warning that the road of the Messiah, and therefore our path as his parents, will not be gentle and pleasant. It frightens me to think of what that might mean. But it is better to be mentally prepared for it, and to pray for

God's strength to endure, than to become so complacent in the love and goodness of this child that separation and loss become unbearable."

"I am ashamed to even ask this question, Mary, and I beg the Lord's forgiveness for my presumption. But I can't help wondering why the angel who has visited us several times already did not simply come and tell us where Jesus was. It would have eliminated a terrible anxiety, one which Jesus himself was surprised we had experienced. Wouldn't we expect an ordinary child to alleviate his parents' concern as much as he could? After all, surely Jesus could have asked that an angel be sent to reassure us in these circumstances?"

"I, too, wondered about that. But I think we have already partly answered the question. The ways of God are not the ways of men. We, as everyone else when they discover who Jesus is, must recognize that basic fact and put our trust in faith. Faith can seem cold and rickety when the storms of life are blowing, but it is the vehicle which God gives us to carry us to Him. There is no other way. Praised be His holy Name! We'll never forget these past three days and the almost unbearable feeling of loss. When other crises come, our faith will be much stronger because of this experience."

"You suggested there might be another reason why we were not informed by the angel."

"Yes. We have been blessed above all other people since the foundation of the human race, Joseph, by being selected to be the earthly parents of the Son of God. Yet in us we see that God has chosen the lowly and the humble for this singular honor. He is telling everyone, I believe, that the standards of the world, where the powerful and the rich lord it over the poor and weak, do not apply to His kingdom of love. His invitation to share in that kingdom is to all. God does not play favorites. If he did, wouldn't he be acting just like the corrupt royalty of Earth, favoring their own sons and daughters, securing privileges for themselves and their friends? And if we were so treated by Him, how would we be able to show our own love in return?

"In a world of hardship and pain, we must live like all others to merit the redemption of the Messiah. Our love for our God and Creator must be pure and uncompromised by personal advantage. This is the way in which God loves us. We must learn to love in the same way if we would be citizens of His kingdom. The only way to give such love back to Him is to bear whatever sufferings we experience with patience, even joy. Love is truly meaningful only when it is hard to give it. So you see that it is because God loves us so totally that He left us alone to search for Jesus as any other parents would do."

"Yes, of course. That makes sense." Joseph went on. "And you have helped me to understand yet another reason why God could not send an angel to remove our fears and our sorrow.

"The story of the Messiah will be told throughout the world until the end of time. He and all of those associated with him will be looked to as examples and models. Other people who lose their children will not have any expectations of heavenly intervention. It will be helpful to them to remember that we, too, experienced loss and pain; that we, too, felt terrible fear and anxiety. Alienation instead of inspiration and consolation would be the result if others saw that we were treated kindly and preferentially by God while they are left in agonizing ignorance. No, love requires sharing. And the sharing of suffering provides the greatest bond of all."

> **"He went down with them then, and came to Nazareth,**
> **and was obedient to them. His mother meanwhile kept**
> **all these things in memory. Jesus, for his part,**
> **progressed steadily in wisdom and age and grace**
> **before God and men."**[22]

---

[22]Lk 2:51-52

PSALM 27:4-6

II

One thing I ask of the LORD;
this I seek:
To dwell in the house of the LORD
all the days of my life,
That I may gaze upon the
loveliness of the LORD
and contemplate his temple.

For he will hide me in his abode
in the day of trouble;
He will conceal me in the shelter of his tent,
he will set me high upon a rock.

Even now my head is held high
above my enemies on every side.
And I will offer in his tent
sacrifices with shouts of gladness;
I will sing and chant praise
to the LORD.

Amen

QUESTIONS FOR REFLECTION

1) What do you think is Luke's main purpose in including this story in his Gospel?

2) What does Luke mean when he says in verse 2:50, "But they did not grasp what he said to them." How many possible levels of meaning can you find in Jesus' words?

3) How do you imagine Jesus as a boy would have been? How would he have related to his peers?

4) Do you think Jesus planned all along to stay behind in Jerusalem when his parents returned to Nazareth? If so, why would he do that? Why might he not want to tell his parents?

5) Why do you think Mary was so anxious about Jesus when she and Joseph realized he had been left behind? She knew, after all, that he came from God and was announced to her as a future king of Israel. What do you think her concerns were? Knowing only what they knew, how would you have reacted?

6) Many modern scholars portray Jesus as barely aware, if at all, of his divine mission, at least until near the end. Given who he was, do you think it likely or even possible that, at the age of 12, he could have successfully debated scripture and theology with these senior Jewish priests and elders?

7) If Jesus was fully aware of his divine nature, do you think he would still have exhibited the characteristics of childhood? Or, are the two conditions incompatible?

8) Why do you think that Jesus, or his Father in heaven, did not send an angel to tell Mary and Joseph that Jesus was safe?

9) What lessons for your own life can you draw from this mystery?

10) Given the circumstances of Roman occupation in Palestine and the tensions between them and the Jews, do you think it likely or unlikely that any member of the Holy Family ever felt threatened?

Father, if it is your will, take this cup from me; yet not my will but yours be done. An angel then appeared to him from heaven to strengthen him. Lk 22:42-43

FIRST SORROWFUL MYSTERY

The Agony in the Garden

The nights were the worst. In the darkness, in the shadows of the subconscious, fears menace the psyche like monsters glimpsed out of the corners of our eyes. Jesus lay on a thin rush mat spread out on the ground, drenched in sweat, fighting panic, trying to stay submerged in sleep as his consciousness rose like a cork through water. He had been having nights like this for years, even back to his boyhood, although then they were only occasional. Now they came every night, unbidden, unwelcome, nightmarish images of bloody, tortured corpses hanging from crosses with bulging, sightless eyes. Wakefulness brought no relief. These nightmares were not merely memories of crucifixion victims that the Romans had displayed as object lessons to the rebellious Jews. They were visions, too; his destiny etched in the stone of centuries of prophecy. Jesus wept and felt better. He prayed—communing with his Father for strength, refreshing himself with the reminder that soon he would be back with Him in the kingdom of heaven. Then he lay down once more and pulled his cloak about him. Fatigue pulled at his eyelids but the icy fear pounded through his veins, driving sleep away. At last, exhaustion prevailed and Jesus slept, fitfully.

It was Wednesday, about midnight. Jesus and his apostles rested in a clearing on the eastern side of the Mount of Olives, away from Jerusalem. Since their arrival in the City of David for the Feast of Passover/Unleavened Bread, they had spent each night in a different location, mostly on the Mount, taking their meals at friends' homes in Bethany and Bethphage. Jesus was tall for his time, about 5 feet 11 inches, and wore over his white linen tunic a seamless beige-colored robe with brown tassels dangling from its hem. On his feet he wore leather sandals. His brown hair hung below his shoulders, longer in the middle than the sides, as was the fashion then among Palestinian Jews. He wore a full mustache and beard, trimmed to about two inches. He was well-built with arms, shoulders and hands strengthened from years of work as a carpenter. His brown eyes were warm and crinkled when he laughed. They were wide-set on either side of a long, straight Semitic nose. His baritone voice was powerful and commanded attention but could also soothe with gentle words and affectionate compliments. He was a handsome man with a ready smile revealing strong, white teeth. People were drawn to him.

There were twelve men traveling with Jesus. These were his apostles, the inner circle of an entourage that routinely numbered more than one hundred men and women, mostly from the province of Galilee. Simon Peter, bold and impetuous, of booming voice and barrel chest, was the first among equals. Jesus had already designated him as such, renaming him "rock" in the process. He and his brother Andrew, a quiet, efficient man, were professional fishermen on the Sea of Galilee, a harp-shaped body of fresh water also called the Lake of Genneserat or Lake of Tiberias for the Roman city which dominated its western shore. Two other brothers, the sons of Zebedee, a prominent businessman who owned several fishing boats, were also apostles. Their names were James and John. They were close friends and co-workers of Peter and Andrew. John was barely fifteen years old when called by Jesus to follow him. His brother was ten years older. Both of them were robust, exuberant individuals. John, in particular, possessed an outgoing personality with a quick and easy grin.

The other apostles included Matthew, tax collector and future evangelist; Thomas, the skeptic, who would likely have been a scientist in the twentieth century; Nathanael, also called Bartholomew, erudite, cultured, witty; Philip, a seeker of truth and close friend of Bartholomew and Andrew; James, son of Alphaeus and Mary, cousin of Jesus and father of Judas, also known as Thaddaeus, a second cousin to Jesus, and, like his father, from Nazareth; Simon the Zealot, of few words but strong convictions; and, last, Judas Iscariot, history's greatest fool.

Hostility toward Jesus from the priests and elders of the Temple, the law enforcers for Judaism, was at a fever pitch. For his part, Jesus had pulled no punches. He had lambasted the pompous Pharisees and scribes, the Temple vanguard for orthodoxy, calling them frauds, hypocrites, fools, brood of serpents, murderers, blind guides and white-washed tombs. He openly challenged their authority and their public image. He ranked them spiritually below prostitutes and tax collectors. As if that were not enough, Jesus had made a whip out of three rough hemp cords and driven the sacrificial animal traders and money changers right out of the Temple precincts! What a sight that was!

* * * * * * *

The day had been glorious. It was Sunday, the first day of the week. Morning rain had drifted away and the lush green of olive, date palm, fig and cypress trees glistened with the jewels of lingering rain drops. A gentle breeze welcomed the cheerful sun and a seventy-degree temperature invited people outside to experience the bright spring day.

Jesus, his apostles, and hundreds of disciples, would-be followers and curiosity seekers had arrived at Bethany about mid-afternoon, after the arduous walk from Jericho almost continually uphill through the Judean Wilderness. Jesus sent word to Lazarus and his sisters, Mary and Martha, that he would be back that night and then went on to the neighboring village of Bethphage located on the eastern, backside of the Mount of Olives. While there, he obtained a donkey. His fame in Israel was so great, even in the snobby city of Jerusalem, that to get that donkey all his disciples had to say was, "The Master needs it."

A couple of the apostles had spread their cloaks over the donkey and Jesus then sat on it sidesaddle. A great roar went up from the crowd as Jesus on the donkey moved forward. By now, word of his arrival had spread like wildfire through the streets of Jerusalem. Visitors to the city, and there were thousands upon thousands of them, caught up in the surging crowd, asked, "What's going on? Who is it?" then listened incredulously as the reply came: "It's Jesus of Nazareth, the prophet! He works miracles. He raised Lazarus of Bethany after **FOUR DAYS** in the tomb! I saw it myself. There has never been anyone like him. Come and see!"

People swarmed out of the gates and across the little stream which trickled along the bottom of the Kidron Valley, then swept like a cloud of starving locusts across the western face of the Mount of Olives. You never saw such excitement! Along the way, they were stripping six-foot branches off the date palms and waving them in the air, shouting about the arrival of the savior of Israel.

The Romans in the Fortress Antonia went to a state of high alert but relaxed when the "people's savior" appeared at the crest of the hill without soldiers or weapons.

By the time the procession was halfway down the Mount on its western side, there were thousands of people throwing their cloaks or tossing reeds on the road, waving their branches and yelling at the top of their lungs:

> **"Hosanna to the Son of David!**
> **Blessed is he who comes**
> **in the name of the Lord!**
> **Hosanna in the highest!**
> **Blessed is the King of Israel!"**[1]

The apostles were amazed and delighted. All their fears vanished. Jesus had warned them time and again that this trip up to Jerusalem would end in his death and they had dreaded their arrival here. But now all was changed! Clearly, the tide of public opinion was overwhelmingly in favor of Jesus and there was no way the Jewish elders would be able to touch him in the face of this popularity. Their newly-found confidence was shaken a bit when Jesus halted his donkey

---

[1] Mt 21:9, Jn 12:13

halfway down the Mount and began to weep profusely. It was hard to hear what he said over the massive roar of the crowd, but the word got around later that he seemed to be deeply concerned about the fate of Jerusalem. It was just one more in a long line of baffling mysteries in the things that Jesus said and the apostles let it pass. They couldn't understand a place for tears on this day of triumph and rejoicing.

The procession continued exultantly on down the hill, across the bridge spanning the stream meandering through the Kidron, and into the base of the Temple Mount through the eastern Susa Gate. The shouts of the happy crowd echoed deafeningly on the ramps which led up from the gate to the Court of the Gentiles. The multitude burst onto the huge span and surrounded Jesus, who had dismounted from his donkey at the gate and had half walked, half rode on shoulders the rest of the way. Children organized themselves into impromptu cheering sections and marched around the court chanting: "**Hosanna to the Son of David!**"[2] As if the crowd weren't large enough already, thousands more people poured in through all of the Temple gates as everyone in Jerusalem, it seemed, reported to one another that Jesus of Nazareth, the prophet from Galilee, had arrived.

The chief priests, scribes and elders, of course, came scurrying over, huffing with indignation and protests. Jesus just glanced at them. This was when he made his whip and started lashing at the dove sellers and money changers. What a commotion! Their tables went flying; cages crashed to the floor and broke apart; liberated, frightened doves flew every which way; and money scattered all over the stone pavement. This, of course, sent the crowd scrambling after the coins, fighting with the money changers who were screaming and cursing and threatening and desperately trying to gather up all their money themselves.

Jesus didn't even pause. He went down the line of those merchants in Solomon's Portico like a tornado through a wheat farm. The Temple guards tried to intervene but were caught up in a sea of humanity sweeping after Jesus. The apostles laughed and danced and encouraged the crowd. Only one of them seemed to be in a state of angry shock: Judas Iscariot. He was, after all, a "financial type" who understood the need for this activity to support the Temple's operations. But he was not above picking up a few coins for his own purse. When he did so, Judas became separated from the other apostles and Jesus who continued on down the portico. All indecision now removed, Judas plunged zestfully into the competition to gather up the spilled silver currency.

A well-dressed, impeccably groomed man about 45 years of age stood slightly apart from the other scribes, Pharisees and elders who, with gaping mouths, watched the chaos caused by Jesus. This was Noam, chief scribe in the Temple, who acted as a kind of modern-day chief of staff to the high priest. He was a thoughtful, calculating man, not given to showing emotion, possessed of a heart as hard and dry as the paving stones on which he walked. He was also an

---

[2]Mt 21:15

excellent judge of character. He had noticed as Judas first tried to deter Jesus and then joined with gusto in the plundering of the money changers. By the time the frenzy in this part of the Temple had died down, Noam had made his way over to Judas, who now looked around furtively to see if anyone had seen him abandoning the Messiah. He jumped when Noam spoke to him.

"You're with the Galilean, aren't you?" Judas' first impulse was to deny that he was a follower of Jesus. But then he realized Noam might demand the return of the coins Judas had grabbed so he decided to bluster instead, knowing the crowd belonged to Jesus and that safety, for this day at least, lay in being on his side. But Noam wasn't interested in the coins Judas had taken and he didn't wait for his reply. He went on: "I can see that you are a clever man, one who understands how the world works. Unfortunately, your Master seems to lack your common sense. I fear that things may not go well for him if this keeps up. The Romans won't stand for it, you know."

"Jesus has powers which could crush these puny Romans!" Judas boasted, glad now to associate himself once again with the Man from Nazareth.

"Yes, you may be right. The problem seems to be to convince him to use those powers that way."

"He'll use them when the time is right. We just need to get him to see that there can be no freedom for the Israelites until the Roman boot is lifted from our necks!"

"And do you think that he sees that now? By the way, what is your name? You seem to me a man of great insight and excellent opinion."

Judas was flattered by Noam's respectful attitude and questions and eager to inflate his self-importance even more. "I am Judas Iscariot. I am one of Jesus of Nazareth's closest confidantes. So much does he trust me that he has given me exclusive control over all of our finances. Without me to manage things, his whole group would collapse."

"Perhaps I could help you. Your master is obviously a great man, perhaps even a great prophet, or more. We should be working together against the Romans, not fighting each other. If you could persuade him to appear before the Sanhedrin, I am sure that we would soon be united. Do you think you could arrange that?"

"Well, I don't know. Jesus pretty much decides for himself what he is going to do. I see the sense in what you are saying but I am not sure I can persuade Jesus to go along with it," replied Judas dubiously.

"See what you can do, Judas. We need to help the Master. If he won't come to us, we will come to him. You just let me know where we can find him, all right? Of course, it will have to be at a quiet time, not with all of these crazed followers around. My name is Noam. I am the chief scribe. You can find me here in the Temple, usually; or at the palace of the High Priest. When we have worked this all out, I see an important role for you in the new government. There will be something for you even before that, of course." Noam spoke unctuously, solicitously to Judas.

Judas was a typical small-time criminal. What he lacked in character and intellect, he made up for in ego and ambition. It was a dangerous combination. He sensed the duplicity in Noam's offer but was enormously flattered to be sought out by such an important official. He who had been a "loner" among the apostles now saw himself as the most important of them, the one whom Jesus needed to bring his mission to fulfillment. Sadly for him, he was right about being needed. "I'll think about it but I'm not promising anything. If *I* decide we should talk more about it, I'll signal you like this:" (Judas then pulled on his beard twice in rapid succession to demonstrate his signal.)

"I'll be looking for your sign, Judas. I knew when I saw you that you weren't like the others. You understand these matters much better." As he walked off to rejoin the other scribes and chief priests, who had been tracking the course of Jesus down Solomon's Portico, Noam turned and gave Judas a little wave of his hand as if to confirm they were already friends working together.

By the time Jesus had traveled about halfway down the colonnaded portico, shouting, "**Scripture has it, 'My house shall be called a house of prayer,' but you are turning it into a den of thieves,**"[3] most of the merchants and traders had grasped what was happening and had hastily gathered up their things and fled to the northern side of the Temple Mount, nearest to the Fortress Antonia.

About this time, another group of traders emerged from the Susa Gate ramps and headed for Herod's aqueduct gate on the opposite side of the Mount. They were pushing a couple of carts piled high with raisins and figs to be sold to the huge influx of Passover visitors. This path was a significant shortcut for delivering merchandise to the vendors in the city. Their timing this day was most unfortunate for them. Jesus spied the little knot trying to push through the crowd and administered the same lesson he had just given to the money changers. In their haste to beat a retreat, the traders upset their carts and tripped over the spilled contents, to the great amusement of the onlooking crowd.

The Pharisees and scribes were almost slobbering with fury. The Roman guards had strict orders not to get involved in any Jewish religious activities and that is what this appeared to be, even if a bit more rambunctious than usual. The Jewish Temple guards were not only vastly outnumbered but many of them also sympathized with Jesus. To top it all off, after his tirade against the profanation of his Father's house, Jesus had calmly set up a kind of station near the Beautiful Gate on the Temple precincts and was curing the blind and crippled! This reduced the crowd to worshipful silence as they beheld the miracles, and they would have torn apart anyone who attempted to seize Jesus in those moments. So the elders seethed and tried to distract Jesus with questions and challenges. He mostly ignored them.

As evening drew on, the crowd began to disperse from the Temple area. Jesus promised to return early the next day and asked that he and his apostles be left alone until then. With that, they left the Temple and retraced their steps over the Mount of Olives to the home of Lazarus in Bethany. Jesus' mother and his

---

[3]Mt 21:13

Aunt Mary had remained there during Jesus' triumphant procession into Jerusalem. Now, however, they were at the house of Simon the leper, who was no longer diseased because Jesus had cured him. Simon had asked to host a banquet for Jesus that evening. Since he had no wife, Martha and Mary and the rest of the women offered to prepare and serve the meal and clean up afterward.

It was a very happy occasion. Only Jesus and his mother seemed uncharacteristically somber in the midst of the festivities. Several times on that day, Mary had been seen weeping quietly by herself. Once, right in the middle of a spirited conversation among the women, when they had been discussing their conviction that Jesus would soon be recognized even by the Temple rulers as the Anointed One of God, Mary had begun sobbing. The other women were astonished. When they asked Mary what was troubling her, she just shook her head and went on quietly weeping. Jesus, you see, had already explained everything to her, how he would be taken into custody by the Temple authorities, condemned by their unbelief, turned over to the Romans and, finally, crucified.

But he also explained to her why it was necessary for the salvation of mankind. He gently asked her to be strong for him, to be there during his ordeal because he would need the strength that only her most perfect of hearts could provide. She embraced him then, unable to maintain her composure any longer while she gazed into the eyes of this Son of hers, sent by God. Of all people on earth, she alone was already spiritually prepared to accept and even to share the viciously cruel sacrifice that loomed only a few days away. She promised to be strong when Jesus needed her, but now in the privacy of their meeting she let her heart break with the agony of it. She did not question. She had learned that lesson well right here in Jerusalem when Jesus was only twelve years old. She did not even wonder, much less fuss about, what would happen to her since she had no other children or husband to look after her. (Joseph had died before Jesus began his ministry). Jesus held her until she could cry no more and then gently wiped the tears from her face with one of the few remaining dry spots on his robe.

At the banquet, Simon the host asked Jesus to offer the prayer of thanks. Jesus spoke from his heart to his Father but no one there except his mother understood that he was addressing his actual Father. Judas tried several times to get Jesus' attention to discuss the possibility of meeting with the Sanhedrin, as Noam had suggested, but Jesus would hardly give him the time of day. This annoyed Judas who felt that he was more in command of the situation now than Jesus. His pride swelled his ego until he soon became that dinner guest that everyone dreads being seated next to. By the Lord's request, Simon had seated Lazarus next to Jesus, followed by Judas, then Peter. Neither of his dinner companions cared for Judas at all nor was interested in listening to any scheme of reconciliation between Jesus and the Jewish authorities. Judas felt belittled and his anger grew.

After the meal had been consumed, Martha's sister, Mary, brought in a small alabaster jar containing about a pound of a very expensive perfume mixed from myrrh, spices and fragrant ointments. She first poured a small portion on

Jesus' head, then knelt at his feet and poured the rest of it over them, rubbing the lovely-smelling lotion into his skin. The fragrance of the balm filled the room. Then, with her heart overcome by her love for Jesus and gratitude for his resurrection of her brother, Lazarus, Mary removed the scarf from her head and let her long, thick, auburn hair fall forward. With this she began to dry the feet of Jesus, lovingly, gently, thoroughly. Everyone at the table was deeply touched. Everyone, that is, except one.

This was the final straw for Judas. He actually stood up and, pointing at Mary, demanded in a loud voice:

> **"Why was not this perfume sold? It could have brought three hundred silver pieces, and the money have been given to the poor."[4]**

The company was stunned by this boorish breach of good manners, not to mention the audacity of Judas in questioning the use of something which had benefited his Master. Mary was both flustered and indignant. She started to respond but Jesus intervened. His face was stern and his voice sharp as he spoke to Judas for the first time that evening:

> **"Let her alone. Why do you criticize her? She has done me a kindness. The poor you will always have with you and you can be generous to them whenever you wish, but you will not always have me. She has done what she could. By perfuming my body she is anticipating its preparation for burial. I assure you, wherever the good news is proclaimed throughout the world, what she has done will be told in her memory."[5]**

Judas reddened and sat down, furious with Jesus for the public rebuke. As of that moment, he vowed to take matters into his own hands. The next day, Monday, while Jesus was teaching in the Temple and berating the scribes and Pharisees, and they, in their turn, vainly attempted to trap him in some comment that would expose him to Roman justice, Judas signaled to Noam. Noam had already briefed the high priest and several other members of the Sanhedrin about Judas. He whispered now to one of these men who, in turn, passed the message on to several other of the chief priests and scribes. Noam led them as a group across the Court of Gentiles to the Royal Portico. This structure dominated the southern end of the Temple Mount, above the main Huldah Gates, and had several meeting rooms used by the Sanhedrin. Judas waited about twenty minutes and then quietly slipped away and followed them there.

"Jesus is not going to come to you voluntarily. But I can help you find him when he will not be surrounded by these crowds. He told us that he is planning

---

[4] Jn 12:5

[5] Mk 14:6-9. Other versions of Jesus' response can be found in Mt 26:10-13 and Jn 12:7-8.

to spend the nights of the Festival on the Mount of Olives. When he settles down for the night, if I can slip away, I will come to you."

Noam smiled broadly and replied, "Excellent, Judas! We will give your Jesus every opportunity to prove to us that he is from God. If he does so, of course, we will then acknowledge him to be the Messiah, the Anointed One of the Lord. You are serving your people well. We will be ready for the time you tell us." Noam rose to leave.

"Excuse me, Noam," said Judas.

Noam cringed inwardly at this familiarity from a man he despised but, nonetheless, turned around wearing a smile. "Yes?"

"I'm putting my neck on the line here. **What are you willing to give me if I hand him over to you?**[6] You said there would be something in it for me now plus a greater reward later when things have been smoothed out with Jesus."

Noam reached into the cloak that he wore over his white linen tunic and pulled out his purse. He had been prepared for this. He knew the little man with the soft hands and close-set, narrow eyes was as motivated by avarice as anything. "Of course, Judas. I'm sorry I forgot. I brought these for you. Here are thirty pieces of silver. Count them if you wish." He tossed the purse at Judas and walked away without looking back. Judas did count the coins, as much for the pleasure of holding them as distrust of the chief scribe, then headed back to rejoin the apostles with Jesus.

Monday and Tuesday of what is now called Holy Week were days of open warfare between Jesus and the Jewish authorities. It was no contest. The best minds in Israel huddled looking for a way to trap Jesus into saying something that could be construed as a threat to Roman sovereignty, which could then be used to bring him up on charges of sedition. Failing that, they hoped to find some issue that would discredit him before the multitudes who hung on his every word and regularly cheered his verbal assaults and ripostes against the pompous chief priests and their allies.

First, they tried to get Jesus to say from where he claimed authority for his pronouncements and actions. To maintain his authority before the people, he could not claim a human source for it, because that would destroy his claim to be the Messiah sent from God. It would also constitute an admission of a political agenda, which would have put him in direct opposition to both the Jewish religious authorities and the Roman temporal rulers. On the other hand, if he said he was from God, he would be asserting a claim that the Jews considered blasphemous, a capital offense for which he could have been immediately stoned to death.

Jesus reversed the conundrum and refused to answer until his questioners stated their opinion of where John the Baptist derived his authority for his baptisms. Now either answer, God or man, exposed the authorities to the wrath

---

[6]Mt 26:15

of the people. For if John had been sent by God, the chief priests and elders had defied I AM by not accepting John's call to repentance and baptism. But they also did not have the courage to deny that John had been a prophet because the people believed otherwise. Something in John's call to repentance and baptism had struck a deep spiritual chord and they revered him as a man obviously sent by Yahweh in the same manner as the prophets of old. So the Jewish authorities refused to answer and Jesus, in his turn, also refused to respond. Round one to Jesus.

The Pharisees huddled. The idea they came up with was brilliant. The hottest political issue in the country was taxation for the benefit of Rome. Those who openly opposed Rome's right to tax were regarded by the Romans as enemies of the state and met a commensurate, unpleasant and rapid end, usually on a cross. Those who upheld the right of Roman taxation were detested and vilified by Jewish patriots. It was the perfect trap question. There was no way, it seemed, that Jesus could avoid being caught on one horn or the other of this dilemma. To make it look like the question was a sincere request for guidance, the Pharisees rounded up some of Herod's people, who were responsible for running the tax collection network in their own provinces. With flattery and honeyed voices dripping insincerity they posed the issue to Jesus:

> "**Teacher, we know you are a truthful man and teach God's way sincerely. You court no one's favor and do not act out of human respect. Give us your opinion, then, in this case. Is it lawful to pay tax to the emperor or not?**"[7]

Jesus glared at them. "**Why are you trying to trip me up, you hypocrites? Show me the coin used for the tax.**" They handed him a small Roman coin, a little shaken that Jesus had seen so easily through their transparent scheme but still smug with the certain success of the trap. "**Whose head is this, and whose inscription?**" Jesus asked.

"**Caesar's,**" they replied.

"**Then give to Caesar what is Caesar's, but give to God what is God's,**"[8] said Jesus as he flipped the coin back to his questioners. They were dumbfounded by his response. In a single sentence, Jesus had enunciated the separation of civic and religious duties, centuries before its practical wisdom would be appreciated, and given them a primary principle for harmonious international relations.[9] Round two to Jesus.

A few of the scribes, who were the lawyers of that age, switched sides after this. Not openly, for they were afraid. But thereafter their hearts belonged to

---

[7] Mt 22:16-17

[8] Mt 22:15-22, Mk 12:13-17, Lk 20:20-26

[9] Jesus may not have been thinking in such geopolitical terms but his advice to honor both our civic and religious duties and, by implication, to keep them separate where there is no intrinsic conflict, is amply vindicated by the terrible experience of history in which religious convictions have been used to deprive the liberty, and lives, of others.

Jesus, the unschooled carpenter from a rural Galilean village, whose genius as much as his miracles testified to his divine origins.

Next the Sadducees decided they would entangle Jesus in one of their favorite theological issues: resurrection of the dead. The Sadducees did not believe in a bodily resurrection. The Pharisees did. The Sadducees knew Jesus preached resurrection and was theologically closer to the Pharisees than to them. So they posed the silly question of the woman married to multiple men, all brothers, and challenged Jesus to say who would be her husband at the resurrection. Jesus replied, in so many words: "Not Applicable." There is no institution of marriage in the next life.[10] As for whether the dead were dead forever, as the Sadducees preached, he reminded them that God had referred to Himself as the "God of Abraham, Isaac and Jacob." There wouldn't be much to His kingdom if Abraham, Isaac and Jacob, etc., were not alive to Him. The Sadducees retired to lick their wounds. Round three to Jesus.

The Pharisees, still reeling from the tax fiasco, but stung by Jesus' attacks, counterattacked with one of their favorite insoluble arguments. Like a gang of kids afraid of a gruff adult, but determined to be defiant anyway, they confronted Jesus as a group. One of their scribes, their "lawyer," was drafted to speak for them. He tried to get Jesus to choose which is the most important of the ten commandments. Jesus sighed. Would they never understand? Patiently he explained that the two greatest commandments were to love God with your whole heart, soul, mind and strength (number 1) and your neighbor as yourself (number 2). These were the foundation for the entire law and all the pronouncements of the prophets, Jesus told them.[11] The scribe who asked the question was so impressed that he expanded the teaching and applauded Jesus! For him, the light finally came on. Round four to Jesus.

Jesus decided to stop the sparring and challenged the Pharisees with an issue that went to the core of their theology. He posed this question to them. **"What is your opinion about the Messiah? Whose son is he?"**

Everyone knew the Messiah would be the new David, his son genealogically and metaphorically. He would be a ruler like David and claim his authority from David's throne.

"David's," they answered.

"Then how is it that David under the Spirit's influence calls him 'lord,' as he does:

> **'The Lord said to my lord,**
> **Sit at my right hand,**
> **until I humble your enemies**
> **beneath your feet.'?**

---

[10]Mt 22:30: "When people rise from the dead, they neither marry nor are given in marriage but live like angels in heaven."

[11]Mt 22:40

If David calls him 'lord,' how can he be his son?"[12]

The Pharisees, once again stymied, retreated in disarray, totally defeated. There would be no further attempts to match wits with Jesus. Only treachery, lies and violence remained as options for the Jewish authorities. They embraced them eagerly.

In between these failed attempts to expose Jesus as a false messiah, he told thinly-veiled parables that warned the chief priests, elders and scribes in graphic language that they themselves were in dangerous waters. With the story of the two sons, Jesus pointed out that God values deeds, not empty words.[13] He warned them of the consequences they could expect by the parable of the tenants in the vineyard, who killed the owner's son, and then were themselves destroyed and replaced by the owner.[14] He referred them to Scripture, to the cornerstone metaphor in Psalm 118, v. 22, a prophetic revelation that Israel and God would part ways permanently because of their rejection of him. Worse, they would be crushed in the process.[15] Finally, he gave them the story of the king's wedding banquet, which the invited guests spurned in extraordinarily defiant ways and, consequently, were destroyed by an army sent by the king.[16] The people loved it. The authorities were merely enraged.

Late Tuesday afternoon, several Greek Gentiles who were interested in converting to Judaism approached Philip, who was from Bethsaida and understood their language, and asked to meet with Jesus. Philip checked with Andrew and the two of them brought the request to Jesus. He received it like a death knell. The inquiry from the Gentiles signaled that Jesus' ministry to the Jews was at an end. His teaching to the people was complete. His hour had come. He trembled slightly and felt fear clutch at his knees and chest. With an effort, he suppressed it and announced to the entire crowd that the hour had come for the Son of Man to be glorified. Using the analogy of a seed, he explained how death was the process which produced the harvest of the future. He called upon those who believed in him to follow him and promised them the Father's reward if they did so. He called upon his Father to glorify His name. And, as the Father had spoken audibly at the beginning of His Son's ministry when baptized by John the Baptist, so, too, did the Father now respond, at the end of that ministry, to His Son's request:

---

[12]Mt 22:41-45

[13]Mt 21:28-32

[14]Mt 21:33-41, Mk 12:1-9, Lk 20:9-16

[15]Mt 21:42-44, Mk 12:10-11, Lk 20:17-18

[16]Mt 22:1-10

"I have glorified it,
and will glorify it again."[17]

But the Jews still did not understand. They did not comprehend what Jesus meant when he said that he would be lifted up but then would draw all men to himself. They listened to his final, almost plaintive, advice to walk in the light, his light, and to keep faith in the light so that they might themselves become sons of light.

Despite the miracles, despite the explicit claims and explanation, despite the predictions, the most astounding of which would come true in time measurable by hours, the Jewish authorities and most of the people would fail to accept him as the long-promised Messiah. So astounding was their stubbornness that John attributed it to God deliberately clouding their reason and numbing their hearts.[18] But the truth was there before them. The invitation to believe, an open door. They hardened their own hearts and closed their own minds. Jesus' kingdom was in another world, manifested by love and kindness. They wanted God's kingdom to be in this world, manifested by power and wealth. The collision was inevitable.

On Wednesday, Jesus stayed with his apostles on the Mount of Olives. As they gazed across at the wall of the Temple Mount towering four hundred feet at its southeastern end above the valley below, he told them how one day soon the Temple would be torn down so completely that not one stone would be left on another.[19] He told them of the final days, for both Jerusalem and the world, and how he would return to earth on the clouds of heaven. He warned them of the Final Judgment and gave them the yardsticks by which all people's lives would be measured then.[20] And the dread within him grew steadily.

Judas kept trying to find out in advance where they would spend each night so that he could pass the information to the chief scribe. But Jesus reserved this decision to himself and Judas was unable to slip away once they had settled for the evening. Further, as he had listened to Jesus' teachings in the Temple and to the apostles on the Mount of Olives, he began to have second thoughts about the arrangement he had entered into. He thought seriously about returning the money to Noam. Jesus was obviously convinced that he was going to come to a bad end here and this made Judas nervous. He couldn't understand it. The populace of Jerusalem loved Jesus. They hung on his every word and many of them spoke openly with absolute conviction that here, indeed, was the Messiah, the savior of

---

[17]Jn 12:28; see 12:24-27 for Jesus' discourse summarized in the preceding paragraph.

[18]Jn 12:39-41

[19]Mt 24:1-2

[20]Mt 24-25, Mk13, Lk 21

Israel. All Jesus had to do was say the word and they would make him king of the entire nation. They would have fearlessly attacked the hated Romans and swept them away. And those who were injured or killed in the process . . . why, Jesus could simply heal them or bring them back to life. At the very least, no one could capture him. He remembered how Jesus had walked through the angry elders in Nazareth two years ago and in the Temple last year at the Feast of Booths[21] and again during the Feast of Dedication[22] when they had decided he had blasphemed and were going to punish him with death. He seemed suddenly to be invisible to all those who were trying to harm him. It was ridiculous for Jesus to talk of being put to death. *It must be a bluff or some kind of tactic,* Judas thought to himself. *I'll be doing him a favor if I help them capture him. Before the Sanhedrin by itself, he can give them a simple demonstration of his power and they will fall into line. Even if that fails, Jesus can walk away, just as he has done every time before. I collect a few shekels, which is only right, Jesus gets pushed into using his power to save Israel, and everyone will see that I masterminded it all. It's perfect, if I can only find out where we are going to be spending each night when Jesus won't be surrounded by all these fawning sheep.*

Thursday morning, Judas got the information he wanted. Andrew called him over and told him that Jesus wanted him to arrange with the owner of the olive press (the *gethsemane*) for exclusive use of the garden that night. They would be celebrating the Passover meal in the city and then returning to this garden afterwards. Judas' face lit up. "Of course. I'll take care of it right away." He got up immediately and left.

Judas is certainly in a good mood today, thought Andrew to himself. *I wish I could say the same for the rest of us. Even the Lord seems extremely subdued. No wonder. He keeps talking about his death like it's going to happen any minute. But why? The people love him and the chief priests and scribes are no match for him. He's proved that over and over. He's certainly no threat to the Romans. Then, too, he does seem to be looking forward very much to tonight's Passover meal. Speaking of which, I better ask Peter where we are going to prepare it.* Andrew went off to find his brother.

Peter took Andrew's question to Jesus, who had already found the solution. On Monday, while Jesus was preaching in the Temple, three men had approached him—a father, his son and a servant. The father's name was Tychus. He was a wealthy Greek who converted to Judaism. He had a wife named Mary and a teenaged son, Mark, sometimes called John, who would one day write the Gospel According to Mark. "Rabbi, the Feast of Unleavened Bread approaches quickly," said Tychus to Jesus. "You will need a place for you and your disciples to eat the Passover supper. I would be honored if you would come to my house.

---

[21]The Feast of Booths took place every year between the 15th and 21st day of *Tishri,* which occurred in September-October of the modern calendar.

[22]The Feast of Dedication, or Lights, took place on the 25th day of the month of *Chislev,* which corresponded to our November/December time frame.

I have a spacious home in the upper city with a second floor room which is large and well-furnished."

Jesus looked at the three men with profound love and gratitude, the same expression he had worn when the Roman Centurion had declared his faith in the ability of Jesus to cure his serving boy by simply giving the order. "I am pleased to accept your offer. As you see, however, your kindness may put you in some danger with the chief priests and the elders as they are convinced that I am a blasphemer. It is growing increasingly difficult for me and my disciples to move about freely. How will we find your house?"

"On Thursday about the third hour,[23] I will send my servant here to the Fountain Gate. He will be carrying a jar of water, which will make him easy to recognize.[24] Send your disciples to the gate. When they see my servant, tell them to follow him. He will bring them to my house."

"Thank you, Tychus," said Jesus. "Your kindness shall reap a harvest for you and mankind beyond your furthest imaginings. Until the end of time, men will bless your faith and your courage. By this means shall the Son of Man provide the Bread of Life throughout the world whenever this meal is commemorated."

Jesus conveyed to Peter the instructions he had received from Tychus. Peter, taking John with him, went off to buy the unblemished lamb, which they would sacrifice in the Temple, and the various other ingredients for the formalized Passover supper. They found the servant as directed and had the Upper Room (known to us today as the "Cenacle") fully prepared when John led Jesus and the other apostles there shortly after dark. Ironically, this room where Jesus would establish the Holy Eucharist, the gift of Himself for the life of mankind, was within two hundred yards of the palace of the High Priest Caiaphas. It was, indeed, spacious, measuring almost 1300 square feet beneath fifteen-foot ceilings.

Meanwhile, Judas had gone to see Noam, the chief scribe, to report that he knew where Jesus would be that night. Noam was delighted. "Excellent, excellent, Master Judas! If you will tell me exactly where to find Jesus, I will arrange for a delegation to go there and bring him back to meet with the Sanhedrin."

"I prefer not to say now, Rabbi," replied Judas. "It will be better if I lead your group. In the dark, you will need me to identify which one of the men is Jesus. Further, I can explain to the other disciples what is going on and prevent any possible violent resistance." Judas' real motive was to ensure that he was recognized as the one who had brought about the acknowledgment by the Jewish authorities of Jesus as the Messiah. That would guarantee him an important place in the new government after Jesus and the Jews drove the Romans out. Even if Jesus "walked" as he had before, Judas could point out that only a man with

---

[23]Nine A.M. The Romans started the day's clock at 6 A.M.

[24]A man carrying water would definitely have stood out because this task was performed almost exclusively by women.

miraculous powers could have escaped their clutches under such circumstances. He would go on to volunteer to continue to work with them by reporting on Jesus' activities and trying to persuade Jesus to use his powers to show that he is, indeed, the One sent by God. *Either way,* Judas chuckled to himself, *I will be the critical intermediary necessary to bring Jesus' mission to fulfillment.*

What Judas in his pride and stupidity did not realize is that the chief priests, scribes and elders had already determined to put Jesus to death. They were uninterested in his message of love and cared nothing about his power to work miracles unless they were to be put in service to the state. Their mind-set was not open to even the possibility that Jesus was who he said he was. Yahweh was One God, in heaven, as far removed from man as the heavens from the earth. Jesus was obviously a human being and, therefore, could not be what he claimed to be.

Caiaphas, the high priest, had persuaded the Sanhedrin after Lazarus had been raised from the dead that either Jesus died or the Romans would sooner or later destroy the nation because of the threat he would pose to their rule. However, Jesus' enormous popularity and the huge crowds present in Jerusalem for the Feast of Passover/Unleavened Bread had about convinced them that they would have to wait until some future time to accomplish their purpose. Judas' timely offer at the last minute seemed heaven sent.

Caiaphas sent a delegation to report to Pontius Pilate that they were about to apprehend Jesus of Nazareth, a dangerous radical who was stirring up the people against Roman rule. This was not true, of course, but Caiaphas knew Pilate would have to investigate the accusation. Because of Jesus' huge popularity and the ever-present threat of riots, they asked for assignment of a substantial Roman contingent to the group that would take him prisoner.

Pilate was skeptical but appointed a tribune to lead a reduced cohort of Roman soldiers to accompany the Jewish Temple guards and those chief priests, scribes and elders who would choose to join them.

Everything was now in place for the culmination of Jesus' ministry on earth.

In the Upper Room, the apostles gathered with Jesus to share the sacred Passover meal. They had no idea then that this meal would be the most sacred one since God created man. Now would the Son of God establish the sacrament that would leave him forever available to all mankind under the appearance of bread and wine. By giving us his body and blood, Jesus made us his true brothers and sisters because henceforth we would share the same flesh and blood, as family members do. The generosity of this act by God is incomprehensible, especially because vicious torture and a cruel death at the hands of the very people he came to save would be required to achieve the primary purpose of the sacrament: to unite God's people with Him in this life and forever in heaven.

The apostles reclined on cushions on both sides of a long table as Tychus' servants served the meal to them. Jesus was in the middle of one side of the low table. On his right sat Peter and to his immediate left was John. Judas was across the table opposite John. The other apostles were spread out to both ends of the table.

Judas was nervous. What had seemed such a good idea before, now seemed dangerous, rash and ill-considered, even to his petty thief's mind. He wondered if he shouldn't just forget about it. After all, he had not told the authorities where to find Jesus and they would not be able to do it themselves without his assistance. If he failed to show up, well, too bad. As long as Jesus remained so popular, and that showed no sign of changing, the Jewish authorities would need him, Judas, more than he needed them. *Maybe I should wait,* Judas thought to himself. *Thirty silver pieces is a paltry price for such a prize. I should have demanded ten times as much. If I wait, I can ask for more next time.*

Judas' thoughts were interrupted by an argument which suddenly erupted among the apostles. They were once again skirmishing with one another over roles and ranks in Christ's kingdom. Jesus listened to them for a few minutes, then raised his hand for their attention. As they quieted, he stood up and removed his cloak. He tied a towel around his waist, poured water into a basin, and, kneeling in turn before each apostle, washed their feet. This was an astonishingly humble act, and Peter, dear, impetuous Peter, initially refused to let Jesus subject himself to such humiliation on his behalf.[25] But Jesus made it quite clear that Peter's refusal would separate him from the Lord permanently, which quickly silenced Peter's objections.

Judas, however, made no protest, although he found the whole thing quite distasteful. This was no way for Israel's Messiah to behave. He was embarrassed for Jesus and his resolve to go to the chief priests strengthened considerably. Judas had never accepted the notion that God would let the Messiah be killed. And if the Messiah were his Son, it was absolutely inconceivable that He would permit such a thing. No man, much less a king, would not use all his power to prevent it and punish anyone who attempted it. It was insane to suggest that I AM would. To Judas' way of thinking, Christ's predictions of his passion and death were tantamount to an admission that he really was not who he claimed to be. Although Jesus had impressive powers, in Judas' mind there would have to be some other explanation for them if Yahweh permitted Jesus to be killed. He was lost in his own thoughts while Jesus explained to his disciples that His way turned the world upside down. Power, control and self-importance were to be replaced in his followers by service, love and humility. After this night, no one who purported to follow Jesus Christ could ever claim that any act of kindness and service, no matter how humble, was beneath their dignity.

Jesus washed his hands, put his cloak back on, and returned to the center of the table. For a moment, he seemed anxious and troubled. Then Jesus looked at Judas with a look of such profound sadness and pity that Judas felt a momentary

---

[25]It was the custom among the Jews to always wash their feet when they entered a home. Jewish hospitality required that the host provide this service for his guests. It was considered the lowliest duty for the most junior servant or least favored slave.

surge of fright. His face flushed and he looked away. Jesus turned to the other apostles and said:

> **"What I say is not said of all,**
> **for I know the kind of men I chose.**
> **My purpose here is the fulfillment of Scripture:**
> **'He who partook of bread with me**
> **has raised his heel against me.'**
> **I tell you this now, before it takes place,**
> **so that when it takes place you may believe**
> **that I AM.**
> **I solemnly assure you,**
> **he who accepts anyone I send**
> **accepts me,**
> **and in accepting me**
> **accepts him who sent me."**[26]

The sorrow which Jesus felt for Judas almost overwhelmed him and he had to fight to regain his composure. Jesus covered his face with his hands and for a long minute or two did not look up. Then, slowly letting his hands fall away from his face, where he blinked back tears, Jesus looked around the table, at the faces of all the apostles who were staring at him, transfixed. He focused directly on Judas as he said:

> **"I tell you solemnly,**
> **one of you will betray me."**[27]

Judas was astounded. Jesus knew! Questions swirled through Judas' mind. *How did he find out? Why did he wait till now to bring it up? Could one of the other apostles also have gone to the chief priests?* This last thought frightened Judas more than any other because he suddenly imagined a competitor stealing away the advantage he had planned for himself.

The other apostles were still in a state of shock over Jesus' sudden and startling revelation. They were already filled with anxiety and apprehension over Jesus' deep solemnity and resignation to his own impending death. It seemed both unreal and unnecessary to them. At the very least, it was unnatural not to resist, not to fight back.

Then Jesus, the Messiah sent from God, performed the ablutions of the humblest slave by washing their feet. True, it was a powerfully effective teaching device since they had just been arguing about who among them was the most important. But it was unsettling. Nothing Jesus did or said was predictable. Often, they could not even understand it. Now this shocking accusation. The apostles were so unsure of themselves that most of them feared that somehow they could

---

[26]Jn 13:18-20

[27]Jn 13:21

perhaps unintentionally betray the Lord. So they asked with trembling voices and pleading eyes: **"Surely it is not I, Lord?"**[28]

Jesus seemed not to hear the chorus of plaintive inquiries. Looking steadily at Judas, Jesus said:

> **"The man who has dipped his hand into the dish with me is the one who will hand me over. The Son of Man is departing as Scripture says of him, but woe to that man by whom the Son of Man is betrayed. Better for him if he had never been born."**[29]

This narrowed the list of candidates considerably. No more than five of the apostles were close enough to Jesus to dip into the bowl of bitter herbs with him. But, then again, there was more than one bowl and perhaps Jesus meant the statement metaphorically to refer to anyone who had eaten with him. The other apostles were now scrutinizing Peter, John, Judas, James and Andrew, the five who sat close enough to Jesus to dip into the bowl with him. Peter, a man of strong and quick opinions, was already agitated by the shocking announcement that there was a traitor in their midst. Now to see the finger of suspicion pointed in his direction was entirely too much. Jesus was sitting upright between Peter and John, so Peter could lean back and get John's attention behind Jesus' back. He silently pointed to Jesus and mouthed the words: "Ask him who!"

John, who had only recently celebrated his eighteenth birthday and tended to treat Jesus as if he were his father, leaned back against Jesus' chest and whispered: **"Lord, who is he?"**[30]

Jesus responded: **"The one to whom I give the bit of food I dip in the dish."**[31] Jesus picked up a small piece of roasted lamb, dipped it into the dish of bitter herbs, and handed it to Judas.

Peter, who had not heard Jesus' response because of the hubbub created by the other apostles arguing about what should be done about the reported traitor, was trying to get John's attention again to find out what Jesus had said to him. But John was staring at Judas, his expression revealing a mixture of shock, revulsion and alarm.

Judas had been looking around at the other apostles, feigning innocence and indignation that one of their number was about to betray their Master, and did not hear the exchange between John and Jesus. He looked at Jesus now and saw the strong hand with the long fingers holding the piece of lamb for him. He smiled and picked up the refrain of the other apostles: **"Surely it is not I, Rabbi?"**

---

[28]Mt 26:22

[29]Mt 26:23-24

[30]Jn 13:25

[31]Jn 13:26

Jesus noted that the other apostles had called him "Lord," while Judas called him "Rabbi." **"It is you who have said it.**[32] **Be quick about what you are to do."**[33]

Judas swallowed the morsel Jesus had given him and got up from the table. He was confused and anxious, unsure of his course. Jesus had not been angry at him, had not ordered the apostles to seize him or worse, yet he knew what was going on. *He even told me to go and do it now,* thought Judas to himself. *So this must be something that he wants to happen. It is just as I planned: Caiaphas, Noam and the rest of them will confront him, he will either show them his power or perform his usual disappearing act, the news of which will get around to all the people, and I will have made it all happen.* But Jesus' warning had been terrible and for a moment had struck fear deep into Judas' heart. *Better to never have been born!!*

The other apostles were looking at Judas now, standing uncertainly across the table from Jesus. They were idly curious about what he was up to, having observed the conversation between Jesus and him but not hearing its exact content. John, of course, knew differently and he looked at Judas with disgust, perplexed as to why Jesus was sending him out since he knew that he was collaborating with the chief priests and Pharisees.

Judas realized there was no going back. In a few moments, all the apostles would know what he had been up to and he would be lucky to escape with his life. When everything worked out later, they would see that he had been right all along. Jesus might even realize he had made a mistake in making Peter his number one disciple instead of Judas. With a surge of recovered confidence, Judas pulled his cloak about him and went out into the night. *How convenient,* he thought, *to be so close to the palace of the high priest. It was all working out perfectly.* Judas vanished into the darkness.

Inside the Upper Room, Jesus told the remaining apostles that he was leaving them now. He explained things in a way they had never heard before, words which spoke to their hearts in language so beautiful it was almost poetic. He warned them that his fate would be theirs as well. He reassured them that he would not abandon them, would, in fact, send the Paraclete who would open their minds and hearts in ways that they could not yet understand. Jesus spoke with such love and sorrow that even without the explicit warnings of sufferings they would have been moved to tears. As it was, many of them could barely sit still. But they were heartened by Jesus' unveiled references to his Father and strengthened by his prayer for them.

With great solemnity, Jesus picked up a loaf of the unleavened bread that had been set before him. Holding it reverently in both hands, he looked up to heaven and gave a blessing of thanks to his Father. Then, looking around at the

---

[32]Mt 26:25

[33]Jn 13:27

apostles, who were watching his every movement, Jesus broke the bread and passed one half in each direction along the table, saying as he did so:

>**"Take this and eat it.[34] This is my body to be given for**
>**you. Do this as a remembrance of me."[35]**

Next, Jesus took his cup and filled it with wine. He raised it in both his hands to his Father, pronounced a blessing of thanks, and said to his apostles:

>**"All of you must drink from it, for this is my blood, the**
>**blood of the covenant, to be poured out on behalf of**
>**many for the forgiveness of sins. I tell you, I will not**
>**drink this fruit of the vine from now until the day when**
>**I drink it new with you in my Father's reign."[36]**

Jesus passed the cup to his right, to Peter first. He drank from it and passed it on, the cup continuing in this fashion until it came around to John who finished it and passed the now empty cup back to the Lord. Jesus was content. He would not feel such joy again in his earthly lifetime. The Sacrament of Union was established. It would bind him and those who believed in him together in a single mystical body for all time. The mustard seed was planted. His death would start its magnificent growth.

Jesus turned his attention to the man who would lead his infant Church. He spoke directly to Peter, charging him to strengthen his brothers. Peter was emboldened by Jesus' singling him out for this responsibility and blustered:

>**"Lord, at your side I am prepared to face imprisonment**
>**and death itself. I will lay down my life for you!"[37]**

Not to be outdone, the other apostles chimed in with similar claims and assurances, all hollow. If the situation had not been so serious, Jesus would have been amused. As it was, he said to Peter with a mixture of affection and sorrow: **"I give you my word, before the cock crows tonight you will deny me three times."[38]**

Peter turned scarlet with embarrassment and frustration. *Why does Jesus say things like that?* he wondered. *I will defend him with my life and whisper his name with my last breath, I swear it!* Then Jesus said something that Peter, the man of action, could finally relate to:

>**"When I sent you on mission without purse or traveling**
>**bag or sandals, were you in need of anything?"**
>**"Not a thing,"** someone replied.

---

[34]Mt 26:26

[35]Lk 22:19

[36]Mt 26:27-29, Mk 14:24

[37]Lk 22:33, Jn 13:37

[38]Mt 26:34

> "Now, however, the man who has a purse must carry it;
> the same with the traveling bag. And the man without a
> sword must sell his coat and buy one. It is written in
> Scripture,
>> 'He was counted among the wicked,'
> and this, I tell you, must come to be fulfilled in me. All
> that has to do with me approaches its climax."[39]

Jesus was finally talking sense. Swords were exactly what they needed to defend him. Excited, Peter exclaimed: **"Lord, here are two swords!"**[40]

Jesus rolled his eyes but merely responded: **"Enough."**[41] Peter was heartened nonetheless. He thought he had detected a willingness in Jesus to let himself be defended, even if he himself would not do so. Peter tucked one of the swords into his girdle inside his cloak. James asked for the other and did the same.

Midnight came. The Last Supper was over. They sang hymns of praise and thanksgiving, strong voices filled with sincerity and hope and love. Then Jesus led them out of the house, down the stone stairs on Mount Zion within shouting distance of the palace of Caiaphas and out of the city through the Fountain Gate. The moon was high and full and cast their shadows at their feet as they walked through the Kidron Valley, past the great white stones of the Temple Mount towering hundreds of feet above them. Jesus walked more slowly than usual, and seemed agitated. The still of the night pressed down ominously all around the little group of twelve men. The sound of their sandaled feet scuffing along the road was unnaturally loud, seeming to thunder their passage to the disapproving darkness. The men shivered against the cold and a terrible feeling of dread. They turned off the road and crossed the arched bridge spanning the little brook murmuring of a rainy season past. The garden of the olive press lay hushed and foreboding amid deep, mournful shadows. Olive trees with gnarled trunks and lacy, silver-green foliage stood motionless among outcrops of craggy, limestone rock. The whole world seemed to be holding its breath.

Although the night was lit by a full moon, the apostles were standing in what was essentially an olive tree orchard. There were numerous shadows and no one's face could be seen clearly. If they had been able to see better, they would have been shocked at the change that had come over Jesus. His eyes appeared to have sunk into his face. His jaw hung slack and his hands trembled. His voice seemed slightly higher in pitch as he told the apostles, **"Stay here while I go over there and pray."**[42] As the apostles looked for places to spread their rush mats,

---

[39]Lk 22:35-36

[40]Lk 22:38

[41]Ibid.

[42]Mt 26:36

Jesus gestured to Peter, James and John to come with him. He led them past thick, old growth olive trees, some of which might have been growing there at the time of Moses, to the edge of a small clearing.

> **"My heart is filled with sorrow to the point of death.**
> **Remain here and stay awake.**[43] **Pray that you may not be**
> **put to the test."**[44]

The three apostles looked at each other anxiously and nodded. Jesus seemed to be on the point of collapse and they were extremely alarmed.

Jesus advanced through the clearing, past a few trees, and into a second small clearing about a hundred feet away. In the center of this space, he fell heavily to his knees, leaning against one of the large outcrops of rock jutting above the ground. Now all of his resolve left him. Terror pounded in his brain, and he was swept by waves of nausea and panic. His heart was palpitating and his entire body was wet with perspiration. He felt so weak he could hardly lift his head. He clasped his hands together feverishly and prayed in words which came in gasps:

> **"My Father, if it is possible, let this cup pass me by. Still,**
> **let it be as you would have it, not as I."**[45]

As though watching someone else, Jesus saw the terrible sufferings ahead. He saw himself bound tightly with cords and pulled angrily about. He saw himself struck in the face and head by fists and sticks. He saw the terrible scourging blows ripping pieces of flesh from his body in a cascade of blood and pain. He saw the needle-sharp spikes of the crown of thorns piercing his head, sending rivulets of blood pouring into his eyes and down his neck. He saw jeering men slapping him, punching him, mocking him, spitting gobs of phlegm directly into his face. He saw himself struggling to carry a heavy wooden beam on legs so weak they could hardly support his own body. He saw himself stumble and smash knees and elbows on hard paving stones. He felt thirst so severe that he could barely unstick his tongue from the roof of his mouth. He saw long, thick nails driven through his hands and feet and himself then hanging suspended on these daggers of pain. He saw the Roman spear enter his right side, pass through his lung and pierce entirely through his heart. Although he would be dead before the spear thrust, the horror of what would happen to his body had almost as severe a psychological effect. These images magnified the normal human "fight or flight" reaction produced by adrenalin released in large doses when the individual is confronted by danger. But Jesus by divine will could choose neither option. Already faint with apprehension and fear of the ordeal which lay ahead, he had to use all of his strength to merely remain still, submissive as a lamb, but without the lamb's blessed ignorance. Nor was anger available to him to steel his nerves and suppress his pain. His sacrifice

---

[43]Mk 14:34

[44]Lk 22:40

[45]Mt 26:39

was one of pure love, for those who would soon torture and kill him as much as for those who loved him. Jesus became absolute vulnerability of mind, body and spirit. He prayed and wept, shaking with convulsive sobs, begging his Father to give him strength to endure what lay so near.

But this was to be Jesus' hour of darkness and the consolation of his Father was no longer there. So Jesus reached out to his closest companions for comfort and help. Rising from where he had lain gripping the rock as if to tie himself to the earth, he returned to where he had left Peter, James and John. There was no empathetic suffering there to console him. The apostles were sound asleep.

Jesus looked at the three sleeping men with pity, but he needed their strength now as he had never needed anything in his life. He shook Peter awake who, in turn, shoved his companions to arouse them.

> **"Asleep, Simon? You could not stay awake for even an hour? Be on guard and pray that you may not be put to the test. The spirit is willing but nature is weak."**[46]

The three apostles flushed with embarrassment and stood up, disoriented from having been suddenly awakened. The moon had passed now to the west and the dim shadows were longer. Jesus looked like a spectre standing before them, hair matted with sweat, clothes clinging to his body and soiled in places that had come in contact with the ground. But there was love in his eyes and as he turned to go back to his place of prayer, he held up his hand to let them know they were not to accompany him.

Once again Jesus fell prostrate against the cold, silent stone. Once again the tidal wave of fear and sorrow rolled over him. Once again he prayed to his Father from the depths of his soul:

> **"Abba (O Father), you have the power to do all things. Take this cup away from me. But let it be as you would have it, not as I."**[47]

Now Jesus' humanity asserted itself. He felt anger rising inside him for the ingratitude and disloyalty of Judas and the hypocrisy and selfishness of the Jewish authorities. He foresaw all the cruelty, greed, lies, wilful ignorance and corruption of future generations, even among those who would profess to be his most loyal followers. His perfect sense of justice clashed with his divine mission of mercy. *It was not right that this should happen to me at the hands of such evil men*, came the thought, pounding with indignation. *They deserve to die in their sins.* He wanted to use his divine authority to cast them away, even into hell, and to give up the struggle as a bad bargain. He was the Son of God, second Person of the divine Trinity, creator of the universe. All power was his by a simple act of will. The submissiveness of his role now in the redemption of mankind required a suppression, an emptying out, of infinite magnitude. But he came to earth to love

---

[46]Mk 14:37-38

[47]Mk 14:36

us, to forgive us, to save us. The burning fire of that divine love blazed up to consume his anger. The victory of love over justice came at an enormous price, however. Emotionally, he was torn apart. Then he thought of his mother, that perfect soul of love, fidelity and trust, and his heart's victory was complete.

But the anguish continued. He had slept poorly for days now and the cumulative effect of fatigue weakened him to the point of total exhaustion. He felt paralyzed, pressed into the very earth, unable to move a single muscle. His breathing came in rapid, shallow gasps and the blood vessels near his skin began to contract, pushing the life-giving fluid back toward the vital organs. His skin, already clammy and cold to the touch, grew paler. His blood pressure and adrenalin levels rose. His human instincts screamed at him to deal with the danger, to either confront and defeat it or flee to safety. His body began to tremble from the severe physical strain of remaining submissive in the face of what he foresaw in all of its horror. Trembling became shaking so violent it resembled convulsions. Jesus held onto the rock to steady himself, fighting the nausea which filled his mouth with fluid and shutting his eyes against the dizziness that dazed his brain. He prayed, and prayed, and prayed. Another hour passed. Desperate, Jesus once again turned to his friends for help.

Peter, James and John had tried to remain awake. Chastened and ashamed after Jesus had left the hour before, they had remained standing for awhile, trying to pray, filled with anxiety themselves, frightened by the sounds of Jesus' anguish that pierced the shadowed silence. But their fear and fatigue weighed them down, and so they sat down to pray, and soon had fallen asleep once more. Jesus found them like that. He did not scold them this time. He merely knelt beside them, pulling John's cloak closer to him where it had fallen away and exposed him to the chill of the night air. He touched the shoulders of Peter and James, drawing strength from their reality and the love he knew they bore him.

As Jesus rose to return once more to his anguished prayer, James opened his eyes and saw his Lord standing there. He struggled to his feet, but Jesus had already moved away. Though James tried to remain vigilant, exhaustion wrapped its leaden arms around his head and pulled him toward the ground. After some minutes, he leaned against an olive tree, then, lulled by the muffled cries of Jesus in the clearing ahead, sank slowly to a sitting position, from where he could resist no longer. Just before he drifted into sleep, he thought he perceived another figure in the clearing with Jesus, but it was shadowy and dream-like and James' exhausted mind simply incorporated it into his slumber.

Jesus walked slowly back to his place of prayer. His shoulders slumped forward and his head hung so low it looked as if he might topple forward. Indeed, he did stumble over a root unseen in the darkness and fell heavily forward onto his knees and hands. Already psychologically and physically tormented beyond human endurance, Jesus could contain his nausea no longer and he retched violently, losing vital nutrients and fluids. Later on that day, their loss would contribute to the intensity of his sufferings and the rapidity of his death by crucifixion. Weeping, Jesus crawled back to the stone and cried out to his Father:

"My Father, if this cannot pass me by without my drinking it, your will be done!"[48]

Now there came a new and more terrible weight than even the vision of his imminent physical sufferings. God laid upon him the debt which he had come to earth to pay. His became the guilt for thousands upon thousands of years of sin, from the first choice of pride by Adam and Eve to the last sin that would be committed before the Final Judgment when Jesus returns in triumph. The degradation and the horror of mankind's offenses would have utterly crushed him had he not been strengthened by an angel sent by his Father.[49] Prayers for strength and endurance poured from Jesus' lips in an unbroken stream. He writhed upon the ground, praying ever more intensely for his Father's forgiveness of all mankind even as visions of human ingratitude and rejection of him played before eyes blinded with tears and sweat. The angel put his arms around his Lord and whispered to him of the multitude of souls who would be with him eternally in heaven only because of this terrible sacrifice.

By now, Jesus' entire outer body was cold to the touch. His blood thickened around his vital organs and in his brain, reacting physiologically to protect the organism which seemed about to perish from mental strains so severe that his heart beat had become irregular. Minute by minute, the hour ticked by. Inch by figurative inch, the Gate to heaven swung open, propelled by the infinite grace being earned by this Suffering Servant for use by uncountable numbers of souls who would appear before God's judgment seat.

At last, all resistance passed, all fear dissolved, all justice surrendered to the divine will of God. Jesus embraced his mission and gave thanks to his Father for letting him reconcile alienated man. Relief and joy swept over him in a cascade of divine Love. In his body, the tension which had been crushing him disappeared and the blood in his veins rushed back into the subcutaneous capillaries they had vacated. The sudden surge ruptured the small vessels intertwined with the millions of exocrine sweat glands, and blood mixed with the sweat that dripped from Jesus' face and body.[50] As a consequence, Jesus' body became almost one continuous bruise as the discoloration from the broken vessels spread beneath his skin and left it highly sensitized. This would act as an intensifier for the blows and lashes of his tormentors in the hours ahead.

The angel left him. Jesus rose slowly, his body aching with fatigue. His teeth chattered and he quivered from the night's cold made worse by evaporation from his sweat and blood-drenched clothing. But now he was at peace, and the

---

[48]Mt 26:42

[49]Luke does not name the angel but what a magnificent creature and friend of the Lord he must be to have been sent by God on such a mission at such a desperate time!

[50]This process, called hematridosis, is described in detail in two books: Frederick T. Zugibe, *The Cross and the Shroud* (New York: Paragon House, 1988), 1-7, and Pierre Barbet, *A Doctor at Calvary*, (Garden City: Doubleday Image Books, 1963), 73-75.

enemy was at hand. He hurried back to his three stalwart disciples, sound asleep. He smiled, remembering their vigorous assurances only a few hours ago of their willingness to suffer death for him. Well, it would not be tonight for them. In fact, this night would be the nadir of their discipleship, a memory of shame and cowardice. But this, too, would serve their Lord's purpose not only by preserving the nucleus of his Church but also by presenting these men as ordinary people, not heroes with greater character than the mass of humanity whom Jesus came to save. Their subsequent heroism and courage in the face of persecution and martyrdom would highlight their transformation by the Holy Spirit and be further evidence of the truth of the Resurrection. Only John would put his life on the line with Christ and he would be rewarded with care of the finest human being in the history of mankind: Jesus' mother.

Among the trees, torches flickered and muffled voices drifted through the still night air. Jesus shook each of the three apostles and said:

"Still sleeping? Still taking your ease? It will have to do. The hour is on us. You will see that the Son of Man is to be handed over to the clutches of evil men. Rouse yourselves and come along. See! My betrayer is near."[51]

Peter, James and John scrambled to their feet. John gasped when he saw Jesus' blood-streaked face and clothing. "Lord, are you injured?"

In response, Jesus pulled a cloth from inside his tunic and wiped his face and neck clean. Any further discussion was interrupted by Judas, who had already entered the little clearing ahead of a crowd of perhaps four hundred soldiers and Jewish officials. He went up to Jesus and, smiling broadly, embraced him, kissing him on the left cheek in greeting. "Peace, Rabbi!" said Judas.

Jesus did not return the embrace but, instead, spoke sadly to Judas:

"Judas, would you betray the Son of Man with a kiss? Friend, do what you are here for!"[52]

The response stung Judas and threw him into momentary confusion. For one horrifying instant, he saw how despicable and hypocritical his actions were. Panic bloomed in his chest but he fought it back, rationalizing again that Jesus was in no real danger. He could easily save himself—and surely would, thought Judas. Jesus had already declared his awareness of the scheme. *I'm only letting events take their proper course,* he told himself. He was confident about their outcome and the benefits that would accrue to him for his initiative. At the palace of Caiaphas, he had explained how he would identify who among the apostles was Jesus by embracing him. He had officiously instructed the Jewish Captain of the Guard, to

---

[51]Mk 14:41-42

[52]This quote combines quotes in Luke (22:48) and Matthew (26:50). In these mystery stories, I have attempted to include as much of each Gospel writer's relevant report as I could consistent with logic and the narrative.

"take every precaution"[53] so as not to injure Jesus or let any violence break out. The Captain merely stared at him coldly, repulsed at having anything to do with a man who would betray his friends so easily.

Jesus stepped around Judas and confronted the crowd of mostly armed men, bearing clubs, swords and spears, holding their torches and lanterns high, who had crowded into the clearing so they could see whom Judas would embrace. The moon had begun to set and the predawn darkness was deepening. **"Who is it you want?"**[54] Jesus asked. He would make it clear that his destiny was not being controlled by Judas. He also intended a subtle message about who he really was.

"Jesus the Nazorean," they replied.

The Jewish temple guards were in front of the group. The Romans were along only in case of substantial armed resistance or to deal with any large crowds that might materialize. But the temple guards were nervous. They had heard about the wonders performed by Jesus, some had even witnessed miraculous cures, and were apprehensive. They half expected Jesus to respond in anger and who knew what he might do then? But now all he did was answer them: **"I am he."**

The nervous guards immediately fell back; some of them even tripped over their own feet and fell down, knocking down others who had been clustering closely together in the flickering light. Jesus' use of the term "I am" to identify himself frightened them thoroughly. It seemed a likely prelude to a possible lightning bolt from an angry God. But Jesus merely asked his question again: **"Who is it you want?"**

"Jesus the Nazorean," they repeated.

"I have told you, I am he. If I am the one you want, let these men go."

The apostles were clustered in a semicircle closely behind Jesus. At Jesus' reference to them, they stirred, suddenly aware of their own involvement in the proceedings. The guards, who were already holding swords, likewise seemed to take notice for the first time that other persons besides Jesus were present. Tensions quickly escalated. Peter, impetuous and quick-tempered, decided now was the time for action. Despite everything Jesus had said, he still did not get it. Jesus was the Messiah, he lived in the world, and, by God, he, Peter, was going to defend him! He would show Jesus that he meant what he said in the Upper Room when he promised to die with him if necessary.

The chief priests, scribes and elders who had accompanied the guards and soldiers had moved to the front of the crowd now, after seeing that there was not going to be any armed resistance. One of them hissed to the guards to take Jesus into custody and several of the guards moved forward and grabbed his arms,

---

[53]See Mk 14:44.

[54]This quote and the ones following for the same scene are from Jn 18:4-8.

pulling them behind his back. James, a burly man, started forward to assist Jesus, asking him, **"Lord, shall we use the sword?"**[55]

Peter did not ask. He reached inside his cloak and drew his sword. With one swift horizontal slashing motion, he swung at the head of the man nearest to him, fully intending to decapitate him.

As it happened, the man was not one of the guards nor even a Jewish official. His name was Malchus, a slave to the high priest, Caiaphas, who had been sent along to observe the arrest and bring back a personal report. Malchus saw Peter's left-handed motion out of the corner of his eye and immediately tried to duck the blow, throwing himself down and to his left. Peter tried to compensate but only managed to catch Malchus' right ear and slice it off. The slave screamed and clutched the bloody wound, rolling on the ground while trying to see if a second blow was aimed his way. Several of the guards, caught by surprise by the attack from men they thought were unarmed, raised their own swords and prepared to strike at Peter, who had turned to confront them and was crouching and swaying, looking for an opening to attack again. The Roman cohort headed by the tribune, consisting of two hundred armed men,[56] also reacted to Peter's attack. For the first time, they unsheathed their swords and lowered their spears, and shouted to the civilians to get out of the way.

In the confusion, the guards holding Jesus released him and he immediately stepped between Peter and the enemy crowd, crying: **"Enough!"**[57] To Peter he said:

> **"Put your sword back in its sheath. Am I not to drink the cup the Father has given me?[58] Those who use the sword are sooner or later destroyed by it. Do you not suppose I can call on my Father to provide at a moment's notice more than twelve legions of angels? But then how would the Scriptures be fulfilled which say it must happen this way?"[59]**

This scolding from the Man for whom Peter had decided to die completely deflated him. He dropped his sword and retreated a few steps. Jesus knelt beside the cowering, moaning Malchus and put his hand on the bloody stump where his

---

[55] Lk 22:49

[56] A full cohort consisted of 600 men. It seems doubtful that the Romans would have sent this many men out to arrest Jesus in the middle of the night, given the nature of the threat he seemed to pose. Because Matthew speaks of a "great crowd" and John mentions the presence of soldiers of a cohort with their tribune, I have arbitrarily picked the number 200 as a plausible element that the tribune might have picked for this particular mission.

[57] Lk 22:51

[58] Jn 18:11

[59] Mt 26:52-54

ear had been. The throbbing pain ceased instantly, replaced by a feeling of warmth that suffused the entire side of Malchus' head and then flowed down his body. Tentatively, Malchus touched the spot where moments before there had been only a soggy mess. It was clean and dry. And there beneath his quivering fingers was his ear, as good as ever. Malchus stared in amazement at Jesus, as much for his kindness as for the miracle he had just performed. He was so stunned by the development and its implications that for nearly an hour all he could do was mumble to anyone who would listen, "He healed me. The carpenter healed me. We're making a mistake. We must let him go. He healed me."

But no one was interested in the mutterings of a slave. Malchus tried to tell Caiaphas what had happened, but the high priest cut him off and thereafter refused to see him. Later, Caiaphas decided Malchus was not a slave he wanted to keep in his household, so he sold him to a wealthy Jew. Malchus became a disciple of Jesus not long after Pentecost.

Jesus stood up and faced the Jewish authorities, who had moved back to the front of the crowd after Jesus had put a halt to the escalating violence. He addressed them harshly:

> **"Am I a criminal that you come out after me armed with swords and clubs? When I was with you day after day in the temple you never raised a hand against me. But this is your hour—the triumph of darkness!"**[60]

At that, the guards grabbed Jesus once again, pulled his arms roughly behind his back, and tied his wrists tightly with cords.

The apostles, prevented from resisting, now let their adrenaline follow the other alternative and fled in all directions into the darkness.

Peter and John stopped after they saw that they were not being pursued. As they halted among a grove of almond trees about 200 yards away, they saw a young man, close to John's age, running toward them without a stitch of clothes on. When he was within a few yards, Peter stepped out in front of him. Before he could ask him who he was and what he was doing there, he recognized him as the son of Tychus, the wealthy, secret follower of Jesus who had provided the Upper Room for them. "What are you doing here? It's Mark, isn't it, son of Tychus?"

"Yes, it's me," gasped Mark, relieved that the burly figure that had suddenly materialized out of the darkness before him was a friend. "I was sleeping in my room when my father awakened me and told me that a large group of soldiers, including many Romans, chief priests, scribes and elders had just passed by our house. He bade me get up immediately and run to warn Jesus. I didn't have time to even put on some appropriate clothing. I simply ran out in my bed clothes. When I arrived at the garden, I realized I was too late. I tried to follow Jesus but some of the soldiers saw me and made a grab for me. I was lucky to escape with my skin, although, as you can see, that is all that I came away with."

---

[60]Lk 22:52-53

Peter said to John, "This boy is about your size. Give him an extra tunic and cloak from your own pack."

"Of course. Come with me, Mark." John led the boy over to where he had been waiting during Jesus' agony and rummaged through a kind of knapsack he had there. Mark, shivering in the night chill now that the body heat generated by his fearful flight had dissipated, quickly donned the tunic and cloak John held out for him.

Peter spoke urgently. "John, you must go and tell Mary and the other women that her son has been taken by the chief priests. I think she had a premonition of this. No, what am I saying? Of course Jesus told her just like he told us. But the women will need to be escorted. Go quickly! The chief priests will take Jesus to the palace of Caiaphas first. In the meantime, Mark and I will go there ourselves and try to find out what is going on. If we cut through the garden, we should be able to catch up to the crowd before they even get across the Kidron."

"Sir," said Mark in response. "I am acquainted with the high priest and his father-in-law, Annas. As you know, our house is quite close to the palace. I am known to his servants, so I believe I can get us inside."

With that, Peter and Mark ran off toward Jerusalem to catch up with Jesus. John ran in the opposite direction toward Bethany to alert Jesus' mother and the other women who traveled with her.

PSALM 88: 2-9

I

O LORD, my God, by day I cry out;
at night I clamor in your presence.
Let my prayer come before you;
incline your ear to my call for help,
For my soul is surfeited with troubles
and my life draws near to the nether world.
I am numbered with those who
go down into the pit;
I am a man without strength.
My couch is among the dead,
like the slain who lie in the grave,
Whom you remember no longer
and who are cut off from your care.
You have plunged me into the bottom of the pit,
into the dark abyss.
Upon me your wrath lies heavy,
and with all your billows you
overwhelm me.
You have taken my friends away from me;
you have made me an abomination to them;
I am imprisoned, and I cannot escape.

QUESTIONS FOR REFLECTION

1) Jesus told the apostles where they would find a donkey for him to ride and what to say if anyone questioned them about taking it. How did he know this?

2) Why do you think that the apostles, especially Peter, could not accept what Jesus told them about his imminent torture and death?

3) Some people deny that there is a hell for lost souls. But, if this is so, how could you explain the sufferings of Jesus? What would be the point of the crucifixion if not to reconcile man and God?

4) The Gospels do not name the angel sent to comfort Jesus in the garden of Gethesemane. What characteristics do you think this angel must have had?

5) Prior to the night of his passion, Jesus had predicted his violent death on several occasions. He said, in fact, that this was why he came into the world, "to give his own life as a ransom for the many."(Mt 20:28; Mk 10:45). Are you surprised, then, that Jesus asked his Father in the garden of Gethsemane to save him from his agony, if possible? Have you had any experiences in which you were brave until the moment of crisis came and then found your courage failing you? What, in your opinion, is the highest form of courage?

6) When do you think that Mary first learned of Jesus' destiny to die by crucifixion? How do you think she reacted? What do you think Mary was doing while Jesus was enduring his agony in the garden? Is it too late for us to share in Jesus' sufferings? If not, how should we do it?

7) Jesus asked Peter, James and John to watch and pray with him but they could not stay awake. Does this experience remind you of your own relationship with Jesus? How might we now "stay awake with Jesus" for an hour or so?

8) Why do you think Jesus bothered to heal Malchus, the slave who lost his ear to Peter's sword? What does Jesus' action say to you about how you should respond when under attack?

9) Why do you think Judas chose a kiss as the sign by which he would identify Jesus to the soldiers? Why not just point to him and say, "There he is!" What similarities do you see between Peter and Judas? What contrasts?

10) In what ways should Jesus' suffering in the garden of Gethsemane be a model for us to follow in our own sufferings? What virtues are represented here? (You should be able to list at least six.)

Upper Agora (Marketplace) and Praetorium of Pontius Pilate[61]

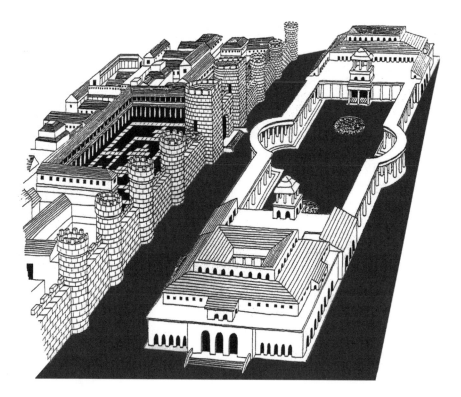

The praetorium of Pontius Pilate would most likely have been the palace of the former ruler, Herod Archelaus. The palace was built by Herod the Great and occupied the highest land in Jerusalem, against the western wall of the city. Note the distinctive pattern of the stone pavement in the marketplace (the Upper Agora) and the archway between the praetorium and the square. This place was also close to the palaces of Caiaphas and Annas and well away from the Temple Mount and Lower City where Jesus' many supporters would have been found.

---

[61]Based upon the Model of Ancient Jerusalem at the Holyland Hotel in Jerusalem, Israel.

Sheep Gate

Fortress
Antonia

Pool of
Bethesda

Damascus
Gate

Gethsemane

Court of
Gentiles

Solomon's Portico

Court of
Women

Via Dolorosa

Jaffa
Gate

Temple of Herod

Ginnoth Gate

Court of
Gentiles

Kidron

(Herod Antipas)

Palace of
Annas

Herod's
Palace

Hasmonean
Palace

"Praetorium"

Upper
Agora

Palace of
Caiaphas

LOWER CITY

JERUSALEM IN
27 - 30 A.D.

Cenacle

Tomb of
David

Gate of
Essenes

Fountain
Gate

[Not to scale]

JERUSALEM WHEN JESUS WAS CRUCIFIED

I gave my back to those who beat me, my cheeks to those who plucked my beard;
My face I did not shield from buffets and spitting. Is 50:6

SECOND SORROWFUL MYSTERY

The Scourging at the Pillar

After tying Jesus' hands behind his back with cords so tight that they bit into his wrists, the soldiers took a long leather leash and tied that around his neck. With this he was pulled roughly forward as the large crowd of soldiers, guards, Jewish authorities and servants made their way back toward the city wall. The predawn darkness was heavy and still. The moon had set and the crowd walked warily along a narrow path that wound through the trees and flowering shrubs. Their torches and lanterns flickered as they hurried, anxious to get their valuable prize safely within the confines of the palace of the high priest. Jesus was expected to keep up. A couple of times he stumbled over objects not seen in the darkness and was dragged a few feet, choking and coughing, before the guards behind him jerked him back to his feet and shoved him along the pathway.

Judas walked with the guards just behind Jesus, who, in turn, was close behind the chief priests. No one paid him any attention now that he had served his purpose. Twice he had tried to protest the rough handling that Jesus was getting but did not get even an acknowledgment that he had spoken. He was beginning to have misgivings about what he had done. The hollowness of Noam's promises became clearer with each step away from the Mount of Olives. And Jesus obviously had not chosen, or been able, to evade capture this time. Judas felt a wave of anxiety pass through him, knotting his stomach and wetting his face with perspiration. Slowly, a terrible truth began to form in his mind. *Jesus is going to let himself be killed! He meant what he said. And I made it happen. I can never face Peter and the other apostles again. Somehow I have to stop this!*

Noam, who was walking with the chief priests and scribes at the head of the procession, beckoned to the Captain of the Temple Guard and whispered something to him. The Captain, in turn, said something to two of his guards. These men told Judas to stay back with them and not to bother the authorities right now. Judas' anxiety grew.

Peter and Mark caught up to the crowd just as the last soldier tramped across the little arched bridge spanning the Kidron. They stayed back far enough to be reasonably hidden in the darkness. Tracking the crowd with its multitude of torches and lanterns was not difficult, especially since their destination was obvious.

The crowd re-entered the city through the Fountain Gate and climbed the steep path up Mount Zion, past the imposing monument marking King David's tomb, toward the palace of Caiaphas. The high priest had put out the call, but not all members of the Sanhedrin, a seventy-one-man group composed of chief priests, scribes (Pharisees) and elders, which constituted the highest judicial body in Israel, had yet arrived. His father-in-law, Annas, had been high priest before Caiaphas, and was a man of considerable influence. It was politic to include him in the decision process dealing with Jesus, and Caiaphas was nothing if not a shrewd politician. He decided to send Jesus on to Annas until the Sanhedrin was fully assembled.

Quintus, the tribune of the Roman cohort, informed Caiaphas that he was taking his men back to the Fortress Antonia inasmuch as Jesus appeared to have no followers who were willing or able to put up any armed resistance.

Pontius Pilate, the Roman governor of Judea, was the latest in a succession of Roman officials who had replaced the Herodian line following Herod Archelaus' disastrous rule more than twenty years before. He occupied Herod's luxurious palace when he was in Jerusalem, especially when his wife, Claudia Procula, accompanied him, as she had this time. By virtue of the procurator's presence, the palace became the praetorium. The palace was large and well-fortified, with its own turreted wall facing the city. There was a large barracks at the north end of the palace where Pilate's soldiers stayed when he was in town. A permanent garrison of Roman soldiers, under the command of Tribune Quintus, occupied the Fortress Antonia at all times.

Pilate's normal headquarters were at Caesarea on the shore of the Mediterranean. He came to Jerusalem reluctantly and as seldom as he had to, but these visits included all of the major Jewish festivals, the time when the likelihood of riots breaking out was the greatest. His wife traveled with him, but without much enthusiasm. Her distaste for the fanatical Jews and their devotion to their God was mollified a bit by the lavish surroundings of Herod's palace with its multiple fountains and lush gardens. It was also about as removed as it could be from the noisy crowds thronging the narrow streets and passageways spread in a tangled web below the wealthy and orderly Upper City. Herod's palace was the highest point within the city, tucked against the western wall and overlooked by three towers Herod the Great had built: the Phaesel, the Hippicus and the Mariamne.

"Tribune Quintus, you know that the palace of my father-in-law, Annas, is not far from the palace where the Procurator is staying. Please take Jesus there on your way. Annas will send him back with some of the temple guards." Quintus nodded to Caiaphas and led Jesus off to the palace of Annas. Once there, the soldiers departed for the Fortress Antonia while Quintus left for the praetorium to report to Pilate.

Meanwhile, Peter and Mark had followed Jesus up to the gateway leading into Caiaphas' palace. There were three arched entrances into the courtyard, each located in the base of three identical buildings standing side by side and forming part of the south wall surrounding the palace. These buildings were the living quarters for the servants, slaves and guards who served the high priest. Each entrance was controlled by a servant who screened visitors. Guards were always nearby in case of trouble. Mark, who lived with his parents in a spacious home just down the street from the palace of Caiaphas, was known to the women who were watching the gates when Jesus was brought in. He received a curious stare but was admitted without question. He was popular with these servants. He had often brought them little treats when he was out and about the city.

Peter started to follow Mark into the courtyard but drew up short before the raised hand of the gate attendant. Her dour stare and crossed arms spoke unmistakably that Peter was not coming inside. Mark, assuming that Peter was right behind him, had hurried on ahead into the courtyard. There he saw the Roman cohort, with Jesus near the front, heading for the main northern gate out of the palace. "Where are they taking the Galilean?" Mark tried to sound casual as he inquired of one of the servants scurrying about.

"Caiaphas is sending him to Annas. But he'll be back soon. The Sanhedrin is gathering for a formal session here in the palace to decide what to do about the blasphemer," replied a servant hurrying past with a jar of water for some unspecified function inside the palace. Mark turned to consult with Peter and realized that Peter was not inside the courtyard. He ran back to the entrance. There was Peter, fuming and protesting that he needed to be inside. Mark spoke to the gatekeeper: "It's all right. I know this man. Let him come in."

The servant girl listened to Mark but seemed dubious. Without moving from the entrance she said to Peter: "**Are you not one of this man's followers?**"[1]

Peter was desperate to get inside so he could monitor what the Jewish authorities would do to Jesus. Without giving it a thought, he said what would accomplish this purpose: "**Not I,**" and brushed past the servant.

Inside, Mark explained the situation to Peter. "Jesus has been taken to see Annas. But his trial will take place here. The Sanhedrin is gathering for that purpose. I know the servants at Annas' palace so I should have no problem getting in there to see what is happening to the Lord. It will be safer if you stay here, now that we have gotten you inside. Jesus will be brought back soon."

Peter was frustrated but he saw the sense in what Mark said, so he nodded his agreement. Mark left him, hurrying off to the palace of Annas.

The night was cold. Peter, who had been perspiring from the pursuit of Jesus and the stress of getting into the palace, now felt the chill. He saw a fire burning in a large circular charcoal brazier located near the middle of the courtyard and went over to it to warm himself. It was already crowded with

---

[1]This quote and Peter's reply are from Jn 18:17.

servants and guards. Peter joined them, trying to act nonchalant but feeling very conspicuous. Mostly he tried to avoid the peculiar acrid smoke which the burning charcoal gave off.

Meanwhile, Jesus had been taken before Annas, a crafty and proud patriarch who had been deposed as high priest some twelve years earlier. Some of the Jews still regarded him as the lawful high priest since appointment to the office was traditionally for life. Caiaphas was careful to remain on Annas' good side. Jesus was brought into a reception room. Many of the guards and servants crowded in behind him, some curious to see up close the man about whom they had heard such amazing things. Mark quietly mingled with them, trying to stay close enough to Jesus to see and hear what was going on.

Annas said to the guards: "Unbind him." One of the guards stepped behind Jesus and, drawing his short sword, sliced through the knotted cords. Then he removed the leash from Jesus' neck. Jesus rubbed his wrists and hands to ease the sharp pain of the blood flow surging into fingers icy and stiff from the retarded circulation. He said nothing, merely looked at Annas and waited.

"Where are your followers, Galilean? They seemed numerous enough on Sunday. You see how fickle these people can be. They will run after anyone who amuses them or gives them hope of getting free bread." Jesus did not reply.

Annas grew annoyed. He was accustomed to having people treat him with great deference, even grovel if they were of low station, like this village carpenter. "I understand you think you can tear down our great Temple and rebuild it in a mere three days. Is it also true that you believe you have the power to forgive sins, that you make yourself equal to God?" Such questioning was actually improper under Jewish legal procedure. Annas knew that Caiaphas was planning to try Jesus before the Sanhedrin, a nighttime trial which was also illegal under Jewish law. An accused was not required to give testimony against himself.

Jesus asserted his privilege against self-incrimination but not directly as a legal maneuver. He deftly reminded Annas of what he already knew—that evidence against Jesus had to come from witnesses who could testify as to what he said.

> "I have spoken publicly to any who would listen.
> I always taught in a synagogue or in the temple area
> where all the Jews come together.
> There was nothing secret about anything I said.
> Why do you question me? Question those who heard me
> when I spoke. It should be obvious that they will know
> what I said."[2]

The fist smashed Jesus on the right side of his face and spun him around. He had spoken evenly and correctly, but his audacity in reminding Annas that he

---

[2]Jn 18:20-21

was violating Jewish law was too much for one of the temple guards. "**Is that the way to answer the high priest?**"[3] he demanded.

Jesus, flushed with anger, felt his lips for bleeding and responded: "**If I said anything wrong produce the evidence, but if I spoke the truth why hit me?**"[4]

Annas studied Jesus. He was impressed in spite of himself. The man obviously knew the law and had been clever enough to assert it without getting tangled up in an assertion that Annas was conducting a trial. They both knew that Jesus' testimony, if he said anything incriminating, would be brought to the trial before the Sanhedrin, and therefore it was illegal to question Jesus that way. But this was not the trial itself. Jesus had been neither intimidated nor lulled into speaking against himself. Annas could see that further interrogation would be fruitless. He rose and said: "Take him back to Caiaphas."

Once again Jesus was bound tightly, this time not only his wrists but also his arms were wrapped tightly against his body. This made it more difficult for Jesus to walk without tripping. The leather leash was replaced on his neck and the temple guards took their places fore and aft. The one who had struck Jesus gave a yank on the leash and he lurched forward through the hostile crowd, out onto the cobbled street. Mark and a few other bystanders followed.

Back at the courtyard of Caiaphas, Peter sat impatiently, wondering what was happening to Jesus and Mark. The servant girl at the gate had been watching him. She beckoned to one of the other servant girls and the two of them spoke together in low tones. The gatekeeper pointed in the direction of Peter. Just then, a commotion arose as the party bringing Jesus from Annas' palace passed through the north gate and into the interior of Caiaphas' palace. Several of the guards and servants sitting with Peter jumped up and ran off in different directions. Peter, too, rose and strained to see whether Jesus had been returned and where Mark might be. Neither appeared to him and he sat back down, leaning forward dejectedly. Across the fire from him, the servant girl who had been summoned by the gatekeeper watched him carefully for awhile then slowly moved around the fire toward him.

"**You too were with Jesus the Galilean,**[5]" she said, pointing her finger accusingly at Peter. All the others turned to look at him.

Peter jumped to his feet and replied hotly, "**I do not know what you are talking about! What are you getting at?**"[6] Peter was angry and scared at the same time. He stalked off in a huff toward the main gate where Jesus had been brought

---

[3]Jn 18:22

[4]Jn 18:23

[5]Mt 26:69

[6]Mk 14:68

in from Annas. He was determined to remain close enough to monitor what was happening to Jesus.

Inside the palace in the great hall, the Sanhedrin was convened to hear the case against Jesus. The seventy men occupied chairs assembled on three rows in a horseshoe shape with the high priest Caiaphas presiding from a raised platform in the center facing the open end of the horseshoe. Jesus stood in a marked area between the extended arms of the assemblage. Witnesses were brought in and seated in an elevated chair situated on the floor to the right of the high priest, facing the person on trial. They took the seat nervously, licking their lips and fidgeting, anxious to remember what they had been primed by the chief priests to say. Some were anxious to testify and needed little prompting. Others spoke for a promised reward, or to avoid a threatened reprisal, and tended to blurt out what they thought the authorities wanted to hear.

It was a circus. Some claimed that Jesus called himself the Son of God. Others argued that he had not said that but had called himself the Son of Man. Still others disputed that, saying that Jesus offered to make everyone sons of God. A few reported that Jesus broke the Sabbath laws. But they could not agree on the details of the transgressions and even some of the scribes pointed out that some of the alleged violations were permitted under exigent circumstances. They argued over whether Jesus had forgiven sins, or merely said that he had the power if he wanted to, or was only assuring people that sins were forgiven by God. Even their ace in the hole, Jesus' alleged threat against the Temple, flopped when the witnesses quarreled over whether Jesus said he would tear down the building himself, or rebuild it by himself, or rebuild it in some unspecified way within three days' time.

The conflicts, confusion and contradictions were ably brought out by two of the members of the Sanhedrin, Nicodemus and Joseph of Arimathea, assisted by a few others who were not willing to sacrifice their integrity to secure a conviction. As it was, there were objections from some of these persons about holding a trial at night at all, since that was clearly forbidden under Jewish law. However, the chief priests explained it was made necessary because of the threat of mob violence from Jesus' followers and promised that any verdict would not be formally rendered until daybreak.

Caiaphas could not believe his ears. Their carefully crafted case against Jesus was in shambles. Unless he could get a condemnation from the Sanhedrin, there was no possibility of getting Pontius Pilate to crucify Jesus. And if they failed tonight, they might never get another chance. Caiaphas glared at Jesus, who stood calmly, staring back at the high priest, both knowing that the trial had failed. Caiaphas was desperate. He resorted to a tactic no good trial lawyer would ever use: he asked Jesus an open-ended question. Rising to his feet, he pointed his finger at Jesus and blustered as if the witnesses had been truthful and effective: **"Have you no answer to the testimony leveled against you?"[7]**

How easy it would have been for Jesus to defend himself, to point out the hopeless contradictions in the witness testimony, to demand that he be released because no case had been made. What an opening to remind Caiaphas and the whole court that Jewish law protected an accused from self-incrimination and that he had no obligation whatsoever to speak. But he remained silent. Caiaphas had one last card to play, a hopeless, futile card doomed to failure if Jesus simply remained quiet.

"I order you to tell us under oath before the living God whether you are the Messiah, the Son of God,"[8] thundered the high priest.

The question reverberated throughout the hall and down the corridors of time. For long seconds, Jesus said nothing. The silence was deafening and Caiaphas knew he had been defeated. For a brief moment, in his rage, he considered ordering the guards to seize Jesus and take him outside and stone him. But the temptation passed quickly. He knew that such an act would rouse the populace to a general uprising that he and his government would not survive.

Then a miracle happened. Jesus answered the question. **"I am; and you will see the Son of Man seated at the right hand of the Power and coming with the clouds of heaven."[9]**

Caiaphas did not hesitate. He ripped his tunic open from its neckline to his waist, signaling that blasphemy had been committed in his presence. **"What further need do we have of witnesses? You have heard the blasphemy. What is your verdict?"[10]**

Pandemonium erupted among the staid members of the Sanhedrin. Most of them leaped to their feet and with wild eyes and shaking fingers pronounced, **"He deserves death!"[11]** Several cried out to Caiaphas, "Stone him now! He has blasphemed the God of Israel! He is an abomination before the LORD! Crush him!"

But Caiaphas merely raised his hand and held it up until the room fell quiet. "Friends, this imposter clearly deserves to die at once. But stoning is too merciful for one who makes such claims and turns the descendants of Moses and Abraham against those appointed to watch over the House of Israel. Further, he has many followers who may try to avenge his death and stir up discontent among the people. We must let the Romans be the instrument of the LORD's justice. Then

---

[7]Mt 26:62

[8]Mt 26:63

[9]Mk 14:62

[10]Mk 14:63-64

[11]Mt 26:66

the blasphemer's followers can deal with them, if they can. If they succeed in bleeding the Romans a bit, so much the better."

Joseph of Arimathea and Nicodemus sat in shocked silence. They were stunned that Jesus had convicted himself when he was so close to freedom. But on a deeper level, they felt a terror for themselves and all Israel that Jesus had spoken the truth, not blasphemy, and now God's chosen people were about to commit an incomprehensible sin. They would kill their own promised Messiah. God had tested their founding father, Abraham, but had stopped him from killing his son, Isaac. Now he tested the whole nation with His own Son. Would He stop them again? As the two secret admirers of Jesus watched the members of the Sanhedrin walk up to Jesus and curse him, slap him, shove him, and spit on him, they knew their answer. They fled the room.

Then the guards got into the act. One of them found a soiled handkerchief which they used to blindfold Jesus. Laughing uproariously, they spun him around and punched him in the face and in the back of his head, knocking him to the floor. **"Play the prophet for us, Messiah! Who struck you?"**[12] they taunted. Blood flowed from Jesus' mouth and nose and matted his beard before dripping from his chin. He struggled to maintain his balance as the unseen hands propelled him back and forth, but he made no sound.

After about fifteen minutes, Caiaphas tired of the spectacle and told his Captain of the Guard to take Jesus to the private dungeon that Caiaphas maintained beneath the guards' quarters. The high priest needed to consult with the Sanhedrin to prepare the formal document summarizing the charges against Jesus. They would take this to Pilate. It could not be adopted, however, until daybreak.

Outside, dawn was approaching. Shouts and cries had been heard from inside the palace but they were muffled. The servants of Caiaphas had not forgotten Peter. They approached him again in a group. One of them was a relative of Malchus and had been with him in the garden of Gethsemane. **"But did I not see you with him in the garden?** You look like the man who struck my cousin, Malchus, with a sword!" Another chimed in: **"This man was certainly with him, for he is a Galilean."** Yet another agreed: **"You are certainly one of them. Even your accent gives you away!"**[13]

Peter was furious. *Why won't these fools leave me alone?* he steamed. He reacted like a cornered animal, cursing and swearing, shouting: **"I do not even know the man!"**[14]

At that moment, the palace guards entered the courtyard with Jesus, shoving him roughly ahead of them. Nearby, a cock crowed. Jesus staggered but

---

[12]Mt 26:68

[13]The three quotes are from, respectively: Jn 18:26, Lk 22:59 and Mt 26:73.

[14]Mt 26:74

caught himself and turned around. He looked at Peter with a look of profound sadness but also love and encouragement, and perhaps just a hint of "I told you so." In that glance, Peter dissolved. His denials of his Lord hammered in his memory and his own inadequacy and foolishness crushed his proud, brave spirit. In that moment of supreme humiliation, when bitter tears burst forth from the big man with the wild hair, Peter the Saint was born. Now he ran, blinded by his weeping, overcome by confusion and failure. He abandoned his Master to his fate.

Jesus was lowered into a dark, musty dungeon by a rope wrapped around his arms pressed against his torso. His wrists remained tied behind his back. A few feet from the bottom, the rope was released and Jesus fell in a heap against the rough, stone floor. The guards laughed, holding their torches over the black cavity to see what condition Jesus was in. He lay on the floor, bruised and with facial abrasions, but otherwise unhurt. When he looked up, he saw half a dozen stairs carved into the limestone wall at the top, ending about twelve feet from the bottom. From there the dungeon walls were a sheer drop to the floor. The guards spit at him and disappeared into the night. Jesus was left in total darkness. He prayed for his captors.

About an hour later, torches reappeared at the top of the cell. A wooden ladder was shoved down the stairs and allowed to fall to the floor. Jesus was barely able to scramble out of the way as it thudded heavily against the stone. The ladder reached past the lowest two steps of the truncated stairway and in a moment two muscular guards were climbing down it. When they reached the bottom, one of them put the leather leash back on Jesus' neck and led him to the base of the ladder. The first guard started up the ladder, pulling on the leash. The other guard placed his hand on the small of the Lord's back and followed him up the ladder. Only the guard's hand kept him from falling backward because his own arms were still bound with his hands behind him. The guards found great sport in joking about letting him fall and hanging him from the leash. They didn't know that angels would have borne Jesus up, if necessary. He had chosen a far worse fate for himself than death by hanging.

A delegation of chief priests, scribes and elders, headed by Caiaphas, was formed to take Jesus to the procurator, Pontius Pilate. The rest of the chief priests and a few of the scribes hurried off to the Temple. It was the preparation day for Passover[15] and their duties this day were numerous and important.

---

[15] One of the enduring Passion Narrative mysteries is on what day Passover occurred vis à vis the crucifixion. The Synoptic Gospels seem to have Passover on the day of the crucifixion, since they refer to the Last Supper as a Passover meal. Remember, the Jewish day began at sundown, not midnight as modern man measures time. But John clearly identifies the day of crucifixion as the *preparation day* for Passover, the day when the thousands upon thousands of lambs would be sacrificed in the Temple beginning at noon. Given the level of activity by Jews in Jerusalem, not to mention Simon of Cyrene coming in from the fields, the day of Jesus' crucifixion was almost certainly not Passover (15th day of Nisan) itself. There have been numerous theories advanced to try to reconcile the Synoptics and John, but none has been entirely satisfactory. For a thorough discussion of the issue, see Raymond Brown, S.S., *The Death of the Messiah* (New York: Doubleday, 1994), 1353-1373.

The whole Sanhedrin, minus Joseph of Arimathea and Nicodemus, had adopted a formal resolution of condemnation as soon as the silver trumpet sounded from the Temple Mount signaling that the first rays of the sun had been sighted over the Mountains of Moab to the east. Another hour was spent preparing a list of charges that would translate Jesus' alleged religious crimes into offenses against Rome. These included charges that Jesus had been subverting the Jewish nation, opposing the payment of taxes to Caesar, and calling himself the king of the Jews. For good measure, they threw in an accusation that he had threatened to destroy the Temple and all surrounding buildings, including the Fortress Antonia; that he encouraged his followers to reject Roman rule; and that he openly opposed military service. There were other charges as well, even more frivolous, the products of Pharisaic hair-splitting and deliberate distortion.

In addition to the chief priests not needed at the Temple, plus most of the scribes, elders, and guards, Caiaphas included in the group to go to Pilate all of his servants and slaves and anyone else whom he considered loyal to the decisions of the Sanhedrin. He wanted to impress Pilate as much as he could with the size of the opposition to Jesus. Pilate would certainly already be aware of the great multitude of people who swarmed around Jesus only a few days earlier when he made his triumphal entry into Jerusalem. Pilate was probably also knowledgeable of the acrimonious verbal exchanges between Jesus and the authorities on Monday and Tuesday. No, he would be no easy mark when it came to Jesus. In fact, he would probably squirm and wiggle and do everything possible to keep from having to deal with him.

Caiaphas understood this perfectly. He shared exactly the same feelings. He wanted the Romans to be responsible for Jesus' death as much as they would want nothing to do with it. First, the execution would be far more cruel and Caiaphas hated the man who had made him and the other Jewish leaders look so foolish so often. Second, if there was any popular revulsion over the execution, better that it be directed to the Romans, who were already resented, than to the Jerusalem Temple authorities. Third, if Jesus were executed as a criminal, he would, according to Mosaic law, be accursed of God. That would make it more difficult, even impossible, for any of his rabble followers to claim later that he had been the Messiah. Caiaphas was determined that Pilate would do his bidding in this matter. And he would stack the deck every way possible to ensure it.

Jesus was brought out, unbound except for his wrists because Caiaphas planned to move quickly through the streets and he did not want Jesus falling down and slowing them up. By now, Jesus' face was swollen over his cheekbones and his right eye was puffy and beginning to discolor. He was very thirsty after the extreme loss of fluids earlier in the night and from the stress and mistreatment since his arrest. He had asked for water but the guards just laughed at him and drank lavishly in front of him, letting ladles of water splash over their chins and onto the ground as Jesus watched. Dried blood was crusted in his beard and his tunic was streaked with blood stains and dirt. He looked like anything but the Anointed One of God.

The party assembled on the north side of Caiaphas' palace, opposite the courtyard where Peter had waited. Judas had been lingering there since Jesus had been brought in. When the Sanhedrin emerged, the word quickly spread that Jesus had been condemned and was to be taken to Pilate for crucifixion.

Judas grabbed one of the servants and demanded: "What happened? Didn't Jesus show the Sanhedrin his power? Don't they understand we need him against the Romans?"

The servant yanked Judas' hand off his shoulder and said: "The blasphemer was convicted out of his own mouth. As for his power, the only power I saw was a guard's fist on his lying face! If he wants to do something against the Romans, he's about to get his chance because that's where the high priest is taking him to be crucified." The servant hurried off after the crowd which had begun to move through the gate.

Judas was stunned and horrified. He had tried to get into the trial before the Sanhedrin but had been rebuffed. He even thought he might be called to testify. He had sent a message into Noam, reminding him of their agreement in the Temple, but Noam had not bothered even to reply. The door remained locked to Judas. The Captain of the Guard, who had been curt the night before, was now openly contemptuous and warned Judas to be gone before the high priest returned. Slowly, the full magnitude of his crime began to dawn on Judas. His mouth opened and closed. Saliva dribbled down his chin as he looked around wildly, desperately seeking some miracle to undo what he had done. He protested to the guards, servants and slaves streaming past him that it was all a mistake, that Jesus was innocent, that they had to stop the execution.

"Get away, scum!" growled one guard who shoved Judas away so hard that he sprawled face down on the rough stones of the courtyard.

Judas lay there in the dirt, sick with fear and self-loathing, until the entire group bound for Pilate's praetorium had passed him. Then he jumped up, forgetting even to brush himself off, and rushed off toward the street which led onto the aqueduct entrance to the Temple. He would give the money back to the chief priests. He knew that many of them would be back in the Temple on this important festival day. *Once I return the silver coins, they will have to release Jesus. That was the bargain. I will explain it was all a mistake, that I was wrong to do what I did. Yahweh will soften their hearts for me.* Judas was like a wild man, crashing through the crowds on the narrow, people-jammed streets, shouting to clear his way, shouting that he had to save the Messiah.

He burst onto the Court of the Gentiles, ran panting past the *Soreg*, beyond which no Gentile could venture without forfeiting his life, and onto the rampart surrounding the Temple precincts. He dashed through the Court of the Women and up the fifteen stairs leading to the Nicanor Gate, careening headlong through the narrow Court of the Israelites and into the Court of the Priests. More than twenty priests and several chief priests moved to intercept him for he was now on turf where he was forbidden to walk.

"**I did wrong to deliver up an innocent man!**"[16] screamed Judas. "Take your money back. Release Jesus. You must not kill him. I was wrong! I was wrong! I was wrong!" Judas held the purse with the coins at arms length in front of him, shaking so hard he could hear them jangling. He offered the money frantically first to one priest, then to another. No one would approach him.

One of the chief priests retorted: "**What is that to us? It is your affair!**"[17] The other priests moved forward then to take hold of Judas, but he evaded their grasp and ran toward the entrance to the Temple. Pausing before the open door he poured the coins from the purse into his trembling hand and threw them inside with all of his strength.

He fled back the way he had come. Judas ran blindly, pursued by demons only he could see. His breath came in hot gasps, white spittle mottling his face and cloak as he shoved through clusters of people who yelled and cursed him in return. He fled through the city and out the Jaffa Gate, turning left then toward the Hinnom Valley which ran beneath the city on the southern side. He seethed with hatred, at first only toward the chief priests, scribes and elders, especially Noam and Caiaphas; then toward Jesus who had "tricked him," he decided, into going through with his betrayal; then toward the apostles whom he now saw as disgusting and weak; then toward God whom he saw as a conspirator in his own shame and failure. Last and most ferociously, he hated and cursed himself, despising his stupidity, but vowing that he would be the master of his own destiny, that *he* would decide his fate, not the God who laughed at Israel and sent a poor wretched creature like Jesus to tease people with false hope.

As Judas descended the steep hill toward Gehenna, the place of refuse and near the refuge of lepers, he found a fig tree, clinging precariously to the side of the hill, leaning out over a slope that plunged precipitously over one hundred feet below. He climbed quickly up the tree, took out his now empty coin purse, tied one end of the leather strings around his neck and the other end around the branch, and leaped into oblivion.

* * * * * * *

All that day, the corpse swayed gently in the wind that blew up from the valley toward the city wall. Judas' body went unnoticed even as the Man he had betrayed hung from another "tree" only a few hundred yards away. Evening came and the Sabbath arrived. Jerusalem became relatively still. The night passed quietly—a long one of shocked disbelief for Jesus' followers, a festive celebration for his enemies. Judas' body passed through rigor mortis and then began to swell with the natural chemical action of decomposition. Late in the afternoon as the Passover/Sabbath neared its end, the swaying action of the body succeeded in

---

[16]Mt 27:4

[17]Ibid.

untying the purse string from the branch and Judas' body plunged to the earth far below, the corrupting flesh bursting open upon impact.

* * * * * * *

After Tribune Quintus left Jesus with Annas and sent his soldiers back to the Fortress Antonia, he went to report to Pontius Pilate at the palace. Pilate had brought his own cohort of soldiers with him from Caesarea and they remained on the palace grounds with him. Quintus, the resident tribune for Jerusalem, had been sent with the fortress soldiers to participate in the arrest of Jesus. Quintus spoke Aramaic and was well respected as a soldier skilled in occupational duty.

Pilate was asleep and had left orders not to disturb him unless there was a threat to the security of the city. So Quintus made a cursory report to the centurion on duty that Jesus had been captured without incident and turned over to the Jews for trial. Then he left for his own quarters at the Antonia.

At about 6:30 a.m., Caiaphas led a large party of priests, scribes, elders, temple guards, and their servants and slaves up the street from his palace. They gathered in the *Upper Agora*, or Upper Market, a large open square surrounded on three sides by a colonnaded portico containing shops. The square itself was paved with stones in a distinctive tile pattern, which led to its being named the *Lithostrotos*, or "Stone Pavement." It was also called the *Gabbatha*, or "Hill Square," in Hebrew and was a popular meeting place, especially for the wealthier residents of Jerusalem. The open end of the square adjoined a street that ran directly in front of the wall protecting Herod's palace, now Pilate's praetorium. An arched opening in the wall was reached by mounting eight steps on either side. On the square side, a raised platform extended to the right of the steps as one stood in the archway. This platform was used to address crowds gathered in the open square and, as appropriate, to pronounce verdicts and sentences for criminals.

Already waiting in the square was a significant contingent from Bethany, including Mary, the mother of Jesus; John, who had brought her here to the square where they knew Jesus would be delivered by the chief priests; Mary, wife of Clopas and sister-in-law of Jesus' mother; Salome, mother of James and John; Mary Magdalene, whose devotion to Jesus was exceeded only by his mother's; and several other women. Most of the male disciples of Jesus stayed away, afraid of being arrested in a general roundup of Jesus' followers. Mark went home after Jesus was taken to Pilate. His parents, seeing his fatigue and fearing for his safety, kept him there. Peter and all the apostles except John stayed away, too.

Caiaphas took his entourage, including Jesus, up to the arched doorway in the turreted wall and demanded to see the Procurator on what he declared to be an "urgent matter of state involving a man who is a threat to the peace and security of Palestine. Tell the Procurator," Caiaphas said to the Roman guard as if he were something a little less than human, "that we cannot enter his praetorium because it will cause us to become ritually impure according to our law. This would be intolerable during the Feast of Passover."

This supercilious attitude by the Jews, especially the religious leaders, was a constant irritant to the Romans and other Gentiles in Palestine. Their claim of preference as God's "chosen people" came wrapped in an all-encompassing religious obsession for worshiping a God who seemed to be fixated on the most minute details of ritual and behavior. Jewish certainty of their moral and spiritual superiority in the face of their obvious temporal subjugation seemed irrational to the Italians and Syrians who made up the bulk of the legions in this part of the empire.[18]

Another source of resentment was that Tiberias had exempted the Jews from service in the Roman army because of their insistence on adhering to their Sabbath rules. The periodic rebel attacks by the Zealots and others merely provided a rationale to the soldiers to do what they already wanted to do: seriously harm any Jew who crossed their path. Jesus, who came to welcome all people to his Father's kingdom, and who entertained no such thoughts of exclusiveness, would suffer terribly for this hostility.

It was about a half hour before Pilate came out in his full military uniform. He had received Quintus' report from the centurion on duty. He already knew that the Jewish authorities were anxious to dispose of Jesus because he was challenging their authority as religious leaders of the people. Pilate hated these internal religious squabbles and wanted as little to do with them as possible. He was in a seriously bad mood as he mounted the steps beneath the arch in the wall that separated the praetorium from the square where the Jews waited.

"Yes, what is it?" Pilate asked irritably.

Jesus was pushed forward to the base of the steps on the square side. He stood there with a dignity and calmness entirely belied by his wretched appearance. His clothing was soiled and stained. His beard was matted with dried blood from the blows he had received in the night. His right eye was black and blue and swollen nearly shut. Pilate looked at him but felt no pity.

"**What accusation do you bring against this man?**"[19] he demanded.

Caiaphas could not resist showing off his authority before the members of the Sanhedrin who stood closely behind him. "**If he were not a criminal, we would certainly not have handed him over to you,**"[20] he retorted.

Pilate glared at him. "Rome has no interest in this man. **Why do you not take him and pass judgment on him according to your law?**"[21]

---

[18]Although there was no nation of Italy in those times, the geographic peninsula bore that name even then. See Acts 18:2.

[19]Jn 18:29

[20]Jn 18:30

[21]This quote and the next one are from Jn 18:31.

"**We may not put anyone to death,**" replied Caiaphas, emphasizing the word "death" to indicate the seriousness of the as-yet unspecified charges against Jesus. "**We found this man subverting our nation, opposing the payment of taxes to Caesar, and calling himself the Messiah, a king.**[22] These are not all of the things he has done to threaten the peace and stability of our people. The charges against him are contained in this list." Caiaphas handed Pilate a rolled-up scroll, sealed with wax.

Pilate took the scroll and glanced over it. He opened his mouth to tell the Jews that he saw no reason to hear anything further in the matter of Jesus but then looked again at the list of charges. He also noted the large size of the crowd watching him. He muttered a curse and, pivoting briskly, walked back into the praetorium, commanding one of the guards as he did so: "Bring him to the south reception hall."

Pilate strode through the soldiers' training ground, past the graceful curved colonnades of the garden entrance and into the cavernous south reception area. He sat down and waited for the guards and Jesus to catch up to him.

Pilate read over once again the list of charges against Jesus. He knew Quintus had an extensive network of informants and agents who provided an early warning system for individuals who constituted a threat to Roman rule. There had been nothing to implicate Jesus, and Pilate considered the charges of subverting the nation and opposing the payment of taxes to be purely bogus. He quickly dismissed most of the other charges as well. Only one troubled him. The crowds on Sunday had proclaimed the man to be their Messiah, sent from God. This was apparently some kind of "king" figure for them. And even though the man obviously did not perceive himself as a king in the traditional sense of armies, power and political rule, the title alone would be unacceptable to Caesar. He looked at Jesus standing quietly before him. *This is about the most pathetic-looking "king" which I have ever seen*, Pilate mused. *If he denies he is a king, I am not going to execute him. Let the Jews and their petty jealousies decide what to do with him.*

"**Are you the king of the Jews?**"[23] Pilate asked.

Jesus' reply was elliptical. "**You are the one who is saying it.**"[24]

Pilate was annoyed by the response. "I'm not saying anything. I'm asking *you* to tell *me*. And what about all these other charges? You are accused of subversion, opposing the payment of taxes, threatening the destruction of public property and a pretty long list of other serious offenses." Pilate held out the scroll for Jesus to examine. Jesus did not even look down, simply stared straight ahead, saying nothing.

---

[22]Lk 23:2

[23]Mt 27:11, Mk 15:2, Lk 23:3, Jn 18:33. All four of the Gospel authors have Pilate presenting this question to Jesus in exactly the same words.

[24]Mk 15:2

for Jesus to examine. Jesus did not even look down, simply stared straight ahead, saying nothing.

Pilate grunted. **"Surely you have some answer? See how many accusations they are leveling against you."**[25]

Still Jesus said nothing, seemingly indifferent to the charges. Pilate was taken aback. Every prisoner he had ever seen fell into one of two categories: either they trembled, denied and begged or bargained; or they spat out their defiance. But this one . . . he unnerved Pilate a little. Pilate looked down at the charges again, saying to himself: _Well, these other accusations are pretty ridiculous. I know for a fact that the man told people to pay what is due to Caesar. There's just the problem of the people calling him a king._ Pilate returned to that issue.

"Are you the king of the Jews?"[26] he asked again.

Jesus looked at Pilate questioningly. **"Are you saying this on your own, or have others been telling you about me?"** It was almost as if Jesus, for a moment, wondered if perhaps Pilate had received an inspiration from the Holy Spirit, that deep inside his selfish heart there might have been a tiny flicker of flame for the truth. Any such hope was soon dashed.

"I am no Jew!" Pilate retorted. **"It is your own people and the chief priests who have handed you over to me. What have you done?"**

Jesus tried explaining:

> **"My kingdom does not belong to this world.**
> **If my kingdom were of this world,**
> **my subjects would be fighting**
> **to save me from being handed over to the Jews.**
> **As it is, my kingdom is not here."**

"So, then, you are a king?"[27] asked Pilate, trying to put Jesus' remarks into the only context that he understood . . . and the one that would enable him to quickly dispose of the matter.

But Jesus was not going to give up on Pilate yet. He tried another tack:

> **"It is you who say I am a king.**
> **The reason I was born,**
> **the reason why I came into the world,**
> **is to testify to the truth.**
> **Anyone committed to the truth hears my voice."**

---

[25]Mk 15:4

[26]This quote and the ones following through Pilate's question about truth are from Jn 18:33-38.

[27]Jesus came to earth to call people away from titles and privilege and toward service and love. He was not about to now assert a claim to be a king, even though it was so true as to be beyond Pilate's comprehension, because to do so would have sent the wrong message to his infant Church. Jesus' model for his followers was washing feet. Those who loved him would understand that in the kingdom of God this level of humility and service was the pathway to greatness.

Pilate snorted. "**Truth! What does that mean?**"

Jesus looked at him with sorrow, sad as he always was when he encountered a soul closed to his invitation, and said nothing.

Pilate pushed his chair back and stood up. He was frustrated and impatient. *Whatever this man is, he's no threat to Caesar. The Jews want him dead because he is a threat to them. Well, I'm not going to do their dirty work for them.* He signaled to his guards to bring Jesus along and went back out to speak to the high priest and his cronies.

"**I do not find a case against this man,**"[28] Pilate announced, hoping the Jews would give up and take Jesus away. But the crowd groaned in protest. It had been growing in size as the chief priests recruited more persons from the ranks of the temple money changers and animal sellers with their family and friends to fill the square.

Caiaphas let the murmurs and shouts go on for a few moments, then held up his hand for quiet. "**He stirs up the people by his teaching throughout the whole of Judea, from Galilee, where he began, to this very place.**"[29]

Galilee! said Pilate to himself. Here was a possible way out. Herod Antipas, who was staying in the Hasmonean palace for the festival, was the tetrarch of Galilee and Perea. Let him deal with the problem. "Is this man a Galilean?"

Caiaphas responded, "Yes," wondering where Pilate was going with this.

"Then take him to see Herod. He's responsible for his own subjects," said Pilate.

The chief priests blinked at this astonishing statement because not long before this Pilate had executed several Galileans without consulting Herod at all. In fact, Herod had been deeply offended by the action, not because he cared about the men who were killed for alleged crimes against Rome, but because his own public image was diminished. He had nursed a grudge against Pilate ever since. Pilate, in seeking to avoid responsibility for dealing with Jesus, would inadvertently heal the breach by appearing to recognize Herod's authority in a very high profile case.

Pilate turned as though he had uttered his final word on the subject and went back inside the praetorium. The Roman guards shoved Jesus toward the Jews and returned to their posts.

It was the equivalent of a door slammed in their faces, so the chief priests, scribes and elders huddled with Caiaphas. Since there was nothing else to do, they sent a runner ahead to tell Herod they were bringing Jesus of Nazareth, an enemy of Israel, to him for his examination. Then they led Jesus off toward the Hasmonean palace, which was located between the palace of Annas and the Temple Mount, next to the three-tier Greek theatre built by Herod the Great.

---

[28]Lk 23:4

[29]Lk 23:5

Herod Antipas was delighted on all counts. First, he took Pilate's action as a public admission that he had been wrong before to deal with Galileans without consulting him. Second, he had been extremely curious to see Jesus in person. There had been rumors that Jesus was John the Baptist, raised from the dead. Herod did not believe this; his spies told him that Jesus did not even look like John the Baptist. But there was still a tiny kernel of doubt. Mostly, he hoped to see Jesus work one of his amazing miracles. He had heard about the raising of Lazarus from the dead and Herod briefly considered killing one of his slaves to see if Jesus would resurrect him. But he thought better of it and instead told his servants to round up a couple of blind and crippled persons. Someone reminded him of the report that Jesus had turned water to wine at Cana and this was immediately seized upon as the perfect miracle for Jesus to replicate. Herod clapped his hands in excited anticipation of Jesus' arrival.

Jesus was ushered into the king's ornately furnished reception hall. Herod sat on a thickly-upholstered chair on a raised platform at the far end. Intricately-woven tapestries hung on the walls and thick carpets covered the floor to a distance of about thirty feet in front of Herod's throne. Jesus was brought up to the edge of the carpet and halted. Herod, smiling broadly, came down the three steps from where he sat and approached him. He was already relieved to see that, indeed, Jesus was not John the Baptist come back to haunt him.

The chief priests and scribes stood on either side of Jesus and vehemently denounced him as a blasphemer and threat to the security of Israel. All the charges presented to Pilate were repeated and many additional ones relating to his alleged religious crimes were shouted out. Herod glared at them and held up his hand for silence.

"Rabbi, we have heard many favorable things about you. But you hear how you are accused of crimes which merit death. What reply do you make to these charges?"

Jesus said nothing. He did not even look at Herod.

"You claim to be the Messiah, the Son of God, do you not? You call yourself the 'Son of Man,' I believe. Such claims are permitted only to he who is truly sent from God. We will free you if you prove to us that you are the Messiah. Work a miracle for us. You see these poor unfortunates on the floor over here." (Herod indicated the blind and crippled beggars he had brought into the hall for this purpose). "Or, if you prefer, I have also ordered these ten jars to be filled with water. I understand you have the power to convert the water into wine. If you are truly from God, show us your power." Herod smiled encouragingly. He was excited at the possibility of seeing a miracle performed right in his own court, at his own command. In the corner of his mind an idea played that he could use this Jesus to make himself very, very important. He gestured again toward the beggars and the jars.

Jesus just stared straight ahead. He made no reply. He did not move. Herod waited patiently for a few minutes, then his face began to darken with anger. The chief priests and scribes saw this and once again began to denounce

Jesus as a charlatan and deceiver of the people. Herod's expression grew grim. He seemed to notice for the first time that Jesus was disheveled, dirty and disfigured. He reddened with embarrassment as the thought occurred to him that he was demeaning his royal personage by placing himself on the same level as this commoner. He walked back up his stairs. But his curiosity got the better of his judgment.

"Many charges have been brought against you, carpenter. How do you answer them? How do you come by your learning? Where are your followers now? Is it true that you have threatened to destroy God's Temple? Would His Messiah do such a terrible thing? Are you here to lead our people against the Romans? Where is your army? Why do you criticize the priests, the servants of God?" Herod's questions went on and on, covering every charge and every rumor he had heard about Jesus since his ministry began nearly three years ago. Through it all, Jesus remained silent, staring straight ahead.

At last, Herod lost all patience and cursed Jesus. He came down from his throne and, walking up to Jesus, spat directly into his face. Jesus did not flinch although a careful observer would have noticed his jaw muscles tighten. "You are a king, all right--the king of dung heaps! Let us pay you homage, O lord of dogs and jackals." Herod spit on Jesus again and the phlegm ran down his cheek. He turned to his guards: "Show our 'king' here how we honor men of his high station."

One of the guards stepped up behind Jesus then and gave him a tremendous kick on his buttocks. It sent Jesus sprawling forward onto Herod's plush carpeting. The room erupted in laughter. Another guard grabbed him by the hair and pulled him away from the carpeting, saying, "Your majesty, please don't crawl on the royal rugs. You'll find the stone more suitable for your exalted Swineship." The guards formed a circle around Jesus and continued to insult him. When he tried to stand up, he was kicked or shoved back down. "Inspect your kingdom, O Lord of dung beetles and rat droppings!"

One of Herod's many courtiers walked up to Jesus and poured his cup of wine on him, saying "Great miracle worker, if you will not change water into wine, perhaps you can change wine into water and bathe yourself!" This greatly amused the crowd surrounding Jesus, who themselves flung insults at him, their faces twisted with hatred.

Not all those in attendance in Herod's court joined in the cruel sport of humiliating Jesus. Herod's steward, Chuza, had long been a secret admirer of the Galilean, and his wife, Joanna, was one of his followers and financial supporters. There were several others as well who were horrified by the mistreatment of the Lord. But they were powerless to intervene and so turned their faces away from the sad spectacle.

It was Herod himself who had the most inspired idea for mocking Jesus and also cementing what he perceived was a blossoming new friendship with Pilate. He sent a servant to bring one of his best robes, made from soft Kashmir goat wool dyed a deep purple and richly embroidered in gold-embossed brocade, hemmed with blue silk and golden tassels. He ordered the guards to bring Jesus forward. "Clean him up a bit," Herod ordered. The guards did as they were told, none too gently, cleaning the dripping wine from Jesus' face and hair and drying him off. Then Herod took the robe and wrapped it around Jesus. "Take our 'king' here back to the Procurator and tell him that we leave him to Roman justice. If he finds that this royal buffoon does not need his robe, he shall consider it my gift to him." Herod ordered his court musicians to play some processional music and laughed uproariously as the delegation of chief priests, scribes and elders led Jesus away in the beautiful royal robe.

Outside, Mary, John and several other women waited anxiously for Jesus to emerge from Herod's palace. They had followed him here and stood patiently across the street from the entrance through which he had been taken inside. When he was led out, bound at the wrists again, they were confused but momentarily encouraged by his new robe and cleaner appearance. But they quickly realized that he was merely being mocked by Herod and sent back to Pilate where, once again, he would face the vicious cruelty of a Roman execution.

Mary prayed without ceasing for her Son and leaned on John for strength. Both knew how this drama would play out because they accepted the truth of what Jesus had told them would happen. Mary Magdalene and the other women, however, could not help hoping that God would intervene to save His Son at the last minute, that the sufferings which Jesus had already endured would somehow be sufficient for the prophecies to be fulfilled. Magdalene in particular, a woman of passion and beauty, once renowned for her prowess as a "lady of the night" and despised by the Jewish wives as a temptress to their husbands, was assaulted all morning with tempests of tears. The emotion that she once gave illicitly, she now gave to the Lord with the same total abandon but made more intense by the shame and sorrow she felt for her years as a notorious sinner.

"Procurator, the Jews are back with their prisoner, Jesus. They request that you come out and sentence the man," said the soldier who brought him the unwelcome news. Pilate uttered an expletive and went out to the arched gateway fronting on the Upper Marketplace where the crowd waited.

Caiaphas stepped forward, holding the magnificent robe that Herod had put on Jesus, and gave it to Pilate. "Herod sends this to you, Procurator, with his compliments." Pilate began at that moment to see Herod in a new, more favorable light. They would become good friends thereafter, reconciled not only by the gesture of friendship that each perceived had been made to him, but bound also by a shared dread that crept through their dreams from time to time.

Pilate decided to dispose of the matter once and for all by explaining to the crowd what seemed perfectly clear to him:

> **"You have brought this man before me as one who subverts the people. I have examined him in your presence and have no charge against him arising from your allegations. Neither has Herod, who therefore has sent him back to us; obviously this man has done**

nothing that calls for death. Therefore I mean to release him, once I have taught him a lesson."[30]

The crowd had grown much larger since Pilate had sent Jesus to Herod. Annas, who was in charge of the financial operations of the Temple, had sent out a call for as many traders, their family members and employees as could be spared from the frenetic trading activity on this day before Passover. They came in droves and packed the square where Pilate addressed the crowd. They were eager to even the score with Jesus who had severely damaged their profits only a few days earlier. With a roar they responded to Pilate's attempt to mollify their blood lust: **"Away with this man; release Barabbas for us!"**

Pilate was caught completely off guard by this sudden demand for the release of one of his most notorious criminals. Barabbas had been captured after stabbing a Roman soldier to death and attempting to incite a general revolt in the Lower City. Pilate looked forward to crucifying this man. Also in a cell at Antonia were several other rebels from Barabbas' band. Two of them were scheduled to be crucified with Barabbas this day: Gestas, a rough and violent man, and Dismas, a young and naive Jewish patriot. Pilate had considered the festival custom of releasing a condemned prisoner his ace in the hole for sparing Jesus. It never occurred to him that the Jewish crowd would prefer the release of an insurrectionist, which they knew would bring a crackdown on them by angry Roman soldiers, to the mild and unthreatening Jesus, whom they were wildly acclaiming less than a week ago. Pilate shook his head and went back inside the praetorium to collect his thoughts.

Inside, his tribune approached him. "Procurator, a group of the Jews has come up from the city to demand your observance of the festival custom of releasing one condemned prisoner. As you just heard, they want Barabbas. Do not give him to them! He stabbed to death a new young recruit from the Antonia, a boy who had hardly begun to shave. He tried to incite a riot in the Lower City and came darned close to succeeding. We were lucky that more of our soldiers weren't killed. As it is, we had to kill half a dozen of the Jews before we got the mob under control. Anyone would be better than this man."

"I have no choice in the matter, Antonius. Tiberias Caesar supports the custom. He thinks it helps pacify the local populace by portraying Romans as merciful, giving the people an avenue of peaceful relief, and keeping the martyr count down. Of course, if we catch them again, there will be no need for a second trial. But we must honor the demand of the people, whomever they may choose. I will try to persuade them that Jesus is a better choice for them."

Pilate went back out and sat on the judge's bench to the right of the archway. He had Jesus brought up to stand beside him. Then he spoke to the crowd again: "You have asked me to honor the custom of releasing a prisoner of your choice at this great festival for the Jewish people. I will do so. But you have

---

[30]Lk 23:14-16

a choice of prisoners, one of which stands here before you. **Which one do you wish me to release for you, Barabbas or Jesus the so-called Messiah?"**[31]

The chief priests, scribes and elders had been circulating through the crowd, as had the deputation which had come up from the city, telling everyone to ask for the release of Barabbas. Most of them already nursed one grudge or another against Jesus and needed no coaching. Mary Magdalene and a few others had frantically petitioned anyone who would listen to ask for Jesus. But the crowd was not a neutral one and Jesus' few supporters found the going rough. When Pilate asked his question, the vote was clear: **"We want Barabbas, not this one!"**[32] The crowd was rambunctious and noisy, shaking their fists at Jesus and screaming ever louder for the release of Barabbas.

As Pilate vacillated over what to do, one of his soldiers handed him a note from his wife. It said: **"Do not interfere in the case of that holy man. I had a dream about him today which has greatly upset me."**[33]

Like many people of his time, Pilate tended to be superstitious in certain respects. He believed that dreams could be prophetic. Everyone knew the story of Julius Caesar's wife dreaming about his death on the Ides of March. But as a civilized Roman, a man of the world, he was skeptical about anyone's ability to identify in advance which dreams should be believed. Claudia's note, however, struck fear in him. There was something about Jesus that had begun to get under his skin. The man made him extremely uncomfortable. And the more time he spent with him, the worse it got. It was clear that the crowd was not going to be easily swayed.

He addressed them again: **"What wrong is this man guilty of? I have not discovered anything about him that calls for the death penalty. I will therefore chastise him and release him."**[34]

But the crowd merely shouted even louder than before: **"Crucify him! Crucify him!"**[35]

Pilate was befuddled. **"Why? What crime has he committed?"**[36]

"Crucify him!"[37] came the cry with so many fists thrust into the air that it looked like the square had suddenly sprouted a forest of limbs. The few cries for

---

[31]Mt 27:17

[32]Jn 18:40

[33]Mt 27:19

[34]Lk 23:22

[35]Mk 15:13, Lk 23:21

[36]Mt 27:23, Mk 15:14

[37]Mk 15:14

the release of Jesus were completely drowned out. The demands for Jesus' execution came like the waves of the ocean, relentless, crashing upon the shore, irresistible. The square was nearly filled with people by now, hundreds of them, seemingly possessed of one thought and one thought only: to see this gentle man before them put to death in one of the cruelest ways ever devised by man. It was surely Satan's proudest moment.

Pilate grabbed Jesus by his arm and pulled him through the archway into the praetorium. He handed him to his guards and said: "Take him and scourge him. Have a little fun with him. Maybe if the crowd sees him afterward that will be enough to satisfy their blood lust."

The soldiers led Jesus to a thick stone pillar about eight feet high. It had an iron ring embedded in the top of it. Jesus was stripped of all his clothes and pressed face forward against this pillar with his arms extended around it. There his wrists were bound tightly together. Another rope was looped at the hands through the circle of his joined arms and pulled through the iron ring. Jesus' hands were pulled up over his head so severely that he was forced to stand on his toes to relieve the biting pain of the rope on his wrists and the strain on his shoulder joints. His face was crushed against the rough surface of the pillar. The rope was secured and two burly soldiers, bare-chested, approached Jesus from either side. Each of them was carrying a Roman *flagrum*, which was a whip consisting of a wooden handle about 12 inches long with three leather strips extending from one end. Each strip had been threaded at its end through two small lead balls placed about an inch and a half apart. The two soldiers stood behind Jesus and to his side, with the one on his right being left-handed and taller than the one on his left who was right-handed.

The two soldiers alternated their blows. The first one struck Jesus across his shoulder blades. Snapping viciously through the air, the little balls shattered his skin in six places. Jesus gasped as his diaphragm heaved inward and sucked his breath away. Almost before his brain could fully register the pain of the first blow, the second came from his other side and created six more bruises on skin already tender from his bloody perspiration in the garden of Gethsemane. The pain exploded in Jesus' head. He stifled a scream and sagged against the pillar. But the rope holding him up tugged at his wrists and strained shoulder joints, cramping the muscles and adding their own voices to the concert of pain that engulfed him.

The next blows struck lower on his back and the fire that burned on his flesh began to spread across his body. Then the soldiers began to work down his torso, striking the buttocks, the thighs, the calves and even as low as Jesus' ankles. His upper arms were also lashed. The first blows essentially destroyed the skin and underlying tissue at the point of impact. His flesh began to swell and reddish-purple welts left angry stripes wherever the flagrum struck. The surface blood vessels burst onto the damaged flesh and subsequent blows raised little geysers of blood as the balls tore into the weakened skin and muscle and exposed nerve endings. By now Jesus' senses were overwhelmed in a crescendo of agony. Behind his tightly closed eyes, he saw only the color red. His entire body began to tremble and sweat poured out of him, aggravating the terrible thirst which choked him.

As the soldiers' blows struck again and again into the blood flowing down Jesus' back, buttocks and legs, pink clouds of bloody mist rose and fell from the splatters of the leaded straps. His heart rate accelerated and his breathing grew so rapid and shallow that it seemed he must surely fall into blessed unconsciousness. But he willed himself to endure and fought off the drowning that beckoned to save him from this bath of suffering.

With each blow, he gasped and groaned involuntarily, but otherwise made no sound. By now he sagged against the pillar and the rope around his hands nearly cut off their circulation. The pressure on his shoulder joints was severe. But he no longer had the strength to push himself up against the pain pulling him down into the dark, roiling sea of agony. Waves of nausea swept over him as his body trembled uncontrollably. Jesus was near death from traumatic circulatory shock.

After the soldiers had struck him thirty-nine times with the now-bloody balls of lead, they paused. Jesus hung limply from the rope suspending his wrists from the iron ring in the pillar. His head fell back and his unseeing eyes stared upward into the bright morning sky. The rope was cut from his hands and he collapsed into a bloody heap at the base of the column. His mouth opened and closed, parched with thirst, and his body shook with involuntary muscle spasms.

The two Roman soldiers with the scourges stepped back and regarded Jesus impassively. The short one said to the tall one: "Pilate has warned us to apply the Jewish rule of no more than thirty-nine lashes. Too many of our prisoners have died here before they could be crucified."

Aramus, a powerful man with a black beard, now dripping sweat which rolled off a long, sharp nose between two small black eyes, regarded his companion. "How many blows have you struck?"

"Nineteen," came the reply.

"And I but one more. We are nowhere near thirty-nine. Turn the Nazorean around and you can see our job is but half finished." The other soldier started to protest but fear of the larger man and indifference to the fate of their Jewish victim silenced him.

Jesus was jerked up from where he lay and shoved back against the pillar, facing outward. His hands were pulled up over his head and around the pillar. They were tied once again, this time behind him. As before, a rope was looped through the bound wrists and secured to the iron ring on top of the column. The position of his arms created an extreme stress on his shoulder joints and the pain which before had been severe now became excruciating. The open wounds on his back pressed their torn and bleeding skin and muscle into the rough surface of the stone column. The soldiers began the flagellating process once more, starting on his upper chest and working downward. There seemed to be no part of his body that was left untouched by the lead-tipped leather whips. As the blows ruptured his flesh, blood, fluid and mucous began to accumulate in and around the lungs, creating a condition known as pleural effusion, or water around the outside of the lungs.

After thirty-five more blows, bringing the total to seventy-four, Jesus had fainted again. His head hung forward, but his body was pinned tightly to the pillar by the rope pulling at his arms. His shoulders were stretched outward to the point of dislocation. His naked body was red with blood from his neck to his feet from the more than two hundred leaded strap marks. He appeared so close to death that even a single blow more might have been fatal. As the soldiers drew back to strike him again, Domitius, their centurion, appeared and halted the scourging.

"You idiots! Are you trying to kill the Jew? Pilate wants him alive. If his sentence is crucifixion, he's to die on the cross, not here! Clean him up and get his clothes back on. Take him down to the barracks until the Procurator calls for him." Domitius strode off, muttering to himself.

One of the soldiers brought a bucket of water and threw it on the unconscious Jesus. That was the extent of his cleaning. Another soldier cut his bonds and the Lord collapsed onto the dirty pavement at the base of the column. His moans faded to whimpers as he attempted to crawl toward his clothes, lying in a heap about ten feet from the pillar. The dirt on the stones ground into his bleeding chest and thigh wounds and forced him to halt. He lay breathing heavily for a few minutes. Then he pushed himself slowly onto his hands and knees to continue. The soldiers were quite amused by his pitiful efforts.

Just as Jesus was about to reach his garments, one of the soldiers took his foot and slid them out of reach. This occurred twice more before the soldiers tired of their sport. When Jesus finally reached his clothes, he trembled so badly that he could not tie his loin cloth. After five frustrating tries, he finally succeeded but his shaking legs collapsed beneath him from the effort. He had to lie on the pavement for several minutes, fighting to remain conscious before he was at last able to stand still long enough to get his tunic back on. He didn't even try to put on his robe; he merely clutched it against his body as if it might somehow protect him from any more of the savage blows. It seemed as if every inch of his body throbbed with pain. But to be free of the searing, shattering bolts of agony created by the lashing metal balls made this new generalized pain almost bearable. With hands shaking, Jesus put his wrists and the backs of his arms to his mouth so that the blood and few drops of water still there might alleviate, if only slightly, his maddening thirst.

Outside in the Upper Market square, the Jews waited in silence, momentarily hushed by the sounds of agony from over the wall. Off to one side, a few women and one young man, a boy really, stood silently, praying for their Lord, desperately trying to send him their love and strength. One woman seemed almost to feel Jesus' blows herself. Mary stood trembling, ashen in color, with her eyes closed, hands clasped so tightly that her knuckles were white. While she could not see the scourging, she could hear the terrible whistle and snap of the flagrum balls as they ripped into the swollen and bloody body of her son.

Pontius Pilate had not stayed to watch the results of his order. He had seen many men scourged, some of them with spiked balls which tore the flesh from their victims in crimson ribbons. The spectacle was not one which he usually enjoyed. Pilate was anxious about other matters. He had gone to find his wife to learn more about the dream that had prompted her warning to him.

He found her pacing the floor in her chambers. She was wringing her hands and seemed to have been crying because her eyes were red-rimmed and puffy. "Pontius, you must release the Nazorean. I have had the most frightening dream about him. In it, I saw the figure of a man, a magnificent person wearing a robe of brilliant light and standing on clouds surrounded by uncountable numbers of other creatures who resembled him but were not nearly so majestic. Before him stood all the residents of earth.

"He pointed his finger at a vast group on his left and spoke in a thundering voice: **'Out of my sight, you condemned, into that everlasting fire prepared for the devil and his angels!'**[38] In this group, I recognized many of the Jewish priests, or at least men dressed like them. And standing beside them, husband, I saw you and me!

"Then suddenly a loud voice cried out from the heavens: 'Kneel before my Son, Jesus the Christ!' At that moment, the earth parted beneath us and, oh, my God, we plunged into a vast sea of flame! I awoke to my own scream and sat upright in bed, shaking, perspiring, frightened out of my wits. Pontius, please, please release him!" Claudia clutched at her husband's neck and clung there sobbing as the terror from her dream seized her again.

"Claudia, it's just a dream—superstitious nonsense. Besides, I am sure the Jews will agree that the wretch should be released once they see his condition after the scourging. Have no fear. We shall not be responsible for the man's death." But Pilate was more shaken by Claudia's words than he let on. He determined that he would not crucify the man no matter what.

———

[38]Mt 25:41

PROPHECIES OF ISAIAH

The Lord GOD has given me
a well-trained tongue,
That I might know how to speak to the weary
a word that will rouse them.
Morning after morning
he opens my ear that I may hear;
And I have not rebelled,
have not turned back.
I gave my back to those who beat me,
my cheeks to those who plucked my beard;
My face I did not shield
from buffets and spitting.

The Lord GOD is my help,
therefore I am not disgraced;
I have set my face like flint,
knowing that I shall not be put to shame.
He is near who upholds my right;
if anyone wishes to oppose me,
let us appear together.
Who disputes my right?
Let him confront me.
See, the Lord GOD is my help;
who will prove me wrong?
Lo, they will all wear out like cloth,
the moth will eat them up.

Who among you fears the LORD,
heeds his servant's voice,
And walks in darkness
without any light,
Trusting in the name of the LORD
and relying on his God?[39]

---

[39]Is 50:4-10

QUESTIONS FOR REFLECTION

(1) Why do you think Pilate was anxious to release Jesus or at least to get someone else, such as Herod, to deal with him? Because he had a basic sense of fairness? Because he sensed something about who Jesus was? Because he was in a good mood? Something else?

(2) What significance does the scourging of Jesus have in your own life? Have you had experiences that made you feel like you were being unfairly "crucified" and then had something else happen that was just too much, something that threw into question your faith and values?

(3) What do you think was the primary flaw in Peter that led him to deny knowing Jesus: Cowardice? Unfaithfulness? Weakness? Pride? Ignorance? Something else?

(4) Christ's sufferings in the scourging are sometimes cited as particularly appropriate for meditation in light of our sins of the flesh. His sufferings under the flagellum were intended to atone for our sins of failing to control our own lustful passions. Would this explain, perhaps, why Christ's scourging was even more savage and brutal than normal?

(5) In the space of a few hours, Judas went from scheming betrayer of Jesus to suicide. What do you think likely motivated this behavior—pride or sorrow? (Despair would have been a component of either motivation.) Have you ever taken pride in punishing yourself and refusing to be forgiven for some transgression?

(6) Do you think the Romans would have really cared if the Sanhedrin had taken Jesus outside immediately after he admitted he was the Son of God and stoned him to death, even though the Romans reserved the right of capital punishment to themselves? Jesus' fellow townsmen in Nazareth attempted to throw him to his death for this claim and, later, Stephen, the first martyr, would be stoned to death while Paul held the garments of the stone throwers. Why were these executions okay in light of Roman policy? Why do you think the Jewish authorities were determined to have the Romans execute Jesus?

(7) Do you think Judas assumed that Jesus could not be harmed by anyone? Was this an attitude shared by the other apostles? How could they think that since Jesus told them repeatedly he was going to be put to death? Why didn't they believe him?

(8) You may have heard the expression that a person "cannot see the forest for the trees." How do you think this expression might apply to the Sanhedrin at the time of Jesus?

(9) Can you see suffering in your own life as a good thing? When bad things happen to you, do you accept them willingly and even thankfully as the means by which you can be a companion to Jesus? Why or why not?

(10) If suffering can be good for our souls, why shouldn't we inflict a little suffering on those whom we love? Do you see any inconsistency in Jesus calling us to accept suffering in ourselves while doing everything we can to alleviate suffering in others?

Weaving a crown out of thorns they fixed it on his head, and stuck a reed in his right hand.
Mt 27:29

THIRD SORROWFUL MYSTERY

The Crowning with Thorns

Jesus, barely able to stand after his savage scourging, was led, half dragged, through the drilling and training grounds between the outer wall and the palace to the soldiers' barracks at the north end of the praetorium. Inside the barracks was a cavernous room where the soldiers assembled in formation. It was also used for recreational activities at other times. One of those activities was the mistreatment of condemned criminals. Usually this particular "sport" took place at the Fortress Antonia, home to Jerusalem's permanent Roman garrison. But when Pontius Pilate was in town, his troops used the barracks. The soldiers especially liked abusing Jewish political prisoners whom they saw as embodying the worst elements of a difficult and arrogant population. When Jesus was brought in under charges of being the king of the Jews, he was made-to-order as a target that would excite the most virulent scorn and cruelty.

"Bring the Jew over here, Servitius," called his comrade-in-arms, Marcellus. Jesus, wearing his tunic but still clutching his robe, was shoved toward the soldier who had beckoned. The man was standing behind a wooden stool. "Sit him down here. Valerius has gone to summon the cohort to come in and meet the new ruler of the Jews. Everyone will wish to honor him appropriately!" Marcellus laughed heartily at his own joke. Jesus was pushed roughly onto the stool. He winced from the sharp pains the sudden impact caused to his deeply lacerated buttocks and then sat quietly, staring straight ahead, trying to control the shaking of his hands and traumatized body.

The cohort[1] filed in haphazardly and formed a rough circle around Jesus. Some of the men enjoyed these spectacles. Others found them cruel and pointless and often skipped them altogether. But Jesus of Nazareth was famous throughout Palestine and nearly all of the Roman soldiers were curious to see the man who

---

[1]A full Roman cohort consisted of 600 soldiers under the command of a tribune. He was assisted by a centurion for each 100-120 soldiers.

had provoked such wild enthusiasm in Jerusalem only five days before. Whatever their expectations, what greeted their eyes now was a man in obviously terrible straits. He sat in his once white tunic, now spattered with blood from collar to hem, streaked and stained with dirt. His beard and mustache were matted with dried blood and his wet hair lay limply on his head. His eyes were sunken in dark circles in a face pinched and pallid with fatigue and suffering. His hands lay folded on his lap, trembling.

A short, stocky soldier approached the Lord and said: "So this is the 'king' who rode into Jerusalem on an ass. How fitting! Marcellus, our 'king' doesn't look very much like one. Where is his royal robe?"

"You are right, Drusus! The Jew needs a royal garment. He must have left his own in his palace." Once again, Marcellus was greatly amused at his own wit. "Bring us one of the officer's cloaks. One Roman officer is worth ten of these provincial kings."

One of the soldiers on the outer edge of the circle ran off and brought back one of the tribune's bright scarlet cloaks that had been torn and discarded. He tossed it over the crowd of soldiers in the direction of Jesus. It did not quite make it and landed on the heads of two soldiers near the front of the crowd. The cohort roared with laughter as the two men struggled to remove it from their faces. The laughter was contagious and the soldiers started to get into the spirit of mocking Jesus.

Drusus took the cloak and had begun to put it around Jesus' shoulders when Valerius called out. "Wait, Drusus! The 'king' still has his commoner's clothes on. We must not mix these 'royal' garments with those."

Marcellus made Jesus stand then and take off his tunic. Few of his scourging wounds were fully clotted yet but even so the action of removing the garment tore at the bloody and ripped skin, accelerating the bleeding in several places. Jesus made no sound, barely even winced at this pain which now seemed quite mild compared to the agony when the wounds were inflicted. When he had sat back down, which was painful in itself, Drusus threw the soiled scarlet cloak around his shoulders. Many of the soldiers then made mocking bows to Jesus as others laughed.

A voice called out from the midst of the soldiers: "A king needs a crown! Where is his crown?" There was silence for a moment as the soldiers considered this.

Then someone else responded: "This 'king' needs a special crown. Give me a few minutes and I will bring him one which is perfect for someone of his high station and breeding!"

While the rest of the cohort flung insults at Jesus and made up lewd jokes about him, the man who had spoken ran to a bin that contained brush and materials for starting fires. Branches from the Acantha bush, one variety of which is now known as the Syrian Christ Thorn, or *Ziziphus spina Christi*, were a common material used for this purpose. This thorn bush, a member of the Buckthorn genus, grows nine to fifteen feet tall and produces sharp spikes that grow close together in pairs 1-2 inches in length. First donning heavy leather gloves, the soldier took several of the branches and plaited them together in the shape of a very prickly skull cap. Then he quickly brought it to Drusus, who had appointed himself to be the Lord's "royal attendant."

"Well done, Publius!" cried Drusus. "This is, indeed, a perfect crown for our 'king' here. Lend me your gloves that I may put it on our new 'caesar.'"

Publius handed him the cluster of thorns with the gloves and Drusus jammed the "crown" onto Jesus' scalp. The thorns pierced through the skin all over his head, from his forehead to the back. Blood immediately spurted out from the many wounds and began to run down the Lord's face and neck. The needle-like points bored easily into the dense layers of nerves that cover the head and face. Severe lancinating pain shot like tiny lightning bolts throughout his face from the injury to the highly-sensitive trigeminal nerve complex. Jesus stifled a cry and tried to hold his head as still as he could because every movement renewed the searing jolts of pain.[2] Some of the blood that flowed down his face, he let trickle into his mouth to relieve the terrible parched dryness of his thirst.

"One thing further is needed," mused Servitius, who had first brought Jesus into the barracks. "This reed will serve as an admirable scepter." He stuck into Jesus' right hand, clenched on his lap from the pain of the crown of thorns, a hard, stiff reed. Then genuflecting before him, Servitius said with mock solemnity: **"All hail, king of the Jews!"**[3]

The other soldiers took up the cry and began to circle Jesus, genuflecting and swinging their arms out in exaggerated postures of fealty. Soon some of the soldiers embellished their mockery by pretending to accidentally strike Jesus with the backs of their hands as they swung them out while kneeling. These blows became increasingly harsh and soon Jesus' lips began to bleed. Then a soldier took the reed from his hand and used that to "salute" him. This became immediately popular and every soldier began to take the reed and to strike Jesus on the crown of thorns, driving them deeper into his scalp. The spikes of pain radiated through his face with each blow.

Some of the soldiers, as they marched around Jesus in mock homage, began to pronounce "*Jews*" in such a way when they hailed Jesus as to literally spit the word at him. This, too, was taken up by the soldiers behind as a competition and soon each was competing to see who could spit the most as he said the word. Then a few got carried away and simply spat large amounts of saliva and phlegm into the face of Jesus. He made no move, merely clenched his jaw and stared straight ahead. Silently, though, he prayed. Not for strength to endure. Not for his Father to punish those who had mistreated him so terribly. Not for his followers

---

[2]Dr. Zugibe describes the case of a man who suffered from a chronic inflammation of these nerves, a disease called trigeminal neuralgia. The pain was so unbearable that the man committed suicide, leaving a note which said: "Forgive me but I can no longer stand the pain." *Cross and the Shroud*, 27.

[3]Mt 27:29, Mk 15:18, Jn 19:3

to escape. Not for relief from the cruel burden he had taken on. Jesus prayed for those who abused him. He asked his Father to forgive those who spat on him. He asked for his Father's grace for the soldiers who nearly killed him with their vicious flagra and for those who now drove thorns as sharp as needles into his very skull. He prayed that someday these brutish men would discover how much he loved them and turn their hearts around so that he could bless them beyond their wildest dreams.

None of these prayers had any immediate effect, however, as the soldiers continued to revel in their nasty mockery of the Lord. One soldier used the reed to strike Jesus in the face. A welt immediately appeared across his cheek.[4] The various blows of the soldiers drove Jesus' head backward and forward and side-to-side. He had to spread his feet to keep from being knocked off his stool. His face swelled from the punches and slaps. One soldier misaimed his slap and stuck himself on a thorn. This infuriated him so much that he punched Jesus squarely in the face, dislocating the cartilage in the bridge of his nose. The head motion increased the darting bolts of fire that raced across his face as the thorns were driven against the irritated nerves by blows from the reed on the crown of thorns. Blood filled his eyes and mingled there with involuntary tears before flowing out and down Jesus' cheeks. The soldiers feigned sympathy while continuing to hit him with reed and hand.

After this had gone on for the better part of an hour, Pilate sent word that Jesus was to be brought back to the archway. "Take the fool's cloak off, Marcellus," said Servitius, who had brought Jesus to the barracks and would now take him back.

"No, wait!" said Valerius. "He was sent to us as the king of the Jews. Let us send him back looking like the 'king' that he really is." So they left the ragged and now blood-stained military cloak and the thorn crown on Jesus and roughly shoved him back the way he had come to confront his people once more.

When Pilate saw him, he approved of the pitiful, ludicrous appearance of Jesus. *If this does not move the Jews to pity, nothing will touch their stony hearts,* Pilate thought to himself. He went up the stairs to his judge's bench and announced to the Jews still waiting in the crowd.: **"Observe what I do. I am going to bring him out to you to make you realize that I find no case [against him]."**[5]

When Jesus emerged at the top of the stairs from the praetorium grounds and stood there framed in the archway, there was a gasp from the crowd, shocked in spite of themselves. Jesus was wearing the prickly crown of thorns, which obscured most of his forehead. Blood still trickled down his face. His face had streaks of both fresh and partially dried blood on it so that he looked almost as if

---

[4]The Shroud of Turin shows a large welt on Jesus' face at about the middle of his right cheek. It seems likely to have been made by a blow from a stick, or similar object. There is another, smaller ridge across his left cheek.

[5]Jn 19:4

he had been colored in warpaint for some purpose. Draped over his shoulders was the scarlet cloak that hung nearly to the ground in back but left the front part of his body exposed, covered only by his loin cloth. In his arms he carried his own tunic and cloak, trying to use them to cover his nakedness. The scourging wounds splotched the front of his body from his collarbone to his ankles with dark bloody welts that looked like dozens of leeches clinging to him.

When his mother saw him, she nearly broke down and wept, but, remembering her promise to be strong for him, she bit her lip, closed her eyes, and prayed with her breaking heart. Magdalene and the other women were not so composed. They burst into tears and cried out to the procurator to have pity on Jesus. Their cries, however, had the opposite effect on the chief priests, scribes and elders, who gestured threateningly toward the women.

Pilate pointed to Jesus and said: **"Look at the man!"**[6]

But the Jewish leaders saw only that Jesus still lived and so they shouted back: **"Crucify him! Crucify him!"**[7] The lust for blood was upon them.

Pilate was completely exasperated and once again tried to evade his responsibility: **"Take him and crucify him yourselves; I find no case against him."**[8]

The Jews were not to be put off so easily. **"We have our law . . . and according to that law he must die because he made himself God's Son."**[9]

Pilate felt his blood chill. He remembered Claudia's dream and fear knotted his stomach. Had he been less unnerved, he might have recognized an opening that would have permitted him to refuse jurisdiction over the case, which is what he had wanted to do all along. For the first time, the Jewish charge shifted from the trumped-up political charges necessary to arouse Roman interest to the real basis for their actions: the accusation of religious blasphemy. Ordinarily, the procurator would have quickly asserted his lack of jurisdiction in such a matter and dismissed the case. But Pilate was now sensing something that frightened him. For the moment, he forgot the political game he had been playing and tried to ascertain the real nature of this man who, despite his terrible wounds and deplorable appearance, still conveyed a dignity and authority that defied understanding. He took Jesus back into the praetorium and asked him: **"Where do you come from?"**[10]

Jesus gave no indication he even heard the question. Pilate raised his voice, barely suppressing his anger and frustration: **"Do you refuse to speak to**

---

[6]In Latin, *"Ecce homo!"* The quotation is from Jn 19:5.

[7]Jn 19:6

[8]Ibid.

[9]Jn 19:7

[10]This quote and the next seven are from Jn 19:9-15.

me? Do you not know that I have the power to release you and the power to crucify you?"

Now Jesus did look at Pilate. With an effort he licked his parched lips and replied:

> **"You would have no power over me whatever**
> **unless it were given you from above.**
> **That is why he who handed me over to you**
> **is guilty of the greater sin."**

Pilate began to sweat. He desperately wanted to release Jesus. He looked at his viciously abused body and already felt some guilt for what he had ordered done. He hated the Jews for putting him in this spot. But he lacked moral courage. Expediency and practicality were his guiding principles. Something in him knew he stood before the true reality but his character was too weak to respond.

As he vacillated, trying to get up the courage to just go out and set Jesus free, he heard a loud cry from the square that struck precisely at his moral Achilles heel.

"If you free this man you are no 'Friend of Caesar.' Anyone who makes himself a king becomes Caesar's rival."

The Jews would not make the same slip they had made earlier. This was a warning that Pilate understood very well. He had lost his chance to dismiss the case. If he released Jesus now, he would have to be prepared to explain to Caesar why he had decided the man was not a king. Yet, in his heart, Pilate knew that Jesus was more than he appeared, much more. His kingdom might be of another world, but he was clearly a king somewhere. The time had come. He had to do something.

He took Jesus back to the archway and sat himself on the judge's bench to the right facing the square filled mostly with people who were determined to see Jesus dead before the day's end. It was now about 11:00 a.m.

Pilate tried again. "**Look at your king!**" But this was playing directly to the strength in the Jews' charges against Jesus. If it was intended as anything but sarcasm, it was pathetically ineffective.

The crowd shouted back: "**Away with him! Away with him! Crucify him!**"

Pilate knew he had been defeated. But he couldn't resist throwing one last bitter question at the Jews. Perhaps he was inspired to do so because in their next two assertions, the Jews first rejected the compact that God had made with them through Abraham and then asked for the consequences to be laid upon them and their children. "**What! Shall I crucify your king?**"

"**We have no king but Caesar,**" replied the chief priests. The crowd surged and took up the cry. Many others, however, protested; particularly the group which had come up from the city seeking the release of Barabbas. They were shocked at the chief priests' recognition of Caesar's authority over Israel. Shoving broke out and then cursing. The Roman soldiers tensed as it appeared the crowd might start to riot.

Pilate raised his hand and the crowd steadied and then grew quiet enough for him to be heard. He called to his attending servants to bring him a basin and a pitcher of water. Holding his hands over the basin, he directed the other servant to pour the water in the pitcher over his hands. As he did so, he called out to the crowd watching him: "**I am innocent of the blood of this just man. The responsibility is yours.**"[11] This was not a decision to release Jesus back to the Jews. He was going to comply with their demands for Jesus' execution. But he wanted them to accept responsibility for it. They did.

"**Let his blood be on us and on our children!**"[12] The cry echoed around the square for a moment. The small group of Jesus' supporters, including the three Mary's, Salome and Joanna, wept while John watched the proceedings in shocked silence, wondering still whether Yahweh might not open up the earth and swallow these men as He had done to the apostate Jews worshiping the golden calf while Moses was on Mount Sinai. But the Father was silent while the Son looked with sorrow and compassion upon His people who rejected their Savior.

Pilate then ordered Barabbas to be released and Jesus to be crucified. He personally directed Centurion Domitius to take Jesus to the Fortress Antonia, link him up with the other two rebels who were to be crucified this day, and have them carry their crosses, as customary, through the streets of Jerusalem as a warning and example to the populace. "You are not to oversee the crucifixion, Domitius. Turn him over to Quintus to handle. Tell Quintus I am sending to the crucifixion site a sign to be placed over the head of this one."

Domitius told his soldiers to take the tribune's cloak off Jesus and to get him dressed in his own clothes. Because the tunic would not fit over it, the crown of thorns had to be removed. This was done, but not carefully. After Jesus had with great difficulty put his tunic back on, he tied it at his waist, hands shaking, with the sash which he used as a girdle.

The soldiers watching him grew impatient with Jesus' exhausted efforts to dress himself. One of them grabbed Jesus' robe and pulled it roughly over his head. Jesus staggered but maintained his balance and slowly completed his own dressing by tying his head covering around him like a belt.

When he was fully dressed, the soldiers shoved the crown of thorns back on his head. This created a whole new set of wounds and once again Jesus' face and neck dripped with blood. Once again the paralyzing pains ripped through his face and scalp. Once again, Jesus made no complaint but merely moved his lips in silent prayer.

---

[11]Mt 27:24

[12]Mt 27:25. Never have words more terrible and unfortunate than these been spoken. God alone knows how many good and decent Jewish people have been oppressed, persecuted and killed by ignorant Christians finding justification in these words of self-condemnation. The irony is that those who commit such acts follow the lead of those who executed Christ, not the Savior whom they purport to worship.

"Marcellus, round up a full maniple[13] of men for taking this man to the Antonia. The streets are crowded with Passover pilgrims and some of them might get excited if they see who this prisoner is. We'll want to keep him inside the group and away from the Jews," said Domitius. "Be ready in ten minutes."

———————

———————

[13] About 50-60 soldiers.

PSALM 86: 14-17

Prayer in Time of Distress

O God, the haughty have risen
up against me,
and the company of fierce men
seeks my life,
nor do they set you before their eyes.
But you, O Lord, are a God
merciful and gracious,
slow to anger, abounding in
kindness and fidelity.
Turn toward me, and have pity
on me;
give your strength to
your servant,
and save the son of your handmaid.
Grant me a proof of your favor,
that my enemies may see,
to their confusion,
that you, O LORD, have
helped and comforted me.

Amen

QUESTIONS FOR REFLECTION

(1) If you had been Pontius Pilate, how would you have handled the case of Jesus? Try to imagine yourself not as a Christian, but as a Roman governor in Palestine around the year 30 A.D., working for the Roman emperor.

(2) What do you think would have been the worst part of the crowning with thorns episode for Jesus—the physical pain, or the mocking and spitting on him? Which would have been the worst for you?

(3) Are you surprised to read in the Passion Narratives of the Gospels that the crowd of Jesus' antagonists who brought him to Pilate for crucifixion were not moved to pity by the sight of him after being scourged and crowned with thorns? Or do you think the effect might have been the opposite; i.e., seeing the Man who had only hours before claimed to be the Son of God in such a wretched condition would have inflamed their conviction that he was a blasphemous impostor?

(4) Have you ever put your trust in someone and then discovered something that made you question your own judgment about that person? How did your error make you feel about that person then? Angry? Scornful? Contemptuous? Embarrassed by your earlier misjudgment? Can you see any parallels here as the suffering, bleeding, and dirt-stained Jesus seems not even remotely divine?

(5) What are the primary spiritual lessons that Jesus teaches us in this episode of the crowning with thorns? Patience? Tolerance? Acceptance of suffering? Love when it seems impossible to do so? Humility? Being undeceived by appearances? Faith? Perseverance? Courage? Dignity under duress? Others?

(6) Have you been falsely accused of anything and punished for it? How did you react? Self-pity? Determined to get revenge? Anger at the injustice of it? Resolved to demonstrate the truth? Shocked that such injustice could happen? What can you learn from Jesus' example here?

(7) What do you think was Pontius Pilate's greatest failing? Can you find any parallels in modern politics?

(8) Why would the Jewish crowd opposing Jesus before Pilate call for His blood to be upon them and their children? Do you think they were proud of what they were doing? Why? What can we learn from this episode about tolerance? Can you think of any parallels in your own experience? In American history? World history?

(9) Are you surprised that all the apostles except John abandoned Jesus? Why do you think they did that? Fear for themselves? Acceptance of Jesus' warning that he was going to be put to death? Indecision about what to do? Lack of leadership? Why were Jesus' women followers more willing than the men to remain nearby during Jesus' trial and execution?

(10) The Jewish authorities shouted to Pilate that they had no king but Caesar. If Caesar represents material comforts, success, power, worldly achievements, and honors, can you see in yourself a tendency to have no king but Caesar? In other words, do you also put worldly success and pleasures ahead of spiritual and moral values and sacrifice?

*Jesus was led away, and carrying the cross by himself, went out to what is called the
Place of the Skull (in Hebrew, Golgotha).* Jn 19:17

FOURTH SORROWFUL MYSTERY

The Carrying of the Cross

When the soldiers had assembled outside the praetorium barracks, Jesus was placed in the middle of them. Although he was tall for his time, it was difficult to see much of his face because the Romans wore their helmets and carried their shields. They marched at a fast pace as well, which caused the civilians in the streets to concentrate on getting out of the way rather than trying to see who their prisoner was. Domitius led his men out the Ginnoth Gate, which was located next to the barracks. They crossed the street that formed the aqueduct bridge to the Temple Mount and descended into the Tyropoeon Valley dividing Jerusalem north to south. Domitius and two of his noncommissioned officers rode on horseback at the front of the column. The streets were packed with Passover pilgrims so the going was slower than normal. Even so, the party arrived at the Fortress Antonia only about twenty minutes after they had left the praetorium. Rumors were already starting to circulate within the city that the Romans had captured some important person whom they had just delivered to the Antonia. Crowds were gathering routinely along the "way of sorrows" to be trod this day by those who had been sentenced by the Romans to death by crucifixion. Very few of the pilgrims and ordinary residents yet had any idea this would include their newest hero, Jesus from Galilee, whom they had missed seeing and hearing in the Temple for the past two days.

At the fortress, Domitius turned Jesus over to Tribune Quintus. He relayed Pilate's instructions and then led his troops promptly back to the praetorium. They would remain on alert for the rest of that day in case riots broke out to protest the execution of Jesus.

Quintus scrutinized the Lord as he stood swaying slightly before him. The walk from Herod's palace to here had been difficult for him, especially climbing up the long flight of steps from the street to the big double-arched gates that were the western entrance to the fortress. He was already desperately weak from the mistreatment he had received and the effects of thirst and fatigue. Quintus expected to see some suffering but he was shocked at the condition of Jesus. His cloak hung open to the waist, revealing a bloody tunic marked with dozens of short, dark stains where blood had seeped from the scourging wounds. His swollen face had streaks of blood, smeared around his eyes where he had wiped them with the back of his sleeve so he could see. So embedded was the mass of thorny brambles on Jesus' head that they seemed to be growing out of his skull. Quintus, who at heart was a decent man, could hardly believe this was the same person he had arrested on the Mount of Olives only about eight hours earlier. Getting him alive to Golgotha, the place of execution for these crucifixion victims, would be difficult, he decided. Jesus already looked half dead. Quintus felt a twinge of pity. He knew that Jesus had committed no crime that merited this punishment.

One of Quintus' best centurions, Longinus, had the execution duty this day. Quintus was glad it was he and not one of his other officers. Longinus would make sure that his prisoners survived to be crucified. "Longinus, take an extra complement of men for this execution. The Nazorean may attract some protests from the people. The high priests have sent over a dozen of their best temple guards as well," said Quintus. "And release Barabbas. He's been given his freedom by the Procurator to honor the Passover festival's custom of a grant of clemency."

Longinus was startled to learn that Barabbas, one of their most notorious criminals, was to be released. The man had murdered one of the young men in his command and Longinus was looking forward to his crucifixion. He started to protest, but the tight-lipped expression on Quintus' face warned him to keep his thoughts to himself.

Inside the fortress, all three men scheduled to be crucified that day—Barabbas, Gestas and Dismas—had been scourged. They, too, had been whipped with the flagrum but had received only thirty-nine blows, and their strokes had been administered less sadistically. Their crucifixion crossbeams, the 75-pound pine *patibula*, had been laid across the shoulders of the three men. Each man had his outstretched arms tied at the wrists behind his beam. If he fell, he would have no way to break his fall except by using his knees on the stone paving blocks and trying to twist his body so that one end of the *patibulum* would strike first. It was difficult to do and nearly impossible for men weakened from a scourging. They stood in the open area at the center of the fortress, waiting for their death processional to begin. Barabbas and Gestas were cursing and bemoaning their fate. Dismas said nothing.

Barabbas watched the Roman soldier walk briskly toward him. For the first time, he noticed another prisoner about thirty yards away, not far from the entrance to the fortress. He had been beaten up pretty badly. *Looks like there's going to be four of us out there today,* Barabbas thought to himself.

"Untie him," said the soldier who had just walked over to Barabbas. "He's been released by Pilate to honor the festival custom. Have him bring his patibulum over to that other prisoner and tie it on him." The soldier pointed toward Jesus.

"What are you talking about?" protested Galenus, the soldier in charge of the prisoner detail. "This man is a murderer. He tried to lead an uprising against us right here in Jerusalem. What's that other Jew done?"

"Best I can determine, he claimed to be the son of the Jewish God. But it don't matter to you anyhow. All you need to know is this man goes free and that man gets crucified in his place."

Barabbas tried to follow the conversation but his Latin was limited. What he knew for sure was that his hands were untied from the crossbeam and he was directed to bring it over to another prisoner and tie it on his shoulders instead. Slowly he realized what must have happened. *Zimran told me he was going to appeal to the procurator to release me under the festival custom,* said Barabbas to himself, remembering. *I never dreamed he would succeed. I wonder who the poor fool is who's taking my place?*

Gestas and Dismas watched enviously as Barabbas walked over to Jesus, carrying his patibulum in his arms. A soldier helped him tie it onto the obviously suffering Jesus, who received it quietly but stood trembling under the added weight.

After it had been secured, Barabbas walked around to the front of Jesus. Their eyes met. With a shock, Barabbas realized this was the alleged miracle worker from Nazareth. He had heard him speak a couple of times, had even met him once when he was teaching the people in Galilee. He had hoped that maybe the stories of this man were true, but he had not seen any miracles and his message was all about love and forgiveness. That was the last thing Barabbas was interested in. He wanted a leader who preached blood and conquest. That was the only language the Romans would understand. So he had dismissed Jesus as just another in a long line of deluded fools who thought they were Yahweh's Anointed One.

"So the chief priests caught up with you, did they? I warned you that your way would never work. Now you see who is being set free and who is going to the cross, don't you?"

Jesus looked at him sadly, without even a hint of resentment that Barabbas's freedom had been purchased with his own life. "You are not free, Barabbas. You are still imprisoned in your sins. And you will die in them, too, unless you repent and follow the way which the Father has set out for all men. I go now to purchase your freedom but you must choose to follow me." Jesus spoke slowly, his voice raspy and dry. But his love and concern still came through clearly.

"Follow you?! You better look around, Nazorean. This is a place to get away from, not to come back to." Barabbas was incredulous at Jesus' remarks. But the Lord had looked into his soul and for a moment he had felt the presence of a profound truth. Later, Barabbas did try to understand what Jesus taught. No matter how he turned it over in his mind, it seemed crazy to him. He looked, but he could not see. He listened, but he could not hear or understand.[1] The habits of force, violence and lust were too ingrained in him. So he returned to his old ways, robbing as needed to support his rebel band's attacks on the Romans. Barabbas did not live long. He was a marked man and the Romans caught up to him in the hills of Samaria.

The Romans formed up the procession for the walk to Golgotha. In front rode Longinus on horseback. Behind him came half a dozen soldiers. Behind them walked a drummer who pounded out a heavy march cadence and a boy who carried a tray holding the nails that would be used to crucify the men who were carrying their crossbeams. Behind the boy came the three condemned criminals, led by Jesus. Three soldiers with whips flanked them on either side. The rest of the soldiers and the high priest's guard detachment followed at the rear. The way of sorrows led through Jerusalem's market section. The streets there were a little wider than those in the residential section in the Lower City. They were still narrow by modern standards, but wide enough to permit crowds of Jerusalem's citizens to flank the sides of the streets to watch the procession pass. It was important that the people have an opportunity to view this walk of death. The Romans wanted to maximize the deterrent effect they hoped to achieve from this most terrible of all public executions.

With shaking legs, Jesus descended the long stairway from the western entrance of the Antonia to the street level. The crossbeam dug into his severely wounded shoulders. The weight of the wood and the protruding crown of thorns forced his head forward so that when he walked he was hunched over with his chin nearly touching his chest. The muscles in his shoulders and upper back were cramping from the strain and angle of extension of his arms. His head swam with dizziness. It was nearly noon and the hot sun glared mercilessly. His mouth felt so parched that his tongue seemed unnaturally large. His extreme thirst was almost worse than any of his other sufferings; as it was, it magnified all of them nearly past the point of his endurance. The steady beat of the drum pounded in his brain. The crown of thorns kept its piercing fingers lodged deep in his scalp. When Jesus raised his head to better see where he was going, the back portion of the crown pressed against the crossbeam, which pushed the thorns deeper into the flesh. Jesus was a strong man, but the agony he had suffered in the garden of Gethsemane, and the lack of rest, followed by the repeated beatings, punches, slaps, scourging, piercings and blows had reduced him to a state of near total exhaustion. He could barely lift his feet. The soldiers cursed his slowness and lashed at him to move more quickly.

---

[1]See Mt 13:13.

After about only a hundred yards, Jesus tripped over a raised stone on the cobbled street. He felt himself pitching forward, unable to stop his momentum, too tired to effectively twist his body away. He landed heavily on his knees, with the left one taking the full brunt of his falling weight, then crashed forward onto his chest and face. The tip of his nose was crushed into the pavement as Jesus struggled to keep the crown of thorns from hitting first and driving its deadly spikes all the way through his skull and into his brain. His nose was severely abraded on the rough stones. The crosspiece on his back fell forward but his arms managed to control it so that the crown of thorns was not pushed against the back of his head.

Longinus halted the column and barked an order: "Get him up and get that bunch of thorns off his head before he kills himself with them!"

Two of the soldiers pulled Jesus to his feet. Another one grabbed the crown gingerly, trying to avoid sticking himself, and pulled it off Jesus' head. He laid the bloody crown on the tray with the nails. The movement of the thorns refreshed the wounds and several of them began to bleed profusely again. Blood flowed down Jesus' forehead and filled his eyes, blinding him. He shook his head and blinked furiously in an effort to clear his vision, but he was only partially successful. As before, Jesus let some of the blood drip into his mouth in a desperate effort to moisten his parched lips and tongue. Longinus saw this and realized that Jesus' thirst was particularly acute. "Give the prisoner a moist cloth to suck on. I don't want him dying of thirst on the way to calvary,"[2] he ordered.

A soldier dipped a linen cloth in a container of water, wrung it out slightly, then put it in Jesus' mouth. He sucked it eagerly and while it did little to reduce his body's agonizing dehydration, it did relieve the dryness of his mouth. Longinus signaled for the drum to begin its cadence again and once more the column lurched forward. To all his other pains, Jesus now had a new one: a severe bruise on his left knee. He limped and teetered as he walked, bowed low under the weight of the patibulum, barely maintaining his balance, peering through blackened, puffy eyes obscured by blood from his bleeding scalp.

John had brought Mary and the other women to a place on the way of sorrows where they knew Jesus would pass and which would offer his mother an opportunity to see him clearly. They had hastened to this spot as soon as Jesus had been taken from the praetorium and brought to the Antonia.

Although Mary remained stoic, the other women could not control their tears. They wept and beat their breasts in frustration and distress. Some of the people they passed inquired about the reason for their tears and were shocked to learn that Jesus of Nazareth was going to be crucified that day. The word spread and the streets filled with people, some horrified, others just curious to see the prophet who had recently captivated all Israel. Those who had accepted Jesus as the Messiah sent by God were the most shocked. They could not understand what

---

[2] "Calvary" is from the Latin *calvaria*, meaning "skull."

was happening. But they were certain of one thing. If Jesus was really the Messiah, he would use his powers to avoid execution. If he was truly the Anointed One, I AM would not permit this unspeakable crime. Thus the very circumstance which the Jewish authorities feared would spur riots and violent protests on behalf of Jesus, a sentence to die as a criminal, was itself a faith-shattering event. Doubt replaced belief. Caution replaced enthusiasm. Wait-and-see replaced individual commitment. The crowd might yet have been mobilized by a leader willing to step up and remind them of the deaths of John the Baptist and some of the prophets and the perfidy of the chief priests, scribes and elders. But there was no such leader. Jesus had seen to that.

Mary, John, and the other women from Galilee stood at a spot close to where the street which the procession was following made a sharp turn to the left. This was also a point at which the street began to ascend up the western side of the Tyropoeon valley. As Jesus approached them, bent over, his eyes fixed on the ground, he was swaying badly. Clearly, he was on the verge of collapse.

When he was about six feet away, Mary stepped out of the crowd and into his path. She had not been this close to her son since Wednesday night. With an effort, he raised his eyes to gaze upon hers, but his vision was obscured by perspiration and trickling and clotting blood. He blinked desperately, struggling to see the face of his mother, needing to see the love that he knew he would find there.

Mary gasped in horror as she looked at the swollen, battered face of Jesus. His right eye was swelled nearly shut and both eyes were sunk deep inside dark rings of exhaustion and pain. Blood, dirt and dried spittle streaked his pallid face. His cheeks were puffy and striped with angry welts. His upper lip was split. The abrasion on his nose from his recent fall bled bright red. His hair was wet with blood and sweat. Sweat beaded his forehead and dripped from his nose and beard. He breathed heavily, nearly gasping. His hands and arms trembled, vibrating the crossbeam to which they were tied. In his eyes was a sadness that mourned all the cruelty and sins of man from the beginning till the end of time.

One of the guards took a step toward Mary to shove her out of the way but suddenly, and briefly, found himself unable to move. In that instant, Mary had stripped the veil from her hair and pressed it lovingly, tenderly against her son's face. His vision cleared and the touch of his mother's gentle but strong hands gave new strength to his heart, if not to his body.

As Mary pulled the veil away, she did not sob or wail. She had promised to be strong for her son and she kept her word. But she could no more have stopped her tears than she could have halted the flow of the Jordan River. They flowed out of her eyes and over her cheeks like a silent tidal wave of sorrow. For several seconds her eyes and those of her son were locked together as their two hearts spoke the language of eternity more eloquently than any other two people before or since. Surely, time itself paused to honor this meeting. Then, almost imperceptibly, Jesus smiled at his mother. Time resumed with the crack of a soldier's whip and his loud curses and demands to move on.

Jesus staggered onward, his whole body trembling with the effort of remaining upright under the crushing burden of the cross on legs that could barely stand. As the street began to ascend, Jesus slowly halted. He swayed back and forth, trying to make his feet take one more step. He fought off waves of dizziness inviting him to blissful unconsciousness and tried desperately to control his shaking. His heart pounded and his chest heaved as his body attempted to mobilize the resources necessary to keep going. But he had no reserves of strength left. His body tried to respond to his will, but it could not. He waited for the sting of the soldiers' lashes and the blast of their curses and threats. Only dimly did he hear Longinus' command.

"Get that cross off him! Can't you see the man is about to collapse? If he dies on the street, you, Galenus, will take his place on the tree!"

Galenus, who had been whipping Jesus to keep him moving, took this message to heart. He looked over at the crowd. At that moment, a husky farmer named Simon, who was from the city of Cyrene in what is today Libya in northern Africa, pushed through the front rank.[3] He had been out working in fields northwest of the city since dawn. Hot, dusty and tired, he had come into Jerusalem through the Damascus Gate and was heading through the crowded streets for his modest home in the Lower City. To get there, he had to cross the streets that formed the way of sorrows to Golgotha. Because the streets were unusually jammed anyway with Passover pilgrims, Simon didn't notice the crucifixion procession until he practically burst upon it. Then he stopped, staring at the suffering men carrying their heavy crossbeams. Before he could retrace his steps, Galenus had hold of his shoulder and was pulling him toward the lead criminal.

Simon resisted, and Galenus and two other soldiers immediately pulled their short swords and explained to him in no uncertain terms that he was going to carry the patibulum for Jesus or they would split him open right where he stood. Simon muttered an oath and moved toward Jesus. He could not believe his rotten luck. Because he was not a criminal himself, the cross was not tied to Simon. In fact, as Jesus had time during this interlude to rest a bit, he regained some strength. Galenus, mindful of the Roman rule that crucifixion victims were required to carry their crosses to their place of execution, decided that Jesus was still strong enough to help carry his patibulum. So Simon carried the back end and Jesus had the front end on his left shoulder with his hands tied around it.

Before the two men were "locked" together along the crossbeam, Jesus looked at Simon, who had been muttering angrily since being drafted for his terrible duty. His appearance alone touched something decent in Simon and he suddenly felt pity for the battered and bloody man before him. But there was more in the dark, mournful eyes than mere suffering. There was gratitude and a promise. Simon felt a powerful surge of emotion sweep over him. He wanted to weep and yet he had not the slightest idea why. It was certainly not from

---

[3]All three of the Synoptic Gospels report this incident. See Mt 27:32, Mk 15:21, and Lk 23:26.

sympathy for condemned criminals, most of whom he felt invited their punishment from the Roman authorities. Simon did not understand his reaction, but he stopped resisting and accepted his share of the crossbeam. He noted which foot Jesus started off with and timed his own pace to match so that he would not accidentally trip him.

Jesus struggled up the steep hill. Even with Simon's help, he could barely make it. He walked bent over like an old man, the cross grinding into his left shoulder with each agonizing step. His arms were so tired that he could only let them hang from the beam, which had the effect of increasing its weight on him.

Simon moved a little closer, trying to take more of the weight on himself. The sun bore down on them. Jesus kept trying to swallow to ease the passage of the air which he was inhaling and exhaling in sharp, dry gasps and to get some tiny relief in a mouth that felt as parched as desert sand. The inexorable pounding of the drum only a few feet ahead of him assaulted his senses. Waves of nausea and dizziness rolled over him. His head throbbed with an excruciating headache that mingled with the bloody thorn wounds in a screeching cacophony of pain. Again and again he felt his consciousness start to slip away and again and again he fought to remain on his feet.

The people lining both sides of the street were mostly silent, though not all. Many were as horrified as if a member of their own family were on his way to Golgotha. Many more felt pity but not a greater degree for one of the criminals than the other, although Jesus was, by far, in the worst shape. Still others were hostile, loudly deriding Jesus for his pretentious claims to be the Messiah and challenging him to call on his Father to save him if he really was who he claimed to be. Some of these persons had been ardent supporters only a few days ago of Jesus' claim to be the Messiah. Now they were embarrassed and angry that they had been duped by this pathetic creature hobbling to his death as a criminal, one who, according to their Torah, was accursed by God.[4] Jesus ignored them, looking straight ahead, seemingly concentrating all his attention on the daunting task of simply putting one foot in front of the other.

A tall, elegant, middle-aged woman of about fifty watched the procession approach. Her name was Seraphia. She was the wife of Sirach, a Temple councillor, and their well-appointed home was just off the way of sorrows. She was an ardent believer in Jesus, although her husband's position required that she be discreet about her support.

The crowd was a living, moving body, engulfing the street from side to side, with gaps for the condemned men and their angry, shouting guards. Catcalls and the crack of whips punctuated the din dominated by the relentless drum cadence.

Through an opening in the flowing river of people, Seraphia saw him. His face was once again begrimed with sweat and blood. His mother's quick brush

---

[4]See Gal 3:13, Dt 21:23.

had done little for the dirt streaking his bearded cheeks and neck. Spittle from antagonists in the crowd was gobbed here and there on his face and hair. Without hesitating, Seraphia darted in front of the Lord and pulled the veil from her head. In one quick motion, she pressed the cloth against his face. The whole thing took no more than five seconds and caught the soldiers off guard. Galenus moved to shove her away but glanced up and saw Longinus pause on his horse and turn around. Longinus raised his hand slightly in a gesture of forbearance and Galenus and the other soldiers backed off.

Jesus whispered, "Thank you," and turned once again to his struggle to make it up the hill. The soldiers shoved roughly past the woman who retreated weeping into the crowd. When she was out of the crush of the noisy bystanders, she looked at the cloth veil. There where she had pressed it against the face of Jesus was his image, eyes closed, suffering face momentarily in repose.[5]

As the long, ascending street finally topped out, Jesus was nearly out of the city. The gate loomed only about fifty yards ahead. Outside the gate, the cries and wails of a large group of women could already be heard. A few of these were professional mourners, paid to weep over any Jew who was about to be crucified so that no one should go to the cross without some sign of sorrow. But most were sincerely moved and wept their tears out of a genuine love for the Lord and a firm conviction that Israel was making the greatest mistake in her history.

Jesus and Simon struggled onward. As the ground leveled out, Jesus was able to stand more erect. But his legs were still shaky and his strength just barely sufficient to keep him moving forward. So exhausted was he by now, that he was almost unaware of the burning pain that inflamed his entire left shoulder. This was caused by the crossbeam that continued to press and grind the deep scourging wounds there.

As he entered the gateway, the ground became rockier and more uneven. Jesus could barely lift his feet off the ground. He wobbled from side to side, almost staggering, as he concentrated all of his attention and dwindling strength on taking just one more step . . . then another . . . and another . . . and another. As he dragged his feet forward, the sole of his right sandal caught slightly in a depression between two little stony ridges. His foot held fast and Jesus had no chance to keep his balance. He pitched forward once again, slightly breaking his fall by hanging onto the crossbeam which Simon was desperately trying to hold up and off the sprawling body of the Lord. By now, Simon was keeping nothing back and was doing everything he could short of bearing the cross all by himself.

But try as he might, Simon could not break Jesus' fall. He fell hard against the stone pavement and scattered rocks, battering his already bruised knees. The side of the patibulum clubbed him in the back of his head and drove his forehead against the ground. His eyes watered with tears from the pain that shot from the

---

[5]We now honor Seraphia as "Veronica" in the Sixth Station of the Cross.

tender, swollen knees. He was dazed by the blow to his forehead where a large lump quickly formed.[6]

Crumpled in the dirt and loose stones, his body one ghastly, throbbing torment from his feet to the top of his head, dehydrated and emotionally spent, Jesus considered where he had fallen. His heart broke with the realization that he had been expelled bodily from Jerusalem, the City of David, the capital of his people, the ones chosen from all time to be the society that would bring God's reconciliation to mankind. He lay gasping on the ground, holding back his tears for his poor, misguided countrymen, waiting for the pounding in his brain and the fog in his vision to dissipate. Then a stab of fear struck him in his stomach as he comprehended the nearness of Golgotha and the culminating torture that awaited him there.

"Get up, you oaf!" shouted Galenus. He cursed the prone Jesus and kicked and lashed him. Jesus struggled to rise under the rain of insults and blows, but his tied hands and exhaustion prevented it. When Galenus saw that he could not get up, he directed two of the soldiers to pull him to his feet.

"Sir, let me carry the cross by myself," said Simon to Galenus. "This man is near death now and certainly cannot survive much more of this punishment." Galenus looked at Longinus, who sat impassively on his horse looking at him as if to remind him of his threat to crucify him instead of Jesus if he let him die on the way of sorrows.

Galenus swore and growled: "All right. Cut him loose and let this man carry the beam for him. Soon enough we'll have his carcass nailed to a tree where it belongs!"

When the soldiers had pulled Jesus erect, Galenus gave him a lash across his back to compensate for not having to carry his own crossbeam. Jesus stumbled, but did not fall, and lurched forward. The drum beat its melancholy dirge and the wail of the women grew louder. Behind him, an even larger crowd pressed through the gate behind the rear guard. In their midst walked Jesus' mother, accompanied by John, Mary of Clopas, Mary Magdalene and several other women followers of Jesus.

As Jesus drew abreast of the women mourners, who shrieked and wailed and beat their breasts in a frenzy of sorrow, the procession ground to a halt. The nearness of Golgotha had compressed the crowds of people and Longinus and his soldiers were temporarily halted as they cursed and shouted at the people to clear the roadway. Jesus turned toward the women and looked at them with eyes filled with compassion. He opened his mouth to speak and they fell silent. The words came out gently from a throat that could barely croak.

"Daughters of Jerusalem, do not weep for me. Weep for yourselves and for your children. The days are coming

---

[6]The computer-enhanced three-dimensional photographs of the Shroud of Turin taken by the electronic VP-8 Image Analyzer reveal what appears to be a large lump on Jesus' forehead.

when they will say, 'Happy are the sterile, the wombs
that never bore and the breasts that never nursed.' Then
they will begin saying to the mountains, 'Fall on us,' and
to the hills, 'Cover us.' If they do these things in the
green wood, what will happen in the dry?'"[7]

But the women did not understand his meaning. They did not begin to
comprehend his metaphor of green wood and dry. Jesus was, and is, the light of
the world, the living vine of God. His followers would become the branches of this
vine, bearing fruit from the sap of his divine grace. From Jesus comes life. Without
him, there is neither life nor growth, neither peace nor reconciliation. By rejecting
her Savior, Israel severed herself from the sustaining action of God who had
conquered her enemies and preserved and restored her for centuries. Now, like a
dead tree, the nation would wither and the Romans would cast it as dry wood into
the fire of its utter destruction in 70 A.D.

All that the women could see now, though, was the imminent fate of this
poor man before them. That a person in his situation would be expressing pity for
their future was beyond their grasp. Those who believed in him may have feared
the just wrath of God for this terrible act, but no one thought that he was warning
them of the total destruction of their nation in little more than a single generation.
They continued to loudly wail and weep and Jesus turned sadly away from them,
grateful for their sympathy but longing for their comprehension of the message of
his ministry.

Centurion Longinus shouted an order and the procession started up again.
They were less than 200 yards from the place of crucifixion and all the condemned
men felt the terror of its approach. Even without the cross to carry, Jesus could
barely walk. He plodded onward, head down, lost in his struggle to stay conscious
and on his feet. Simon whispered encouragement to him, a kindness that Jesus
appreciated more than he was able to show.

After passing through the gate, the procession wound along the path
outside the city's western wall. Ahead and to their left loomed the stark outline of
the crucifixion knoll in the middle of the quarry, looking like its namesake, a
grinning skull with "eyes," "nose" and "mouth" marked out by rock formations
and a fortuitously placed tomb. Its summit was nearly 25 feet high and was
reached by a gradual rise from the southeastern side of the quarry. On the north,
the rock face dropped off abruptly and it was this side that gave the place its
name. The top of the knoll was about twenty yards across and crisscrossed with
paths to facilitate coming and going by soldiers, officials, family members and
spectators. Bristling on the top were six upright posts, the *stipes* portion of the
cross. Each one stood about eight feet from ground to tip. A mortise was cut into
the post at the seven foot level and into this groove the patibulum was fit and
nailed. After the victim, or *cruciarius* as he was called, had died, it was relatively

---

[7]Lk 23:28-31

easy to hammer the patibulum out of its groove and re-use it at times when the number of executions was unusually high.

Jesus walked slowly, stumbling but catching himself, staring at the stark hillock and its deadly spikes. Here the sacrifice of the Lamb of God would take place in mere minutes. The sun beat down from a bright blue sky. There was not a cloud to be seen. Among the crowd of people present, only one person fully understood what was about to transpire here. Only the Son of God knew that this grim spot would change the destiny of countless human beings for all eternity. Less than one-half mile away, thousands of lambs were about to be slaughtered to commemorate the deliverance of Israel from physical bondage to Egypt. In a vastly crueler fashion, one Lamb would deliver the souls of all people from bondage to sin. Jesus, exhausted, tormented by severe dehydration and thirst, suffering excruciating pain all over his body, too tired to weep or mourn, rejoiced that the compact his Father had made with Abraham was about to be fulfilled. That joyful reunion, whose divine dimensions are beyond our comprehension, was mere hours away.

But there was a terrible abyss of suffering between that moment and this one when Jesus was still on his way of sorrows. Apprehension increased his trembling and distracted him from the rocky path which he trod haltingly. For a third time, he lost his footing and sprawled heavily into the dirt. For a third time, his body crashed against the unforgiving stones, bleeding and bruised. This time, Jesus' hands were free to break his fall, and he rolled slightly to his right to spare his nearly broken kneecaps. The stones tore at the flesh on his palms and elbows and left deep contusions on his side from his shoulder to the calf of his leg. He lay stunned for a few moments, weary to the point of death, until the soldiers began to kick and lash him, cursing and yelling at him to get up. Slowly, he did so. Then, looking once more at the crucifixion knoll, he seemed almost to draw energy from the sight. His step grew firmer and he walked with grim purpose. The last 75 yards passed and Jesus stood at the foot of his cross. His journey was almost over.

FIRST LETTER OF PAUL TO THE CORINTHIANS

The Wisdom and Folly of the Cross

The message of the cross is complete absurdity to those who are headed for ruin, but to us who are experiencing salvation it is the power of God. Scripture says,

> "I will destroy the wisdom
> of the wise,
> and thwart the cleverness
> of the clever."

Where is the wise man to be found? Where the scribe? Where is the master of worldly argument? Has not God turned the wisdom of this world into folly? Since in God's wisdom the world did not come to know him through "wisdom," it pleased God to save those who believe through the absurdity of the preaching of the gospel. Yes, Jews demand "signs" and Greeks look for "wisdom," but we preach Christ crucified—a stumbling block to Jews, and an absurdity to Gentiles; but to those who are called, Jews and Greeks alike, Christ the power of God and the wisdom of God. For God's folly is wiser than men, and his weakness more powerful than men.

I Cor 1:18-25

QUESTIONS FOR REFLECTION

(1) If you had been one of Jesus' many believers, but not an apostle or close disciple, how do you think you would have reacted to seeing him carrying his cross on his way to be crucified?

(2) What can we learn from the example of Simon of Cyrene who helped Jesus carry his cross but only after being forced to do so?

(3) What can we learn from the example of Seraphia (Veronica) who braved the hostility of the authorities and the rejection of the crowd to help Jesus?

(4) Jesus said that if anyone wishes to be his disciple he must take up his cross and follow him (Mt 16:24, Lk 9:23). What did he mean by this? How can you apply Jesus' instruction to your own life?

(5) St. Louis de Montfort wrote: *"Wisdom is the cross and the cross is Wisdom."* What does this mean to you?

(6) "Barabbas" means "son of the father" in Hebrew. Do you find it ironic that the "son of the father" should be spared while the "Son of the Father" is crucified in his place? Or, can you see a powerful symbolism here?

(7) In speaking to the women of Jerusalem, what did Jesus mean by comparing "green wood" to "dry wood?" Do you see any parallels to other periods in history, even our own time?

(8) What thoughts do you think Mary might have had when she encountered her Son on his way of the cross? Do you think she had doubts, questions, fear . . . or perfect acceptance? Or all of the above?

(9) Do you imagine that Jesus gave his mother instructions about what to do and not do during his carrying of the cross to Golgotha? Or do you think he simply left it to the grace of his Father and his mother's perfect Heart to determine her response?

(10) What are the burdens, sorrows and difficulties that make up your own way of the cross? Do you see how Jesus wants to be your Simon and Mary your Veronica to help you on your journey? Have you asked them? Do you see how Jesus wants you to help others to bear their burdens of sorrow?

Seeing his mother there with the disciple whom he loved, Jesus said to his mother,
"Woman, there is your son." In turn he said to the disciple, "There is your mother."
Jn 19:26-27

THE FIFTH SORROWFUL MYSTERY

The Crucifixion

The climb to the top of the knoll known as Golgotha had been steep and difficult. But Jesus, despite his wounds and weakened physical state, had seemed almost eager to get there. Dismas and Gestas, the two insurgents who were to be crucified along with Jesus, had shown no such enthusiasm. Dismas' step had slowed noticeably, which produced the predictable lashing and cursing by the Roman soldiers, but he was otherwise quiet. Gestas protested, threatened and cursed the whole way. In the last fifty yards, fear devoured his strength and pride and his knees buckled under him twice. Each time, he was lashed, kicked and cursed until the torrent of abuse overwhelmed the dread that paralyzed his limbs.

At the top of the knoll, the Roman soldiers, experienced in this particularly gruesome function, went to work efficiently. First, they extracted the wooden wedges that held the upright stipes in their vertical position. Then they pulled the posts out of the holes in the rock that had been carved for them and laid them down. About a foot from the top of the stipes was a mortise into which the crossbeam would be laid and fastened with three nails.

Following the soldiers, Jesus had led the way up the steep path to the top of Golgotha. Behind him, Simon labored to carry the heavy patibulum. He was followed by the other two men to be crucified. At the top, two soldiers took the crossbeam from Simon and ordered him off the knoll. He paused before heading back down the path, a solitary figure moving against the upward bound traffic of soldiers, spectators, Jewish officials, and followers of Jesus. He wanted to apologize to Jesus for not being able to do more to help him, but Jesus cut him off with a whispered *"Thank you,"* and a promise of his Father's blessing to Simon and his family.[1]

While the two pieces of the cross were being nailed together, the condemned criminals were stripped of their clothing. Gestas and Dismas, coming out of the dungeons at the Fortress Antonia, wore only a ragged tunic over their loin cloths and sandals. Jesus was more completely dressed with his cloak, now

---

[1]Two of Simon's children, Alexander and Rufus, later became disciples and probably priests in the infant Christian church. cf. Mk 15:21.

soiled and stained, over his tunic. Their clothes were roughly stripped from each of the three men. Scourging wounds, particularly on Jesus who had been much more savagely beaten, were torn open and bled anew as the cloth, adhering to the wounds as they had scabbed over, clung to the damaged flesh. Ordinarily, Roman crucifixion victims were hung naked on their crosses. But in Palestine, the strong Jewish aversion to nudity had produced a compromise that permitted even condemned criminals to retain their loin cloths. The clothing of the three men was tossed in separate piles near their crosses.

Jesus was crucified first. He was shoved down roughly on his back on the stipes and his arms were pulled out along the crossbeam. Two soldiers were at each hand. Holes had been bored in the wood at the point where the hands were expected to reach. However, the placement of these holes in the newly-cut patibulum had been measured hurriedly and based on the arm length of Barabbas, who was nearly as tall as Jesus with unusually long arms. As a consequence, Jesus' hands near the wrists, where the nails would bind them to the wood, were significantly short of the holes.

"Galenus, what do we do?" asked one of the soldiers, pointing to the gap between Jesus' wrists and the nail holes. "We'll never get these nails through that wood without predrilling the holes but no one brought an auger."

"The Jew will just have to grow longer arms," chuckled Galenus. "Start with his right hand first."

Jesus was pulled to his right until his right wrist lined up with the hole in the wood. One soldier knelt on the inner part of his lower arm, crushing it against the wood, while the other expertly placed the sharp point of the square crucifixion nail in the thickest part of the *thenar furrow* of the palm.[2] The nail was angled back about 20-25 degrees so that when the cruciarius hung from the cross, the weight of his body would pull the nails into the wood. The nail would be driven through a slight opening in the hand/wrist bones before emerging in the back of the hand at the wrist. This path placed the nail firmly in the bone structure, although it did not break any of them, so that it would not rip out of Jesus' hands as his 175-pound body weight generated some 200 pounds of gravitational force on *each* arm.[3] When the six-inch nail was placed, the soldier raised his square-headed iron hammer high and drove the nail through Jesus' hand and deep into the wood. The nail ran along the trunk of the median nerve, one of the most sensitive nerves in the body and the one that gives the hand its extraordinary sense of touch. Jesus' body arched and his fingers reflexively curled toward the nail as the pain

---

[2]This furrow is located at the base of the muscle prominence where the palm swells at the base of the thumb. It is the curved fold in the skin which is formed when you touch the tip of your thumb to the tip of your little finger.

[3]This is according to the laws of physics that say that the pull on each arm is a factor of weight and the angle of the arm from the vertical. The greater the angle, the greater the pull. Zugibe, *Cross and the Shroud*, 53-57. Of course, once Jesus' feet were nailed to the stipes, he would no longer be hanging free so the total pull on his arms would have been less. Nonetheless, the gravitational tug would have seemed crushingly powerful.

exploded in his hand and arm. He clenched his teeth to stifle the scream that sought to escape his swollen, bruised lips. The nail was thick and required many powerful blows before its bell-shaped head, nearly one inch across, came to rest in Jesus' palm, pinning it tightly against the wooden beam. The point of the nail protruded more than an inch through the back of the beam.

Next the soldiers turned to Jesus' left hand, which was short of the drilled hole by nearly the length of his hand. Galenus put a slip knot in a piece of rope and tied it around Jesus' left wrist. "You two—grab hold of this rope and pull the Jew's arm until it's long enough to put the nail in the hole," he told the soldiers. Gesturing to the two soldiers who had nailed Jesus' right hand, he said, "Hang on over there and make sure the nail doesn't pull the hand apart."

The soldiers managed to force Jesus' left hand far enough to put the nail in the hole, although his shoulders were nearly dislocated in the process. Jesus' suffering was indescribable and even some of the soldiers squirmed a bit from watching the infliction of such agony. As the nail tore through his left wrist, the lightning bolt of pain seemed to shatter his arm. Blood spurted out of the wound but subsided as pressure from the nail head compressed the bleeding veins. Damage to the median nerve in both hands left them feeling as if a fire burned within them. Combined with the torture of his over-stressed shoulder and elbow joints, the pain overwhelmed his senses and drove Jesus into incoherent, semi-conscious moaning.[4]

When Jesus' hands had been nailed, the soldiers turned to his feet. His knees were bent and drawn up until the feet lay flat against the stipes and provided a solid nailing surface. There were already numerous holes in the post from previous crucifixion victims of differing heights and leg lengths. Ordinarily the feet were placed side-by-side and nailed separately because this was easiest to accomplish and the effect was about the same. But today, Galenus interjected: "Wait. Our 'king' here should not be nailed like any common criminal. He needs something to distinguish him. Put his left foot on top of his right and nail them together."

Soranus, the Roman soldier holding the hammer and nails about to be driven into the Lord's feet, objected: "Crucifixion is bad enough, Galenus, without twisting the legs and feet to increase the muscle cramping. Besides, it's easier to nail them separately."

"I'm in charge of this detail, Soranus, and you'll do it the way I tell you! If you don't like it, tell the centurion you're feeling sorry for the Jew. When you do, be sure to remind him about the soldiers he has lost to these Jewish bandits."

---

[4]This description of Jesus' nailing is based upon the visions of the Venerable Anne Catherine Emmerich who described Jesus' arms as being torn from their sockets with distended shoulders and disjointed elbows. *Life of Jesus Christ and Biblical Revelations*, v. 4, 272. This horrific description is supported somewhat by the Shroud of Turin where the image of Jesus' right arm does appear to be longer than the left. Even if merely an excess of morbid imagination, the scene so pictured helps one to understand why crucifixion was considered too terrible a punishment for any Roman citizen, no matter his crime.

Soranus shook his head but gave up the argument. "All right, hold his feet steady," he said to the soldier helping him. "And give me one of the extra long nails, too." He started to call for a third soldier to assist, but Jesus voluntarily put his left foot on top of his right and tried to hold it there against the trembling that shook his entire body. Soranus placed the nail midway up the left foot where the metatarsal bones converge and drove it in a single blow through both feet and into the wood of the upright. Several more heavy blows were required to anchor the feet solidly. Each one drove the square iron nail roughly past the plantar and peroneal nerves which, like damage to the median nerve in the hands, caused a vicious burning sensation as if his hands and feet had been literally set ablaze. Although he managed not to scream, Jesus could not suppress a groan that sounded as if his very skeleton was being sundered. His face contorted in agony and his fingers clutched the heads of the nails pinning his hands to the rough wood of the crossbeam. His lips moved in silent prayer and his eyes were tightly closed.

As Jesus lay there, a soldier from Antonius' command at the praetorium came running up to Longinus. "Pilate has sent this sign to be placed on the cross of the Nazorean." Longinus took the sign and read it. It consisted of three lines, one each in Hebrew, Latin and Greek, all of them declaring:

JESUS THE NAZOREAN
THE KING OF THE JEWS.[5]

Longinus looked down at Jesus. Hardly a spot on his body, from the top of his scalp to the bottoms of his feet, was not bloody, bruised or torn. The muscles in his arms and legs were tensed against the pain of the nails binding him to the cross beneath him. His eyes remained crunched slits above jaw muscles locked in rippled knots. Lines of blood had left meandering downward trails on his forehead and face. Fresh blood dripped down the sides of his hands and feet. *Not much of a king,* thought Longinus. *Still, there is a dignity, almost a majesty, about him that shows through all his suffering. A strange man, indeed.*

Longinus gave the sign to one of his soldiers and told him to nail it on Jesus' cross above his head. As the soldier did so, some of the chief priests and scribes crowded forward to see what the sign said. They were deeply offended. "You can't write that! This man was not our king. He only pretended to be one."

"If you have a problem, take it up with the Procurator. He's the one who made the sign," replied Longinus disdainfully. He did not like the Jews, especially their pompous leaders.

So a delegation of the chief priests and scribes headed back down the little knoll and hurried along the city wall, passing through the Jaffa Gate and then the

---

[5]Jn 19:19

Ginnoth Gate. When they reached the archway leading into the palace, they demanded that Pilate come out.

Pilate refused to see them. But the Jewish leaders did not go away quietly. They insisted that the guard at the entrance to the praetorium take their message to the procurator: **"You should not have written, 'The King of the Jews.' Write instead, 'This man claimed to be King of the Jews.'"**[6]

When Pilate received the message he was livid. He was already angry with himself for letting the Jews pressure him into executing a man whom they all knew posed no threat to Rome. Now they wanted to be free of any taint of scandal that might suggest they had been disloyal to their own country. They had cleverly manipulated Roman authority to their own ends. *Well, now they can just live with the results,* fumed Pilate. "Tell the Jews that **what I have written, I have written,**"[7] Pilate instructed his messenger and stalked out of the room.

While Jesus was being nailed to his cross, Gestas and Dismas were also being nailed. Four nails were used on them as their feet were nailed separately.

When all three men had been fastened to their crosses, the soldiers picked them up one at a time, Jesus first. Four men lifted the cross and placed the foot of the stipes back in the hole that had been carved in the rock for it. At each end of the patibulum there was a round iron ring with a rope passed through it. Two soldiers held each rope to guide the cross and keep it from tipping left or right as two others pushed it upright. The victim on the cross felt the agonizing pains in his hands and feet increase exponentially as he was raised into a vertical position and all his weight came to bear on the three or four iron spikes suspending him above the ground. Worst of all was the drop when the stipes was vertical enough to plunge into the hole. Most men, no matter how stoic up to that point, could not stifle a scream from pain so severe it felt as if their hands and feet were being torn apart. With the cross in its upright position, the wooden wedges were quickly hammered back between the stipes and the edges of the hole to hold it firmly in place.

The three men, momentarily delirious from the pain and traumatic shock of the crucifixion process, hung from their crosses, Jesus in the middle. Gestas on his left and Dismas on his right moaned incessantly as drool and perspiration dripped from their open mouths and contorted faces. Jesus also sweat profusely but managed to keep his teeth tightly clenched as he continued to pray fervently and silently.

As Jesus' cross thudded into place, Galenus noticed that his crown of thorns remained on the tray on which it had been carried during most of the way of sorrows. He remembered that Jesus had been wearing the crown of thorns when Pilate sent him to the Antonia. *Obviously the Procurator intends that the Nazorean be crucified with his 'crown' on,* thought Galenus. *He even sent over a sign announcing that*

---

[6]Jn 19:21

[7]Jn 19:22

he is the king of the Jews. By standing atop one of the wedges holding the cross in place, Galenus could just reach the top of Jesus' head. Straining, but holding the thorns gingerly, he shoved the "crown" onto the bowed and bloody head. Jesus, already under mortal assault from his multiple wounds, seemed hardly to notice the piercing, needle-sharp thorns.

With their victims successfully nailed to their crosses, the soldiers turned to dividing up their clothing as the spoils of this particular punishment. Jesus' clothing had value not only because it was superior to the rags that Gestas and Dismas wore but also because he was famous throughout Israel. The Roman soldiers knew that his fame would raise the price of his clothing in spite of the method of his death. The soldiers started to argue among themselves about who would get what, but Longinus cut it short by announcing that he would distribute the goods. First, he tossed Jesus' tasseled cloak to Galenus, an ironic reward for the soldier who had been the most abusive of Jesus. But Galenus was the foot soldier in charge, so he received the best garment. Next, the head scarf that Jesus had worn around his waist as a binding for his cloak was given to another soldier. Then the sash girdle that had bound his tunic at the waist was given to yet a different soldier. Last, Longinus threw the sandals to a fourth member of the guard. That left only Jesus' tunic. The centurion saw that it was a fine garment, woven in a style that had only recently come into fashion as improvements in these ancient looms had permitted the garments to be created in one piece. Prior to this time, they had been woven in two pieces and sewn together horizontally at the waist.

"Galenus, this tunic is too good to rip apart. You and the other men can cast lots to see who gets it," ordered Longinus. One of the soldiers produced a pair of dice which he carried in his purse. With these, the distribution of the Lord's clothing was completed and the prophecy of King David in Psalm 22 was fulfilled:

**They divided my garments among them;
for my clothing they cast lots.**[8]

As the soldiers huddled around the base of Christ's cross, groaning and cheering as their respective interests were affected by the roll of the dice, a shadow seemed to pass over the sun. Few paid any attention at the time, but some looked up, expecting to see a cloud drifting through the sky, wondering if it presaged a change in the balmy Spring weather. There was no cloud. Only the sun shining down through a clear sky. Nonetheless, it was noticeably darker. It was only half past noon, but the light conditions suggested late afternoon already, with dusk rapidly approaching.

Numerous people gathered on the knoll to witness the crucifixions. Most interest focused upon Jesus. Large numbers of Passover pilgrims were passing by

---

[8]Jn 19:24, Ps 22:19

on the two roads that converged near Golgotha. By now the word had spread throughout Jerusalem that the prophet from Galilee had been crucified by the Romans. Nearly everyone who heard this was shocked. The signs and wonders performed by Jesus had been overwhelming. Most of the people had been convinced he was the Messiah and were simply waiting for him to assert his claim with a call to action against the Romans. Even those who were not completely convinced admitted that there was no other explanation for his powers if God was not with him. Therefore, to see him now hanging in disgrace in this most cruel of executions was a stunning reversal. Despite all the evidence to the contrary, somehow Jesus must have performed his miracles without Yahweh's assistance, they decided. It was simply inconceivable to them that I AM, the creator of the universe, the God who had brought His people out of Egypt and defeated Pharaoh and the Egyptian army in the process, could let His Son be killed like this. Having concluded that Jesus had to be an imposter, these people turned on him angrily, demanding: **"So you are the one who was going to destroy the temple and rebuild it in three days! Save yourself, why don't you? Come down off that cross if you are God's Son!"**[9]

Although their taunts were cruel and motivated by anger, frustration and embarrassment, there was also a tiny, lingering hope that maybe it was all a secret plan to demonstrate Jesus' awesome power and authority. This little hope glimmered that maybe, just maybe, Jesus was the Messiah after all and would yet prove it. The hope was, of course, perfectly founded and shortly to be vindicated, only not in the way they wished. But at this moment, almost no one grasped that death was the doorway to a life both eternal and unimaginably better than the one we know, and that Jesus, the Son of God, was on the cross to teach us this infinitely more important truth. What a hollow triumph it would have been if he had come down from the cross, established a world kingdom for Israel and then left mankind without hope for anything more than the brutal struggle that characterizes so much of human life on earth. We would have been given the triumph of the strong and the powerful, the privileged and the gifted, whom the world already rewards. But the poor and the unfortunate, the ignorant and the misguided, the weak and the powerless would have been spurned as always, confirmed in their wretched fate. The Messiah as world conqueror, no matter how wise and benevolent, would only have changed the names on the place cards. It would still be a world of competition and struggle, of winners and losers. The Kingdom of God is a place with no losers, no underclass, a place where the common currency is love and joy. Such treasure is granted by the generosity of God for helping, serving, loving and supporting others, not ourselves. We are upside down on this planet. No wonder it was so difficult for his contemporaries to comprehend Jesus' teachings.

---

[9]Mt 27:40

Still, he must have been tempted to demonstrate his power, especially in the depth of his sufferings and to those who mocked him. But he was far too loving to do this. He remained hanging in agony, enduring the taunts and jeers of those he came to save. Who can comprehend a love which under these circumstances would cry out: **"Father, forgive them; they do not know what they are doing."?**[10] That cry was not merely for the Jews and Romans who had condemned Jesus to death. That cry was for everyone who has sinned or will sin, from Adam to the last human born of his line. That cry was for you and me. That cry was the turn of the key unlocking the Gate of Heaven. If Jesus had come down from his cross, the door would have remained closed for all time. The souls of mankind were not compatible with the infinite Love that resides in Heaven until the sacrifice of Jesus paid our collective debt and gave us the means (grace) to wash ourselves clean of the stain of our sin.

The chief priests, scribes and elders still saw the promised Messiah as someone who would be sent from God to restore power and authority to Israel, under their leadership, of course. Their sin was the age-old one of pride, the very sin that first cast mankind out of God's favor. The same tendency is still prominent in nearly all of us. We desire God to support our opinions and views of how things should be done. Despite repeated admonitions in Scripture that God's ways are not our ways and that we must place our trust in Him the way little children place their trust in their parents, most of us seem unable to do it. We are certain that we know what is best for us, from career success to good health to being right in matters religious, and if life does not follow the path we have outlined, we become convinced that God has turned His back on us. Like Adam and Eve who sought to be like God, we demand that God bless our endeavors in this world and then reward us in the next life as well.

But happiness can only be found in doing the will of God, as painful (ask Jesus) as that may be sometimes. We are called to serve, not to be served. It is only in giving that we can receive, only in forgiving that we can be forgiven, only in loving that we can find love, only in surrendering that we can be victorious.

The Jewish authorities gathered on the knoll before Jesus and jeered him. They encouraged and incited the onlookers to scorn the crucified Christ:

> **"He saved others but he cannot save himself! So he is the**
> **king of Israel! Let's see him come down from that cross**
> **and then we will believe in him. He relied on God; let**
> **God rescue him now if he wants to. After all, he claimed,**
> **'I am God's Son.'"**[11]

Gestas, hanging in agony at Jesus' left, transferred his anger and bitterness to the Lord. Like the people who laughed at and scorned Jesus out of disappointment over his failure to fulfill their expectations of Messianic triumph,

---

[10] Lk 23:34

[11] Mt 27:42-43; see also Mk 15:31-32 and Lk 23:35.

so Gestas cursed the man who seemed to have the power to save them all. "**Aren't you the Messiah?**" he asked contemptuously. "**Then save yourself and us.**"[12] Surely he hoped that his angry challenge would provoke Jesus into doing what he, Gestas, thought best, a judgment shared by almost everyone there. But Jesus did not then and does not now respond to taunts and jeers. To do so would make him an accomplice in our sin.

Dismas, on Jesus' right, gathered his strength against the overwhelming pain of gravity trying to pull his body through the nails that held him to his cross. "**Have you no fear of God, seeing you are under the same sentence? We deserve it, after all. We are only paying the price for what we've done, but this man has done nothing wrong,**" he gasped in rebuke of Gestas. Then Dismas said something so astonishing that even Jesus was amazed. "**Jesus, remember me when you enter upon your reign.**"[13]

Where did such faith come from? What did Dismas see that no one else, except Jesus' mother and maybe a few disciples, could see? How could he see the victory of Christ through the disgrace and horror of death by crucifixion? Of all the miracles in the New Testament of sight being restored to the blind, none compares to the insight that Dismas displayed at this moment.

Slowly, Jesus raised his head and turned to look at Dismas with wonder and gratitude and joy. Here at a moment when his humanity may have been waging its own struggle with despair, came a gift from his Father, a reminder that Jesus' sacrifice could ignite the flame of love and faith in the deepest pit of darkness. Despite his unbearable agony, Jesus managed almost to smile as he replied: "**I assure you: this day you will be with me in paradise.**"[14] And so Saint Dismas was born, the only Saint personally and publicly attested to by our Lord and Savior, Jesus Christ.

The public revilement went on for awhile but gradually dissipated as the sky grew darker and darker. The sun occupied its correct place in the sky but now, like a fire's embers exhausted by the effort of keeping a long night's darkness at bay, barely glowed. A kind of hush fell across the scene, disturbed only by the labored breathing and groans of the crucified men. In addition to the excruciating pain emanating from their hands and feet where gravity tugged the raw flesh relentlessly against the metal spikes, their whole bodies trembled from the muscular strain of hanging in such a vertical position. Their upper thighs burned and had long been cramping severely. It was a pain threatening madness as the men sought some way to relieve the unbearable strain. Elbows and shoulders shrieked with pain, especially when the legs were relaxed in an effort to gain some respite from the torture in the legs and feet. Pushing upward against the nail(s) in

---

[12]Lk 23:39

[13]This quote and the one from Gestas are from Lk 23:39-42.

[14]Lk 23:43

the feet produced some slight relief but only at the cost of magnifying the pain there nearly to the point of fainting. For Jesus, this solution was doubly terrible because his feet were nailed one on top of the other. To gain any relief from the vicious pain in his hands and along his arms, he had to mash his left foot down hard on top of his right one as both of them crushed their raw wounds against the nail. In addition, the strain on his right thigh muscles was increased dramatically because it was the primary brace for the body's weight.

As if this were not enough torture, Jesus could not straighten his neck to relieve the agony in his cramping shoulder muscles. The crown of thorns prevented that.

The circulation of each cruciarius was so adversely affected that very quickly their limbs became cold to the touch and their toes and fingers icy. Yet the inner sensation was of arm, leg and torso muscles and nerves in flame. Their breathing was labored and shallow, not because of the risk of asphyxiation, because there was none with their arms outstretched, but because their normal physical functioning was so disrupted by the severe pain and circulatory stress. Traumatic, circulatory and hypovolemic shock from the loss of fluids due to perspiration and bleeding led to low blood pressure and put enormous strain on their hearts. Jesus in particular, whose pre-crucifixion agonies and fluid loss had horribly exceeded those normally experienced by even the most heinous crucifixion victim, struggled to remain conscious and alive.

At the foot of the cross, standing perhaps ten feet away, one person suffered almost as much as Jesus. His mother leaned heavily on the young John, praying and begging God to let her bear as much of her son's pain as possible. The perfect empathy that her sinless nature gave her for the divine Son who suffered before her eyes filled her own body with his wounds, her own soul with his grief over his rejection by his people. Besides John, her companions willing to stand courageously before the world's condemnation included the wife of Clopas (Mary, her sister-in-law, who was the mother of James and Joseph) and Mary Magdalene. Nearby, Salome (the mother of John and James), and some of the other women who followed Jesus from Galilee waited as well.

In the deep twilight darkness that now covered the land, Jesus opened his eyes and beheld his mother and John standing with his arm around her. Barely able to speak, Jesus said slowly: "**Woman, there is your son.**" Moving his eyes toward John, he gasped: "**There is your mother.**"[15]

By this act near the last moments of his life, Jesus conveyed at least four very significant messages to the world: First, he gave his Blessed Mother to all humanity, a role that she has played perfectly down through the centuries through her appearances on earth and by serving as our primary intercessor in heaven. Second, John represents all of us, and in Jesus' words to him we also are told to embrace Mary as our mother and treat her accordingly. Third, Mary's patience is

---

[15]Jn 19:26-27

a model of virtue and faith because Jesus' death would have left her without husband or child to care for her. And while we can be confident that she would have been provided for by the many who loved her for herself besides being the mother of the Anointed of God, her example of trust is still powerful. In the Jewish culture of the time, without family, she would have been socially homeless. Fourth, Jesus had a plan for his mother. He chose not to state it until he was on the very verge of death. So, too, we must have faith in the goodness and providence of God. Jesus has assured us that His Father loves us more than we can fathom.[16] Through his mother here, he reminds us that our trust in him will never be misplaced even when all appears lost.

Minute by interminable minute, the time crawled by. Even seconds seemed endless. Insects landed on the bleeding and open wounds of the crucified men, or walked across their sweaty faces, adding a new torment to their death agonies. Because of the angle of crucifixion (about 65 degrees) the weight on each arm of the cruciarius actually exceeded his total body weight. Muscle spasms and cramps attacked Jesus' legs, chest and arms. Shifting positions on the cross to relieve these maddening pains caused the square-sided nails to scrape bits of the bone away inside his feet and hands and widened the holes made by the nails. The already inflamed median and plantar nerves sent bolts of agony up his limbs each time he moved. Arching his back to relieve the unbearable muscle spasms in his legs not only caused such pain in his shoulders as to nearly cause him to faint, but it also jammed the crown of thorns against the upright and renewed the piercing stabs into his scalp.

Mary felt her soul being torn apart by the unspeakable suffering of her son. Slowly, ever so slowly, the minutes became an hour. Surely death must come soon, prayed all those who loved the Lord and watched in horror as his face and body contorted themselves into gross distensions. But death did not come. The debt of mankind's sins was not yet paid. Eternity came and went, but only two hours passed on the cross. In the third hour, Jesus' inner resources began dwindling rapidly. The trauma to his body was overwhelming its ability to maintain its vital systems. Jesus floated in and out of a crimson sea of pain and semi-consciousness. His muscles contracted involuntarily, locking themselves into excruciating knots, and waves of nausea and perspiration swept over him. Finally, the third hour passed.

Without warning, Jesus suddenly stiffened on the cross and cried out: **"'Eloi, Eloi, lama sabacthani?' which means, 'My God, my God, why have you forsaken me?'"[17]**

---

[16]See Mt 6:26-33.

[17]Mk 15:34, Mt 27:46. We cannot know the depths of anguish that produced this terrible cry. But it completely dispels the notion that Jesus was insulated in any way by his divine nature from the full measure of his sufferings. Clearly, he looked into the same pit of despair and hopelessness that afflicts the rest of humanity for more mundane causes such as intractable illness, cruel oppression and persecution, the unbearable emotional distress

The shout from Jesus startled those who stood by and his words were not understood clearly. Some of them said to one another: **"Listen! He is calling on Elijah!"**[18]

The cry was shattering to his mother. For the first and only time in her life, she felt torn between her love for her son and her trust in his Father. Why had I AM abandoned His Son? Throughout all the trials of her life, the unwed pregnancy, the difficult journey to Bethlehem, fleeing into Egypt, life as a humble carpenter's wife, early widowhood, loss of her son to his three-year ministry, the gibes and taunts of her neighbors in Nazareth, and now this heart-crushing vigil as her son suffered the least deserved and most agonizing death devised by a cruel humanity—all were accepted without a single doubt, without a single question, in humble and absolute submission to the Lord's will. The Son of God, her son, had been her consolation and her happiness, the rock of her faith, all her hopes for herself and Israel, the final triumph of good over evil. Yet in the midst of suffering more horrible than she could ever have imagined had she not stood at the foot of the cross and shared those pains with her perfect, sinless empathy, Jesus cried out to a silent God. Teetering on the brink of desolation and anger, Mary collapsed to the ground and prayed, *Oh my God, my God, my God! Please help Jesus. Please end his sufferings. He is your beloved Son. Please, please, please help him!*

Jesus, ashen-faced and trembling uncontrollably, eyes shut against his suffering, muttered a hoarse whisper: **"I am thirsty."**[19] Without question, he was suffering from a physical thirst and dehydration that is incomprehensible to anyone who has not nearly died from fluid loss and deprivation. His parched and swollen tongue and sand-dry mouth created a sensation of nausea and choking.

But more than the physical affliction, Jesus' call was for souls to love him. His own eternal love longed with a desire akin to severe thirst to be reunited with those whom he had created and who had been separated from him by their sin. Now in the last moments of his life, he called once again to us to come to him and believe and accept our places in his Kingdom.

Those hearing him, of course, understood none of this. One of the Jewish spectators ran to a nearby jar of cheap, sour wine, which had been drugged with myrrh, a common analgesic offered to crucifixion victims. Jesus had earlier tasted

---

that often accompanies the loss of a loved one, or even prolonged unemployment.

But scholars have also noted that the words of Jesus are the first two lines of Psalm 22, David's prophecy of the sufferings of the Messiah. The psalm graphically describes mistreatment precisely like that borne by Jesus. But it ends on a note of hope and triumph in the Lord and this, too, was probably a component of Jesus' exclamation only a few minutes before he surrendered his spirit to his Father.

Finally, the connection with Psalm 22 was likely also intended as a reminder to the world that Jesus' crucifixion had been foretold and, therefore, voluntarily undergone. In other words, God was still in charge, despite the apparent hopelessness of Jesus' situation.

[18]Mk 15:35

[19]Jn 19:28

it but refused to drink it. The soldiers, indifferent to the sufferings of the men on their crosses, made no move to interfere. The man took a sponge, soaked it in the wine, impaled the sponge on a reed and held it up to Jesus' mouth. Jesus tasted it, but once again refused to do more.

Other bystanders chastised the man with the sponge, saying: **"Leave him alone. Let's see whether Elijah comes to his rescue."**[20] Even now, those watching half expected Jesus to accomplish some miraculous rescue of himself.

But Jesus merely sighed in a barely audible voice: **"Now it is finished."**[21] His body sagged against the nails. His trembling subsided. His breathing slowed, almost stopped. Death beckoned, but with a last great effort, he forced himself up. Looking up to heaven, he cried out in a great, triumphant shout that echoed off the walls of Jerusalem and cascaded into the valleys and hills beyond. As the sound died away, his lips moved in a soft whisper: **"Father, into your hands I commend my spirit."**[22]

With one last convulsive shudder, Jesus collapsed. His knees buckled and his body dropped a few inches until it was pulled taut by the nails holding up his arms. His face fell forward, eyes open and staring unseeing at the ground. His breathing had ceased and his body was still. Fresh blood oozed from the nail wounds caused by the lurching of his body. At a little past 3:00 p.m., Jesus was dead.

They felt it before they heard it . . . the ground shaking. Then the rock forming the top of the Golgotha knoll cracked and the rumble of a powerful earthquake rose around them. The people on the knoll screamed and clutched at one other. Longinus' horse reared and whinnied, backing frantically away from the seam that had suddenly opened in the rock, splitting earth and boulders before diving under the Jerusalem outer wall, heading for the Temple.

On the Temple Mount, the Passover sacrifice of lambs was drawing to a close. The giant altar was drenched with the blood of the lambs slaughtered for the thousands of Passover pilgrims. Inside the Temple, past the ornate, gold-encrusted outer doors, past the curtain that hung just inside those doors, to the thick, two-story, overlapping tapestry before the Holy of Holies came the rumble of the earthquake. The indestructible curtain, decorated with symbols of God's creation, was ripped apart in a single stroke from top to bottom. The magnificent Temple would stand for another forty years or so, but the thirty foot cubicle sanctuary, built over the rock where Abraham nearly sacrificed Isaac, and, according to some legends, the ground where Adam himself was buried, was now truly empty. The covenant was both fulfilled and broken. Henceforth, the temple of God would be the souls of people who loved Him.

---

[20]Mt 27:49

[21]Jn 19:30

[22]Lk 23:46

Around Golgotha, some of the tombs that had been carved in the rocks opened. The quivering earth rolled back the stones that blocked their entrances. Seeing all this in the heightened suspense of the unnatural darkness and the sudden earthquake at the moment of Jesus' death, Longinus and his soldiers saw the hand of God at work. **"Clearly this was the Son of God!"**[23] exclaimed Longinus, staring at the body of Jesus.

They calmed down a bit, however, when no ghosts nor bodies emerged from the tombs, the earthquake subsided and the strange darkness gave way to normal midafternoon light.

Most of the spectators left after this, seeing that Jesus had died. They were shaken by the events, though. The forlorn body of the man whom many of them had proclaimed to be the Messiah only five days earlier somehow seemed to gain the credibility in death that Jesus had lacked as a brutalized victim of Roman "justice." In death, his spiritual dimension reasserted itself in their minds, and they left Golgotha confused and fearful that perhaps God's chosen people had committed the unthinkable act: they had misunderstood I AM's plan and had executed their long-promised Messiah.

The chief priests, scribes and elders, satisfied that they had accomplished their purpose by eliminating another blasphemous pretender, who also happened to be a serious threat to their own worldly status and comfort, left to return to the city. On their way, a few of them diverted to see Pilate and requested that he not leave any of the crucified men on their crosses during the rapidly approaching Sabbath, a day which would also be a solemn feast day. Pilate refused to come out to see them so they sent a request in to him through one of his guards to have his soldiers break the legs of the *cruciaria* so that they could be removed and disposed of before the feast day began at sundown. They made no mention of Jesus' death, not caring whether the Romans broke his legs so long as his body did not profane their sacred holiday. Gestas and Dismas were still very much alive. Their deaths would have to be hastened, something which, despite its brutal method, would be welcomed by both.

Pilate acceded to the wishes of the chief priests and sent a soldier to tell Longinus that the legs of the crucified men were to be broken and their bodies released to the Jews as soon as they had expired. There was a special tool used for this purpose. It was an iron bar formed in a triangular shape. The edge was rounded, not sharp, so that the legs would not be cut, but the focused edge was very efficient, indeed, in smashing the shin bones.

The Roman soldiers were always happy to perform the leg breaking. It meant their execution duty was about to end and they could return to their barracks. For the most part, too, they intensely disliked the Jews who tended to disdain them as inferior for being Gentiles, a judgment that they arrogantly asserted came from their God. They were always protesting or even rioting over

---

[23]Mt 27:54, Mk 15:39. Luke quotes the centurion as saying: "Surely this was an innocent man." 23:47

some affront to their prickly God, and many of them formed rebel bands that attacked small Roman patrols and detachments. Killing a Jew, therefore, especially in a brutal way, was usually quite satisfying to them.

Galenus picked up the iron bar and approached Gestas first. Despite his agony and the relief he knew that death would bring, Gestas' heart pounded with fear for this new torture. He closed his eyes tightly and waited for the blow. Galenus swung hard and the bar smashed into Gestas' shins, shattering them both about five inches below the knees. Gestas screamed and fainted as the pain of the broken bones exploded through his body.

Dismas watched the soldiers approach. He did not close his eyes but looked over one last time at Jesus, who hung lifeless from his cross. With a prayer on his lips, Dismas, too, felt the sudden tidal wave of pain crash into his brain as his legs crumpled under the blow of the iron bar.

The two men immediately went into severe traumatic shock from the overwhelming pain of their smashed legs. Though collapsed, the limbs could not escape the crushing gravity that jammed the broken bones and torn nerves together. Already suffering from mild circulatory and hypovolemic (loss of fluids) shock, and incipient congestive heart failure, the weight of their bodies was now borne entirely by the nails in their hands. This generated additional severe pain plus pressure on their chest cavities. They also suffered a decline in blood pressure from the blood loss from the broken legs. In a few minutes, both men experienced convulsive, fatal heart attacks.

The soldiers had skipped over Jesus, seeing that he was apparently dead. But now Galenus drew back the iron bar to break his legs anyway, both for the satisfaction and to insure that death was irrevocable. But Longinus intervened.

"Forget it, Galenus. The man is dead. I'll make sure of it." Taking his lance, Longinus shoved it into Jesus' right side between the fifth and sixth ribs and pushed until it passed through his heart and into his ribs on the other side. As he withdrew the spear from the right atrium of Christ's heart, the blood that had gathered there flowed out in a thin stream. It was immediately followed by a stream of clear liquid, the pleural effusion that had collected around the outside of Jesus' lungs from the severe scourging he had received that morning. Thus flowed the blood and water reported by John in his Gospel.[24]

Mary, who had been on her knees in prayer at the moment of Jesus' death, had been forced to rise and move out of the way when the soldiers were breaking the legs of the two men still alive. She watched in horror as Longinus thrust his spear into the exposed side of her helpless, dead son. As the thin, sharp edge of the blade sliced through the pale, blood-streaked skin, Mary clutched at her own heart and fell against John. He staggered from the unexpected push but recovered and managed to keep Mary from collapsing to the ground. She who had empathetically and mystically shared in the sufferings of Jesus, now experienced

---

[24]Jn 19:34

the piercing of his heart as well. Now was the prophecy of Simeon more than thirty years before completely fulfilled: "**. . . and you yourself shall be pierced with a sword . . .**"[25] Mary would have joyfully taken all the pain of Our Lord's passion and death exclusively unto herself. As it was, the piercing of his heart was hers alone to bear since he was already dead. Forever after, her Immaculate Heart and his Sacred Heart would be joined and symbolized by that terrible spear thrust.

When the chief priests, scribes and elders had left Golgotha after Jesus died, Joseph of Arimathea had observed their return to the city. Most of them had gone off in the direction of the Temple, but another contingent had headed for the praetorium. Joseph had stopped one of his Sanhedrin colleagues and asked what had happened.

"The Galilean is dead but the other two criminals are still alive. Some of our members have gone to the procurator to ask him to break the legs of these men so that they will not remain hanging on their crosses to profane the solemn feast day tomorrow," replied the Jewish elder.

Joseph heard only the words "the Galilean is dead." He and Nicodemus, who had tried unsuccessfully to defend Jesus during the trial before Caiaphas, had been unable to bear witnessing his death march on the way of sorrows or his crucifixion agony on Calvary. Joseph whispered a prayer to I AM, begging His forgiveness for their sin of executing one who was, at a minimum, entirely innocent but who was also, in all probability as Joseph saw it, sent directly from I AM as the Messiah He had promised for so many centuries. *The sin is so monstrous as to be . . .* Joseph could not find words to finish the thought, so horrifying was it to him. He determined that he would do all that he could to provide Jesus' remains with a decent burial. Fortunately, he owned a new and unused cemetery plot in a part of the Golgotha quarry that had been reclaimed for burials. But the day was growing late. He had to hurry.

Joseph went first to find Nicodemus, his ally on the Sanhedrin, and one who was also a secret admirer of Jesus. He was not quite as converted as Joseph, but he was not far behind. In any case, he shared Joseph's horror at what the Sanhedrin had done to a man who was at the very least one of Israel's greatest prophets.

Nicodemus told Joseph he would purchase burial spices (myrrh and aloes) and bring them to Golgotha. Joseph said he would obtain the appropriate grave cloths to wrap the body in. "I will need to go to Pilate, too, to get his release of the body." The two men hurried off on their respective missions.

At the praetorium, Joseph asked to meet with Pilate. He hoped that Pilate would come out to the gate, but he was prepared to commit an act of ritual impurity by entering the residence of the Gentile procurator, if necessary. He remembered Jesus' impatience with the nitpicking rules of the Pharisees and their

---

[25]Lk 2:35

inability to see that it was the human virtues of people that gave them merit, not their ethnic or social status.

The guard took his request and sauntered off to deliver it to Pilate. Joseph waited. He paced as the time passed, fretting while he watched the sun descend toward the horizon. It was already after four o'clock. Finally, the guard reappeared and told him that the procurator had no intention of coming out to the gate any more that day. But if Joseph were willing to come inside, then he, the guard, would bring him to Pilate. Almost before the guard finished speaking, Joseph said: "Let's go!"

Pilate received him in the room where he had interrogated Jesus.

"Procurator, Jesus of Nazareth is dead. I humbly request your permission to remove his body and bury it in a tomb that I own nearby," said Joseph.

"So, his legs have been broken then?" asked Pilate.

"No, Procurator. He died sometime ago of his wounds. I know nothing of the condition of the other cruciaria," responded Joseph.

Pilate was greatly surprised that Jesus had died so quickly. True, he had been beaten up pretty badly, but the man was strong and young. Pilate, of course, had no real comprehension of the torments and sufferings that Jesus had undergone since the night before. But he was suspicious by nature. The Jewish authorities had not mentioned anything about Jesus being dead when they asked him to order the legs of the cruciaria to be broken. Now here came this other obviously well-to-do Jewish leader asking for permission to remove Jesus' body with his legs unbroken. "Have a seat, Joseph. I will grant your request but first I must be sure the Nazorean is dead. Perhaps my order to break the legs of the cruciaria was delayed for some reason. You may wait here until we find out."

Pilate called for Antonius, his tribune. "Have the centurion in charge of the crucifixions today sent to me."

Antonius sent the order and thirty minutes later Longinus appeared before Pilate. "This man has requested the body of the Nazorean for burial. Is he dead already?" asked Pilate.

"Yes, Procurator," replied Longinus. "All of the criminals are dead. The Galilean died first and I speared him in his heart to make sure that he was in fact expired. The other two men had their legs broken and they have died as well."

Pilate turned to Joseph and said: "You may take the body and bury it. Longinus will accompany you back to the site."

Joseph bowed and thanked Pilate but explained that he had to go and buy some burial linens first. He could make his own way to the crucifixion site. He hurried out of the room. Longinus delayed a moment to speak to Pilate.

"Procurator, there were some very odd things that took place today. I believe they were connected with the death of this man, Jesus. I'm sure you noticed the strange darkness that fell for most of the afternoon. And the earthquake. It split the rock upon which the Nazorean was crucified. The man was more than he seemed. These signs . . ." Longinus did not finish his sentence.

Pilate had turned beet red with anger before he exploded at the centurion: "I don't want to hear another word about the Nazorean! He was a man, nothing more! He bled like any man, he suffered like any man, he died like any other man would. He said his kingdom was in some other world. Good! He's gone from here. Let him rule there. Now get out of here!"

Longinus saluted the angry governor and quickly left. He returned to Golgotha, made one last check of the cruciaria, and took his soldiers back to the Fortress Antonia. Removal of the bodies and their disposition was not a matter of interest to him or to Rome. In a couple of days, when reports of Jesus' body being stolen would begin to circulate, his interest in Jesus would be rekindled. What he would find out later from the apostles led him to become an early convert to Christianity.

By the time Joseph purchased a fine linen burial cloth, one that was long enough to encompass the body from foot to head and back again, plus the cloth bindings which would be wrapped around this single cloth, and the napkin to tie his jaw closed, it was after five o'clock. The sun was low on the horizon. Joseph felt a rush of panic that the Sabbath would catch them before they had been able to bury Jesus. He and two of his servants accompanying him hurried as fast as they could walk, nearly running toward the Jaffa Gate and the path to Golgotha.

Nicodemus was waiting for him on the knoll, pacing back and forth. Dismas and Gestas had already been removed and sent to unconsecrated ground for burial with other criminals. No one was left on Golgotha except Mary, John, Mary of Clopas, Salome, and a few other disciples of Jesus who had ventured closer now that the Romans and Jewish authorities had all left. Only two temple guards remained to watch and report on any irregularities or religious rule violations that might occur.

Nicodemus had also brought a ladder. With this, the servants mounted the cross behind Jesus and inserted a sheet behind his back, looping it under his arms before pulling it back over the patibulum and tying it around the stipes. This held his body tight, even if his arms pulled upward, and secured him while the nails were driven and pulled out of Jesus' hands and feet. Carefully they removed the crown of thorns and passed it down. The feet were freed first, then the hands. They worked quickly but the task was painstaking. After about twenty minutes, Jesus swung quietly from the sheet which tugged at his underarms. Disconcertingly, his body retained the shape of its crucifixion. Rigor mortis caused the arms to remain outstretched, the left foot to be arched over the right with the left knee slightly more bent, and the head jutting forward.

The men lowered him to the ground where his mother waited, sobbing now that her promise to be strong for her son no longer applied. John helped to lay the Lord in his mother's arms as she knelt on the rocky knoll, then stood by for a few minutes to allow her to grieve. Clutching Jesus as tightly as his awkward position would permit, she rocked him gently, wailing while her body convulsed in wracking tears for the agony he had suffered, the loss of her only child, and the cruelty of a world that could do this to someone so innocent and so good. After a few minutes, Joseph whispered something to John and he knelt beside the weeping, broken-hearted woman.

"Mother, we must bury the Lord very soon, before the sun sets. We must act now. I am sorry."

Mary looked up, her eyes filled with the tears that streamed down her cheeks, looking so vulnerable and so sad as she held the stiff, lifeless form of Jesus in her arms that no one seeing her could hold back their own tears. Even the temple guards were moved and looked away. Wordlessly, she nodded, and let John and the other men pick Jesus up to carry him toward Joseph's tomb in the small garden about forty yards away. Jesus' body was laid upon the sheet that had been used to support him while he was being unfastened from the cross. Two men held the ends of the sheet and two others grasped the cloth on either side. It was now six o'clock and the sun would set in mere minutes.

Near the tomb, the party laid Jesus out on a slab of stone. Joseph's servant hurried over with a jar of water and cloths to wash Jesus' body. One of Nicodemus' servants helped him perform this duty, the two men working rapidly and thoroughly to clean the clots and dried sheets of blood that nearly covered the entire face and body of Jesus.

Next, three of the men picked Jesus up and Joseph and Nicodemus laid out the long, linen burial cloth on the stone slab. Jesus was laid back down. His arms were forced down against their rigor mortis and placed across his body, left hand on top of the right. Next his legs were straightened as best they could be. The left knee remained slightly bent. His head was pushed back but still continued to lean forward slightly.[26] His jaw was tied with the handkerchief by wrapping it under his chin and knotting it on top of his head. Two Roman coins, *leptons* (the widow's mite), were placed on Jesus' eyes to keep them closed. Next, the fourteen foot linen cloth was folded over the front of Jesus' body. He was then bound at his ankles, knees, waist and upper arms. It was 6:10 p.m.

Quickly the men carried the body of Jesus into Joseph's tomb, being careful to hold him level and prevent the eye coins from falling off. The entrance was low and they had to bend over to pass him inside to place him on the stone bench in the 75 square foot chamber with its seven-foot ceiling where his body would be interred. Nicodemus hastily packed the mixture of myrrh and aloe spices that he had brought, nearly one hundred pounds worth, all around the body. They laid the sheet that had been used to carry Jesus' body beside the bench. Then the men backed out of the tomb. Finally, four of them rolled the large round stone, which had been anchored to one side with a chock in its groove, in front of the tomb. Jesus' burial was as complete as it could be.

The long, piercing cry of the ram's horn *shofar* echoed off the hills around Jerusalem. The Sabbath had begun.

---

[26]This description is based upon the appearance of the image in the Shroud of Turin. See Zugibe, *Cross and the Shroud*, 131-132.

Mary Magdalene and Mary of Clopas carefully noted the tomb in which Jesus was laid and made plans to return as soon as the Sabbath was over. They would then have time to clean his body and prepare it thoroughly with the burial spices and perfumed oils.

Because of the Sabbath movement limitations, John, Mary and the other women returned to the home of Mark's parents, Tychus and Mary. The other apostles were already there, hiding in the Upper Room where Jesus had celebrated the Last Supper only the night before. Joseph of Arimathea and Nicodemus, of course, went to their respective homes.

That evening, many of the Sanhedrin members met with Caiaphas and Annas to discuss the day's events. They congratulated one another on disposing of the latest Messiah imposter and doing it so cleverly that it appeared to be the Romans' doing. "Hardly a voice was raised in protest, much less any rioting," gloated Caiaphas. "What a pleasure it was to see that faker hanging on a cross!"

His father-in-law, the former high priest, Annas, was thoughtful. "Yes, well, the man is certainly dead. But I recall him predicting that this would happen. And he had opportunities to defend himself and let every one of them pass. Does it bother any of you that we seem to have done exactly what he wanted?"

"The man was deluded, that's all," responded Caiaphas. "He no doubt thought that his God would save him and prove to everyone that he was the Messiah. Near the end, he himself called out to the LORD asking why He had abandoned him. Clearly, his plan went awry when the God of Israel refused to acknowledge him. We even challenged him to come down from his cross. But, of course, he could not and now he is beyond doing anything at all."

Annas persisted. "The man was quite clear in predicting his death. Now he is dead as he foretold. Perhaps we should be thinking about what else he said would happen."

One of the Pharisees spoke up then. "Surely you do not mean his preposterous prediction that he would rise from the dead on the third day?"

"That's precisely what I mean," said Annas, fixing the Pharisee with an icy stare. "Let's not forget the man has disciples. The only way they can profit from the loss of their leader is to fulfill his prediction for him."

"I see what you mean," said Caiaphas. "We need to guard the Nazorean's tomb for at least three days to make sure that his followers do not steal the body and then go around pretending he rose from the dead. Alexander[27] can take a delegation to see Pilate in the morning and arrange to have a Roman guard put on the tomb for the next three days."

This plan was adopted and the meeting disbanded.

Early the next morning, while the city lay still and silent under the strictures of the Sabbath/Feast of Unleavened Bread, Alexander led a group of

---

[27]This Greek name, Alexander, may seem an odd choice for a member of the Jewish Sanhedrin. However, Acts 4:6 lists him and a man named John, along with Annas and Caiaphas, as among the "high-priestly class."

chief priests and Pharisees to Pilate's residence. The procurator, who had not had a good night, was in a surly mood as he came out to the gate to meet with the Jewish leaders. "What is it today? Have you got some new pathetic 'threat' to Rome that you want me to crucify?"

Alexander was unruffled:

> **"Sir, . . . we have recalled that that imposter while he was still alive made the claim, 'After three days I will rise.' You should issue an order having the tomb kept under surveillance until the third day. Otherwise his disciples may go and steal him and tell the people, 'He has been raised from the dead!' This final imposture would be worse than the first."**[28]

The chief priests and Pharisees with him gravely nodded their agreement.

Pilate studied the little group of ornately dressed Jewish men with their elegant white tunics made of the finest linen under rich woolen robes of royal blue, fringed with tassels of golden bells and pomegranates. Although their request seemed preposterous, he knew that only a very real concern would have brought them to see him on this important Sabbath/feast day. Their faces were serious, frowning. His initial reaction had been to scoff at the request and simply leave them standing at the gate. But he remembered his own reaction to the remarkable self-assurance of the Galilean who stood patiently before him yesterday. And his wife's dream! Then Centurion Longinus from the Antonia garrison, a tough, veteran soldier with a distinguished battle record, had been clearly shaken by the strange darkness and earthquake yesterday afternoon. *Maybe guarding this man's tomb is not so ridiculous*, Pilate thought. *But it will not be with Roman soldiers. If the Jewish God is, indeed, going to raise this man back to life, Roman spears and swords will not prevent it. On the other hand, if he stays in his tomb, which is highly likely, I would be a laughing stock in Rome when word got back that I was using soldiers to keep dead men in their tombs.*

Pilate said to Alexander: "Yesterday when their leader was still alive, the Galilean's followers were too afraid to show their faces, let alone attack my troops to save him. It is not likely that they will now be willing to risk harm by stealing his body. **You have a guard. Go and secure the tomb as best you can.**[29] But I warn you." Pilate paused as he stared with cold menace at the elegant Jewish men. "At your insistence, this man was deemed an enemy of Rome. If anything happens to his body, your guards will find themselves rowing Caesar's battle ships!" Pilate turned sharply on his heel and went back inside.

Alexander reported Pilate's refusal to Caiaphas. He, in turn, called his Captain of the Guard and had him immediately post a nine-man detail at Christ's tomb. The guards, who would serve in two-hour shifts of three men each from

---

[28]Mt 27:63-64

[29]Mt 27:65

midnight till 6 A.M., first sealed the tomb completely with a thick wax. Then they took up their post directly in front of the large, round stone that covered the tomb's entrance. It was mid-morning on what would soon become Holy Saturday.

———

PRAYER BEFORE A CRUCIFIX

Behold, O kind and most sweet Jesus!
I cast myself upon my knees
in your sight.
And with the most fervent desire of my soul,
I pray and beseech you to
impress upon my heart true sentiments of
faith, hope and charity
while with deep affection and grief of soul
I contemplate
your five most precious wounds,
having before my eyes the words which David spoke
in prophecy of you, O good Jesus:

"They have pierced my hands and feet;
they have numbered all my bones."

Our Father . . . .

Hail Mary . . . .

Glory Be . . . .

Amen.

QUESTIONS FOR REFLECTION

(1) The Jews believed that anyone who was crucified was accursed by God and, therefore, would be damned. Why do you think Jesus chose to die this way? What lessons does he want us to see in the cross? Do you see the message of the cross as good news or bad news?

(2) Why did Jesus have to die at all?

(3) If you have suffered tragic loss in your life, has it been a comfort to you to meditate upon Christ's crucifixion? Why or why not?

(4) Why do you think the Jewish authorities would not accept Jesus as the Messiah? Would the same be true today? How open are you to the signs of God's presence, especially when they come unexpectedly? In your life, have there been such signs? If so, how have you responded?

(5) Jesus may have felt abandoned on the cross by God. Yet he persevered and not long afterward surrendered his spirit to his Father. How do you respond when God appears to be indifferent to your sufferings and problems?

(6) What parallels can you see between Christ's birth and his death?

(7) When people mistreat you, how do you react? Do you subscribe to the advice, "Get even, not mad?" Do you consider the example of Jesus on the cross to be "Not Applicable" to your own life in the world? If so, why?

(8) What do you think motivated the centurion, Longinus, to declare Jesus after his death to be the Son of God?

(9) Dismas and Gestas, the two criminals crucified with Jesus, reacted very differently to being with Christ. How do you think you would react in similar circumstances? How do you react now when bad things happen to you?

(10) What do you think were the Blessed Virgin Mary's thoughts and feelings as she stood at the foot of the cross?

He has been raised, exactly as he promised.
Mt 28:6

FIRST GLORIOUS MYSTERY

The Resurrection

Somewhere in the distance a cock crowed, its rusty hinge squawk ripping the thick predawn silence. Mary slept in a small room by herself in the home of Lazarus, Mary and Martha in Bethany. Her sister-in-law and best friend, Mary of Clopas, was staying in Jerusalem, about one and one-half miles away on the opposite side of the Mount of Olives. She and several of the other Galilean women, including Mary from Magdala, the woman who loved Jesus perhaps more than any other person on earth, next to his mother, spent the night restlessly in the home of Mary and Tychus, parents of Mark. All of the apostles were there, too, except, of course, poor foolish Judas Iscariot. They and about two dozen other male followers of Jesus had locked themselves in the Upper Room (Cenacle) where Jesus had celebrated the Passover meal with them as he himself became the Paschal Lamb for all mankind. In the darkness, occasional moans and cries drifted upward from the sleeping figures as nightmare images replayed the horror of Christ's passion and their own terror.

Mary had declined to stay in the city, not out of fear of the Jews and Romans but because she did not intend to go with the women to her son's tomb this morning to more properly prepare Jesus' body for burial. The other women had been terribly upset by the haste with which he had been buried on Friday. They wanted desperately to perform these last ablutions as a final devotion to the Master who had so ignited their lives with love and hope. When they invited Mary, she merely smiled and replied, "Thank you, but I don't think it will be necessary." In the evening on Saturday, after the Sabbath had ended at dusk, John had escorted her to Bethany and then returned to stay with the other apostles.

Mary slept peacefully on a slim pallet stuffed with wool. She had believed and accepted what her Son had told her about his fate in Jerusalem when they came up a week ago out of the Judean Wilderness. She had followed him on his way of sorrows and shared his pains on the cross, taking unto herself entirely the spear thrust into Jesus' still heart. Old Simeon's prophecy had been more than fulfilled. A sword through her own heart that would have ended her life would have been merciful. But God had called her to share in the sufferings of His Son. She had done so willingly, courageously, joyously even, regretting only that she could not bear them entirely for the God-Man who was also her child.

The light gently filled the room, nuzzling into the dark corners and scattering shadows. In the center of the light, a Being of Love coalesced into the outline of a man, then a man with features, and, finally, a man with wounds in his hands, feet and side from which the light streamed even more brightly.

"Mother." The voice was liquid velvet. Mary's eyes opened slowly, almost languidly as she rolled over and faced the voice.

"Jesus!" She leaped from the bed and threw her arms around her risen Son. He laughed and hugged her back. He thanked her then for being with him during his Passion and for easing his sufferings by her perfect love and her total empathy. Although Mary had complete confidence that Jesus' predictions about his resurrection would be fulfilled, still, to see him in the flesh with his beautiful smile and twinkling brown eyes seemed like an impossible dream come true. She stepped back and looked at him from head to foot, trying to replace the memory of his tortured body hanging lifeless from bloody nails.

All at once she realized that this Jesus was no longer her son the way she had known him: a talented carpenter, miracle worker, preacher, prophet, emissary from God, citizen of Galilee, Jewish man. He had come into his glory as the Son of God; her son, nonetheless, but her Creator and Lord as well. Mary fell to her knees in homage.

But Jesus would have none of it and, reaching down, took her by her hands and pulled her gently back to her feet. "I have completed my work on earth and shall soon return to my Father to stay. The doors to my Father's kingdom are now open and the world must learn that through me all are invited. You must remain here a little while longer to help my infant church to grow. Peter and the others will need your wisdom, your great love, and your good sense, but mostly they will see me in you and that will give them strength and comfort. My beloved and faithful servant, John, will be your son and provide for you as if I, myself, were still here. And, of course, I shall be with you constantly, though you may not always recognize my presence."

Outside the windows of the house, the first glow of dawn above the mountains to the east pushed against the blue black of the fading night. Jesus vanished and Mary knelt again, enraptured, lost in prayers of thanks and joy for the event that would transform human history.

Meanwhile, in Jerusalem, Mary Magdalene; Mary of Clopas; Salome, mother of the two apostles, James and John; and Joanna, wife of Herod's steward, Chuza, gathered quietly in a room downstairs from the Upper Room. Mary, the mistress of the house, a maid servant named Rhoda;[1] Susanna from Galilee; and two other women were also present. The women checked their supply of perfumed oils, spices, aloes and fresh linen cloths, which they had purchased the evening before as soon as the Sabbath had ended just after six o'clock. Normally, the vendors did not open for business until the following morning, but Mary of Tychus used her influence to persuade one of the shopkeepers in the Upper Market to open up long enough to sell the women the burial materials that they needed.

Carrying torches to light their way, the women left the house and walked north along the street that ran beside the palace of Caiaphas, between the Upper Market and Herod's palace, and through the Ginnoth Gate. From there, they would make a sharp left turn and exit the city through the Jaffa Gate. It was still dark outside, although dawn was near. Jerusalem's roosters had already begun to announce its arrival. The Levite who stood high on the Temple pinnacle to catch the first rays of sunlight over the Mountains of Moab was poised to signal the birth of the new day.

Rhoda, the maid servant, asked one of the other women as they hurried along the narrow, silent city streets, "Isn't it too late to perform this anointing? Jesus has been in the tomb since Friday. Surely his body will have begun to decay?" She said it as a statement but it came out as a question.

Mary of Clopas overheard the conversation and replied, "It is the Lord who is in this tomb. Don't you remember Lazarus? In the tomb *four days* and brought forth in his burial wrappings as fresh and healthy as on the best day of his life! Surely God will do no less for Jesus, whom He sent to work signs and wonders like no other prophet in Israel's history."

"And if the body has indeed begun to decompose, we will certainly notice it after we enter the tomb," added Joanna, joining the discussion. "In that case, we will simply sprinkle the Lord's body with our perfumed oils and depart."

The long piercing cry of a silver trumpet echoed out from the Temple precincts, declaring the new day to have officially begun. The sky was noticeably lighter to the east; but it still looked like night where the women walked, and they held their torches high. Mary Magdalene led the way, walking with firm step and a determination to match. She had fretted throughout the Sabbath about their failure to anoint Jesus properly for his burial, and now she was set upon rectifying that grievous omission.

She had tried to persuade some of the apostles and other male disciples of Jesus to come with them to the tomb this morning, but all had refused. They were convinced that the Jewish authorities intended to round them up, or instigate the Romans to do it, and crucify them as they had Jesus. After all, they had supported his "kingship" and so would seem to be as guilty of threatening the Roman state as he had been. Peter had openly declared Jesus to be the Son of the

---

[1]See Acts 12:13.

living God, which was all that was needed to get him, and the rest of them as well, executed by stoning. None of them seemed even to recall Jesus' oft-repeated promise to rise from the dead. They had all seen crucifixion victims. John's and the women's description of what had happened to Jesus made it clear that his death had been even more terrible than usual. To his followers, especially the men who had been willing to follow him into battle but not to submit like sheep, Jesus was horribly, incomprehensibly killed and now their own lives seemed likely to fall as easily, and as cruelly. None of them knew about the temple guards that Caiaphas had posted to watch Jesus' tomb. Certainly that would have confirmed the apostles' worst fears.

As the women began their descent into the garden areas surrounding the barren and rocky knoll near the center of the limestone quarry known as Golgotha, Mary Clopas whispered to Mary Magdalene: **"Who will roll back the stone for us from the entrance to the tomb?"**[2]

"I don't know," said Mary Magdalene. "None of the men would come with us. I am hoping that we can get the man who tends the gardens and maybe some passersby to help us. I have money to pay them. There may also be some workers in the quarry, although there doesn't seem to be any mining here at present. When we get to the tomb, we will pray that the Lord will send us some help."

Mary Clopas looked dubious but said nothing. All of the women fell silent as they concentrated in the dim light on navigating the rocky trail downward. When they reached the quarry floor, about 100 yards south and east from the tomb where Jesus was buried, they stopped dead in their tracks. Flickering light and voices drifted toward them in the dew-laden morning air. Soldiers! It had not occurred to the women that anyone would put a guard on a dead man's tomb. At almost the same moment, however, a great cracking sound boomed forth and the ground shook beneath their feet. Terrified, the women rushed together in fright, staring wide-eyed toward the tomb where the noise had come from. There were no longer any voices to be heard. Even the flickering firelight had been suppressed by a much brighter light that shone above the shrubs that blocked their view of the tomb.

After a few minutes, with no further shaking of the earth, the women regained their courage and rushed toward the tomb to see what had happened. On the ground before the entrance, nine Temple guards lay unconscious, scattered about like rag dolls. The great round stone, four feet in diameter, that had covered the entrance to the tomb, had been rolled back and chocked in place with a wedge-shaped stone block. The mouth of the tomb stood open, dark and silent.

As the women stared open-mouthed at the strange scene, unsure of whether to proceed or return to the Upper Room and demand that some of the men come back with them, a brilliant light suddenly appeared above the rolled-

---

[2]Mk 16:3

back tomb stone. The light took flesh as a young man, resplendent in a dazzling white robe and shining with a light that illuminated the area around him. It was as if he stood at the center of a ten-meter ball of incandescence. He smiled at the women and took a seat, almost casually, on the stone. They, in turn, were nearly paralyzed with fright. Some of them whimpered on the verge of tears. Two had already collapsed to the ground.

"**Do not be frightened,**" the angel reassured them. "**I know you are looking for Jesus the crucified, but he is not here. He has been raised, exactly as he promised. Come and see the place where he was laid.**" The angel gestured toward the open tomb. "**Then go quickly and tell his disciples: 'He has been raised from the dead and now goes ahead of you to Galilee, where you will see him.' That is the message I have for you.**"[3] With that, the angel disappeared.

The tomb was too small for all the women to enter. Anyway, some of them had lost heart and could not stop shaking and crying from fear. The guards remained unconscious where they had fallen. This, too, was unsettling for the women. But Mary Magdalene did not hold back. She rushed toward the low, open doorway. Mary Clopas and Salome hesitated, then ran after her. The burial supplies which they had brought lay on the ground where they had been dropped and forgotten.

The women thrust their torches before them as they stooped to enter the darkness of the tomb. The flickering flames struggled against the blackness, leaving eerie shadows dancing upon the walls. Once inside, they could stand easily beneath the high ceiling. They gasped in sequence as each looked at the stone slab upon which the body of Jesus had been laid. It was empty. The burial cloths lay on the floor. Not sure whether to believe their own eyes, they moved forward together, hearts pounding in anticipation that Jesus might suddenly appear wrapped as Lazarus had been, or materialize as a spirit, a thought which terrified them. As they reached out to touch the spot where Jesus should have been lying on the stone bench, another young man in a glowing white robe was suddenly before them, sitting to their right at the end of the bench. All three women stifled screams and stumbled backwards, hands raised in defense, beginning to weep hysterically.

Then a curious thing happened. An enormous, overpowering sense of peace and love enveloped them, caressing their minds, comforting their hearts, filling them with a sense of being loved like they had felt only occasionally in the presence of Jesus himself. Bright light illuminated even the chamber's corners. The angel spoke softly and their hearts leaped to hear the message of the other angel repeated:

> "**Why do you search for the Living One among the dead? He is not here; he has been raised up. Remember what he said to you while he was still in Galilee—that the Son**

---

[3]Mt 28:5-7

of Man must be delivered into the hands of sinful men,
and be crucified, and on the third day rise again."[4]

With that, the second angel vanished, and the shadows rushed back in.

The women quickly exited the tomb. All of Jesus' predictions about his death and resurrection came vividly back to them. The three shared what had just transpired with the six who had remained outside the tomb. Then the six women had to go into the tomb to confirm what they had been told, although Rhoda was still too frightened to pass the entrance. She merely crouched down and peered in. The tomb remained silent and empty.

When the women emerged, everyone began talking at once. They were thrilled at the news, though not quite able to grasp its reality, but most were still trembling from shock.

Mary Magdalene was the first to recover. "Come! We must tell Peter and the others. The Lord is not here. He has risen as he promised!"

Some of the women still doubted, however. After all, they had not seen Jesus himself. And while the angels looked solid enough, they might have been mere ghosts, who were notoriously unreliable in popular superstition. But despite these concerns, they chattered excitedly as they rushed off to report to the apostles.

When the women had left the garden area and passed through the Jaffa Gate, the guards on the ground began to awaken. They looked toward the tomb and saw the stone rolled back. Two of them ran inside the now dark tomb and then quickly emerged. "The Nazorean is gone!" This produced consternation among the remaining guards, all of whom had to crowd into the tomb to see for themselves.

Jehiel, the captain of the guard, cursed. "We're in for it now. The procurator has already threatened to send us as galley slaves to the emperor's battle ships if anything happened to the Galilean's body. We'll be lucky to convert that sentence into death."

"But, Jehiel, we did nothing wrong!" protested one of the younger guards. "You saw what happened. The earth shook and then a spirit looking like the LORD himself rolled back the stone. There was nothing we could do. We cannot fight such beings!"

"Yes, we all saw it, Elam. But who will believe us?"

Gloom settled on the group as they all realized they had no acceptable excuse for what had happened. The truth would be instantly rejected. Falling asleep on guard duty was a capital offense which was almost always punished with execution because such behavior jeopardized the lives of the entire troop. Claiming that they had been overwhelmed by the disciples of Jesus would also ring hollow in light of their lack of casualties, not to mention the near impossibility of no one noticing such a large body of men clashing with the guards. There was nothing to do but go into the city and report to the chief priests.

---

[4]Lk 24:5-7

"Elam, you and Kemuel come with me to report to Jotham (the Captain of the Jewish Temple Guards). The rest of you clean up this campsite and return to your regular duties," Jehiel ordered.

The three men headed off toward the Jaffa Gate while the other men gathered up their weapons and personal items before following them into the city.

Once on the Temple grounds, Jehiel found Jotham making his rounds of the various guard posts. He explained what had happened and then endured 15 minutes of furious cursing and interrogation. Unable to shake the men's story, Jotham finally uttered one last expletive and said, "Well, there's nothing to do now but tell Caiaphas and Annas that the Galilean refuses to stay dead. You better pray that they find your story more believable than I do!"

Jotham led the three men to the Royal Portico at the southern end of the Temple Mount. The chief priests had offices there. It was also the location for the Grand Court of the Great Sanhedrin, the 71-member body of elders, scribes, chief priests and the high priest who governed Israel in all matters religious. Noam, the chief scribe, was talking to Alexander and John, two of the chief priests, when the four guards approached.

Jehiel repeated the story of the brilliant flash of light and the lightning-like burst of energy that seemed instantly to roll back the great stone sealing Jesus' tomb, leaving shards of wax strewn along its path. He attempted to describe the dazzling white figure within the explosion of light but Elam and Kemuel began to argue, insisting the figure was 10 feet high and fully armed with sword, shield and breastplate. Noam listened to the men carefully, studying their faces. He had seen thousands of men lie before. He rarely failed to discern when it was happening. *These men,* he thought to himself, *are telling the truth. Or, at least they think they are telling the truth.* Noam held up his hand for silence and the men stopped talking.

"Jotham, gather all of the men who were on guard duty last night and bring them here. They are to remain under guard until the High Priest decides their fate," said Noam. Then he left with Alexander and John to inform Caiaphas and Annas.

Caiaphas, in turn, directed a convening of the full Sanhedrin in the Grand Court. Joseph of Arimathea, Nicodemus and a few other known sympathizers of Jesus were deliberately excluded from the meeting.

Annas began the discussion by informing the assembled body of what the guards had reported. "This story, of course, is nonsense. Most likely the guards simply drank wine half the night and fell into a drunken stupor. During this time, the followers of the Nazorean came and stole his body away."

One of the elders protested: "But these men are among the best of the temple guards! Jotham hand-picked them himself. Jehiel is well-known to many of us as a man of integrity and courage. I find it hard to accept that their behavior would be as you describe."

An elderly man, slight of stature and deferential in his manner, spoke up hesitantly. "Given the character of these men, should we not consider the possibility that their report is true? What if this Jesus was, in fact, raised from the dead? We cannot overlook, either, the unexplained destruction of the great tapestry in the Temple that shielded the Holy of Holies. Perhaps, brothers, we have made a most terrible mistake. Perhaps we should don sack cloth and ashes, as the Ninevites did in the time of Jonah, and petition the Lord of Hosts for His forgiveness."

Caiaphas could not believe his ears. He turned nearly purple with rage. He stood up in his formal high priest robes and, shaking his finger at the elder who had just spoken, shouted: "The God of Israel is the creator of the universe! He would never, never, never send the Messiah, His Anointed, as a lowly carpenter who ate and drank with notorious sinners—with prostitutes and tax collectors, people accursed in the sight of God! Which of us would permit our son to be killed, much less crucified, if we had it in our power to prevent it? It is unthinkable that the Lord would do otherwise. If this carpenter is no longer in his grave, it is either the Evil One who has reclaimed his son or the man's followers who seek to perpetuate their attack on the faith of our fathers."

Annas was much calmer than his son-in-law. "Brothers, Caiaphas speaks wisely. Have we not dedicated our lives to following, teaching and implementing the law of Moses, the very law given to our people by the Lord God himself? Is it possible that God would send His Messiah to lead Israel to its long prophesied greatness outside of we who have striven so hard to serve him? Do we not even now stand ready to embrace the true Messiah as soon as the LORD shall reveal him to us? If this Jesus is that Messiah, where is he now? Why does he not appear before us so that we may acknowledge him as Lord and Savior?" Annas paused for effect, holding his arms out wide, and looking all around as if in welcome for a guest who has deliberately failed to show up. Most of the members of the Sanhedrin nodded at the apparent wisdom of Annas and looked contemptuously at the mortified elder who had dared to suggest that Jesus might have been who he claimed to be.

"What, then, shall we do?" asked one of the chief priests. "If the guards continue to say they saw a being of light who opened the Galilean's tomb, many of our people will accept him as the Messiah. This would create the greatest threat to the faith of our fathers since Abraham's time. There might even be civil war eventually. Shouldn't we have these guards executed immediately?"

Noam spoke up. "Killing these men would only make them martyrs and confirm the sincerity of their claims. The people would be sure to believe them then. No, we must persuade them to change their story, to tell everyone who inquires that the Nazorean's disciples stole his body while they slept. And we must protect them from Pilate's wrath as well, for if he tries to harm them they may revert to their original story to save themselves."

The members of the Sanhedrin saw the sense in Noam's advice. There was a brief period of discussion and then his plan was adopted. He, Alexander and John were sent to meet with the guards and convey the Sanhedrin's decision.

Jotham had gathered all nine guards in a room within the Royal Portico, not far from the Grand Court. Some paced nervously, increasingly agitated that their fate would be death or worse. Others slumped against a wall, heads down. A couple of them, however, were thoughtful. They pondered the significance of what they had seen and resolved to keep an open mind on the subject.

When the three Jewish leaders came into the room, a hush fell immediately. The guards were confused but heartened by the friendly demeanor of Noam and the two chief priests.

Noam spoke first: "The members of the Great Sanhedrin have deliberated all morning upon the story you have given us. We believe it to be nonsense, however sincere you may be in believing it yourselves. However, we know you are true sons of Israel who wish to do nothing evil in the sight of our God who has chosen us to lead His people in these difficult times.

"The Nazorean was a faker. If his body is no longer in its tomb, it can only be because it has been taken away by men or spirits of evil intent. Somehow, you were prevented from stopping that. Perhaps a spell was cast upon you by Beelzebul.

"If your story circulates among the men of Israel, however, many will believe that the Nazorean fulfilled his promise to rise from the dead. Many will follow him then, to the great sorrow of Israel and displeasure of the Lord. Therefore, you are to say, **'His disciples came during the night and stole him while we were asleep.'**"[5]

Several of the guards protested strenuously: "If we say that, Pilate will have us hanging from trees ourselves! We know that he has already threatened to send us to Caesar's fleet if we failed to protect the Nazorean's tomb."

"If any word of this gets to the procurator, we will straighten it out with him and keep you out of trouble,"[6] said Alexander.

Jehiel was angry. "I have been a soldier of Israel all my life and have always fought bravely and with honor. I will not now claim that I failed in one of the most basic of a soldier's duties: remaining awake while on guard!"

"Jehiel, we know you are one of Israel's finest soldiers," said Noam soothingly. "But there is no other way to keep the errors of this man from being spread throughout Palestine. We are not unmindful of your sacrifice and its costs. For that reason, each of you is to be given 200 denarii from the Temple treasury as an expression of thanks from the people of the One God. As the captain of the guard detail, you will receive an additional 100 denarii."

This was a great sum of money for the guards since one denarius was equivalent to a day's wage. The bribe for their silence was more than six months' wages; Jehiel's nearly a year's.

"In addition, each of you shall be given the guard assignment of your choice for the next year. Of course, if you refuse to cooperate with this generous offer and to do your duty by Israel, then we will have no choice but to turn you

---

[5]Mt 28:13

[6]Mt 28:14

over to the procurator," said Noam evenly but with just a hint of menace in his voice.

It did not take long for the guards to realize that they had no alternative but to accept the deal. Their story became the stock explanation of the Jewish authorities who continued to deny the reality of Christ's resurrection. A couple of the guards ultimately renounced their lie when they saw the miraculous works of the apostles and became convinced that Jesus of Nazareth really had risen from the dead on that Sunday morning. But by then the false story was entrenched and Jews who followed the line of reasoning of their leaders clung to it.

The women returning from the tomb hurried along the street toward the Upper Room where the disciples hid behind locked doors. They were still dazed by their experience with the two angels at Christ's tomb and wondered how they could convince Peter and the other apostles of what they had seen. Some were not sure themselves of what had transpired. They understood that Jesus' body was no longer in the tomb, but what it meant in terms of his ministry on earth was very confusing to them. In the daylight of early morning, their memory of the shimmering brilliance of the angelic figures seemed more like a dream, even if a vivid one.

As soon as they arrived at the house of Mary and Tychus, Mary Magdalene, followed by Mary Clopas, Joanna and Salome rushed upstairs and pounded on the door to the Upper Room. The rest of the women soon followed and crowded together on the landing at the top of the stairs. Behind the door, there was no response, since the disciples feared just such a moment and now trembled with fright, imagining Roman soldiers standing on their doorstep with weapons in hand. "Let us in! It is only us. A great thing has happened. The Lord has risen! God has sent His angels to tell us this!"

Footsteps approached the door cautiously on the other side. It creaked open and Peter's face appeared in the crack. Mary Magdalene shoved against the door and the women rushed inside, practically knocking Peter over. All began talking at once: "We have seen angels!" "Beautiful, glowing spirits at the Lord's tomb." "And there was a mighty earthquake!" "The soldiers looked like dead men." "The tomb was empty and we saw a young man standing in it." "It was terrifying!" "Jesus is not there!" "The angels told us to tell you that Jesus is risen." "He is going to Galilee to show himself to you." "Remember how he told us?" "Hurry now! We must leave the city at once." "The Master is risen!!"

The apostles attempted to follow the excited, overlapping voices, and understood that the women had found the tomb empty. Apparently, they had seen one or more spirits who told them the Lord was risen. But they had not seen the Lord himself. "Dead soldiers" also came through, which greatly alarmed the men. Who could have killed them? If Roman soldiers were casualties, there would be a real massacre in retaliation. Finally, after a lot of shouting back and forth, Peter took control of the situation and made Mary Magdalene explain it all over again while the other women were told to remain quiet. When she was finished there was silence in the room. The men looked at the women as if they had lost their senses.

Peter spoke first. "All you have seen is an empty tomb guarded by soldiers who may have been asleep. The Lord said he would rise but we have not seen him, and I gather you have not, either. And where in Galilee are we to go? To Nazareth? To Capernaum? To Mount Tabor? It is dangerous for us to be seen on the streets of Jerusalem, especially so close to the palace of Caiaphas. What you saw may have been a trick of light, perhaps the rising sun reflecting off the soldiers' fallen shields? If the soldiers were sleeping and not dead—and you did say there was no blood or sign of a struggle—it must mean that the body of the Lord was removed during the night. That would explain the empty tomb.

"I want to believe you, but you know yourselves how little sleep you have had since before the Sabbath and how we are all nearly destroyed by the cruel death of our Lord."

The other apostles and disciples, except John, murmured their agreement with Peter's skepticism. In the face of this disbelief, the women themselves began to doubt their own witness, still protesting that they knew what they had seen, but with less and less conviction. Some of them began to cry.

Thomas, who flatly rejected the women's story, told Peter that he was going into the city to try to find out what was going on; i.e., whether the Jewish authorities were seeking them and what had happened to the soldiers and Jesus' body. Peter nodded and Thomas left.

John, who had been excited by the women's story and was prepared to believe them, had been lingering impatiently near the door. Finally, he could wait no longer. "Peter, the Lord told us he would rise on the third day. Today is the third day. We must go to the tomb and at least see what has happened there."

James, John's sturdy and sensible brother, was alarmed. "What these women are saying is nonsense. It is too dangerous to go out there now. Let us wait another day at least. Besides, it has only been two days since the Lord was crucified, not three."[7]

But Peter agreed with John. "I'm going to the tomb. If anyone wishes to come with me, come on!"

But only John was willing to go. With that, Peter and John scurried out the door and ran down the stairs and out onto the street. Free at last to follow his impulse, the teen-aged John took off running as fast as he could go while the burly Peter huffed and puffed behind him.

Behind Peter, Mary Magdalene also followed by herself. Stung by the men's refusal to believe them, she had to go back to the tomb to reassure herself that she and the other women had not been hallucinating that morning. Mary

---

[7]Although it was only around forty hours since Jesus had died, the Jews reckoned time from sunset to sunset. Thus, Jesus died on Friday (Day #1). Day #2 began at sundown and ended on Saturday at sundown. Day #3 began Saturday at sundown, so Jesus did rise on the third day by the "clock."

hurried but did not run. She correctly feared the attention that such flight by a woman would attract.

John raced past Pilate's praetorium (Herod's old palace), shuddering as he remembered the vicious suffering that Jesus had endured there only the day before yesterday. Through the two gates and down the gentle slope he ran, into the garden area next to the place of crucifixion. As he burst through the last clumps of shrubbery, he saw the open doorway of the tomb provided by Joseph of Arimathea. There were no guards nor any trace of them around. The place appeared to be completely abandoned. When he reached the tomb's entrance, John bent down to peer in. He saw Christ's burial cloths, including the sheet which had been used to carry his body, lying on the ground. The stone slab where the body had been laid was empty.

As he stared, wondering, Peter came rushing up and, almost without pausing, bent over and scooted into the tomb. With the rise of the sun into early morning, the tomb's contents were visible, at least after one's eyes adjusted for the change in lighting. Peter saw the long binding strips that had been used to wrap around Jesus' body at four points to keep it straight and flat upon its bench. Then something caught his eye. It was the main shroud, which had enfolded the entire body, including the face. It was lying by itself in a corner of the tomb, near the head of the stone upon which Jesus had been laid, folded into a square. There were blood stains on the cloth, but also a faint outline that encompassed the stains and gave the whole thing a curious shape.

As Peter stared at the cloth, John came into the tomb and interrupted his gaze. Silently, Peter pointed to the cloth.

John looked more closely and exclaimed, "Peter, it is the Lord's face! He has left us his image!"

Peter stared at John, but shook his head. It did look like an image, but graven images were forbidden in the Jewish religion and Peter was not prepared to accept that Jesus had left a portrait of himself on his bloody burial shroud, which itself would make a man unclean from merely touching it. He looked around the tomb once more. It was empty all right. But there were no angels or young men or anything else out of the ordinary. Nor was Jesus around.

Peter backed out of the tomb, leaving John standing quietly in the middle of the chamber, staring first at the burial shroud and then at the empty stone slab. Suddenly, John knew. Jesus *had* risen! He had told them repeatedly that he would rise on the third day. His brother was simply counting wrong. The women had been telling the truth. Evidently, the Lord had already left to return to Galilee. But why? Why had he let himself be tortured and killed in such a terrible way if he intended to simply rise again a couple of days later? And why go back to Galilee? The heart and head of Judaism was here in Jerusalem. Wouldn't Jesus want to now assert his authority and accept the people's, even the leaders,' acknowledgment that he is indeed the Messiah? It was all baffling to him.

On their way back to the Upper Room, John and Peter discussed the situation. There seemed to be far more questions than answers. John was convinced that the women had reported their experience accurately. Peter was not so sure. He wanted more time to think about it all. He rejected John's suggestion that they leave for Galilee at once. "Another day or two's delay will not hurt. Surely the Lord would have told us before his death if he had wanted us to return to Galilee right away. I think we must remain here and pray for God's guidance, at least for a few days. Thomas is out in the city now trying to learn what the chief priests and the Romans are up to."

Mary Magdalene saw the two men walking back, engrossed in their conversation, but hid herself so they did not see her. After they had passed, she hurried on to the tomb.

Arriving once again at the empty tomb, Mary looked around expectantly. But only the chirping of a bird in the brush and the sounds of caravans and travelers passing on the road nearby broke the stillness. Mary bent down and peered into the darkness, blinking her eyes to adjust them to the dim light filtering in through the opening. Her emotions overwhelmed her then and she began to cry. Relief and joy and doubt and fear and hope and excitement and sorrow all combined to produce a cascade of tears as Mary's body shook with sobs.

"**Woman, why are you weeping? Who is it you are looking for?**"[8]

Mary was so startled by the unexpected company and question that she nearly shrieked as she spun around to face the voice. Swallowing hard and blinking back her tears, she looked at the tall man who stood gazing at her inquisitively but very kindly, too. He was dressed in a white tunic with a brown cloak and ordinary leather sandals. His dark brown hair hung to his shoulders. He was impeccably groomed but Mary was confused and emotionally distraught so she simply assumed he must be the gardener who tended the shrubs and flowers planted here as the quarry was reclaimed to be used as a cemetery. Her tears had brought back all the terrible memories of Jesus' crucifixion and prompted a desperate desire to behold her Lord once again. The message of the angels seemed far, far away in the cold reality of the empty tomb and the recollection of the torn, bruised and bloody body of Jesus.

"**Sir, if you are the one who carried him off, tell me where you have laid him and I will take him away.**"[9] Mary gestured toward the open entryway.

"**Mary!**" he exclaimed, and in that single word, Jesus was revealed to her.

Mary gasped and blurted out, "**Rabbouni!**"[10] as she fell to her knees and attempted to hug Jesus' feet. She felt her tears coming back when she saw the nail wounds in the feet and then could hold them back no longer as she blamed herself for not recognizing Jesus at once. *What is the matter with me? How could I be so blind?* "Forgive me, Lord. I was crying too much, I guess, to see it was you. You are risen!

---

[8]Jn 20:15

[9]Jn 20:15

[10]Jn 20:16. *"Rabbouni,"* John tells us, is Hebrew for *"Teacher."*

Risen just as the angels said!" Mary attempted to kiss Jesus' feet but he reached down and gently pulled her up by her hands.

"Do not cling to me, for I have not yet ascended to the Father. Rather, go to my brothers and tell them, 'I am ascending to my Father and your Father, to my God and your God!'"[11]

"Lord, come with me. I have already been to see the brothers and they do not believe me. If you come, they will know that I have spoken the truth." But before Mary had finished speaking, Jesus had smiled at her and vanished. Tentatively, she put her hand into the space where he had been standing. There was nothing. But now Mary was convinced beyond all possibility of doubt that Jesus lived. She had seen him. She had spoken to him and he to her. She had touched him.

Forgetting her earlier caution, she practically flew back to the Upper Room. A few of the soldiers at the praetorium eyed her suspiciously and one or two passersby started to ask her if she needed assistance, but most just got out of the way of the wild-eyed woman running laughing and skipping down the street.

Once again she raced up the stairs and pounded on the Upper Room door. Peter answered it quickly. **"I have seen the Lord!**[12]** Not merely angels this time, but the Lord Jesus himself!" Hardly able to contain her excitement, Mary related all of the circumstances, how she had been crying and had not even recognized Jesus, mistaking him for the gardener, until he spoke to her. She told them what he had said about his ascension.

"What about Galilee, Mary?" asked Andrew. "Did the Lord say anything about us leaving to go home and where we are to look for him?"

Mary's face, rapturous as she had told of her encounter with Jesus, clouded slightly. "I'm sorry. I forgot to ask him. But he vanished so quickly that I am not sure I could have asked even if I had remembered."

The apostles, who had hoped to finally resolve their doubts, remained troubled. The messages were confusing and Jesus' conduct now was so different than their experience of him before his death. How could Mary not recognize him? She adored him and had been following him for well over a year. No matter how upset she had been, it did not make sense to them that she had not recognized Jesus instantly. They found themselves wondering once again if perhaps Mary was simply so emotionally overwrought that she was imagining everything she had reported. Jesus' vanishing made him sound like a ghost, which was a very different matter in their minds. Ghosts occupied a different sphere of existence from humans and were greatly feared because of it. John, on the other hand, had no doubts. He had been convinced of the reality of Jesus' resurrection since seeing the empty tomb and the burial cloths that morning.

---

[11]Jn 20:17

[12]Jn 20:18

Peter rubbed his chin but said nothing. Something definitely seemed to be happening but what exactly? Why didn't Jesus appear to the apostles directly? Why were the women, who were not allowed in Jewish law even to be witnesses, the ones who were receiving all of the messages? He regretted that he had been unwilling to go with them to the tomb that morning. It had all seemed so futile and foolish then. *Well, I guess I have my answer,* said Peter to himself. *Only the women have shown any faith today. Jesus told us many times that we had to have faith to follow him. I remember how astonished we were when he scolded us and said if we had only the faith of the tiny mustard seed we could order a mountain to move itself.*[13]

Peter folded his arms and walked back toward the table where the apostles and disciples had been arguing over their next course of action. Already the group was splintering. He thought of Cleopas and his brother, Aaron, who had left for the small village of Emmaus shortly after he and John had returned from the tomb. When Peter and John had come back without seeing any angels or anything but the empty tomb, Cleopas and Aaron had given up any hope they might have had that Jesus was alive and well. John mentioned the image on the burial shroud, but that had made no impression at all. It really needed to be seen to be understood. Otherwise, it sounded like seeing faces in the bark of trees or in clouds.

After telling her story, Mary Magdalene had left the men to return downstairs to the other women. The disciples locked the door after her and resumed their debating, praying, watching and wondering in the Upper Room.

Meanwhile, out on the road to Emmaus, which was about seventeen miles west of Jerusalem, Cleopas and Aaron walked along with the sun at their backs, oblivious to the beauty of the bright Spring day with its swooping birds and gently waving white and yellow roadside daisies. They were engrossed in a spirited exchange about the terrible events of the weekend and who Jesus might have been, after all.

"Obviously, Jesus was a great prophet, perhaps the greatest in Israel's history," said Cleopas to his brother. "No one could work such miracles and move people's hearts the way he did if he were not sent from God. The mystery is in his death. He seems to have been mistaken in his greatest claim of all, that is, that he was the Anointed of God, the Messiah, the Son of Man, as he called himself."

Aaron shook his head sadly. "Could a great prophet be mistaken about such a basic question as his identity and mission? This Jesus, whom we all loved and followed with such great hopes, seems to have been repudiated by the Lord God. He whom Jesus called 'Father' as if He were, indeed, his actual father, was nowhere around when His son was being crucified. The women told us that Jesus himself questioned his abandonment by God shortly before he died. Something is very wrong here. I cannot explain the man's miraculous powers. And in his presence, I felt total love. Everything in the world seemed to make sense when he

---

[13]Mt 17:20

spoke. Yet he let himself be brutally murdered without even a peep of protest. Why? It makes no sense."

"Perhaps you are right, Aaron, but I cannot help feeling that we are missing something," said Cleopas.

"What we are missing is hope for Israel!" exclaimed Aaron bitterly. "The Roman yoke lies heavier upon our necks than ever. The Messiah was supposed to save Israel. All Jesus seems to have done is force our own leaders to compromise themselves with the Romans. We are no nearer to the glory of the Kingdom of David than before Jesus came."

"Well, the apostles, including Peter, who was always blustering about dying for Jesus, certainly did not distinguish themselves. At Gethsemane, everyone ran like rabbits when the authorities came to take Jesus prisoner," replied Cleopas. "Only John was brave enough to follow Jesus to Golgotha. The women put us all to shame that day."

Aaron, embarrassed by the truth of the charge, protested vigorously: "That's not fair, Cleopas! Peter tried to defend Jesus at Gethsemane but he would have none of it. How could they sacrifice their lives for someone who would make no effort to save his own life? He even let that traitorous rat, Judas, embrace him when he knew that he had betrayed him. No wonder none of them knew what to do, so they just ran away to save themselves."

As the two men walked along, arguing and commiserating, the road led through a cleft in one of the small hills along their way. As they emerged on the other side, a stranger came walking down the grassy hillside. Cleopas and Aaron paused and watched him approach. After first making sure that he was not a threat, they invited him to join them in their journey. This was customary for the time, reflecting not only the prevailing sense of courtesy, but also the fact that there was always more safety in numbers in those days. They did not recognize the tall stranger in his white tunic, brown cloak and dusty leather sandals.

They exchanged introductions: "I am Cleopas, and this is my brother, Aaron, of the house of Tobias in Emmaus."

The stranger replied, "I have been in Jerusalem this past week and am now on my way home to my father, a great journey from here."

No other information was offered and, out of politeness, the two disciples did not inquire further. The three men continued along the road to Emmaus.

"What are you discussing as you go your way?"[14] asked the stranger.

The question astonished Cleopas and Aaron and they immediately stopped walking and turned to the stranger in amazement. Cleopas responded to his question with a question of his own: **"Are you the only resident of Jerusalem who does not know the things that went on there these past few days?"**[15]

"What things?" asked the stranger.

---

[14]Lk 24:17

[15]This quote and the next one are from Lk 24:19.

Cleopas and Aaron both started to speak at once, but then Aaron yielded to Cleopas, who replied:

> **"All those that had to do with Jesus of Nazareth, a prophet powerful in word and deed in the eyes of God and all the people; how our chief priests and leaders delivered him up to be condemned to death, and crucified him. We were hoping that he was the one who would set Israel free. Besides all this, today, the third day since these things happened, some women of our group have just brought us some astonishing news. They were at the tomb before dawn and failed to find his body, but returned with the tale that they had seen a vision of angels who declared he was alive. Some of our number went to the tomb and found it to be just as the women said; but him they did not see."[16]**

The stranger was not in the least apologetic for his apparently inexcusable ignorance. He replied with some indignation: **"What little sense you have! How slow you are to believe all that the prophets have announced! Did not the Messiah have to undergo all this so as to enter into his glory?"[17]**

Before the two disciples could answer, the stranger began to explain his meaning. "Through Moses, the God of Israel gave you the Feasts of Passover and Unleavened Bread to commemorate the deliverance of Israel from Egypt by His mighty hand. The blood of lambs was used to mark the homes of the Israelites and save them from the avenging angel. You will remember that in establishing the feast, the Lord forbade you to break any of the bones of the lamb to be sacrificed.[18] This was a foretelling that the Lamb sent by God to save His people from their sins was to be sacrificed without breaking any of his bones.

"Remember what David prophesied in his psalms:

> **'All who see me scoff at me;**
> **they mock me with parted lips,**
> **they wag their heads;**
> **"He relied on the LORD, let him deliver him,**
> **let him rescue him, if he loves him."'**

"And, again:

> **'They have pierced my hands and my feet;**
> **I can count all my bones.**
> **They look on and gloat over me;**

---

[16]Lk 24:19-24

[17]Lk 24:25

[18]See Ex 12:46, Nm 9:12.

> they divide my garments among them,
> and for my vesture they cast lots.'[19]

Does this not describe the contemptuous rejection of Jesus by the leaders of his people and his death by crucifixion?

"So, too, did Isaiah prophecy:

> 'A voice cries out:
>
> In the desert prepare the way of the LORD!
>
> Make straight in the wasteland a highway
> for our God!'[20]

"This voice was that of John the Baptist, sent by God to announce the coming of the Messiah. Did not Zechariah instruct you:

> 'See, your king shall come to you;
> a just savior is he,
> Meek, and riding on an ass,
> on a colt, the foal of an ass.'?[21]

The prophet speaks of the entry of the Messiah into Jerusalem, the heart of Israel. Recall how Jesus entered the city in exactly this fashion just one week ago today.

"Elsewhere, Zechariah told you that the Lord's service to Israel would be valued at thirty pieces of silver. The Lord told him to throw the paltry sum into the treasury in the house of the Lord and thus was the sacred covenant between the Lord and Israel broken.[22] You did not know, but this was the sum given to Judas, who betrayed Jesus to the chief priests and elders and later threw the money into the Temple.

"In Zechariah, you will also find this prophecy:

> 'I will pour out on the house of David
> and on the inhabitants of Jerusalem
> a spirit of grace and petition;
> and they shall look on him
> whom they have thrust through,
> and they shall mourn for him as one mourns
> for an only son,
> and they shall grieve over him as one
> grieves over a first-born.'[23]

Thus was the Messiah pierced on his cross by a Roman spear.

---

[19]Ps 22:8-9, 17-19

[20]Is 40:3

[21]Zec 9:9

[22]See Zec 11:12-13.

[23]Zec 12:10

"Isaiah foretold the sufferings of the Son of Man and explained very clearly what his purpose was:

'I gave my back to those who beat me,
my cheeks to those who plucked my beard;
My face I did not shield
from buffets and spitting.'[24]

'He was spurned and avoided by men,
a man of suffering,
accustomed to infirmity,
One of those from whom men hide their faces,
spurned, and we held him in no esteem.

Yet it was our infirmities that
he bore,
our sufferings that he endured,
While we thought of him as stricken,
as one smitten by God and afflicted.
But he was pierced for our offenses,
crushed for our sins;
Upon him was the chastisement
that makes us whole,
by his stripes we were healed.
We had all gone astray like sheep,
each following his own way;
But the LORD laid upon him
the guilt of us all.

Though he was harshly treated,
he submitted
and opened not his mouth;
Like a lamb led to the slaughter
or a sheep before the shearers,
he was silent and opened not his mouth.

Because he surrendered himself
to death
and was counted among the wicked;
And he shall take away the sins of many,
and win pardon for their offenses.'"[25]

---

[24]Is 50:6

[25]Is 53:3-7, 12

These were not all the passages of Scripture that the stranger explained to Cleopas and Aaron. In fact, as they walked along the quiet, country road, he interpreted every passage that described the mission of the Messiah, his manner of coming, and the meaning and character of his life on earth. The two disciples listened with growing excitement as they saw the Messianic prophecies in a whole new light. Suddenly, they seemed crystal clear and what had seemed like incomprehensible, tragic folly a few hours ago, now appeared as an equally incomprehensible but magnificent gift of love and sacrifice from the God of Israel Himself.

The three men arrived at a crossroads just outside the village of Emmaus. The stranger smiled at Cleopas and Aaron and said: "So you see that what you have seen as disappointment is truly cause for rejoicing. Share with all whom you meet what I have taught you." The stranger started to walk away from the two disciples, following the dusty road that curved south around the village.

"**Stay with us,**" pleaded Cleopas. "**It is nearly evening—the day is practically over.**"[26]

The stranger turned around at the invitation and thanked the two men graciously for their hospitality, saying that he was very happy to accept. Cleopas and Aaron took the stranger to their father's house. He was introduced to Tobias and all the members of the household and all were invited to join together for the evening meal.

At the table, Tobias invited him to pronounce the supper blessing. As they bowed their heads, the stranger took a loaf of fresh bread into his hands and, looking up to heaven, he gave thanks to God: "Father, we thank you for the bounty of your Hands which feeds the bodies and souls of your children. In your mercy and goodness, you have given glory to your Son that all those whom he loves might share in the glory and love you bestow upon those who live in your kingdom. Grant that through his words, which you have given him to speak, and through this bread, which is the body he has given up for all those who love him, they may come to love you and to serve you in that Spirit which we share forever and ever. Amen."

The stranger's words struck deep chords within Cleopas and Aaron. They stared intently at him, as if they could not quite focus their eyes. He then broke the bread and passed one half in each direction along the table. As he did so, the two disciples leaped to their feet, saying in perfect unison: "It is the Lord!" Jesus looked at them, smiled, and vanished.

"**Were not our hearts burning inside us as he talked to us on the road and explained the Scriptures to us?**"[27] said Cleopas to Aaron. "Father, the stranger whom we invited to share our dwelling and our meal was Jesus himself, raised from the dead as he promised! We were not permitted to recognize him

---

[26]Lk 24:29

[27]Lk 24:32

until he explained to us the meaning of his suffering and death and then broke the bread for us as he himself was sacrificed upon the cross. We must return at once to Jerusalem to tell the apostles and all the others who have followed him that he is alive! The women spoke the truth and we were wrong not to believe them."

"Of course, you must return at once!" agreed Tobias. "But take two of our camels. That's the only way you can get back to Jerusalem tonight."

Cleopas and Aaron got up then and immediately set out on the return trip to Jerusalem. They spurred their camels and traveled back considerably faster than their trip out. Even so, it was well after dark before they reached the Jaffa Gate. The two men arrived breathless at the home of Mary and Tychus, who expressed surprise to see them back so quickly. "We must see Peter and the others at once! We have the most wonderful news. We have seen the Lord!"

"You, too!" exclaimed Tychus. "This is truly a day which the Lord has made! Go quickly upstairs. You will find them still gathered there. They will rejoice to hear your report."

The two men dashed up the stairs, followed closely by Tychus, and pounded on the still-locked door.

"Who is it?" came the muffled query.

"Cleopas and Aaron. We have wonderful news to share! Open the door. Hurry!"

The door was flung open and James, the brother of John, stood there with the remaining apostles and disciples gathered in a large knot behind him. Before Cleopas and Aaron could say another word, James, grinning from ear to ear, announced: **"The Lord has been raised! It is true! He has appeared to Simon."**[28]

Peter had gone back to the tomb early in the afternoon to collect the burial cloths of Jesus. The Lord had appeared to him then as he had to Mary Magdalene earlier. The apostles and disciples had no problem believing the word of Peter, who was a man and their recognized leader. They had spent the afternoon in prayer and excited discussion about what the Lord's resurrection would mean for Israel and their hopes that he would return and lead them all again, as before.

After Peter's experience, most of the remaining apostles and disciples had gone out in separate small groups to the tomb, but they had not seen Jesus nor any other heavenly personage.

Cleopas and Aaron were the center of attention as they recounted their whole experience with the mysterious stranger, relating as best they could all that he had explained to them about the Scriptural prophecies concerning the Messiah. They described how their hearts had filled with love and excitement in the presence of this stranger, and how they felt they would burst with joy during his blessing. When he broke the bread to distribute it to them, they suddenly saw him as Jesus, and realized that his word and his bread had been needed to uncloud their minds. As with Peter, this incredible news of Jesus' appearance caused a

---

[28]Lk 24:34

great deal of excited comment among the apostles and disciples. But no one was prepared for the thrill they were about to receive.

As Cleopas and Aaron had finished describing their experience, the other men in the room had tended to spread out a bit as they discussed among themselves the wonderful report they had received. Some of them thought of additional questions and moved back toward the two disciples to ask them. In the middle of this hubbub, Jesus was suddenly just *there*, standing in their midst.

"**Peace be with you,**"[29] he said calmly.

Those who were facing the spot where he appeared out of thin air gasped and fell back, momentarily stunned into silence. Then everyone turned to see the source of the familiar voice. The general reaction was to retreat in terror as if the appearance of Jesus could be explained only if he were a ghost. Despite the manner of his earlier appearances, the disciples still expected Jesus to knock at their door, and to otherwise behave as any normal human being. For them, resurrection meant a return to life as Lazarus had, with final death only postponed. They still had barely a glimmer of understanding that the true reality to which Christ had come to bring them was not the world they inhabited, but the life on the other side of death's door.

"**Peace be with you,**"[30] Jesus repeated. "Why do you fear me? Can you not see that it is I? Do I look and sound like a ghost?" Jesus was kind, but his voice conveyed his impatience as well. Even after all his miracles, and his walking on the water during the storm upon the Sea of Galilee, and his transfiguration on Mt. Tabor, they were still constantly surprised and alarmed by him. He continued to challenge them:

> "**Why are you disturbed? Why do such ideas cross your mind? Look at my hands and my feet; it is really I. Touch me, and see that a ghost does not have flesh and bones as I do.**"[31]

Hesitantly, the disciples moved closer now. Jesus held out his hands with the nail holes low in the palms and gestured for those standing near him to actually touch the wounds. They did so timidly and in awe. Jesus pointed to his feet where two gaping holes pierced them just where the bones and flesh began to arch upward toward the ankles. Then Jesus opened his cloak and, through a split in his tunic, showed them the two-inch narrow oval of the spear's entry wound in his right side. Again, he gestured to those nearest to him to actually place their fingers into the opening so that they would see he was made of real flesh and blood.

---

[29] Jn 20:19; see Lk 24:36.

[30] Jn 20:21

[31] Lk 24:38-39

The apostles and disciples were overwhelmed by their emotions. A few began to cry, moved to tears by the sight of the Lord's cruel wounds. Many were grinning crazily, still confused but joyous, waiting for Jesus to take charge and tell them what to do. Some were still not convinced. *How could flesh and blood walk through walls?* they wondered.

So Jesus said to them: **"Have you anything here to eat?"**[32]

On the table there were still some leftovers from the evening meal, left uncleared by the tumultuous arrival of Cleopas and Aaron.

"Here, Lord, are fish and bread. And some cheese and wine," said one of the disciples, eager to please. Jesus walked over to the table and sat down. He picked up one of the cooked fish, blessed it and proceeded to eat it. The disciples watched as Jesus ate the fish and drank the wine, just as he had for innumerable meals in the years earlier. Clearly, he was no ghost.

When he had finished, Jesus beckoned to them to gather around him at the table. The apostles and a few disciples sat; the rest stood. First, Jesus took them to task a bit for their lack of faith: "Why were you not prepared to believe that I had risen today? Did I not tell you on several occasions that I would do this? When the women came to you to tell you of the message of the angels I sent, you refused even to consider the possibility that they might be telling the truth. When John told you of my burial cloths and the image thereon, you paid him no heed. It was my desire that you leave this city and return to Galilee, but you had so little faith that you would not consider doing so until I personally told you where to go. Did you think I could not find you? Since you have remained this long, I desire that you stay a little longer here."

Jesus' rebuke for their unwillingness to leave for Galilee made Peter, who had repeatedly counseled delay, turn scarlet. When the Lord had appeared to him personally, it had been brief and he had said nothing other than to remind Peter that he had prophesied his resurrection.

Jesus continued: "Your weaknesses and slowness, however, shall be a consolation to those who will learn from you and follow me. Despite their errors and their failings, I shall love them with the love that my Father gives to me so long as they put my words into practice. Of you I shall make a great Church and those who love me will understand that the glory of the Father, Son and Holy Spirit are manifested most powerfully in the weakest of God's children."

With the apostles and disciples appropriately chastened, Jesus turned to building his new Church: **"Recall those words I spoke to you when I was still with you: everything written about me in the law of Moses and the prophets and psalms had to be fulfilled."**[33]

As the men looked into the face of Jesus, they all experienced a great flash of insight. Of course! All at once, just like that, the Scriptural passages that referred

---

[32]Lk 24:41

[33]Lk 24:44

to the Messiah stood out in their minds in bold relief. And they saw how those writings had explicitly predicted the passion and death of Jesus. They were not yet clear on the *why* of it, that would not come for another fifty days, but they saw how the plan of God had been prescribed and then fulfilled.

Jesus let their new understanding sink in and then continued:

"Thus it is written that the Messiah must suffer and
rise from the dead on the third day. In his name,
penance for the remission of sins is to be preached to
all the nations, beginning at Jerusalem. You are
witnesses of this. See, I send down upon you the
promise of my Father.[34]
As the Father has sent me,
so I send you."[35]

Jesus extended both his arms out from his body, encompassing the entire group of men who hung avidly on his every word. Then, turning from left to right, he breathed in their direction, saying when he had completed the semi-circle:

"Receive the Holy Spirit.
If you forgive men's sins,
they are forgiven them;
if you hold them bound,
they are held bound."[36]

With these words, Jesus established the Sacrament of Penance, his first post-resurrection gift to his infant Church. In the confessional, we have Jesus' assurance that the Holy Spirit is present and the priest speaks in His name with the very authority of heaven.

Jesus stood, and as he did so, there was a loud knocking at the door to the Upper Room, where they were gathered. All heads turned toward the sound.

"It is I, Thomas. Let me in. I have much news to share with you!" As the men turned back to see Jesus' reaction to the arrival of Thomas they were shocked to discover him gone, vanished as quickly and silently as his arrival had been. They looked all around, but, indeed, Jesus was no longer in their company, at least not visibly.

Thomas knocked again, more insistently. "There is no danger. Let me in!"

Two of the disciples hurried to the door and opened it to Thomas, who pushed brusquely past them. The room erupted into a cacophony of voices: **"We have seen the Lord!"**[37] "Thomas, it is true! The Lord was just here in our

---

[34]Lk 24:46-49

[35]Jn 20:21

[36]Jn 20:22-23

[37]Jn 20:25

company." "He is alive and well. And not a ghost!" "We touched him and felt his wounds." "We saw him eat a fish and drink wine!" "Only when you arrived did he disappear, the same way he came." "The Lord is truly risen!"

But Thomas could not accept it. He was a man of logic and reason. It was inconceivable to him that God would let His Son die on a cross without intervening. In his mind, it diminished Yahweh, made Him less than an earth father, any one of whom would do all that could be done to save a son under similar circumstances. Similarly, Jesus' failure to save himself convinced Thomas that, in the end, Jesus lacked the power and authority which he had claimed. Despite all that he had seen: the incredible miracles, the profound wisdom and insight of Jesus, the unique power of his personality, Thomas could not reconcile the vicious and violent death of crucifixion with a God who loved and cared about His people. In his mind, they were as incompatible as square circles or warm ice: oxymorons. With his deep-set, black eyes, he stared at the other men as they excitedly described the risen Lord. Sadly, but with chilling conviction, he replied: **"I will never believe it without probing the nail-prints in his hands, without putting my finger in the nail-marks and my hand into his side."**[38]

"But, Thomas, that is what we have already done," explained his good friend, Matthew. "He stood practically where you stand now and showed us his wounds and invited us to touch them all. Several of us did." But the words did not soften Thomas' disbelief.

After awhile, the men gave up trying to convince him and let him tell what he had learned during his all-day sojourn into the city. He had observed activities at the Fortress Antonia as well as at Pilate's praetorium. The Romans showed no sign of interest in them or anyone associated with Jesus.

At the Temple, the Feast of Unleavened Bread continued to be celebrated. There had apparently been a convening of the Great Sanhedrin in the morning. It was Temple guards and not Roman soldiers whom the women discovered at the tomb. They had been called in to meet with Noam, the chief scribe. "No one knows yet what that was about, but they were not taken into custody so the chief priests must have been in an uncharacteristically charitable mood. There is a rumor going around that the guards saw something but won't talk about it now. Others said the guards had had a party and gotten drunk.

"Most of the people I spoke to are still in a state of shock and sorrow over the death of Jesus. The chief priests and elders, however, were strutting around like peacocks. I spoke to one of the priests in the Court of the Israelites. He told me that the chief priests and elders were afraid that the followers of Jesus would steal his body, so that is why they posted the guard. Isn't that a laugh?! We were all cowering here in this room, afraid we would be the next victims.

"The authorities expect that we will simply disappear, like all the other followers of false messiahs before Jesus. All in all, there seems little risk to us now,

---

[38]Jn 20:25

but it would probably be safer if we remained out of sight, at least as a group, for another week or so.

"As for where Jesus' body has gone to, and who took it, nobody seems to know. It may have been the Romans, or even Joseph of Arimathea, whom I was not able to find."

Several of the apostles shook their heads at Thomas' reference to the missing body of Jesus. They were annoyed that he refused to accept the truth.

Having concluded his report, Thomas headed for the supper table, for he was very hungry. He had at first been too nervous and then later too busy to eat while he was out and about in Jerusalem. The disciples and apostles continued to try to convince him that Jesus was, indeed, resurrected in the flesh, but finally gave up when he stubbornly responded that there was only one way in which he could be convinced of that, and that was in the manner he had already described.

One week later to the day, the men were once again assembled in the Upper Room for prayer, discussion of when they should leave for Galilee, and dining. The doors were still kept locked. By now, they had learned that the Temple guards were claiming that followers of Jesus had stolen his body away. This had cheered them somewhat because it confirmed Jesus' physical resurrection. But it alarmed them, too, since there now existed the possibility that the Jewish authorities, or even the Romans, might seek them out to punish them for the reported transgression.

As they prayed, Jesus appeared before them and said: "**Peace be with you.**"[39]

No one was more astonished at the appearance of Jesus than Thomas. His eyes widened beneath their bushy eyebrows as he opened his mouth to speak, but closed it when no words came out. Jesus beckoned to Thomas to come toward him. Thomas did not move, merely continued to stare, seeming not to hear Jesus' words.

"Thomas, the Lord is calling to you! Go to him!" hissed Bartholomew, who gave him a nudge to get him moving.

Thomas walked slowly toward Jesus, mouth opening and closing but still unable to find anything to say. Jesus smiled, amused in spite of himself. But he had an important lesson to convey to his skeptical apostle, and through him to all the rest of us down through the ages who would try to believe and follow Jesus. So he spoke rather sternly to Thomas: "**Take your finger and examine my hands. Put your hand into my side. Do not persist in your unbelief, but believe!**"[40]

---

[39]Jn 20:26

[40]Jn 20:27

Jesus' words snapped Thomas out of his awestruck reverie and mortified him at the same time. Blushing from shame, he dropped to his knees and bowed before the Lord, saying: "**My Lord and my God!**"[41]

Jesus reached down and grasped Thomas by one of his upper arms and helped him to his feet.

> "**You became a believer because you saw me.**
> **Blest are they who have not seen**
> **and have believed.**[42]

Go now, all of you, into Galilee. You will see me there."

With these final words, Jesus left them once again. The events of his resurrection were at their end. Forevermore, what happened on this first Easter Sunday would be the pivotal event in the history of mankind. It is the foundation upon which all Christianity rests. It is the foundation of all our hopes; the happy solution to the mystery and sorrow of our lives on earth.

---

[41]Jn 20:28

[42]Jn 20:29

THE RESURRECTION

Tell me, if Christ is preached as raised from the dead, how is it that some of you say there is no resurrection of the dead? If there is no resurrection of the dead, Christ himself has not been raised. And if Christ has not been raised, our preaching is void of content and your faith is empty, too. Indeed, we should then be exposed as false witnesses of God, for we have borne witness before him that he raised up Christ; but he certainly did not raise him up if the dead are not raised. Why? Because if the dead are not raised, then Christ was not raised; and if Christ was not raised, your faith is worthless. You are still in your sins, and those who have fallen asleep in Christ are the deadest of the dead. If our hopes in Christ are limited to this life only, we are the most pitiable of men.

. . . .

Now I am going to tell you a mystery. Not all of us shall fall asleep, but all of us are to be changed—in an instant, in the twinkling of an eye, at the sound of the last trumpet. The trumpet will sound and the dead will be raised incorruptible, and we shall be changed. This corruptible body must be clothed with incorruptibility, this mortal body with immortality. When the corruptible frame takes on incorruptibility and the mortal immortality, then will the saying of Scripture be fulfilled: 'Death is swallowed up in victory.' 'O death, where is your victory? O death, where is your sting?' The sting of death is sin, and sin gets its power from the law. But thanks be to God who has given us the victory through our Lord Jesus Christ.

—From the First Letter of Paul to the Corinthians, chapter 15, verses 12-19, 51-57.

QUESTIONS FOR REFLECTION

(1) Given the astonishing miracles that Jesus worked during his ministry, why was it so difficult for the apostles to accept the reports of his resurrection? How would you have reacted? Is it still difficult for men to believe what women tell them?

(2) Why do you believe that the resurrection of Jesus actually took place?

(3) Why do so many other people not believe it took place? In other words, why isn't everyone Christian?

(4) Why do you think the Jewish authorities would not accept the reality of Christ's resurrection, even after their own guards' testimony? Have you observed a similar propensity on the part of other government officials to lie rather than accept an embarrassing truth? Other persons? Yourself? Give some examples.

(5) Do you think that Jesus appeared to his mother on Easter morning? If yes, why is it not reported in Scripture, do you think?

(6) It has been said that the establishment of the Eucharist by Jesus created a relationship between man and God superior to that with Adam and Eve before they sinned. In other words, man's loss to Satan was converted by God into a victory, and the sharing of humanity between man and God more than offsets all the sin and suffering in the world from the beginning until the end. Do you agree?

(7) Some Bible scholars say that even if Jesus did not rise from the dead his teachings should still be followed because of their advocacy of love and good will. But Saint Paul says Christians are the biggest of fools if there was no resurrection. Who do you think is right? Why?

(8) There were no human witnesses at the moment of Jesus' resurrection. Can you think of any reason why God did it this way?

(9) Between His death and resurrection, Jesus freed the souls from that place where they were held pending the opening up of Heaven to them. How do you imagine this encounter between Christ and all these souls patiently waiting for their liberation? A huge mob scene like a post-holiday sale?

(10) Given the fact of Jesus' resurrection and the promise of our own, why do nearly all of us still fear death so much? Why do we mourn and weep over the death of loved ones who appeared to live good lives or who were reconciled with God at their deaths? What more would you like God to do for you to make you feel more secure about dying?

This Jesus who has been taken from you will return, just as you saw him go up into the heavens. Acts 1:11

SECOND GLORIOUS MYSTERY

The Ascension

After Jesus left the apostles and other disciples in the Upper Room following his appearance and encounter with Thomas, they began to make plans to leave Jerusalem for Galilee as Jesus had requested. He still had not specified a particular place in Galilee for them to go to, but neither Peter nor anyone else saw this as a problem any longer. They understood now that they were to go about their lives in ways which to them seemed best, while being careful to always include prayer and open hearts and minds in their decision-making. God would intervene as needed to direct them when the time was appropriate.

Mary and Tychus remained in Jerusalem, but their son, Mark, traveled with the disciples. Mary, the mother of Jesus; her sister-in-law, Mary of Clopas; Salome, the mother of James and John; Joanna, the wife of Herod Antipas' steward, Chuza; Susanna; and several other Galilean women accompanied the men, glad to be returning home. If the truth be told, everyone was happy to leave Jerusalem. They had numerous family and friends in Galilee to whom they were anxious to tell the glorious news of Jesus' resurrection. Of course, it would be a mixed message for those who had not yet heard of his crucifixion. They would be horrified to learn that that had been the Lord's fate, even as he had warned.

There were other reasons, too, for being happy about leaving Jerusalem. There was the very real possibility that the Jewish authorities might seek to prosecute the followers of Jesus, especially if they perceived them to be a continuation of the threat that Jesus had presented to them. This apprehension was heightened by the spread of the report that the disciples of Jesus had stolen his body from his tomb in order to claim that he had been raised from the dead. Finally, there was the unpredictability of Pontius Pilate. He had been reluctant to crucify Christ, but having made that decision, he might decide that logic impelled him to crucify the Nazorean's followers as well. All in all, the apostles and other disciples were excited to be departing the city for the pastoral and tranquil beauty of Galilee.

"Peter, do you think the Lord will stay with us once we get back to Galilee?" asked John, as he loaded the water jugs, tents, provisions and extra clothing on the backs of the small donkeys who would accompany the party on their journey.

"I hope so," replied Peter. "All Israel will follow him after they see him risen from the dead. No one will doubt any longer that he is the Messiah, the Son of God sent from his Father. It will be like Moses when the Lord led our people out of Israel, only this time we will follow the Lord himself in reclaiming his people and his land for God."

Matthew, overhearing Peter and John, jumped into the conversation. "I don't know, Peter. What you say seems obvious to us in light of the prophecies as we have understood them. But the Lord has constantly surprised us. And didn't he just explain to us how the Scriptures pointed to his suffering and death so that our sins could be forgiven? And why not appear to the leaders of our people now? Or, better yet, last week when so many pilgrims were here for the Feasts of Passover and Unleavened Bread? There are still many, many unanswered questions. I hope everything will be made clear to us when we get home to Galilee."

Now Bartholomew joined in. "We all want Jesus to lead us like he did before. But he's not the same as he was then. Since his resurrection, his body—which I touched myself—seems very different. In his presence now, I sense an overwhelming power. Remember how the Magdalene and Cleopas and his brother, Aaron, did not even recognize Jesus at first? He had to empower them to see him. With Cleopas and Aaron, he revealed himself in the bread which he broke for them, perhaps a reminder of the bread that he gave to us at the Passover supper we celebrated the night before he died. Before, Jesus seemed like one of us. But now, he seems to be visiting us from someplace far more significant than this world."

Peter and John glanced at each other, remembering how they had felt after the Transfiguration of the Lord on Mount Tabor before his final, fateful journey to Jerusalem.

"Well, I, for one, have learned my lesson!" declared Thomas. "The plan of God is far more clever than I am. We have the prophets and they have given us the words which the Lord spoke to them. But there were no dates attached and that makes everything difficult to sort out. From now on, I am going to be a good listener. The Lord has asked us to go home, it's a beautiful day for traveling, and I say, let's get going!"

The apostles, disciples and the Galilean women returning with them had assembled at the home of Lazarus, Mary and Martha in Bethany. Just over a hundred people would be making the trip. Since most of them were headed for their homes around the Sea of Galilee, they followed the route down through the Judean Wilderness to the road that ran along the western side of the fertile Jordan River, which itself flowed out of the southern end of the great lake.[1]

---

[1]The "Sea" of Galilee is a bit of an exaggeration. It is actually a good-sized fresh-water lake more than 600 feet below sea level. In the shape roughly of a harp, it is 6 miles wide and 15 miles long, 32 miles around, and approximately 150 feet at its deepest point.

This path also took them past Mount Quarantal, the mountain near Jericho where Satan offered Jesus all the kingdoms of the world if he would follow his path instead of God's.

The Blessed Virgin Mary and her sister-in-law Mary did not return to Nazareth. The village had not been a hospitable place for them since the time the villagers had attempted to kill Jesus for proclaiming himself the Anointed of the Lord. When Clopas' son James, and his grandson Jude Thaddaeus, had become apostles of Jesus, James had relocated his family to Magdala, a village about halfway between Capernaum and Tiberias. Jesus' mother stayed in Magdala as a guest of Mary Magdalene.

Once back in Galilee, the disciples gathered together every day at first, awaiting another appearance from Jesus. But a week went by and Jesus did not appear. It was now three weeks since his resurrection and two weeks since anyone had reported seeing him.

Peter, an impetuous man by nature, grew increasingly impatient. He felt completely inadequate for the task of leading Jesus' followers without the Lord's personal presence. More than once he considered simply quitting and going back to his life as a fisherman. As the days passed without any appearance from Jesus, the belief that he was inadequate to the task to which the Lord had called him grew more and more toward a firm resolve to return to his former life.

Several of the other apostles were either staying at Peter's house, or spent their days there. Included in this group were the "Sons of Thunder" (and of Zebedee), James and John; Bartholomew (also known as Nathanael); Thomas; Philip and Simon the Zealot. Late one afternoon, Peter could contain his restlessness and doubts no longer. He had been pacing back and forth, stopping every so often to stare out across the lake which was lapping at the rocks only a few meters from his doorstep. Abruptly he stopped and announced: "**I am going out to fish.**"[2]

The other apostles present, as anxious as Peter and even more convinced that their mission was hopeless without the presence of Jesus, quickly seized the opportunity to do something and declared, "**We will join you.**" The lure of their previous, relatively carefree, life was strong in all of them.

The men tossed off their good cloaks and hurried out the door of Peter's house toward the dock where his and several other boats were kept. The seven apostles, temporarily enthused by the opportunity to divert their mounting anxiety to this constructive pursuit, threw themselves into casting off, searching the waters for likely spots, and rowing as the slack wind required. Peter stood at the till as they headed out into the lake. About 300 yards off shore, they let down their anchor. Reports had indicated favorable fishing conditions and the apostles looked forward to doing something both enjoyable and profitable.

---

[2]This quote and the next one are from Jn 21:3.

They threw the round, weighted net over the side of the boat and let it sink out of sight. The net contained small stones inside a hem that circled the outside edge of the net. The stones (sometimes lead weights were used) pulled the net down into the dark waters like a giant, porous pancake. A small circle was left open in the middle of the net. Through this small circle, a rope line was connected to 22 brail lines that were fastened with equal spacing to the outer edge of the net. When the net had completed its descent, encompassing whatever fish got in its way, the rope line and brails pulled the bottom of the net together, trapping the fish in the pocket formed by the outer edge of the net being pulled inward toward the small, center hole. As the net broke the surface of the water, one or more of the other fishermen would use hooked poles to grasp the net and help pull it into the boat. If the net was too full to do that easily, the men rowed the boat ashore, towing the net full of fish behind.[3]

This day, however, no such effort was needed. The net came up almost as effortlessly as it had gone down, because it came up empty. Not one single fish. The men threw the net over the side again and waited a little longer this time for the net to sink lower. When they pulled it up, there was again nothing in it. After another half dozen tries, all of which produced not one wriggling, shiny inhabitant of the murky waters, they pulled up their anchor and moved to another spot about 50 yards away. Again and again and again the net went down and each time came up empty.

This cycle went on as darkness fell and midnight came and went. Torches flickered at key points along the sides of the boat. The nonfishermen, Bartholomew and Simon the Zealot, were ready to call it a night. But Peter, James and John felt their pride was on the line. Besides, the fishing at least kept their minds occupied and away from the constant wondering where Jesus was and what his plans were for them and himself.

All night long, the men toiled. Casting, pulling, finding nothing, moving the boat, repeating the cycle. The brilliant white band of the Milky Way stars sparkled for hours, then gave way to predawn blackness, which, in turn, yielded to a dark gray, then a deep purple, and finally a cerulean blue as the cheerful gleam of the yellow sun peeked over the horizon. The bottom of the boat was as clean and uncluttered as when they had set out with such high hopes the afternoon before.

Besides Peter and the two sons of Zebedee, Thomas and Philip were also experienced fishermen. All of them were baffled. There was no reason why they should have had such poor luck. The day before, other fishermen had reported that the fishing was good and had themselves returned with bountiful catches.

---

[3]This technique was known as cast net fishing, used more commonly by fishermen standing in the shallows. Two boats working together used a method known as dragnet fishing in which they suspended the net between them and gathered all the fish in the way.

From time to time, the men had even seen schools of the shiny fish[4] glistening as they darted in unison just beneath the surface of the water. Eagerly they had cast their nets in the places where the fish should have been. But they caught nothing. By daybreak, the boat had moved about one-half mile north and east of Capernaum and was approximately 100 yards offshore. The men were working in shifts now. It did not take all of them to pull up an empty net.

The man on the shore watched them for a few minutes, then called out: **"Children, have you caught anything to eat?"**[5]

All seven men on the boat stopped what they were doing and looked in the direction of the friendly voice that had boomed across the water to them. With the sun not fully risen, it was still somewhat dark on shore and the apostles could not make out the features of the man who had spoken.

"Not a thing," replied James irritably. He was annoyed by the stranger's reference to the breakfast which they did not have.

The voice came back, **"Cast your net off to the starboard side and you will find something."**[6]

James and John looked at Peter, who shrugged and picked up the net as he moved toward the starboard side of the boat. Peter tossed the net into the water and watched it fade once again into the depths. Philip, Bartholomew, Thomas and Simon the Zealot were all standing now, watching to see if the stranger's advice would be any good. They were prepared to help on the rope or hook the sides of the net with their long poles, if needed, but almost no one gave that requirement any thought in view of the night's frustration. However, when the men started to draw the net back up, it became immediately clear that this was going to be a dramatically different experience.

"Grab your poles!" cried Peter as he clung to the rope which plunged straight and taut into the opaque waters. The load was massive. Slowly, the net shimmered into sight. The top and sides of the net bulged with leaping, wriggling fish, each one a prize catch, flashing silver as the sunlight glinted off their sides. Perspiring, the apostles struggled to contain the net and haul it into the boat. But it was impossible. The net was swollen to the breaking point. The apostles gaped in amazement but there was no time to dawdle. Peter barked orders and the men hurried to weigh anchor in preparation for rowing the boat into the shallows of the lake. They would have to tow the fish to shore behind the boat and then pull them onto the beach.

---

[4]The most popular edible fish in the Sea of Galilee today is known as Saint Peter's fish, or *tilapia galilea*. Legend has it that this is the fish from which Peter pulled the coin to pay the temple tax (Mt 17:27) and that it bears his fingerprints as markings which identify the species today.

[5]This quote and the next one are from Jn 21:5.

[6]Jn 21:6

Maybe it was his sharp young eyes, or maybe it was some response of his heart, but John was the first to recognize the stranger. He grabbed Peter's arm and pointed toward the shoreline: **"It is the Lord!"**[7]

Peter stared and then whooped with joy. He had been wearing only a loin cloth against the sweat and splash of the work and sea. Now he grabbed his tunic, pulled it over his head, and dove headfirst off the bow. He was already swimming before his head broke the surface. The men in the boat, towing the net full of fish, followed.

When Peter reached the shoreline, he clambered over the sandy bank and ran toward Jesus. "Master!" he cried. "We have longed to see you." Forgetting himself, and that he was soaking wet, for a moment, Peter hugged the Lord, who returned the embrace wholeheartedly. Then Peter remembered and fell to his knees, "Lord, forgive me. I forgot myself."

"Peter," replied Jesus laughing, "such enthusiastic love, even if a bit damp, needs no apology. Your joy gladdens my heart and matches my own for you!" He looked up then at the boat which had just landed. **"Bring some of the fish you just caught,"**[8] Jesus called out to the apostles on the boat.

Peter, still dripping water, ran back toward the boat and the bulging net of flopping fish. The other apostles quickly jumped to his assistance and together they hauled the fish on shore. There were an astonishing 153 of them, yet the net had not a single strand torn.[9]

When they were all on shore, wearing the rough workmen's cloaks that were kept on board, Jesus gestured toward a charcoal fire that was already burning nearby. A cooked fish lay simmering on the grill and near it was a loaf of fresh bread. **"Come and eat your meal,"**[10] he said to them.

The apostles stared at the Lord. It was clearly he, they knew it was he, but there was something different about him, too. There was a kind of majesty about his appearance, a way he had of looking at you as if he were speaking directly to your soul. Around him everything seemed brighter, as if Jesus were his own light source. Yet there he was in a real human body. His hands and feet still bore the holes from the nail wounds. Perhaps it was the clothes he wore. They seemed like the usual tunic, sash girdle and robe, but their colors were brighter, nearly glowing it seemed. Plus, there was the psychological factor of dealing with someone now fully revealed to be divine but standing, nonetheless, before them as flesh and

---

[7]Jn 21:7

[8]Jn 21:10

[9]"Ancient Greek zoologists held that there were precisely this number of species of fish in existence, so the catch can be seen as representing the entirety of humankind and the universality of the gospel." Porter, *Jesus Christ: the Jesus of History, the Christ of Faith*, 43.

[10]Jn 21:12

blood. The apostles weren't sure whether they should fall to their knees and bow to Jesus or behave as they used to around him.

But Jesus had no uncertainties. "Come, come! Put a couple of your fish on the fire here. I know you are hungry."

When the apostles had gathered around the fire, Jesus removed the fish and put it on a plate. Then he took the warm bread, offered a blessing of thanks for it to his Father, and gave it to the seven men. Next, he took the fish and cut it into small pieces and passed that around to them. When they had eaten these, he said to them: "I have called each of you, and your brethren, to be fishers of men. As you have by yourselves caught nothing throughout the night in a sea filled with fish, so, too, you cannot bring men into the safe harbor of my Father's kingdom unless you do so in my Name. Through me, however, your harvest will overflow your greatest expectations. You will melt the hardest hearts and capture the cleverest minds, for my grace beckons to an innate hunger in every human soul. The fish you have netted this morning at my direction represent all the elect who shall respond to my invitation until I return in glory. They will come from every nation and speak every tongue, be of every race, tribe, kingdom and age. Their numbers will be countless and their joy complete and everlasting. Not only shall you bring these souls to my Father through me, but through me you shall also feed them. Recall what I did the night before I suffered. That bread was the bread which came down from heaven. Then, as now, and until the end of time, I am the bread of life, the nourishment of body and soul for those who love me and love my Father."

Indeed, the apostles were hungry and they ate accordingly. Never had food tasted more delicious. More fish were added to the grill as needed until all were filled. The bread loaf fed them all with multiple pieces and yet, at the end of the meal, appeared to have been untouched.

When everyone had finished eating, Jesus turned to Peter and said: **"Simon, son of John, do you love me more than these?"**[11] As he said this, Jesus gestured toward the fish and Peter's boat, indicating the life that Peter was about to leave behind forever.

"Yes, Lord," replied Peter, **"you know that I love you."**

Jesus looked lovingly and entreatingly at Peter as he said: **"Feed my lambs."**

Peter nodded but Jesus did not remove his eyes from this man he had already named the "rock" upon which he would build his Church.[12]

A second time, Jesus spoke: **"Simon, son of John, do you love me?"**[13]

---

[11]This quote and the next two are from Jn 21:15.

[12]See Mt 16:18.

[13]This quote and the next two are from Jn 21:16.

Peter squirmed a bit but responded immediately and just a little defensively: "**Yes, Lord, you know that I love you.**"

Jesus continued to stare intently at Peter as he commanded: "**Tend my sheep.**"

Peter nodded again, more vigorously this time. Still Jesus' eyes bored into him. "**Simon, son of John, do you love me?**"[14]

At that moment a little puff of wind swirled around the embers of the charcoal fire and blew wisps of smoke toward Peter. The pungent smell brought back an instant memory of the night, only three weeks earlier, when he had stood warming his hands over a similar charcoal fire in the courtyard of Caiaphas, the high priest. Peter flushed with shame at the recollection of his denials of knowing Jesus. But he had not meant to renounce Jesus; he had only been resisting an accusation that was likely to get him ejected from the courtyard. It was a painful lesson, nonetheless. He had not trusted the truth, and he had not stood up for his Lord before the world, as he knew he should have. As he responded to Jesus' question, Peter wondered if the three questions were somehow intended to cancel out his three denials. Further, the lesson of the fish had not been lost on Peter. Never again would he consider returning to the life he had led before being called by Jesus. He knew that their failure to catch any fish on their own had been the Lord's way of telling them that their past was closed forever.

"**Lord, you know everything. You know well that I love you.**" Gone was the braggadocio which filled Peter when he swore at the Last Supper that he would give his very life for Jesus. Jesus had known him better than he knew himself. Peter's flaw was not cowardice; it was a failure to listen and to comprehend. Painful as it was, he had learned his lesson well. But through it all his devotion and love for his Lord burned fiercely within him. Jesus knew this and Peter knew that he knew it. The purpose of the three-fold question was not to ascertain Peter's feelings, but to cleanse his conscience and to emphasize both his primacy and his responsibility in carrying out Christ's mission. And, it was a reminder to Peter that service to the Lord was a service of love.

Jesus was satisfied but his demeanor remained serious and his tone was urgent as he told Peter, "**Feed my sheep.**" Whether the metaphor was fisherman or shepherd, Peter was reminded of his selection by God through His Son to become the head of His fledgling Church. He was strong of heart and conviction, courageous and bold, a natural leader—all qualities that would be vitally needed to convey Christ's spiritual sustenance to those who would accept Him in the new faith. His leadership would be needed to form and shape the organization that would sustain the community of Christian believers. After him, other men would fill his shoes and, successively, be the final human link between Church and Christ, the one charged with ultimate responsibility for making the decisions that would feed and care for the souls in the vast spiritual sheepfold of the Lord. Only

---

[14]This quote and the next two are from Jn 21:17.

in this way could Christ ensure the continuity that would keep his Church whole and faithful down through the centuries and millennia until he comes to fulfill it with his own direct rule.

Jesus looked away now, across the placid waters toward the hunkering bluffs of the Golan Heights separating Palestine from Syria. Peter felt relieved. He looked around and saw the other apostles watching him curiously. He felt the responsibility of the Lord's charge but also some pride as well.

Perhaps Jesus picked up on this in those channels of communication that are hidden from us in this world, for he turned around and addressed Peter again, very seriously: **"I tell you solemnly: as a young man you fastened your belt and went about as you pleased; but when you are older you will stretch out your hands, and another will tie you fast and carry you off against your will."**[15] Jesus looked sadly at Peter. He was warning him in very explicit terms that his future held suffering and a death much like Jesus' own.

Through these words to Peter, and like the words old Simeon spoke to Mary and Joseph in the Temple so many years before, God reminds us that those who best do His will are not immune to suffering and violence. Often they are the most egregious victims. All of the apostles, except John, died martyrs' deaths. According to tradition, even John was lowered into a vat of boiling oil but was miraculously spared from harm; thereafter, he was exiled to the island of Patmos, where he wrote or directed the writing of the Book of Revelation.

In a world full of violence, cruelty, injustice and selfishness, those who love God and His Son, Jesus Christ, must lead the way through these formidable obstacles and death itself to the eternal bliss of heaven which God promises to all who love Him. After Pentecost, the apostles would fully understand this. Then they would rejoice at their opportunities to suffer for the Name.[16] But on this bright Spring day filled with excitement, hope and contentment, suffering still seemed like defeat. So Jesus said it as directly as he could to Peter: **"Follow me."**[17]

Jesus turned around then and started toward the boat. Peter was still smarting from what had seemed too much like a lecture from the Lord, and was not comfortable at all with the dire prediction Jesus had just given him. As John walked by, hurrying to stay next to the Lord whom he loved so dearly, Peter asked Jesus: **"But Lord, what about him?"**[18]

---

[15] Jn 21:18

[16] See Acts 5:40-41.

[17] Jn 21:19

[18] Jn 21:21

Jesus stopped immediately and faced Peter. **"Suppose I want him to stay until I come, how does that concern you? Your business is to follow me."**[19] Peter got the message and shut up.[20]

As he approached the shoreline, Jesus stopped and faced the men who had been trailing behind him. "Gather my followers on Mount Tabor. I will see you there." Raising his hand in blessing, Jesus vanished.

After a few moments of the usual stunned surprise, the apostles rushed onto their boat, anxious to get back to Capernaum and report to the other apostles and disciples of Jesus. Then James remembered all the fish that they had left on shore so he and John remained with the catch while Peter and the others returned to Capernaum and sent the fish traders up the road to where James and John waited.

It took about three days to get the word to the villages in Galilee where the followers of Jesus could still be found and another three days to gather them on top of the 1,000-foot Mount Tabor. The "mountain," which is more accurately described as a high hill, rises out of the Plain of Megiddo like a giant inverted half watermelon. But from the summit the views are magnificent. The vistas stretch in all directions and the sensation of seeing the world as God sees it is powerful, indeed. Here was Jesus transfigured before Peter, James and John only weeks before his crucifixion. Summoned now by the risen Lord, more than 1,500 men,[21] women and children made their way laboriously up the narrow road that curved sharply back and forth as it ascended to the top. The crest is flat and spacious and easily accommodated the assembled people.

It was late morning when Peter called them together and led them in prayer. He had his eyes closed and his arms lifted to heaven when he heard a collective gasp from the crowd. Opening his eyes and looking to his right, he saw the Lord himself standing beside him. Jesus smiled as the front ranks of the crowd moved cautiously to approach him.

Many people, especially those who had been dubious about coming at all because they were doubtful of the resurrection reports, fell to their knees and exclaimed, "Praised be the God of our fathers and His Anointed, the Lord Jesus Christ!" A few of the bolder souls reached to touch his garments or his arms and hands to satisfy themselves that he was present in the flesh and not a ghost.

---

[19] Jn 21:22

[20] Some of the other apostles, however, were confused by Jesus' rhetorical question and thought he had said that John would live until Jesus came in glory at the Second Coming. This notion was not so hard to accept during the first 50 years or so when most of the first Christians believed that Jesus intended to come back in their lifetimes.

[21] Saint Paul reports in 1 Cor 15:6 that Jesus appeared to "five hundred brothers at once," although he does not say where this took place. Since only men were counted in these ancient "crowd reports," I have tripled the number to include the women and children who would undoubtedly have been there.

Jesus welcomed them all, moving through the crowd, greeting many by name, even picking up a few of the children and carrying them with him for awhile but always making sure they got back to their parents when he put them down. When everyone had a chance to see that Jesus was truly risen and present to them here and now on this mountain, he returned to the front of the crowd and gestured for quiet. It took a few minutes for the last hosanna and hallelujah to die away. Then Jesus spoke:

> **"Full authority has been given to me both in heaven and on earth; go, therefore, and make disciples of all the nations. Baptize them in the name 'of the Father, and of the Son, and of the Holy Spirit.' Teach them to carry out everything I have commanded you. And know that I am with you always, until the end of the world!"[22]**

As he finished speaking, he rose from the ground, extended his hand and blessed the assembled people. Even the birds hushed as the words of the Lord's blessing fell gently like a misty rain upon the upturned faces. He smiled and vanished from their sight.

The following day, Jesus appeared privately to his cousin, the apostle James the Less, and told him to tell Peter to lead the apostles and those disciples who wished to go, back to Jerusalem. Of course, his mother Mary and her friends would need to go as well. Three days later, the traveling party of about 50 apostles and disciples departed Capernaum, passed through the Gentile city of Tiberias on the western shore of the Sea of Galilee, and made their way back to Jerusalem, arriving on the 35th day after Jesus' resurrection. Along the way, there was much excited speculation about whether Jesus was now going to establish his kingdom in Israel and use his divine power to drive out all uninvited foreigners, especially the Romans.

When they reached Bethany, Mary and the other women elected to remain there in the home of Lazarus and his sisters, Mary and Martha. The apostles and most of the disciples went on to Jerusalem to the Upper Room, or Cenacle, in the home of Mary and Tychus, parents of Mark.

After they were settled and had explained to their eager hosts all that had happened in Galilee, they settled into a routine of day-long prayer and discussion. Some of the men were ready to go to the Temple grounds and spread the word about Jesus' resurrection. Others advocated caution. They were worried about a hostile reaction from the chief priests and elders. But they had no answer to the question of *when* the apostles and disciples should go out and carry the message of Jesus throughout Palestine. Thomas suggested that their uncertainty was itself a sign that God did not intend for them to go forth just yet. The discussion grew quite heated from time to time. Finally, Peter, who found the arguments of both sides convincing, appealed to the mother of Jesus for her advice. She and several

---

[22]Mt 28:18-20

of the other women had been coming into the city each morning for the past three days to join the apostles in the Upper Room.

"Thomas is right, Peter. If my son wished for you to begin your mission to Israel now, he would certainly have told you so clearly. When his followers are so divided, it is a sign that the time is not yet right. There will be no such differences when it is our Lord's will that you proceed."

"But Jesus told us in Galilee to go and make disciples of all the nations," protested James, John's brother. "How long are we to keep ourselves locked up in this room?"

Andrew spoke up, "Jesus told us through James, his brother, that we should return to Jerusalem. If he had wanted us to go out from Galilee, he would have told us then. Mary is right. No one knows the heart of her son better than she. Obviously, the Lord Jesus wants us to have this time of prayer and reflection. He will tell us when the time is ripe."

"Peter," said Mary, "tomorrow is the fortieth day since Jesus rose. Let us gather together all those who love him on the Mount of Olives. He will surely hear your prayers and give you the guidance that you need."

The next morning, the apostles and disciples from Jerusalem made their way to the top of the Mount of Olives. The women, Lazarus and a number of other disciples came to the same place from the opposite side of the Mount. The sun sparkled at their backs and gleamed off the golden crown of the Temple standing proudly on the Temple Mount about 400 yards across the Kidron Valley below them. It was a Thursday and crowds of people streamed back and forth across the Court of the Gentiles, going in and out of the Court of the Women in the Temple precincts, mostly through the Beautiful Gate which faced the Mount of Olives. There was the usual commotion and noise of people buying and selling animals and exchanging money for most of the length of Solomon's Portico, the high colonnaded porch that ran the entire length of the eastern side of the Mount. Israel's (and the world's) Messiah had come and gone and life went on pretty much as it always had. But the dark shadow of history lay across the Jerusalem Temple. It was now no more than a piece of architecture, splendid to look at and exciting to visit, a magnificent monument to Jewish history and culture. Its Soul was gone, however; gone to take up residence where It would be more welcome: in human hearts where grace could create edifices of spiritual beauty vastly beyond the glory of marble, wood, gold and precious jewels. These new temples of the Lord God were eternal. The old one would lie in ashes in just over 40 years, a period remarkably symmetrical to the number of days since Israel's leaders crucified their Messiah and slammed the door on the *nation's* spiritual future.[23]

As the group of about 100 disciples prayed on the Mount of Olives, Jesus appeared and stood in their midst. A few of the disciples, who had not gone to Galilee, saw him for the first time since his resurrection. These fell to their knees

---

[23]This is not a judgment of individual Jews, of course, who are no less holy and loved by God than are Christians.

in awe. As always, Jesus made it a point to touch them personally, not always with his hand but just as powerfully with a look and a smile. Everyone felt the urge to kneel in the Lord's presence, but the love and affection he exuded kept them on their feet, excited and rejoicing to be in his physical presence once again.

"To each of you I bring my Father's blessing. Today I am returning to my Father and your Father. But I shall never abandon you and whenever you shall call upon me I will hear and answer you.

> **"Go into the whole world and proclaim the good news to all creation. The man who believes in it and accepts baptism will be saved; the man who refuses to believe in it will be condemned. Signs like these will accompany those who have professed their faith: they will use my name to expel demons, they will speak entirely new languages, they will be able to handle serpents, they will be able to drink deadly poison without harm, and the sick upon whom they lay their hands will recover."[24]**

"Lord," asked Peter, "when shall we go forth to the children of Israel and to the world? Shall it be today?"

Jesus replied:

> **"Wait, rather, for the fulfillment of my Father's promise, of which you have heard me speak. John baptized with water, but within a few days you will be baptized with the Holy Spirit.[25] Remain here in the city until you are clothed with power from on high."[26]**

Philip then asked the question that had been on the minds of many of them for weeks: **"Lord, are you going to restore the rule to Israel now?"[27]**

The answer they all wanted was "Yes." After all that Jesus had said and done, they still longed for the earthly kingdom of perfect peace and justice which the Hebrew Scriptures had been promising for generations. They understood now that the prophets had also warned of the Messiah's necessary suffering and death. They accepted Jesus' explanation that that terrible price had been required to reconcile sinful mankind with their Father in heaven. But they still did not really get it. They thought that God's kingdom meant a restoration on earth of something

---

[24]Mk 16:15-18. These extraordinary gifts of grace are granted by the Holy Spirit when needed. The small band of apostles and disciples needed them all to grow the tiny mustard seed of Christ's Church. Such gifts are rarely needed now to support evangelization efforts. It would be a rash person, indeed, who assumed he or she was blessed with these simply because they had professed faith in Jesus Christ. As Jesus said to Satan when tempted in the desert: "You shall not put the Lord your God to the test." (Lk 4:12).

[25]Acts 1:4

[26]Lk 24:49

[27]Acts 1:6

like the Garden of Eden, with Israel in charge and the Gentiles on the outside looking in.

Jesus knew what they wanted and he also knew that what he was giving them, and us, was an inconceivably greater prize. But for the time being, he answered them as God often answers our own requests to know His plans:

> **"The exact time is not yours to know. The Father has reserved that to himself. You will receive power when the Holy Spirit comes down on you; then you are to be witnesses in Jerusalem, throughout Judea and Samaria, yes, even to the ends of the earth."**[28]

This was the Lord's last joint instruction to his fledgling Church. As he finished speaking, he raised his hand in a final blessing and began to rise into the clear, blue sky. As he rose, a cloud of extraordinary brightness enveloped him and took him higher and higher until it passed from sight. For several minutes everyone remained in place, peering into the sky, hoping for one last glimpse of the risen Lord. Because of their fixation, they did not notice the two strangers dressed in brilliant, glowing white robes who quietly joined them.

"Men of Galilee," they said, **"why do you stand here looking up at the skies? This Jesus who has been taken from you will return, just as you saw him go up into the heavens."**[29] The two angels, for that is who they were, did not wait for a response but vanished immediately. They achieved their purpose. The apostles, disciples and the holy women with them understood that Jesus' mission on earth was ended and that the torch had been passed to them now. After falling to their knees in prayer to acknowledge Jesus as Lord, they returned to Jerusalem singing and shouting the praises of God, rejoicing with (and startling) all whom they met. They went back to the Upper Room and began what would be nine days of prayer, reflection and waiting. On the 10th day, a truly miraculous transformation would occur. Jesus had planted the seed. It would bloom spectacularly in the fertile soil of the Holy Spirit.

---

[28] Acts 1:7-8

[29] Acts 1:11

THE APOSTLES' CREED

I believe in God, the Father almighty,
creator of heaven and earth.
I believe in Jesus Christ, his only Son, our Lord.
He was conceived by the power
of the Holy Spirit
and born of the Virgin Mary.
He suffered under Pontius Pilate,
was crucified, died, and was buried.
He descended into hell.
On the third day he rose again.
He ascended into heaven
and is seated at the right hand
of the Father.
He will come again to judge
the living and the dead.
I believe in the Holy Spirit,
the holy catholic Church,
the communion of saints,
the forgiveness of sins,
the resurrection of the body,
and the life everlasting.[30]

Amen

---

[30]See *Catechism of the Catholic Church,* following ¶184, pp. 49-50.

QUESTIONS FOR REFLECTION

(1) Why do you think Jesus sent the apostles back to Galilee after his resurrection?

(2) How do you imagine the apostles spent their time in Galilee between appearances by Jesus?

(3) How do you imagine the apostles viewed the Lord after his resurrection—with reverential awe or do you think once the initial shock wore off they relapsed into their old patterns of fellowship? How do you think Jesus would have wanted them to react to him? How does he want you to respond to him?

(4) Why do you think John's Gospel reports the exact number of fish ("153"—Jn 21:11) that the apostles caught when Jesus told them where to cast their nets after a night of fruitless effort? Can you think of anywhere else in the New or Old Testament where a number is used symbolically?

(5) St. Paul tells us that Jesus appeared to as many as 500 "brothers" at one time (1 Cor 15:6). How do you visualize this encounter—warm, personal, exciting, joyous? Or perhaps majestic, triumphant, solemn, awesome? How will you react to Jesus when you see him? How will he react to you?

(6) Just before he rose into heaven, Jesus told those on the Mount of Olives to be his witnesses even to the ends of the earth. How do you see this applying to you? How can we be effective witnesses for Jesus? How can we be evangelists in our daily lives?

(7) In describing the ascension of Jesus at the conclusion of his Gospel, Luke says the apostles were "filled with joy." (Lk 24:52). Why would the apostles have been filled with joy when Jesus left them?

(8) Imagine yourself on the Mount of Olives a few moments after Jesus has disappeared from view as he ascended into heaven. How would you feel? There are no Christian churches in which to worship, no hierarchy, very little awareness in most of the world that Jesus had even existed. Most of the apostles and disciples were "blue collar" workers. The leaders of their faith, the faith that God had given to Abraham and Moses, were actively opposed to the message and person of Jesus. Would it have seemed an impossible task to consider evangelizing the world without Jesus physically present to help them? Yet they did it. What message does this give us about "impossible tasks" to be done in Jesus' name? With His help can we confidently adopt the slogan: "The difficult we do immediately. The impossible takes a little longer"? Are there any examples from your own life when you overcame what seemed like impossible odds after asking God for help?

(9) Luke tells us that Jesus ascended in a cloud,[31] which may indicate they lost sight of him well before the cloud disappeared. Have you had times when Jesus seemed hidden from you as you searched anxiously to find Him? Saint John of the Cross refers to times like these as the "dark night of the soul." Yet these difficult times are the means by which God tries and proves us and prepares us to grow in holiness. In a very short time after Jesus ascended, the Holy Spirit would transform the apostles from men of society into men of God. Have you had times when your spiritual life seemed particularly arid but suddenly blossomed into a much closer relationship with Jesus?

(10) Why do you think Jesus physically ascended at all? He had previously just appeared and disappeared. Why not do that again? What point do you think he was making for the apostles and us? Do you think he was telling us in some way that heaven is "up there" and not to be found on earth? Can we look at Jesus ascending as a reminder that we, too, are called to rise above earthly desires, concerns and fears and remember that our life's destination is "up there?" Or do you think that Jesus was simply using this means to emphasize to the apostles that this departure was final, that henceforth his mission on earth would be accomplished through his followers?

---

[31]"No sooner had he said this than he was lifted up before their eyes in a cloud which took him from their sight." Acts 1:9

Tongues as of fire appeared, which parted and came to rest on each of them. All were filled with the Holy Spirit. Acts 2:3-4

THIRD GLORIOUS MYSTERY

The Descent of the Holy Spirit

Jerusalem thronged with hordes of happy pilgrims and visitors. They were there mostly to celebrate one of the most joyous festivals of the year: the Feast of Shavuot. It was also called the Feast of Weeks because it fell on the day following completion of seven weeks, or fifty days, after the start of Passover. The Greek word for fiftieth is *pentecost*, so the holiday was known by that name, too, even before it became a Christian holy day. The holiday celebrated the grain harvest and each adult Jewish male who came to Jerusalem was required to bring to the Temple two loaves of leavened bread made from the newly harvested crop. Although the holiday was naturally celebratory, it was also brief: only a single day. Yahweh himself had commanded the Israelites to be merry for this particular festival.[1] The time interval of fifty days also coincided approximately with the journey of the Israelites from Egypt to Mount Sinai where Yahweh gave the Ten Commandments and other laws to Moses. This, too, was commemorated at this feast.

In the Upper Room, or Cenacle, the apostles Peter, Andrew, James and John, Philip, Bartholomew, Matthew, Thomas, James the Less, Jude Thaddaeus, Simon the Zealot, and their newest member, Matthias, were all gathered in prayer. Matthias had been selected by lot only a few days earlier to replace Judas Iscariot. With them were the Blessed Virgin Mary, Mary of Clopas, Salome, Mary Magdalene, Joanna, Susanna, Seraphia, Mary of Tychus and a few other women followers of Jesus plus numerous male disciples, including Tychus, the owner of the house, and Mark, his son. All in all, the number of those present was about 120. It was 8 A.M. on the tenth day following Jesus' bodily ascension into heaven. Here was Christ's entire Church, gathered together in a single place, awaiting its birth. Their plan for the day was the same as it had been every day

---

[1] Dt 16:11

since Jesus told them to wait in Jerusalem for the Spirit whom he would send. They would pray, sing hymns, and read the Hebrew Bible, especially the Psalms, Isaiah and the other prophetic passages which described the time of the Messiah. They visited the Temple every day, as well, to pray there as other faithful Jews did. The nine days they spent in prayer and anticipation from the day of the Lord's ascension to this moment have been described as Christianity's first novena.[2]

As they gathered that morning, Simon the Zealot approached Peter with a worried expression: "Peter, do you think that Jesus will return to lead us as he did before?"

"No, Simon," said Peter. "I think the Lord will not return in that way until the great day when he comes to establish the New City of Jerusalem as the Holy City of God. Until then, we must carry his message for him."

"But who will listen to me, a man not skilled with words or explanation?" fretted Simon. "For that matter, who will listen to any of us? How can such an unlearned and insignificant group convince our people that Jesus was the Messiah when they refused to believe him in spite of all the miracles he worked? I feel very inadequate to this task which the Lord has laid upon us."

"I understand, Simon," responded Peter with a shake of his head. "I wonder myself how we can accomplish such a mission. But I am sure the Lord has a plan that will answer all our concerns. We must wait for him to reveal it as he told us he would do through the Spirit."

Outside in the city of Jerusalem, there was excitement in the air this morning. Some of it was the normal festivity that marked the Feast of Weeks. But there was something more, too, a kind of crinkling in the atmosphere like the static electricity that sometimes rolls in with thunderstorms. It was odd because the sky was clear, the temperature a beautiful 74 degrees, a gentle breeze stirring every so often. Flora and fauna alike proclaimed the joyousness of life. Nature's stage was set for the spiritual cataclysm about to take place.

The sound was faint and distant at first. Down near the bottom range of human hearing, it was more felt than heard. Slowly, but steadily, the intensity increased, rising to an audible drone coming from the east. In a few minutes, passersby on the street had stopped and were looking up at the sky, seeking the source for what seemed like the rumble of distant thunder. The sun continued to smile cheerfully from its cloudless blue home. All at once, the distant rumbling exploded overhead. It swooped down from nowhere and everywhere, roaring like an angry and ferocious wind, but turning not a leaf, ruffling not a feather. Jerusalem paused. Then, hearing the great roar centered in the Upper City, near the monument marking the tomb of David, thousands of people rushed in that direction. A huge crowd converged on the house of Tychus.

Inside the Upper Room, they heard the rushing, roaring "wind" and clutched one another for support as the house itself quaked under the onslaught.

---

[2]See, e.g., John S. Johnson., *The Rosary in Action* (Rockford, IL: TAN Books, 1954), 253.

They did not realize then, not that it would have mattered, that theirs was the only property in Jerusalem that was physically reacting to the strange commotion.

As suddenly as it began, the shaking stopped. As the followers of Jesus began to relax, a fire burst forth in their midst, leaping with flames that dazzled but did not burn, suspended above them as if all the energy of the universe had concentrated itself into this small space. One hundred and twenty people,[3] for the first time, saw and felt the universe as it really is—God at the center as Creator and Sustainer, the interconnectedness of all life, Love as the glue bonding all living things together. Each person present was filled with the Holy Spirit according to his or her capacity and future destiny within the Kingdom. Inside those 120 souls, the Holy Spirit opened their minds and hearts to the mystery of God's wisdom and reality.

As the Holy Spirit imparted His gifts to each person present, a small flame split off from the radiant central fire and reappeared above that person's head, blazing in red, yellow, and white brilliance. Instantly, all that Jesus had taught them MADE SENSE! They saw clearly for the first time in their lives. God is the reality! This world is a way station, a time of testing and trial, a place of confusion and obscurity, of fleeting pleasures and distractions. Like sparks dancing and twirling above a massive bonfire, the small flames flaring above their heads signaled the rapture of souls consumed in the fire of the Paraclete, the Spirit of God, the Third Person of the divine Trinity, the living Love shared by the Father and the Son. They knew as they were known by God. They loved as they were loved by God. They were turned right side up and saw that the existence for which we are made, the kingdom to which we are all invited, is on the *other side* of death's door.

The blessed souls upon and within whom those flames burned were like Plato's prisoner[4] who has been led outside the dark cave he has inhabited all his life and shown the magnificence of God's natural creation. He shouts back to his fellow prisoners (all humanity): "Reality is here, outside! It is magnificent, indescribable, beautiful beyond comparison!" But they, still chained with their faces toward shadows dancing on dim walls, cannot comprehend the reality described. Who could explain colors to people who had seen only black, white, and shades of gray all their lives? Who can convincingly describe the kingdom of God to those who cannot see past the pleasures and beauty of the natural world? On this first Pentecost morning, the birthday of the holy catholic Church, 120 people looked outside the entrance to the cave and saw the gift that Jesus had purchased for us. In every sense of the word except physically, they were re-created and reborn. Not one of them would ever again view this world as anything

---

[3]Luke says "there must have been a hundred and twenty gathered together" in the Upper Room when Matthias was chosen to replace Judas Iscariot. It is unclear whether the "120" figure refers only to the men present, or to everyone. Acts 1:15.

[4]Plato, *The Republic*, Jowett trans. (New York: Vintage Books, 1991) Book VII, 253 *et. seq.*

more than a training ground to prepare us to take our places with God in His world in a communion of mutual, total and eternal love. No longer did they wonder how or when they were to begin spreading the Gospel message. Now they burned with an overwhelming desire to tell that story to everyone in the world.

The Paraclete began then to infuse each of them with the gifts they would need to deliver the message that they finally understood so vividly and completely. The apostles leaped to their feet and began to proclaim the eternal truths as prompted by the Spirit. Each spoke in a foreign tongue, expressing the universality of God's invitation.[5] All understood what each said, representing the oneness of citizenship in the kingdom of God. From simple, uneducated, rural villagers, the apostles were changed far more completely than the transformation of caterpillar to butterfly, of dry wood to crackling flame, or even ignorance to genius.

They threw open the door to the Upper Room and stormed out onto a balcony which overlooked the street. Below them, the enormous crowd was curious—pointing, discussing, wondering, called together by the "tornado" centered on this house. The apostles spoke in turn, faces lit with excitement and conviction, voices thundering the proclamations of the Holy Spirit, understood by their listeners in all the languages of the world. Luke describes the reaction of those astonished people:

> **"'Are not all of these men who are speaking Galileans? How is it that each of us hears them in his native tongue? We are Parthians, Medes, and Elamites. We live in Mesopotamia, Judea and Cappadocia, Pontus, the province of Asia, Phrygia and Pamphylia, Egypt, and the regions of Libya around Cyrene. There are even visitors from Rome—all Jews, or those who have come over to Judaism; Cretans and Arabs too. Yet each of us hears them speaking in his own tongue about the marvels God has accomplished.' They were dumb-founded, and could make nothing at all of what had happened."[6]**

A few in the crowd could not understand the apostles. They heard only gibberish. They laughed and jeered at the wonderment of the others, calling out: **"They have had too much new wine."[7]**

Peter heard the raucous catcalls of the skeptics and rose to challenge them—but not by attacking them. Peter with the sword was dead. The new Peter was strictly a fisherman and shepherd. The Holy Spirit gave him the bait to use.

---

[5]Speaking in tongues apparently became quite popular as Christianity spread. Saint Paul felt constrained in 1 Cor 14:6-28 to point out that if the speaker could not be understood, then speaking in tongues was pointless and valueless.

[6]Acts 2:7-12

[7]Acts 2:13

"You who are Jews, indeed all of you staying in Jerusalem! Listen to what I have to say. You must realize that these men are not drunk, as you seem to think. It is only nine in the morning![8] No, it is what Joel the prophet spoke of:

'It shall come to pass in the last days,
says God,
that I will pour out a portion of my spirit on
all mankind:
Your sons and daughters
shall prophesy,
your young men shall see
visions
and your old men shall
dream dreams.[9]
Yes, even on my servants and handmaids
I will pour out a portion of
my spirit in those days,
and they shall prophesy.[10]
I will work wonders
in the heavens above[11]
and signs on the earth below:
blood, fire, and a cloud of smoke.
The sun shall be turned to darkness
and the moon to blood
before the coming of that great and
glorious day of the Lord.
Then shall everyone be saved

---

[8]Acts 2:14-15. Besides stating the obvious that even alcoholics are usually not drunk as early as nine in the morning, Peter may also have been referring to a feastday fast requirement whereby the celebrating could not begin until noon. See Johnson, *The Rosary in Action*, 260.

[9]Acts 2:16-17. Remember the angel's method of speaking to Joseph, the husband of Mary, was through dreams. In these stories we have seen that such dreams are not the ordinary kind of shadowy, surreal, hard to remember imagery, but instead are vivid, direct and unforgettable.

[10]Acts 2:18. Peter is using the prophet Joel here to remind his audience that the power of God may be manifested even through the lowlier members of society. From our vantage point of 2,000 years later, we have seen that Marian apparitions and other private revelation have *usually* been to children and other "unimportant" members of society.

[11]Acts 2:19. From here on, Joel's prophecy seems on its face to be more of a reference to the Last Days, the time before Jesus' Second Coming.

who calls on
the name of the Lord.'"[12]

Peter continued: "**Men of Israel, listen to me! Jesus the Nazorean was a man whom God sent to you with miracles, wonders, and signs as his credentials. These God worked through him in your midst, as you well know.**"[13]

A murmur of assent ran through the crowd which had packed into the street and spilled over into the neighboring properties below the balcony where the apostles stood. Many of the people there had personally witnessed Christ's actions, especially at the time of Passover nearly two months ago. His execution had been a shocking repudiation because he had seemed to possess the very power of Yahweh Himself.

"**He was delivered up by the set purpose and plan of God: you even made use of the pagans to crucify and kill him,**"[14] said Peter.

Again, a ripple of comment stirred the crowd. Many protested they had not known of Christ's being delivered up to the Romans by the Jewish authorities. But others pointed out that no one protested during his way of sorrows from the Fortress Antonia to Golgotha, nor during Jesus' time on the cross. Some even had taunted him as he hung dying. A few argued that Peter said it was all according to God's plan, so perhaps there was no guilt on their part. But then others responded that that only meant that God knew the terrible things that would happen because of the hardness of human hearts. It did not excuse their sin.

Peter went on: "**God freed him from death's bitter pangs, however, and raised him up again, for it was impossible that death should keep its hold on him.**"[15]

There was silence and rapt attention among the thousands of faces that listened intently to Peter's words. There had been rumors of the resurrection of Jesus of Nazareth, but the Temple priests had put out the word that his body had been stolen from its grave, probably by his followers, and hidden somewhere. People were eager to learn the truth and to visit the grave of this great prophet if they could find where he had been laid. Peter was the leader of the apostles. He would certainly know where Jesus was. His confirmation of the rumor of resurrection was startling to them. Peter turned to Scripture and one of Israel's most revered figures, David, to buttress his claim:

"**David says of him:**

    '**I have set the Lord ever before me,**
      with him at my right hand I

---

[12] Acts 2:19-21; see Jl 3:1-5.

[13] Acts 2:22

[14] Acts 2:23

[15] Acts 2:24

shall not be disturbed.
My heart has been glad and my
tongue has rejoiced,
my body will live on in hope,
for you will not abandon my soul
to the nether world,
nor will you suffer your faithful one
to undergo corruption.
You have shown me the paths of life;
you will fill me with joy in
your presence.'[16]

"Brothers, I can speak confidently to you about our father David. He died and was buried, and his grave is in our midst to this day. He was a prophet and knew that God had sworn to him that one of his descendants would sit upon his throne. He said that he was not abandoned to the nether world, nor did his body undergo corruption, thus proclaiming beforehand the resurrection of the Messiah. This is the Jesus God has raised up, and we are his witnesses."[17]

Peter's explanation gave new insight into these words of David. All knew that David's body had not been spared corruption. He had died and been buried like any other mortal. So his words obviously referred to someone else, someone whom God would call His "faithful one." That this would be Jesus made sense in light of the signs, wonders and miracles he had performed. If David predicted a resurrection, the apostles' claim that Jesus was risen from the dead completed a critical loop in the Messianic prophecies from King David, the forebear, to Jesus Christ, his descendant. Peter continued to explain:

"Exalted at God's right hand, he first received the promised Holy Spirit from the Father, then poured this Spirit out on us. This is what you now see and hear."[18]

Someone in the crowd yelled out: "Brother, how are we to know that Jesus of Nazareth now sits at the right hand of God and has sent the Spirit down today to work the signs we have seen this morning?"

Peter replied: "David did not go up to heaven, yet David says,
'The Lord said to my Lord,
Sit at my right hand
until I make your enemies
your footstool.'

---

[16] Acts 2:25-28; see Ps 16:8-11.

[17] Acts 2:29-32

[18] Acts 2:33

"**Therefore let the whole house of Israel know beyond any doubt that God has made both Lord and Messiah this Jesus whom you crucified.**"[19]

Peter's quote reminded his listeners that David had acknowledged a Lord in heaven who was seated at the right hand of God. David himself was not in heaven when he wrote the psalm and, according to Pharisaic belief, would not go there until the Last Judgment and the resurrection of the dead by God. Therefore, someone else superior to him (and to anyone not divine) was being referred to. Jesus himself had used this quote from David a few days before he died to refute the Pharisees' assertion that the Messiah would be David's son.[20] Thus, Jesus' miracles, the claim of resurrection, and David's words 1,000 years earlier all tied together to make a powerful case for accepting Jesus as the Messiah.

Most people in the crowd were horrified by the realization that Jesus of Nazareth was, indeed, the Christ, the Messiah promised for centuries by God for the salvation of Israel, and what they had done, or permitted to be done, to him. Surely, God's wrath would descend upon them now. In fear and trembling, they cried out to Peter and the other apostles: "**What are we to do, brothers?**"[21]

Peter answered: "**You must reform and be baptized, each one of you, in the name of Jesus Christ, that your sins may be forgiven; then you will receive the gift of the Holy Spirit.**"[22]

"But how can this be? We have the blood of the Messiah on our hands!"

Peter reassured them: "God's mercy is unlimited. The suffering of His Son was foretold. He let himself be sacrificed as the Lamb of God so that all our sins might be forgiven. **It was to you and your children that the promise was made, and to all those still far off whom the Lord our God calls.**"[23]

Peter continued: "The kingdom of God is not of this world. He invites all men to share his kingdom of everlasting peace and joy, which is with Jesus Christ in the kingdom of heaven. There love reigns, not the power and domination that men seek in their earthly kingdoms. The Messiah came not to restore Israel's power on earth, but to make of her God's instrument of salvation for the Jews and for all peoples of the earth. For this, it was necessary that Jesus the Christ take upon himself the sins of mankind so that in him whom the Father loves, we might find our own forgiveness. It was for you that Jesus gave his life! Wash yourselves

---

[19] Acts 2:34-36; the quote from David is from Ps 110:1.

[20] See Mt 22:41-45.

[21] Acts 2:37

[22] Acts 2:38

[23] Acts 2:39

clean in his blood and put on the garment of salvation. **Save yourselves from this generation which has gone astray.**"[24]

Hundreds of people in the crowd surged forward in response to Peter's invitation. He and the other apostles came down to the street and began to baptize from jars of water in the name of the Father, and of the Son and of the Holy Spirit, as Jesus had commanded them on Mount Tabor in Galilee during one of his post-resurrection appearances.[25]

Others in the crowd moved away, unable to accept the enormity of Israel's crime if, indeed, Jesus of Nazareth was the Anointed One of God. Many of these also could not reconcile themselves to receiving a message of such earth-shaking importance from these uneducated "country bumpkins" from Galilee. But some just needed more time to think about it. Many of these hesitant persons did become Christians subsequently when they saw the miracles which Peter and the others worked in the name of Jesus. All told, about 3,000 Jews joined the Christian Church that morning of her birth.

In the midst of the jubilation and excitement of the mass conversions, Peter called out to Simon the Zealot: "Simon, do you still question how you will fulfill the Lord's mission without him here to lead us?"

Simon paused, his baptizing cup momentarily suspended in the air, and shouted back: "No, Peter, because now I know that the Lord *is* here to lead us! He is in me and acts through me. I see with His eyes. I hear with His ears. I speak with His tongue. I baptize with His hands. It is I who am no longer here. Now Jesus the Christ lives through me!"

And what of Jesus' mother and the other holy women in the Upper Room that glorious morning? Their testimony was worthless in the Jewish culture of the time. Jesus had not forgotten them, though. He had already favored them with his first Resurrection announcement and appearance. In the eyes of history, they would become not only acceptable as witnesses but they would occupy the first place. The Holy Spirit was the mystical spouse of the Blessed Virgin Mary. She had been shaped and developed by this union so that on Pentecost she became love united to Love. The other women, too, were devoted, faithful, courageous, passionate disciples of Jesus. Their souls were like tinder ready to respond to the flame of God's love. The ecstasy of that holy union carried them into the very presence of the Trinity, a place to which we all long to go, a place called Heaven.

---

[24]Acts 2:40. Luke tells us in this verse that Peter used "many other arguments" to convert these first Jewish listeners on Pentecost morning. It seems reasonable that those arguments might have run along the lines of the fictional dialogue presented here, at least in part.

[25]See Mt 28:19.

COME, HOLY SPIRIT

Come, Holy Spirit, Creator, come
From thy bright heavenly throne!
Come, take possession of our souls,
And make them all thine own!
Thou who art called the Paraclete,
Best gift of God above,
The living spring, the living fire,
Sweet unction, and true love!
Thou who art sevenfold in thy grace,
Finger of God's right hand,
His promise, teaching little ones
To speak and understand!
O guide our minds with thy blest light,
With love our hearts inflame,
And with thy strength which ne'er decays
Confirm our mortal frame.
Far from us drive our hellish foe,
True peace unto us bring,
And through all perils guide us safe
Beneath thy sacred wing.
Through thee may we the Father know,
Through thee, the eternal Son,
And thee, the Spirit of them both,
Thrice-blessed Three in one.
All glory to the Father be,
And to the risen Son;
The same to thee, O Paraclete,
While endless ages run.
Amen

V. Send forth your Spirit, and we shall be re-created.
R. And you shall renew the face of the earth.

Let us pray.
O God, who by the light of the Holy Spirit, has instructed the hearts of the faithful,
Grant that in the same Spirit we may be truly wise and ever rejoice in Your consolation.
Through Christ our Lord.
Amen.

QUESTIONS FOR REFLECTION

(1) What arguments would you use today to convince unbelievers that Jesus is the Son of God, sent by Him as the Messiah promised to the Jews and to us?

(2) Who is the Holy Spirit to you? How would you explain Him? What is His nature? What is His relationship with Jesus and the Father?

(3) What did Jesus mean when he said that all sins can be forgiven except blasphemy against the Holy Spirit (Mk 3:29; Lk 12:10)?

(4) The descent of the Holy Spirit at Pentecost could be described as the first Christian Confirmation. What is the purpose of the Sacrament of Confirmation and in what way does it relate to the Holy Spirit?

(5) The miraculous signs associated with the Paraclete (Holy Spirit) at Pentecost include the speaking in tongues understood in the many native languages of the people in Jerusalem, inexplicable flames burning above the heads of the followers of Jesus, and the strange climatic disturbances focused upon the house where the apostles and disciples were staying. What would you consider the greater miracle—these signs or the willingness of 3,000 Palestinian Jews to accept a crucified criminal as their Savior?

(6) Have you in your lifetime had an "Ah, ha" moment when suddenly you were aware of the reality of God? Could you compare that experience to Pentecost?

(7) Consider the seven gifts of the Holy Spirit: wisdom, understanding, counsel, fortitude, knowledge, piety, and fear of the Lord (*Catechism of the Catholic Church* ¶1831). St. Paul tells us that the gifts of the Holy Spirit are given to us for the benefit of the community.[26] Which gifts have you received and how have you applied them to serve the Lord?

(8) There are 12 fruits of the Holy Spirit: charity, joy, peace, patience, kindness, goodness, generosity, gentleness, faithfulness, modesty, self-control and chastity (*Catechism* ¶1832). Which of these do you have? In which are you lacking?

(9) The *Catechism* (¶s 694-701) lists the following as symbols of the Holy Spirit: water, anointing, fire, cloud and light, seal, hand, finger and dove. In what way do these things represent the Holy Spirit?

(10) An expression popular in the 1970's was "the medium is the message." Could this expression be applied to the Holy Spirit? How?

---

[26]1 Cor 12:7

Who is this that comes forth like the dawn, as beautiful as the moon, as resplendent as the sun, as awe-inspiring as bannered troops? Sg 6:10D

FOURTH GLORIOUS MYSTERY

The Assumption of Mary

Jesus had called Herod Antipas, tetrarch of Galilee, a fox[1] and so he was. But he was no match for his nephew, the cunning and arrogant Herod Agrippa I. Agrippa, raised in the courts at Rome, was dissolute and vain, but played the Caesarean political game masterfully. By befriending Caligula, he gradually succeeded to the rule of the Palestinian lands, beginning with Herod Philip's territories east of the Jordan River in 37 A.D., then Herod Antipas' Galilee and Perea in 39. When Caligula was assassinated in A.D. 41, Agrippa supported Claudius in the competition to become the new Roman emperor. He was rewarded with the kingship of Judea and immediately set out to consolidate his rule, which now approximated that of his grandfather, Herod the Great (37–4 B.C.).

The Herodian family was never fully accepted by the Jewish population. Agrippa determined to remedy this estrangement as much as he could by winning over the Jewish religious authorities. By the year 42, Christianity was perceived as a significant challenge to the Jewish religion and persecution was active. Herod Agrippa saw in this situation another political opportunity and immediately had one of the leading apostles, James, brother of John and son of Zebedee, seized and beheaded. James was the first of the apostles to be martyred.

Next Herod imprisoned Peter during the Feast of Unleavened Bread with the aim of trying and executing him after the Passover celebration was completed. Peter was guarded by four squads of soldiers, presumably Temple guards. He was freed, however, by the intervention of an angel and escaped Herod's designs. The hapless guards were executed after a search for the apostle proved fruitless.[2]

The Christian community in Jerusalem laid low for awhile. Soon, Herod, who had no personal interest in the Christians one way or the other, tired of the

---

[1]Lk 13:32

[2]See Acts 12:1-19.

demands and complaints of the chief priests and Pharisees and departed for his palatial residence in Caesarea on the shores of the blue-green Mediterranean.

Far to the north and west, on the coast of the Aegean Sea in what is today modern Turkey, in the city of Ephesus, the mother of Jesus resided with the Apostle John in the company of a few women companions. She had been brought to this house, located on an isolated mountain peak about 10 miles from the predominately Greek city of Ephesus, by the Apostle John not long after the stoning of Stephen, the first martyr to follow Christ into death for the new faith. Ephesus was a main metropolis of Asia, the fourth largest city in the Roman Empire, with a population estimated at 250,000 during that time. The city was a major trade center and seaport, linking the sea routes to the west with the land routes to the east. Ironically, it was also a principal center for magicians and pagan worship. It is not surprising that Mary kept a discreet distance from the (ancient) world-famous Temple of Artemis. Nonetheless, Ephesus became a Christian triumph. Paul spent more than two years there and one of his letters in the New Testament is the "Letter to the Ephesians."

Paul's good friend and frequent companion, the physician and future Gospel author, Luke, traveled with him and spent considerable time in Ephesus. Besides attending to the medical needs of the small community, he loved to visit Mary at her home outside of town. It was the next best thing to being with the Lord Himself, who, of course, was their favorite topic of conversation. Luke was especially curious about the birth and childhood years of Jesus. Mary explained how she had learned from the visit of a beautiful angel one afternoon of her destiny to be the mother of the Messiah. It was a topic she obviously enjoyed. The more Luke learned about how God had arranged all this, the more awestruck he was to be in the presence of this remarkable woman.

"How did your parents and Joseph respond to this news?" Luke asked Mary.

Mary chuckled as she thought back to those moments. "I think my parents were somewhere between astonishment and consternation. That the Messiah was finally coming to save his people was incredible enough, but that I, a poor girl in Nazareth, should be his mother and without a human father's involvement . . . well, it's not hard to understand why they were in a state of shock. My parents, of course, immediately thought of the potential repercussions to me as an unwed mother. That was one reason they agreed I should go immediately to visit my kinswoman, Elizabeth. She was well beyond her child-bearing years so if she was indeed pregnant as the angel had said, then all was confirmed. It's funny, though. I was never concerned about these things. If the Lord could do what He was doing to me, I knew He would take care of these other details as well."

"And Joseph?" asked Luke.

"Poor, dear Joseph!" exclaimed Mary. "I didn't have a chance to tell him before I left to visit Elizabeth because he was away from Nazareth. By the time I got back, my condition was beginning to be pretty noticeable. When we told him what was happening, he wanted to believe, I know, but he just couldn't accept such an explanation. Just imagine how you would have reacted if you'd heard a young girl claiming to be pregnant by the direct power of God Himself."

Luke thought for a moment and shook his head, "I could never have believed it."

"After Joseph left that night, I thought my parents were going to have a nervous collapse. My poor father was convinced that Joseph would report me to the Synagogue and I would be taken out and stoned to death. My mother was a little calmer. She could see that the Lord must have a plan to deal with this problem, but she was still very anxious about it. Looking back, I see the wisdom of God even here in these difficult, painful moments. He sent the angel to reassure Joseph and after that everything was beautiful. But Joseph had been tested first. He had proved his love and his generosity by deciding not to expose me to the law and, instead, to help me in every other way . . . short of marrying me, of course," said Mary, laughing.

"Even knowing the truth did not save him from a lot of kidding and embarrassment. It was scandalous in Nazareth to conceive a child during the period of betrothal. On top of all this, dear, dear Joseph saw immediately that the conception of this Child by the Spirit of God constituted a kind of divine marriage that took precedence over our earthly one. Even though this meant he would not have any children of his own, he never complained. He was always the most generous of husbands and the most loving of fathers to Jesus. I have missed him very much all these years." Mary looked sad for a moment as she thought back to Joseph's premature death from illness when Jesus was in his mid-twenties. But it was only a moment. She knew with absolute certainty that Joseph was re-united with her Son and that both were waiting for her in the beautiful courts of heaven.

"Did you tell your cousin, Elizabeth, about the coming of the Messiah?" asked Luke.

"I was so excited about it I couldn't have kept it in if I had tried," laughed Mary. "But I was concerned about how to tell the story. It did seem pretty hard to believe on its face. I had not seen Elizabeth for a few years so I wasn't sure she would recognize me. As soon as she opened the door, however, she not only knew who I was, but she also knew that I was to be the mother of the Lord! Praised be our kind and gracious Father in heaven! He spoke the truth directly to her heart. Dearest Luke, I cannot begin to describe to you how the Lord has surrounded me with His blessings and His care all the days of my life!"

"The people of Israel long expected the Messiah to be a warrior-king to drive out foreign invaders and restore the earthly kingdom of David. Was that your thought as well?" asked Luke.

"All Israel thought that," replied Mary, "but from the moment the Child was conceived in my womb, I began to see a different mission for him. It was mainly because I was so engulfed in love which poured down upon me from the Lord that violence and armed conflict just seemed incompatible with what was happening to me. Later, though, when we were returning to Nazareth and the old priest Simeon prophesied in the Temple that Jesus would be the downfall and rise of many in Israel, a sign of opposition, and that I would be pierced by a sword, it seemed that maybe the Messiah would someday take up arms against Israel's enemies. Poor Joseph was terribly upset by this. He couldn't understand the Lord not protecting the mother of His Son. How little we understood then!"

During the rest of that afternoon and for many visits thereafter, Luke discussed with Mary the early years of Jesus' life. He learned the details of the Angel Gabriel's visit to Zechariah and the presentation in the Temple. She explained to him all about the incident with the teachers when Jesus was left behind in Jerusalem at the age of 12. There were many other things which Mary shared as well but which were not included in Luke's Gospel.[3]

John made Ephesus his base of operations and traveled to and from it when he was not in Jerusalem. He was there with Mary in late June when the courier, dusty and tired from the difficult hike up the mountain, brought the news of his brother's death. The letter was from his birth mother, Salome:

My dearest John,

It is with the greatest sorrow that I write to tell you of your brother's death. James was called to follow our Lord into His Kingdom shortly before the Feast of Passover. The chief priests and elders stirred up King Herod against him and all of our community. At his trial, his testimony for our Lord and Savior was powerful. But this is a stiff-necked people and they were not to be satisfied until they had spilled his blood by beheading him, as the great prophet, John the Baptist, had died before him at the hand of Herod Antipas.

We have laid James' body in a tomb here in Jerusalem. Your father is well though he grieves deeply for his son.

Herod also arrested Peter, but he was freed by an angel sent from the Lord to remove his chains and rescue him. Praised be the God of Israel! He was led from his prison cell in the very midst of guards who slept beside him and many others who stood watch all around. This has caused a terrible uproar among the Sanhedrin and the Temple soldiers and I fear it will not go well with these men. Peter and the other apostles have left Jerusalem for now. Pray for them and for all of us. Do not return here until you hear that it is safe.

Please convey my deepest affection and devotion to Mary, your other mother. We are all honored beyond saying by her presence in our

---

[3]There is an old tradition that Luke was an artist as well as a physician and writer. Some believe that he painted a portrait of Mary known as the *Hodegetria*, which inspired the Byzantine style of icon portraits of Mary. The most famous of these today is Our Lady of Perpetual Help. The original of this picture, painted on wood, hangs above the high altar in the Redemptorists' church of Sant' Alfonso in Rome. The *Hodegetria* itself was destroyed when Constantinople fell in 1453 to the Turks.

family. Her sister, Mary, and all those who miss her and love her, send her greetings.

Your loving mother,

Salome

When John showed the letter to Mary, she read it in silence and then hugged him tightly. After a few moments, she stepped back and, taking both of his strong hands in hers, said, "James is very blessed to be with my Son so soon. You cannot imagine the happiness he has found. Because time is different for him in heaven, he sees that we shall all be reunited very, very soon."

John nodded and said, "Thank you, mother, for your kind words. I know that James is with our Lord. But I am sad that I shall not see him for perhaps many, many years for I must live by earth's calendar. And I know my parents' pain is great."

For the rest of that day, Mary remained in prayer and solitude. The following morning at breakfast she said to John: "I would like to return to Jerusalem to convey my sympathies to your mother and pay my respects at the tomb of James. I have spoken with my Son and learned that my time with you and the others grows short. It is also my heart's greatest desire to revisit the places of His suffering before I leave this world. We need not fear the persecution of Herod. He will be gone from Jerusalem before we arrive."

"Of course, mother," replied John. He had long since learned that when Mary spoke with authority, she should never be doubted. He was deeply concerned, however, by her reference to leaving the world. She seemed to be in perfect health, but death came in many guises. In any event, there was no point in arguing with her. The Lord's will would be made known in due time. For now, John was excited about returning to Jerusalem. He wanted very much to comfort his parents and to make his own farewells to his fierce older brother who had looked out for him for so much of his life.

It was a week before Mary and John were ready to set out. Mary Magdalene, who was probably the closest to Mary among the women with her, insisted on going with them. Mary was pleased to have her company. They traveled with one servant, who was sent back with their horse-drawn cart after they reached the seaport. There, John found an inn where they stayed while he searched the docks for an outbound ship which shared their destination and had room for three more passengers. He was lucky. In just two days, he found passage on an Egyptian grain ship that was returning to Alexandria with a load of boxwood, a wood prized for making fine furniture. The ship planned a stop along the way in Caesarea. Since the winds at this time of year favored eastbound travel, the journey would require no more than seven or eight days.

The morning they had left had been sunny, bright and beautiful. Mary was lost in thought as she walked around the little house and grounds where she had lived for so many years. She had exchanged tearful farewells with the women who had accompanied her to Ephesus and then stayed to make their home with her. The social atmosphere among the women in those years was not morose nor always somber. The women were good friends and spent many hours together in domestic projects, prayer, and conversations about events great and small. Although their company could not be characterized as jovial, they exulted in the joys and beauties of their grace-filled existence, even occasionally laughing over some antic by one of the domestic or small wild animals that scampered around the property.

But the death of Jesus and the struggles of His infant church were serious business. The apostles and disciples passing through, including Saul (Paul) of Tarsus, brought them news of the triumphs and difficulties of the followers of Jesus. Most of the news was good and always included wonderful stories of miracles and multiple conversions. These moments were probably the most light-hearted that the little mountaintop Ephesian community enjoyed. News of persecutions, of course, were very troubling and frequently precipitated many tears among these loving and empathetic women.

All of the women took upon themselves the role of prayer and sacrifice as their way of sharing in the work of the male disciples. There was little else they could do in the culture of the time. Certainly, prayers from the mother of Jesus were a mighty boon to anyone who was their beneficiary, as they still are. Under her direction, a commemorative series of stations were built on the grounds of their compound to recall the details of Christ's passion. Mary's little Way of the Cross began with a small garden with some olive trees, shrubbery and flowers. It was a place to reflect upon Christ's agony in the garden of Gethsemane. Her stations concluded with a life-size wooden cross on a small mound. As she retraced these terrible steps nearly each day, she would often become so emotionally overcome that others would have to help support her. It is not surprising that there was not much levity in this tiny Christian community at Ephesus.

But for all that, there was joy, a deep, abiding joy that grew from the living presence of the Holy Spirit and the full consciousness that death was merely a brief barrier to incomparable happiness and beauty. All of them longed to pass through that doorway whenever Jesus should say to them: "Come you blessed of my Father into that Kingdom prepared for you from the foundation of the world!" Now, as Mary had looked around one last time, she had been sure that she was about to receive that invitation from her Son.

As the ship carrying the two Marys and John sailed through the calm late summer waters, some of the apostles began to re-surface in Jerusalem. Herod Agrippa had returned to Caesarea and there, besides the usual political machinations, was enmeshed in plans for a spectacular series of games to be hosted in honor of the Roman emperor, Claudius. Mary of Clopas' son, James the Less, was the bishop of Jerusalem. His son, Jude Thaddaeus, was present, as were Matthew, Andrew and Bartholomew. Peter was not far away. Thomas had gone to India, but was reportedly on his way back to Jerusalem for a visit. The other apostles, too, as well as Paul, seemed to be heading back to the City of David for a coincidental variety of reasons. For some of them, this would be their last visit.

Because of the Jewish persecutions, Lazarus and his two sisters, Mary and Martha, had left Bethany some years before. Mary, Mary Magdalene and John, therefore, went into the city to the house of Mary and Tychus. Rhoda, the long-time maidservant, who had accompanied the women to the tomb on the morning of the Resurrection, answered the door. She shrieked with delight when she saw the mother of Jesus, Magdalene and the beloved apostle standing there.

"Mistress Mary, it is the mother of the Lord, Mary Magdalene, and John!" Rhoda called out to Mary Tychus, who hurried from the kitchen where she had been supervising the preparation of the day's meals.

"Now has the Lord's blessing truly come upon this house!" exclaimed Mary as she hugged the two women and John, in turn, and escorted them all inside. They were glad to be off the street, especially so near to the palace of the high priest. They were also tired from their travels. Mary was 63 years old and looking quite wan. John was 33, the age of Jesus when he was crucified. Mary Magdalene was younger than Mary by a good bit, but, in her late forties, not as resistant to the rigors of travel as she once was.

On the ninth day after their arrival in Jerusalem, Mary asked John and Peter to accompany her on a retracing of her Son's sorrowful journey to Calvary. They began early the next morning among the gnarled, ancient olive trees and limestone outcroppings of the garden of Gethsemane, near the base of the western slope of the Mount of Olives. The visit brought back disturbing memories for both Peter and John as they once again showed Mary where they had waited for Jesus and the small glade about thirty yards away where he had gone to pray by himself. It was not necessary to tell her anything further. She seemed to see the scene clearly in her mind, as if she were experiencing it herself. She collapsed to the ground and began to perspire heavily and to groan softly. John and Peter watched her with growing alarm but hesitated to disturb her ecstatic trance. Shortly, she began to weep and to exclaim over and over, "Oh, my Son! My poor Son!" After about thirty minutes, Mary gave a great sigh and looked around. Her cheeks were wet with tears and her eyes were red. Although she was composed, her face was very pale.

The three of them next followed Jesus' path back across the little arched bridge over what was at this time of year a dry stream bed at the bottom of the Kidron valley. They passed through the Fountain Gate and headed up the steps on Mount Zion toward the Upper City. They paused outside the gates to the palace of Caiaphas but did not linger there. Instead they went on to the Upper Agora, the marketplace and open square that served the wealthy residents of Jerusalem. Here, Mary, John, Mary Magdalene and several of the other Galilean women had waited and watched when Jesus had been condemned by Pilate after the crowd had rejected the procurator's offer of clemency and had demanded repeatedly that Jesus be crucified.

Mary returned to the place where so many years before she had stood, leaning heavily on John, listening to the hiss and snap of the scourgers' *flagra* raining down upon the bare flesh of her Son. The near-fatal beating had occurred on the other side of Herod's palace wall, which Pilate was occupying at the time. But then, and certainly now, Mary seemed somehow to be able to visualize the terrible scene as well as hear it. Jews shopping among the merchants spread out in the colonnaded portico surrounding the large open square stared curiously at the two men kneeling beside an elderly, weeping woman. At this place, Mary's tears were fierce and her body heaved with sobs. John felt his own tears running silently down his cheeks. Peter did not cry, but was too emotional to speak, remembering his own agony that day after denying three times the night before that he even knew Jesus.

John looked toward the silent, arched opening in the high stone wall with its crenellated battlements. A token detachment of Herod Agrippa's soldiers were on duty there now. It seemed like only yesterday that Jesus had been led through the arch and made to stand on the elevated platform to the side, patiently enduring the demands of his countrymen for his execution by the Romans. He had swayed slightly from side to side, blood-streaked from a crown of thorns that had been driven into his scalp and rips in his flesh up and down his body from the lead-tipped *flagra*. The Roman soldiers had been amused to dress him in a scarlet tribune's cloak to mock the Jewish accusation that Jesus was claiming to be a king. An hour passed before Mary recovered her composure enough to continue.

The three of them next passed the Hippicus and Mariamne Towers built by Herod the Great and left the Upper City through the Ginnoth Gate. They walked down the city streets that sloped into the Tyropoeon valley splitting the city within its walls. Their destination was the Fortress Antonia, or, rather, a place about 200 yards from it just where the street begins to climb up the western side of the little valley.

As they passed one of the narrow corners, crowded with a cluster of small shops and street vendors, a small voice called out to them: "Please, could you give us just a copper coin? My brother and I are very hungry."

Mary stopped instantly and looked in the direction from which the words had come. Sitting on the dirty pavement, hunched against the limestone wall of a small cheesemaker's shop, were two children. One was a girl of about eight and the other a small boy, perhaps three years old. They were dressed in tunics torn and soiled and had bare feet scratched and bruised from the rough cobblestones of the streets. There was hardly a clean spot on their faces and the ubiquitous dirt was streaked from past tears that had left forlorn trails of sorrow down the small, gaunt cheeks.

"Oh, Peter, John, look at these poor angels! Children, where are your parents?" said Mary as she knelt on the street beside the two ragged urchins.

"My father was killed in an accident and my mother is home with our other brothers and sisters. We live in a tent near the valley[4] where the trash is burned and the lepers live. We are all very hungry. If you can give us anything at all, the Lord will bless you," begged the girl.

Mary turned toward Peter, but he already had his purse open. He gave the girl two silver denarii, which was two days' wages in that time, and watched as her face lit up with joyful gratitude. "Children," said Mary. "Have you heard of Jesus of Nazareth, the Messiah who has visited his people?"

"No, dear lady. Who is he? Can he help us?"

"Oh, yes. And those who love the Lord will help you, too. But first, tell me your names."

"I am called Tamaria and this is my brother, Joshua," said the girl shyly.

"Take your brother now and go to the house of Tychus in the Upper City. It is near the palace of Caiaphas, across from the Tomb of David, and has an upper floor with a large balcony. You will probably hear people inside singing the praises of the Lord Jesus. Tell whomever answers the door that the mother of the Lord sent you and asks that you and your family be given shelter and food. They will tell you also about the wonderful, wonderful news that has been given to Israel and to all the world by the grace of God. Hurry now!" Mary helped the two children to their feet.

"But we are so dirty and poor! How can we go to a rich man's house without being chased away with stones?" said the girl while clinging to Mary's hand.

"These are people who are rich in the love of our Lord Jesus and desire nothing more than to help people just like yourselves. Do not be afraid. I will see you when I return and make sure you are comfortable. I promise it!"

Reluctantly, the child let go of Mary's hand and turned in the direction of the Upper City. John said then, "Wait here and I will take them through the Ginnoth Gate and make sure they know where they are going from there."

When the children arrived at the house of Tychus, nothing more was needed than to say the mother of the Lord had sent them. They were taken in at once, cleaned and fed, and a servant was sent with Tamaria to invite her whole family to leave their squalid circumstances and join the fledgling Christian community. This was an offer gladly accepted for multiple reasons, as might be imagined. When she saw her mother, Tamaria could not stop talking about the lady who had helped her. "Oh, mother, she was so beautiful! When she smiled at me I felt like I was in heaven. She promised to come and see us when she returns from wherever she was going. I can't wait for you to meet her!"

After getting Tamaria and Joshua on the right track, John rejoined Mary and Peter at the street corner where they met the children. From there, they resumed following the way of sorrows that Jesus had trod on his way to Golgotha.

---

[4]This was called the "Valley of Gehenna" during the time of Christ. He used the imagery to warn of the perils of dying in sin.

It was only a couple of blocks to the place where Mary and John had waited for the procession of soldiers and condemned men to pass them. The two of them shuddered as they stood on the corner and remembered the exhausted Jesus struggling to stay on his feet, staggering under the weight of his crossbeam, dirty, bloody, battered and swollen. The horror of that scene remembered struck to their souls' depths and left them in shock. Mary and John hugged each other tightly, eyes closed against a memory that could not be shut out. Mary thought back to how she had tried to mop up the drops of Jesus' precious blood with her mantle. It was Peter who finally touched John's shoulder and suggested they move on. Mary's face was showing the strain of this melancholy journey. She had dark circles under her red-rimmed eyes and her face was drawn and pinched. The two apostles were deeply concerned.

"Mother, I think we should go back to the house to rest now. This journey is too much for you. We'll finish it tomorrow or when you are feeling stronger," said John.

"No, my son. The journey must be made now. Tomorrow will be too late, I'm afraid. I'll be fine. Just let me lean on you and Peter as I need to, my dears."

They continued to follow Jesus' path to Golgotha, past where Simon was forced to help the Lord carry His cross, past the place where Seraphia (Veronica) braved the soldiers and the hostile crowd to show Jesus a bit of kindness, past the places where he fell and where the mourning women of Jerusalem wept and wailed for the fate of the men being crucified that day.

They passed through the Jaffa Gate and stood at the top of the limestone quarry now largely converted to a cemetery sprinkled with gardens.[5] They stared at the high outcrop with its rough skull shape and remembered the price of their salvation. The apostles wanted to turn back at this point, but Mary insisted they go on and ascend to the very spot where Christ's cross had been anchored in the ground. Since Herod Agrippa had been restored to the throne of Judea, Golgotha was no longer being used for crucifixions so there were neither uprights nor victims present. The cross to which Jesus had been nailed had long since been removed by his followers and kept as a prized relic of His Passion. When they reached the place where Jesus had hung dying, Mary once again collapsed to the ground. She lay still for a long time, perhaps in some mystical way experiencing more than the sufferings she had endured 15 years earlier. When an hour had passed, John once again bent to rouse her. This time, however, there was no response. He shook her a little more firmly. Still no response.

"What's the matter with her, John?" asked Peter anxiously. He bent over the still figure and turned her face upward. Mary's face was in repose, her eyes closed, her breathing labored and slow. "Oh, my Lord, she's not well! We must get her back to Tychus at once."

---

[5]By the time of the Jewish Revolt in A.D. 66-70, this area would be included within Jerusalem's city walls by the Third Outer Wall which nearly doubled the size of the enclosed city.

Peter, who was still a strong and robust man in his late forties, picked Mary up in his arms and carried her by himself. John followed closely behind. They hurried back through the Jaffa and Ginnoth Gates and down the street toward the house of Tychus. Inside, they rushed her to a bedroom on the first floor, near the back of the house. She had not regained consciousness.

"Is Luke in the city?" demanded Peter.

"Yes," said Mary of Tychus.

"Send for him at once! Tell him that the mother of our Lord is very ill."

When Luke arrived, he went directly into the room where Mary lay unconscious. He emerged about half an hour later. "Our mother is not well. I cannot find a cause, but her life seems without a doubt to be slipping away. It would be well to summon the apostles and all those who love her. There may not be much time left to say goodbye. Whether she will regain consciousness is impossible to say. I hope so. But for that we must pray and pray very hard!"

****

The first warning bells had rung throughout the heavenly realm when Luke announced that Mary appeared to be dying. Benjamin and Natali, aged five and seven in earth years, respectively, were practicing swoops and dives with their newly assigned "wings"[6] when the glorious chimes rang out. The two children were recent arrivals in heaven. Each was an only child and had been killed in unrelated accidents, one by drowning, the other by a fall. As young children, they especially missed their mothers. Rumors had been buzzing around heaven for some time now that the Mother of Jesus, the Son of God, would be coming home soon. Everyone rejoiced at that thought and regarded her arrival as no less than the return of their own mothers, even if they were also in heaven already. Family relationships are dramatically expanded, you see, in the kingdom where God reigns Personally, because His love tends to transform everyone into brothers, sisters, children, parents and best friends. It stood to reason, therefore, that Mary, the Blessed Mother of God, would be mother to all. For the very young children, however, this meant a little something extra: they would have a very, very, very special mother until their own mothers could join them when it was their time to leave earth. I need not describe to you the level of excitement among all the "orphans" in heaven over the news that the number one mother of all time would soon be there.

Benjamin and Natali had arrived at the "Pearly Gates" at just about the exact same moment. They had been welcomed together and had been best friends ever since. But they still missed their mothers. So when they saw the posted notice

---

[6]The angels and saints in heaven do not wear wings with feathers as they are often portrayed. In fact, they have no such appendages at all. But they do have the facility to fly and this capability may be thought of as "wings" for our present purposes.

that volunteers were sought to go to earth to escort the mother of the Lord back to heaven, they read it eagerly:[7]

ATTENTION,
ALL RESIDENTS OF HEAVEN!

Mary, the blessed mother of our Lord and Savior Jesus Christ, will be coming home soon. All residents of heaven are cordially invited to join the escort party which Gabriel and Michael are forming to go to earth and bring back the body and soul of the Holy Mother of God. Participation will be limited, so apply early!

All members of the entourage must bring a flower of their own choosing. Roses, the most beautiful of flowers, and lilies, the most pure, are recommended for these will be associated with Mary for all time.

To sign up or for further information, see the aforementioned Archangels, Gabriel or Michael.

P.S. Don't be late!

The note was signed by Moses as "Acting Gatekeeper," standing in for Saint Peter until he would arrive in another 25 years or so and become the official gatekeeper for heaven.

Benjamin and Natali immediately flew off to find Gabriel or Michael. It wasn't hard because there was already a huge crowd of souls and angels around them, clamoring to join the escort party. When the two little children saw the huge crowd, their faces fell. There was no way, they were sure, that they would ever get on the list with all these other people in front of them.

But that little tug of disappointment set off an internal alarm in the Holy Spirit, the living Being of Love who emanated from the Father and the Son. He was the Energy source for the divine realm but, more than this, provided a kind of universal communications net which kept all of the Blessed in touch with one another. No unhappiness was permitted in heaven. The Spirit whispered to Gabriel to be sure to reserve two small places in his group for two special souls who would be representing the Son of God Himself! Gabriel was surprised, but delighted as well, and looking out across the vast throng of holy residents waiting to sign up for the journey to earth, he saw Benjamin and Natali standing patiently in the very back of the crowd. The two little spirits had their fingers crossed, which might seem to you like a forbidden superstition but was actually just a form of physical prayer.

All at once, the great crowd parted and a pathway opened up directly from Benjamin and Natali straight to the feet of the great Archangel Gabriel

---

[7]There is no illiteracy, even among the very young, in heaven.

himself! The children gaped and then gulped as they saw Gabriel beckoning to them to come forward. Slowly, and a little bit awkwardly because their flying skills were still pretty rudimentary, they sailed down the long pathway until they tumbled to a halt in front of the magnificent archangel, who regarded them lovingly but also somewhat dubiously.

"I have but two places remaining in the escort party for the Blessed Mother," Gabriel informed the two children standing awestruck at his feet. "It seems that Someone has penciled your two names in. It won't be long before we'll be leaving. The time for departure will be signaled by three rings from the Crystal Chimes which stand at the entrance to heaven. Don't be late because when the final chime rings, the gates will be closed until we return! I suggest you two work on your flying skills in the meantime. And be sure to find a suitable flower for our Queen!"

The children were too overwhelmed to actually speak so they merely stared up at the dazzling face of Gabriel and nodded with their little mouths hanging open. When they had recovered and let their excitement take full charge of their senses, they immediately set off to search the entire expanse of the heavenly kingdom for the very best flower to give to the Blessed Mother. As for the saints and angels who were unable to join the escort party, there was no disappointment because in heaven everyone is in perfect synch with the will of God. Natali and Benjamin would not have felt disappointment either had it not been the will of the Father that they be part of the escort party.

The two little saints looked high and low at an endless stream of beautiful flowers. In heaven, the flowers have much more vivid colors with far lovelier fragrances than even the most delicate and beautiful ones on earth. They live in a way, too, that vegetation on earth does not. They can vary their colors and appear at the same time two different ways to two different persons. But none seemed quite right to Natali and Benjamin, who were determined to find the very best flower in all the heavenly realm for the woman who would be elevated above all others. Of course, in heaven, the higher your elevation, the greater your love and the dearer you are to all the other residents of that glorious place. Stations in heaven are nothing like the often stiff and intimidating social structures on earth, nothing at all!

The children looked in the public gardens but although each flower seemed more beautiful than the one before, and each tried different color combinations, none was exactly right.

Next, they searched the gardens of the Patriarchs, including Abraham, Joseph and Moses. There were some stunning beauties there, but still not one which was just perfect.

From there, they went to the gardens of the first Christian martyrs. The Holy Innocents had a very special place filled with Fairy Roses, Baby's Breath, Bluebells, yellow Santolina button flowers, Primroses and many others in all the colors of the rainbow. Natali had a hard time pulling Benjamin away from this charming place which was especially designed by the Hand of God to please and delight small children. But still they did not find a flower which was perfect for Our Lady.

After this, the children climbed up through the various levels of heaven, visiting the magnificent gardens of the nine choirs of angels: the Angels, Archangels, Principalities, Virtues, Powers, Dominions, Thrones, Cherubim and Seraphim. And while the flowers in each successive garden were indescribably more beautiful, none seemed quite beautiful enough for the Mother of God.

At last, when it seemed that Natali and Benjamin had searched the entire kingdom of Heaven from top to bottom and side to side, going here and there, thither and yon, as saints and angels suggested places for them to search, they did something they probably should have done in the first place. They went to see the Lord Jesus Christ. He seemed to expect them for they no sooner had made the decision to visit Him than, lo and behold, He was standing right beside them! The joy and love that radiated from the Second Person of the Divine Trinity were so powerful, and the light so dazzling, that the children almost forgot what they wanted to ask Him. But Jesus knew and He knelt down beside them and invited each of them to come closer. When they did, He put one arm around each small shoulder and whispered a secret in each upturned ear. Then He laughed, kissed them both, and went back to His great central throne around which all of Heaven revolves.

"Natali," asked Benjamin excitedly, "what did the Lord say to you?"

"He told me that His mother always loved pink roses the best. What did He say to you, Benjamin?"

"He told me that He has been preparing a secret garden to be just for His mother and He told me where to find it!"

"Benjamin, where? We must go there at once. Most certainly the perfect flower will be found in this most special of all gardens!"

Benjamin screwed up his face in the most intense concentration he could muster. He turned around and pointed to the north. Then he wavered and pointed toward the west. Then he wavered some more and pointed to the south, hardly pausing there before he swung on around to point to the east. But that didn't seem right either. "I forgot already!"

"Oh, Benjamin, think! Concentrate with all your might!" But it was no use. Benjamin could not remember the way that Jesus told him to go to get to His mother's secret garden no matter how hard he tried and no matter how many times he turned around and pointed in every direction, it seemed, on the compass.

Just then a beautiful chime with all the best notes of all the magnificent symphonies ever composed rang out across heaven. The escort party was leaving! And the two smallest members of that party not only had no flower, they could not even figure out where to go and search.

Natali threw up her hands and sighed. "Well, Benjamin, we tried. I guess we better go tell Gabriel and Michael to go without us." With that, the two little saints rose into the air, sadly, and started to turn toward the towering archway that marked the entrance into heaven.

But no sooner had Benjamin's little feet left the ground than he was picked up as on a homing beam and swept off in the direction of the Throne of God. Natali was so surprised she almost sat back down again, but then she recovered her presence of mind and raced after him.

As she drew closer, she could hear the boy yelling: "Now I remember what the Lord told me! He said that if I just flew in any direction that His love for His mother would capture us and sweep us swift as arrows right into her secret garden."

Around the Throne with its throngs of angelic attendants the two children flew at incredible speed. Jesus waved at them as they zipped past. Suddenly they were at the entrance to the garden. They looked around. It was stunningly beautiful. The Throne of God was very near; the children could see the brilliant light from the Holy Trinity who resided there glowing above the sparkling green trees and shrubs, laden with flowers and fruit, which surrounded them in what seemed to be the most secluded spot in all Heaven. And the fragrances! Truly this was the most blessed place in all the universe. In the center of the garden there was a beautiful chair which gleamed with the fire of precious diamonds. Benjamin approached it curiously. Tentatively, he put out one small pudgy hand to touch the seat. It yielded gently to his touch. He thought about climbing in, but Natali said, "No, Benjamin! That chair is for Our Blessed Mother and you may sit in it only if she invites you. Now, come on! We must find the pink rose which the Lord said was her favorite flower."

It wasn't hard to find. It was growing right beside the beautiful chair. A magnificent rose with delicate petals in translucent pink that were so vivid that the color itself appeared alive. The fragrance from the flower filled the garden and was so light and lovely that it seemed to capture the most beautiful essence of every flower that had ever existed on earth. But this rose was no ordinary flower. It was nearly 12 inches across! The stem was over an inch thick. Benjamin stared at it and swallowed hard. "Natali, how can we pick it? It is too big!" As these words emerged from his lips, the two children heard the second chime echo across the vast reaches of the heavenly realm.

This galvanized Natali into action and she fell on her knees before the rose. "Dear little flower, you are the most magnificent rose in all of Heaven. But you were created to be the first gift for the holy Mother of God, who will soon be here. Won't you help us to take you to her so that you may be the first sign of the glorious treasures which her Son has created for her in her eternal home?"

If a flower can smile, this one did. Its petals rustled ever so softly and with just a slight twist it severed itself from the ground and floated before the children. Because it was so large, the two of them got on either side of it and carried it together. Once they had it in their grip, they felt themselves being drawn back into the current that flowed from the mighty Throne and flying faster than they had ever flown before, faster even than they had ever seen any of the great Archangels fly, faster than an eye can blink!

But the gleaming archway was very far away. Before they reached it, the third chime rang out, and the glorious welcoming party of angels and saints departed for earth rejoicing with songs so beautiful and smiles so radiant that they cannot begin to be described here.

In the distance, Benjamin and Natali were tiny specks flying at the top speed allowed in Heaven, carefully embracing their precious cargo of the beautiful pink rose. But the rest of the escort group was already out of sight and the gate was closing rapidly. They couldn't make it. It was just too far. Natali realized that not only would they not make it through the gate in time, but at their astonishing speed they would almost certainly not be able to stop, either. "Hang on, Benjamin! We're going to crash!"

But we know that these two precious children with the gift which Jesus had arranged especially for them to deliver to His mother were not going to smash themselves and their stunning rose against the gate of Heaven. At the last minute, the gate paused in its closing and stayed open just long enough for the two little saints to zip through and on down the long, long tunnel toward earth.

****

Meanwhile, in Jerusalem, all of the apostles except Thomas, and many of the disciples and holy women, gathered at the bedside of Mary. She remained in the coma into which she had fallen after collapsing on Golgotha the previous day. All day and into the evening they prayed and wept and prayed some more, all hoping against hope for just one more word, one more smile from the lovely mother of the Anointed of the Lord. But it was not to be.

Over the previous week, since Mary had arrived in Jerusalem from Ephesus, she had quietly and unobtrusively made her farewells with each person individually. She had thanked each one for their faithful service and devotion to her Son and to her and asked them to continue to grow in love and generosity for one another. She reminded them that they were building the holy Church which the Lord had left behind to be the visible manifestation of His mystical Body and the means of salvation for all peoples on earth. She stressed the Real Presence of Jesus in the Eucharist and His promise to always be present when two or more gathered in His name. Then she gave each one a personal message for him or her alone. Whether this was an inspiration from her Son, Jesus, or the wisdom of the Mother of God, no one reported. But each person came away filled with awe and joy and ever after treasured these special moments as a most precious gift from heaven.

When the end came, it was so silent and still that a few minutes passed before those gathered for the vigil in Mary's room noticed that she was no longer breathing. Luke immediately stepped to her side to confirm that life had ceased. When he solemnly nodded, a great weeping and wailing burst forth in the room. When that subsided a bit later, Peter called Mary of Tychus aside and asked her to prepare Mary's body for burial. He and most of the mourners then left the room.

Mary was dressed in a beautiful white silk tunic with a gold sash and gold slippers on her feet. A blue mantle was draped over her dark hair and folded carefully along her sides. Although her breathing had ceased, Mary's face was in perfect repose, eyes closed naturally, complexion still fresh and healthy looking. It made the women uneasy, especially in the flickering light of the olive oil lamps by which they worked. Luke was called back twice more to ensure that Mary was indeed deceased. He, too, marveled at her appearance but carefully ascertained that she had no pulse and, by the polished bronze mirror he used, no breath. He shook his head and told the women to continue with the burial preparations.

They prepared a bier for her body by laying new perfumed linen cloths as a base and spreading flowers around and over the body. On Mary's head they placed a garland of miniature roses and crossed her arms across her breast. When the body was fully prepared, the bier was carried in a solemn processional to another building not far from the home of Tychus and Mary. There Mary would lie in state tomorrow for no more than a single day, assuming the condition of her body permitted it, for visits by the thousands of Christians in Jerusalem who were learning already by word of mouth that the mother of Jesus had died. Wrapping in a linen shroud would follow and burial would take place in a new tomb on the Mount of Olives, very close to the garden of Gethsemane. At least, all of this was the plan.

After Mary had been properly dressed for her burial and taken on the bier to the neighboring building, which had more room for mourners to visit her, she was left alone. Those who loved her so much had little sleep since the day before and needed now to rest and compose themselves for the funeral that would be conducted the next day. Two of the servants were left to stand watch at the door.

With no one in the room, there was no one to see the arrival of the escort party from heaven. Thousands of angels and saints, in their incorporeal bodies, led by the Archangels Gabriel and Michael, crowded into the room where Mary lay quietly on her bier. Gabriel took her by the hand and said, "Mary, arise! Your Son awaits you."

Mary's eyes blinked open and she looked around, smiling to see so many beautiful, heavenly faces. She was overwhelmed by the flowers they brought as each lay his or her selected bloom upon the bier, floor and wherever space could be found. Soon the room was overflowing with flowers, mostly joyful roses and trumpeting white lilies, which filled the space with a most heavenly fragrance.

As Mary stood up, helped by the Archangel Michael to her feet, there was a sudden commotion at the back of the group which had spread out around her. Everyone looked in the direction of the disturbance. They saw what appeared to be a bundle of four arms, four legs, two heads and one enormous pink rose precariously balanced. The entire conglomeration was tumbling frantically toward an imminent collision with the bier upon which the Blessed Mother stood fascinated. Her eyes opened wide as she watched the two little saints, Benjamin and Natali, come whirling to a halt in a clump at her feet. The rose they had been carrying slipped from their grasp and floated up in a gentle arc right into the hands of Mary.

"Oh, dear! What have we here?" asked Mary.

"It seems the two youngest members of your entourage have arrived, my Queen," explained Gabriel. "Somewhat tardy, I'm afraid, and not very skillfully but not lacking in energy or enthusiasm, as you can see."

By this time, Natali had regained her composure and had helped Benjamin to his feet as well. "We're sorry, Blessed Mother, but we searched and searched and searched all over Heaven for the most beautiful flower until your Son, our Savior, helped us and then we couldn't find the garden at first 'cause Benjamin forgot what Jesus told us and then it was so big and we had to both carry it and when the Lord helped us fly we just flew too fast to stop and that's why we're here like this now and do you like the rose? It was sent to you especially by your Son," explained Natali as she finally paused and took a deep breath. She related her story in much the same way as she had made her entrance.

"It is the most beautiful flower I have ever seen," said Mary with a smile. "Do you think I might take it with me? And since you obviously know the way to my Son so well, would you lead me to Him?"

Well, this was quite an astonishing invitation for the two children. Even Gabriel and Michael were taken aback. A murmur of surprise, and, truth be told, of delight as well, swept through the assembled spirits. Benjamin's mouth fell open again, which was his usual response to the unexpected. He looked at Natali, then at Mary, then back at Natali who was in the process of curtsying deeply as she said most humbly: "Blessed Mother, we will be honored for all eternity to do whatever you wish."

"Me, too!" said Benjamin as he tried to mimic Natali's curtsy but tumbled over instead. Gabriel helped him back to his feet.

"Dearest Gabriel," said Mary turning now to the majestic Archangel whom she remembered so well from his visit long ago in Nazareth, "before we leave the earth there is one thing I must do yet. May I make a last visit?"

"My Queen, never was there any soul more in tune with the will of God. Whatever it is you ask shall always be granted. Where would you like to go?" replied Gabriel.

"There is a young girl whom I promised to visit. I would like to keep my word to this poor child." Mary had no more said the words than she was in the room with Tamaria, the impoverished little girl whom she had encountered begging with her little brother when Mary, Peter and John were following the way of the cross the day before. The child, now reunited with her mother and siblings, slept peacefully in a corner of their crowded room. Joshua was curled up next to her, drawing strength and hope from his big sister. No one awoke to see the heavenly light that filled the room with its dazzling brilliance. Mary, still wearing her funeral garland of flowers, bent over and kissed Tamaria on her cheek. She whispered to her, "Though you cannot see that I have kept my promise to you, I make you one further promise. Whenever you or anyone whom you love seeks my protection or asks my help, it shall be granted to you. In heaven, I will ask my Son to prepare a special place for you and for all the children of all times who have had their childhoods stolen by the cruelty and injustice of life in a sinful world. Before you have scarcely noticed the passing of the years, we will be reunited in the eternal joy of our Father, His Son and their Holy Spirit of Love." The Blessed Mother then reached up and, taking off her garland, placed it tenderly on the sleeping head of Tamaria.

"Children, I am ready to see my Son now," Mary said to Natali and Benjamin. Holding her magnificent pink rose in one hand, with her other hand clutched tightly by the two little saints, Mary was drawn up into the glorious realm of Heaven, leading a resplendent band of angels and saints who surrounded her with light and music so beautiful and so joyous that to hear it once would make further existence on earth unbearable.

The following morning, Tamaria awoke first. She found the mysterious garland of flowers on her head and noticed the beautiful floral scent which filled the little room. She awoke her mother, who was as mystified as Tamaria as to where the flowers and the fragrance had come from. Later on that day, they learned that the Blessed Virgin Mary, the mother of the Savior, had died the night before. This was crushing news to Tamaria, who was bitterly disappointed that her mother and the rest of her family would not have an opportunity to meet the beautiful lady who had helped her and Joshua. But the disappointment was soon replaced with astonishment and wonder when Mary of Tychus explained that Mary's body had disappeared. The circumstances had made it absolutely clear that Mary had experienced the first fruits of her Son's resurrection.

When Tamaria heard that the holy women had made a garland of flowers for the crown of the deceased Virgin, but were now supposing that she had taken it with her to heaven, Tamaria immediately ran to her new home and brought back the garland she had found that morning. When Mary of Tychus saw it, she fell to her knees and exclaimed, "Where did you find this, child? This is the garland that I formed myself to be the crown for the Blessed Mother of our Lord."

Tamaria explained how she had discovered it on her head that morning and offered to return it. But Mary saw that the Blessed Virgin Mary herself had given it to this child, and so she graciously declined its return. Tamaria took the garland home and kept it in a place of honor. Days went by and the flowers remained as fresh and as lovely as the day they had been picked. Weeks and then months passed and still the flowers sparkled and dispensed their heavenly fragrance. The garland became a wonderful source of devotion and many persons reported miracles in response to their prayers to the Blessed Mother before the beautiful floral crown.

Early in the morning, about the time Tamaria was awakening, the Apostle Thomas came to the place where Mary's bier had been set up. He had finally arrived from India and had received the sad news of Mary's death with enormous sorrow and regret that he had not arrived in time. Now, he hurried to pay his respects and to look upon her beautiful face one last time. Peter, John, Andrew and James the Less accompanied him. The two servants were sitting, sound asleep, outside the door to the room where Mary's body had been laid. The apostles left them resting peacefully.

Peter grasped the handle to the door and opened it carefully. He was nearly engulfed in a flood of flowers that half tumbled, half floated through the doorway. When he and the other apostles recovered from their astonishment, they made their way into the room, carefully pushing aside the beautiful, if unearthly, flowers that rested lightly on the floor nearly three feet deep. They halted before the empty bier where Mary had lain then looked upwards at the ceiling. Even Thomas forgot his disappointment as the men marveled that the holy Mother of the Lord Jesus Christ now lived body and soul with Him in everlasting glory.

PRAYER

Mother of Christ,
we rejoice in you,
created to be the wheat
for the Bread of Life.

When the dark winds and the rain
drove the harvest field
to a storm of gold,
locked in His love
you were unique to God
among the multitudinous wheat,
the chosen grain for the Host.

Now, the red sheaves are bound,
the grain sifted and threshed,
the wheat in the bread.

Now, the Creator's hands
that sheltered you,
like a fended flame in the wind,
reach down from a Heaven of cloudless blue,
receiving you into eternal light.

Amen

—Caryll Houselander

QUESTIONS FOR REFLECTION

(1) Do you think there is fun in heaven? Do children play there? Do people have different personalities like they do on earth?

(2) Why do you think Jesus did not explain more about what heaven is like? He did not say too much about hell, either, and nothing about purgatory. Could it be that he wants us to focus on love and living our lives in ways that develop us as loving people? Does Jesus want us to seek heaven because we love God and our fellow human beings and not for our self-interest (to gain the good things of heaven and to avoid the horrible things of hell)? Is it possible that knowing too much about the wonderfulness of heaven would be a problem for us because it would be much more difficult to separate our own self-interest from a genuine love for others? Or is this just another unanswerable mystery for us to ponder?

(3) We have the example of St. Francis of Assisi, St. Catherine of Siena, the Venerable Anne Catherine Emmerich, and many others who mystically shared in the Passion of Christ. Do you think the Blessed Virgin Mary would have done so, as well, in the years following Jesus' ascension?

(4) What do you imagine Mary's daily activities were after Christ died and before she was assumed into heaven?

(5) What do Mary's many apparitions down through the centuries, including Guadalupe, Lourdes, Rue de Bac, La Sallette and Fatima, suggest to us about the state of the physical body in heaven? Compare Mary's reported appearances with the fact that she would have been in her early sixties, according to the best tradition, when she died and was assumed into heaven. Also, like Jesus, she appears and disappears without regard to physical barriers.

(6) Would your devotion to the Blessed Virgin Mary be the same if she had not been assumed bodily into heaven? If not, in what way would it be different?

(7) Mary is honored by Catholics as the model for Christ's Church in her obedience and discipleship and as Queen of Heaven and Earth. To what extent do you think these honors are dependent upon her having been bodily assumed into heaven and, therefore, having already achieved what Christ has promised to all of His faithful after the Last Judgment?

(8) How do you envision Mary's assumption taking place? With a multitude of angels and attending souls? With Jesus present or awaiting her in heaven? Jesus alone to take her to heaven? Other?

(9) The Blessed Virgin Mary has played a central part in salvation history. Yet there is very little written about her in Scripture and no contemporary writings outside of the New Testament books. Despite this, Mary has assumed a dominant role in the Church and in the devotions of the faithful. What message does this convey to us about patience, humility, the ways of God, worldly fame and success, and the triumph of the Spirit?

(10) Mary's bodily assumption into heaven is irrefutable proof of her sanctity and perfect holiness. Can you think of any other instances where God has demonstrated that the sanctity of a life on earth has physical consequences after death?

A great sign appeared in the sky, a woman clothed with the sun, with the moon under her feet, and on her head a crown of twelve stars. Rv 12:1

FIFTH GLORIOUS MYSTERY

The Coronation of Mary

All heaven eagerly awaited the arrival of Mary and the huge entourage of angels and saints sent to accompany her from earth. Jesus was at the entrance when Mary appeared being led by the two beaming little saints, Natali and Benjamin. This was not Jesus as mere human, however, but Jesus Transfigured as on Mount Tabor. Now revealed in his glory as the Second Person of the Holy Trinity, Jesus was a Being of Light, a transcendent brilliance in which all the love in the universe appeared to be centered. Mary, too, as she entered the heavenly realm, appeared in the spiritual glory she had merited as the Mother of God, or *Theotokos* ("God Bearer"). They, and all the other residents of heaven, remained recognizable in their human forms, but the limitations of the physical body no longer applied. Rather, like the bodies of all the Elect will be following the Last Judgment, Mary's glorified body was one that was able to transition from the solidity of flesh to the freedom of her spiritual essence.[1] This essence, or soul, contains all of the individuality of the person and manifests the holiness achieved during his or her time of testing on earth by its ability to contain and reflect the glory of the Triune God. Mary shone like the sun itself. But light in heaven is never hurtful. This light does not blind, it illuminates. Where the light is greater, the sense of union and love are greater. One "sees" with one's being, not with eyes as we use them.

---

[1] In theological terms, Mary's body took on four remarkable characteristics: it became *agile* (instant responsiveness to the wishes of the soul), *subtle* (not subject to the limitations of time and space), *impassible* (immune to pain and suffering), and possessed a *clarity* of beauty that was breathtaking. Federico Suarez, *The Afterlife* (Sinag-tala Publishers: Manila, 1989) 80-81.

Mary was unaware of her own shining brilliance. She had eyes only for her beloved Son who stood before her resplendent in incomparable beauty, kindness and goodness. To describe the infinite with finite words is, of course, far more impossible than to describe the natural beauty and qualities of the "blue planet" to people who, like Plato's cave captives, understood existence only in terms of a black-and-white-and-gray world of flickering light and shadows. But this analogy may help you to grasp the inadequacy of language in a task such as this one. In God is all existence, actual and uncreated (His own), created and potential. The "energy" or essence of God is love—love for what is good and joyful and delightful and pleasing to all the senses. Our senses in heaven are heightened so we may experience full reality as God has made it. Souls are like unblemished, sparkling crystal containers, filled to the brim with God's Love. Anyone who has ever been passionately in love knows that that condition transforms one's perception of the world. Everything appears brighter, happier, lighter, more exquisite. Sorrow and depression are totally incomprehensible when one is transported by love. Even gravity seems overcome with the sensation of floating upon smiles that have wings. Such moments seem rare on earth and flat out impossible to maintain in a world darkened by the consequences of Original Sin. But no matter how fleeting, they are probably our best insight into the unfathomable joys of heaven.

Mary was the perfection of human creation. Even more than Adam and Eve, who began in perfection, she was made immaculate from sin from the moment of her conception because she would conceive, bear and raise God the Son when He became man. Her perfection for this role, and her manner of loving and living the life God willed for her on earth, which included severe hardships and suffering, now revealed itself in heaven as love embodied in light second only to the infinite Trinity. Love seeks above all things to serve and to give, and so matching Mary's radiant splendor was a total surrender of herself to the will of God. The honors that He had planned for her generated no sense of pride or superior achievement. Such feelings do not exist in heaven. There, the greatest and holiest beings desire the most to help others in every possible way. This desire to love radiates outward from them so that all others in that joyful realm are more attracted to them than to anyone or anything else.

As Jesus extended His arms to welcome His mother to heaven, Natali and Benjamin stepped aside, brimming with the joy of being in the presence of this perfect union. The mother they had sought exceeded even their heavenly expectations. The knowledge that this would be a mutually-shared joy for all eternity was so overwhelming that the two little saints felt like they could fly right up there with the seraphim and the cherubim, the highest of the angels. Benjamin, whose five-year old spirits made him even more exuberant and perhaps a tad less sound in judgment started off to do just that, but Jesus caught him by his robe and pulled him back.

"Whoa, Benjamin. You have, indeed, mastered your flying skills and both my mother and I thank you for accompanying her here with such grace and enthusiasm. I know she will want to hear later all about your experiences, but for now I would like you and Natali to come with me to see my Father."

We already know what always happens to Benjamin's little mouth when he is surprised and this time was no exception. It fell open. Everyone in heaven sees the Face of God at all times because He is the essence of all creation. But it is still possible to have a closer encounter with Him when He wills it. Neither Benjamin nor Natali had ever had such an experience and, thus, to be invited by Jesus to visit His Father was an honor that would have caused them to faint if such a thing were possible in heaven.

"And bring the special rose you found for my mother with you. My Father has a special use for it," said Jesus to the two astonished little saints. Then He took His mother by the hand and led her away up toward the Throne of God. She reached down and handed Natali the splendid pink rose, which seemed even more beautiful since its return to heaven in Mary's possession. It was as if the flower had its own internal light which had suddenly been intensified. The color of the petals glowed with a sparkling effervescence, and a fragrance of exquisite delicacy and sweetness enveloped it.

The Throne of God was the centerpiece of heaven. Great choirs of angels and saints surrounded it in spiraling circles of magnificent colors and shapes. From here came the ineffable music that gently graced the entire realm. Each being in heaven heard this music in a format and intensity perfectly matched for her or his preference and state of holiness achieved on earth. This music was the Vision of God expressed through the ears of His blessed creatures. Such perfect love and joy were communicated through the harmony of these heavenly notes that even if all other senses were suspended, the happiness in heaven would be perfect, indescribable and unending.

On the Throne of God was to be found the Source, who is the Father, and His Self-Knowledge and Expression, who is the Son, and the Living Love, who is the Holy Spirit proceeding from Father and Son. The residents of heaven were intended to occupy different places in that Kingdom, some farther away, some nearer to this Triune Source of Life. But God could, and often did, enable those He loved to come closer than their normal proximity for special purposes. He did this by increasing the capacity of these souls to accept the blaze of His infinite love. This increase was obtained by sharing from all the residents of heaven who thereby participated in the glorification that God bestowed on these occasions. For creatures whose joy derived entirely from the love they shared, this was an increase in heavenly happiness above what had already seemed to be an impossibly joyous existence.

From the very heart of the great Circle of Light, the Three Persons of the Trinity shared their Divine Life with those who loved God. Included in that Circle was a special place for the Blessed Virgin Mary, the Holy Mother of God. She alone of all God's creatures had the capacity to remain in such proximity to the

Trinity without "borrowing" from the other residents of heaven. On the contrary, God's infinite grace and blessings for mankind would flow through her so that she would be an unending source of assistance and support to those on earth who sought to draw upon her special relationship with her Son, the Second Person of the Holy Trinity.

Jesus brought His mother here to the Center of Life to be honored for her life of service and love. All heaven gathered around to share in the ceremony. The vast multitude of souls and angels formed the petals of a gigantic living rose in which the Trinity formed the heart. In heaven, there are no bad seats, no blocked views, no video screens to compensate for distances that exceed reasonable human perception. What God sees, He can make available to all those who share His home. The sensation of having a front row seat is experienced by all.

Mary stood before the Throne of God, shining with a light nearly as bright as that of her Creator because her perfection permitted its reflection with almost no loss of brilliance. Jesus presented her to His Father and to the Holy Spirit, who was her spiritual Spouse. She knelt in perfect adoration. Her parents and Joseph were nearby and would soon have an opportunity to welcome Mary to heaven personally. But, for now, they stood in attendance upon the ceremony by which God would bless mankind ever after with a perfect friend and mother for all those who would ask for her assistance in coping with the trials, struggles and sufferings of earth.

"Children, give me your precious rose, please," said Jesus to Natali and Benjamin. They handed it over and Jesus took it, removed its stem, and placed it in the air, about three inches above Mary's head. The rose stayed where it was placed, suspended, then began to turn slowly, showing its perfect beauty and majesty to the four corners of heaven.

Then God the Father spoke, and as He did so, the rose blazed into a crown of magnificent golden effulgence, shooting off rays of white light and sparkling with flashes of living colors like a phosphorescent jewel. "Daughter, you have borne my Son, shared His life and sufferings, and enabled Him to redeem mankind from the sins which had kept all people from sharing in this glory that I have prepared for them from the foundation of the world. It is fitting, therefore, that this crown shall signify that henceforth all of the graces that shall be conferred upon mankind by my Son, earned through the infinite merits of His sacrifice for them, shall pass through your hands. By this crown, you shall be recognized as my *'Mediatrix of All Graces.'*"[2] The great circles of human souls and angelic spirits surrounding God's Throne stirred with appreciation and homage to the new Queen of Heaven.

When God the Father had finished speaking, Jesus stepped before His mother, who was still kneeling humbly before the Throne, and opened His hands

---

[2]In *Lumen Gentium*, Vatican II's Dogmatic Constitution on the Church, November 21, 1964, (§62), Mary was officially given the title of "Mediatrix," without further definition or explanation.

as if to release a small bird enclosed there. Instead of feathers, however, there appeared a small orb of dazzling white light, flashing rays in all directions, a miniature star burning with the brilliance of the Christmas Star that had once lighted the pathway of the first Gentiles to worship the Incarnate Word of God.

Taking the star, Jesus placed it in an orbit around the blazing golden crown above Mary's head. "By this star, Mary, the first in your eternal crown of glory, I declare that whatsoever you shall ask of me for mankind shall be granted. This star shall identify you as friend and intercessor until my Father's kingdom shall be restored under my hand on a New Earth when I have returned in glory. Nothing that you seek shall be denied. No favor sought for any child of earth shall be refused. Your heart, so perfectly attuned to the will of my Father, so responsive to my needs on earth, shall be a repository of love for all those who choose to come to me through your mother's understanding and concern. Accordingly, you shall be known as *'Our Lady of Perpetual Help.'"*

The Living Love at the core of the Throne which burned with the white-hot intensity of millions of suns, brilliant beyond description in its crystalline purity, emanating Itself as Spirit throughout infinity, presented Himself beside the Son before Mary. The voice which spoke from the Holy Spirit was the caress of every lover since time began, the coo of every contented baby, the touch of every healer, the joy of every sin forgiven: "Mary, this second star that I place upon your crown acknowledges your *'Immaculate Heart'* whose love for all things holy and whose faithful service to the will of God made you my fitting spouse and the Mother of God made man. In your Immaculate Heart shall all those who are called to the religious life find inspiration to seek lives of absolute selflessness and perfect purity. In your Immaculate Heart shall all people find their hope and their model for lives that are faithful to the commandments of God. In your Immaculate Heart men and women shall find the strength to turn away from corruption and easy pleasures. In your Immaculate Heart nobility shall be reborn in robes of grace."

As He placed the star in orbit with the first star around Mary's crown, the Spirit transformed into a swirl of evanescence which bloomed in fiery gold and then swept back into the Light that was Creation. All of the angels and saints felt the touch of His kiss and the fountain of love that sprang up to mark His passage. The star of the Spirit danced in flames of crimson, gold and white, incandescent with the very essence of joy and exultation.

Jesus took Mary's hands now and gently raised her to her feet. Then he turned her to face outward as he gestured toward an inner "petal" of the vast throng who were formed in layers around the Throne as a rose spreads its petals around its heart. From this circle came a delegation of souls who had died as babies and children. One small child, orphaned at birth, deprived of any other human love by cruel circumstances on earth until she perished in loneliness and neglect, carried a snow white square pillow resembling a cloud. Upon this cloud pillow rested a third star, sparkling in a multitude of bright and happy colors. When the small group arrived in front of Mary, a young boy who had given his life to save his family by going back into their burning home to rouse them, lifted the star from the pillow and, with a gentle push, launched it into orbit with the other two stars.

Jesus spoke for them and for all humanity: "Mary, this star marks you as the *'Mother of All Souls,'* especially for those who have been deprived of the maternal affection and nurturing that my Father intended all children to have. You shall be the special patron of those who have no voice, of unborn babies who are cruelly and wantonly destroyed in the womb, of children whose very souls are jeopardized because they are not shown that love exists. For them, you shall be their mother and shall grant My graces most generously to all who open their hearts to God.

"Your perfect motherhood shall be a model for all mothers on earth and your heart especially attuned to their prayers, pleas and needs for understanding, wisdom and right counsel. In your humble selflessness, all parents, fathers as well as mothers, shall see that love, self-sacrifice and service are the qualities that ennoble them and unite them to Me. In the glory that my Father confers upon you here, my people shall see that these are the qualities that define true success."

The fourth star for Mary's crown was brought forward by two people who were the ancestors for all other saints present. This star had a tiny spark gleaming within a crystal sphere of perfect clarity and, as it rotated, gave off pulses of pale blue light like lasers.

The woman spoke: "Mary, this star represents your *'Immaculate Conception'* by which you were created to be the 'New Eve.' My husband and I brought sin into the world by seeking to be like God and so we were separated from Him longer than any other human beings on earth. Your Son has borne our sins and all those which followed from our progeny who, as our children and descendants, were born with rebellious and sinful natures. In you, mankind was given a second chance. In your fidelity, redemption was made possible. In you, humanity has achieved what God intended for Adam and me. But you have greatly transcended the goodness with which we were first blessed. The price of redemption was infinite and required a New Eve far greater than I to be the mother of the Son of Man." Adam placed the star in the circle that was slowly forming around Mary's fiery golden crown.

Now came three people who truly gladdened Mary's heart to see them. They were Joachim and Anne, her parents, and Joseph, her devoted and beloved husband. *What perfect happiness to have my family with me for all eternity,* thought Mary, as the three of them approached. With them came a very impressive trio, indeed, for a woman steeped in the Jewish faith and raised in first century Palestine: Abraham, Moses and David. The star they brought gleamed like a many-faceted diamond, casting flashes of fire and color in all directions, winking its mysteries from out of its depths.

Abraham presented it before Mary and said, "Beloved daughter of Israel, O faithful one, this star designates you to be the *"Mother of All Virtues."* The first of these is faith, faith and trust that the promise of the Lord to you would be fulfilled, just as His promise to me for all the nation has been fulfilled in the salvation of God our Savior."

Moses stepped forward then to stand beside Abraham. "The second of the principal virtues is hope. On you, the hope of all mankind depended for your willingness to be the Mother of the Anointed of the Lord, the Messiah sent by God, from God, of God. As the people of Israel placed their hopes in the Lord for rescue from Egypt and protection during their exile, so the Lord placed His trust and care in your hands during His years of dependency. As Israel carried the commandments of God in the Ark of the Covenant, so you bore in your womb the Son of God. He would fulfill the law of the first Covenant with the love of the New Covenant. All of the hope of the world now rests in Him to whom you gave birth. Forever, mankind will call you 'Blessed' but, in you, mankind is equally blessed and finds its hope of salvation in your example of trust and service."

Next came David, the single most renowned and accomplished figure in Jewish history. Mary smiled to herself as she remembered her youthful expectations that the Messiah would be a "New David." He turned out to be so much more!

"Mary," said David, "it is my great honor to acknowledge you as the Mother of Love and Courage. Selfless was your life, generous were all your actions, courageous was your faith in the face of hardships and violence. What I foresaw in prophecy about the sufferings of the Messiah, you lived through and with your Son. Where I defended Israel against Goliath, you defended your Son and our Savior against the evil intentions of Herod. You stood bravely at the foot of the cross in opposition to those who crucified your Son. In you forever shall all humanity find an example of absolute love and unflinching courage."

Anne and Joachim followed David to stand before their daughter. "God has been pleased, Mary, to permit us to testify before all creation that in you all of the virtues were perfected," said Anne.

"Never did we observe a single flaw," agreed Joachim. "With perfect patience, humility, kindness and generosity you graced our time with you. Therefore, it has pleased God that you who succeeded so well in overcoming sin and temptations, and who lived a perfect and exemplary life, shall be a source of His grace until the end of time for all those who turn to you in prayer for help in becoming more virtuous."

Finally, Joseph addressed Mary: "Dearest and most holy Mary, it is my joy to say that in you I found the fullest flowering of the Holy Spirit. In you were always perfect goodness and friendship. From you I learned the full meaning of gentleness, self-control, chastity and fidelity. The home you made for our Lord and me was a beautiful perpetual garden blooming with peace, joy and love. How honored I am now to be your witness before Eternity that by this star God makes you the inspiration and help for all who struggle to achieve holiness."

The six people raised their hands to the brilliant diamond glowing above and before them and it immediately took its place in the corona of Mary's splendid crown.

The sixth star was placed upon Mary's crown by John the Baptist. He had been the last and greatest of all the Messianic prophets. He had called the people of Israel to repent, reform their lives, and thereby make a straight path for the Lord into their hearts. Now John was chosen to name Mary the *"Gate of Heaven."*

As John's star joined the other five, he said to Mary: "God graciously appointed me to be your Son's first herald, a role that I embraced even in the womb when you visited my mother. But while I announced the coming of the Lord, you were the gateway to earth for the redemption that would become the doorway to heaven for souls seeking salvation. To you are to be entrusted all the graces needed to ensure a happy death. Your life of obedience and service will forever be the model of the most perfect way to live. It pleased God to make me both symbol and messenger to call man out of the wilderness of sin and alienation. Your life teaches all how to live with the greatest assurance of being accepted into God's heavenly kingdom at the end of one's life."

From the third tier of the grand rose formation came a familiar face but one that Mary had a difficult time placing. Of course, in heaven communication is instant and nonverbal so the answer followed instantly upon the question. Here at the Throne of God, among the holiest and mightiest souls in mankind's history, stood one who had been a terrorist, robber and thief, and fervent Jewish patriot. Mary recalled the grotesque death agony that had so disfigured the face and body of Dismas as he hung crucified on his cross next to her beloved Son. To see him now resplendent in his robes of light was pure joy. Dismas carried his star high where everyone could see its golden brilliance.

"Most holy Queen of Heaven, I am honored to include in your crown of stars one that shall acknowledge you as *'Refuge of Sinners.'* I was saved by the grace of our Lord and Savior, Jesus Christ, on the very threshold of damnation. As I hung upon the cross in the most unbearable of agonies, I saw in the love of your silent attendance something more than the loyalty of a mother. There was a transcendence there, a holiness that bespoke the presence of God. Then I knew that contrary to all human reasoning, the Savior of the world hung next to me. It was you, Blessed Mother, who prompted my faith for in your eyes I beheld a world beyond that of earth. What you gave to me in opening my heart shall be available to all sinners who seek your help in the ages to come, no matter how heinous their sins or late their repentance." With that, Saint Dismas, the Good Thief, placed his star in the circle of six already rotating around Mary's head.

Another group of saints descended from a tier of the vast spiral rose and approached Mary. These were four Old Testament prophets: Isaiah, Zechariah, Jonah, Jeremiah and one, Simeon, who spanned the two divine covenants. The crystalline star they bore was tear-shaped but sparkled with joyful colors and piercing rays of dazzling white.

"My Queen," spoke Isaiah, "by the design and mercy of God, we were called to be His witnesses to our people of the sorrows that would befall them and the suffering of the Servant who would be sent to save them. We place this star in your crown to signify that you shall be known as *'Our Lady of Sorrows.'*

"There was much suffering and hardship in your own life, beginning with the gossip and scandal you endured because the Lord was begotten in your womb before your wedding date to Joseph. After that, you journeyed to Bethlehem on a donkey's back when you were great with child and gave birth to the Holy Infant in a humble stable in a cave. You were forced to flee your country to save your Child from an attempt to kill Him and to endure the rigors of that journey to and from the land of Egypt. In the Temple you learned from God's holy servant, Simeon, who stands here before you now, that tragic conflict lay in your future. Later, you would suffer terrible anxieties as you searched for the Child who had been left behind in the Temple. God was pleased to make you a widow at a young age and then to commit your Son to a public ministry which removed Him from your company. You experienced the fright and disillusionment of seeing your neighbors and friends in Nazareth attempt to kill your Son who had lived in their midst and served them well as friend and carpenter for more than 20 years. Later, you watched as your Son was condemned to the most terrible death reserved for the worst criminals, carried His cross before you, and suffered and died while you stood helpless and silent in the face of a monstrous injustice. You, yourself, were a victim of persecution and forced to live in a foreign country after your Son's death. When you longed to be reunited with Him in heaven, you were left on earth for many years to counsel and support His infant Church. Throughout your life, you were required to remain silent and patient in the face of difficulties, misunderstandings, threats and sufferings caused by your countrymen who did not understand and accept your Son and His mission. You received little recognition and few honors for all your service. All this you bore in perfect submission to God's will. Now it pleases Him to offer you to all mankind as their sorrowing mother when those whom He loves so much cry out in their sufferings against the silence of their Father in heaven."

The five prophets were immediately followed by a young woman. The star she bore was a miniature fountain of fire which flowed like a magnetic field around a ruby red heart glowing from the flames within. Her smile was so beautiful, and her eyes conveyed such love and sympathy that no one could look upon her face without being wonderfully consoled. Ever so gently, she placed her star above the crown and then said to Mary: "I am Rachel. I have mourned for the terrible sufferings of my people, Israel, when the tramp of foreign armies resounded across her lands and the cries of widows and orphans bewailed their fate. I have wept for the tragic slaughter of the babies of Bethlehem when our Lord Himself was in peril. As we have heard from our brother, Isaiah, you have experienced the tragic results of injustice and cruelty. You have wept endless tears for your own sorrow and the sorrow of others. In your sinless nature and uncompromised empathy, love has been made perfect. The sufferings of others have become your own. You were the consoler and helpmate, the great listener, for all those around you in your lifetime. Therefore, no one will ever bring a hurt, no matter how great or small, to you, O Blessed Mother of God, without gaining a sympathetic and comforting ear. For that reason, my star announces that you shall be the *'Comforter of the Afflicted.'"*

Mary, who had prayed regularly for the suffering families of the innocent baby boys slaughtered at Bethlehem, after she learned of their tragic fate, embraced Rachel. Then she said to her: "Those who suffer and mourn but persist in seeking God and in loving their neighbor will always be my special concern. We shall be good friends here."

The tenth star for Mary's crown was brought forward by the only apostle who had preceded her in death. James, son of Zebedee, brother of Mary's beloved "adopted" son, John, cradled his dazzling star close to his heart. Glowing, translucent colors of blue, pink, yellow, green, and lavender rotated through and around the little star's core of radiant white.

"Mary, mother of my Lord and Savior, Queen of Heaven, bright star of wisdom and understanding, by this star you shall be known as *'Our Lady of Good Counsel.'* As you nurtured and taught your Son, Jesus, as a child, so you nurtured and sustained His infant Church by your guidance, prayers and advice. As you helped His physical body to grow, so you have helped His mystical body. I and all the apostles joyfully acknowledge you as our mother in the spirit of the Lord whom we serve. In the centuries ahead, especially in the dark days when Satan's power shall seem to grow stronger even than the Lord's, you will be sent back to earth to remind those whom the Lord loves on how to defeat the Evil One and preserve their souls. Through children you shall speak. Signs and wonders shall accompany you. For those who heed your words and your example, you shall provide an invincible armor against the evils of that age."

From far, far up on the top tier of the surrounding host of angels and saints, three little figures flew toward Mary. As they neared, she saw they were a young soldier, or at least that was his dress, a young woman and a child, whom Mary understood to be his family. The young man spoke: "Blessed Mother, I am a nameless soldier, one who died in faithful service to my country. I gave my life for my countrymen, my family and my fellow soldiers in defense of their freedoms and their right to worship the One God in peace and according to their own rituals."

Then his wife spoke: "Blessed Mother, I am the widow of this soldier. He died to protect my freedoms and my rights but I was left alone, bereft of his love and his companionship for the many, many years remaining in my life."

Last, the child spoke: "Dear Blessed Mother, I am the child of my father who was a soldier and left me alone to be raised by my mother. She raised me true in the love of our God and the service of our people. But I missed the love and guidance of my father so much that never did I have a day without feeling the pain of his absence. As I grew up, he was not there to give me the guidance and assistance which I so often needed."

Then the three of them spoke in perfect unison: "Our star, Holy Mother of God, salutes you as the *'Queen of Peace.'* We who have suffered, and all those uncountable other souls who will yet suffer in the future because of men making war on other men, place ourselves under your special protection. Even when strife and violence wound and destroy their bodies, those who love the Lord and His Blessed Mother will find peace in their souls and salvation in their future through His grace and your prayers." The little family raised its star, a multi-pronged burst of blue and pink light which pulsated with the rhythm of a beating heart, and set it carefully among the others now streaming quite close together around the radiant gold of the rose crown.

Then from the tier next to the Throne of God itself came a magnificent angelic creature. Mary knew him instantly. She had met him in a small house in a poor village in Galilee when she was only 14 years old. He had brought a simple request. She had given a simple reply, a humble "Yes." From that tiny seed God had made the cornerstone for the Kingdom which now engulfed all the universe around her. Gabriel knelt before his Queen and echoed the words he had first said not quite half a century earlier: "**Rejoice, O highly favored daughter! The Lord is with you. Blessed are you among women.**"[3]

The first time she heard these words, Mary had been deeply troubled, disturbed in her profound humility by such a greeting from such an astounding messenger. No less humble now, she was no longer troubled by the greeting because she was in the presence of the Triune God Whom she had served so well. Her will was absolutely and completely attuned to the divine will. She accepted the honors that God bestowed upon her not in pride and satisfaction but as the servant of the Lord who would serve in heaven according to His most holy will.

Mary smiled and said, "Thank you, dearest Gabriel. You have been my special friend and companion all the days of my life. From you I learned of the Holy One's mysterious and magnificent plan of salvation. You speak truly; I am blessed among all women of all times because of the goodness and generosity of our Lord. As it pleases Him, I will magnify those blessings upon all who seek my help to find Him, to love Him, and to serve Him."

Gabriel's star, which identified Mary as the *"Queen of Angels,"* glistened with an astonishing array of the purest and most intense shafts of golden light. As he placed it into the final vacancy in Mary's crown, all heaven burst forth in a celestial hymn of praise to God for the woman He had crowned Queen of the Universe. Never before or since has heaven sung more beautifully. But the song is often replayed; in fact, its sublime melody is the first song heard by a soul who comes to God through Mary's loving intercession, or is led by her from the cleansing desolation of purgatory into the glorious beauty of the heavenly realm. As you can imagine, there is a great deal of "Mary's Theme" played there now.

As for Natali and Benjamin, they live joyfully with their families and an uncountable number of friends in the breathtaking splendor of heaven. They are

---

[3]Lk 1:28. This quote is from the 1970 New American Bible translation. The 1986 edition deletes Gabriel's words, "Blessed are you among women," because this statement is now ascribed solely to Mary's cousin, Elizabeth. Whether or not spoken by Gabriel at the Annunciation, the statement is highly appropriate for the occasion of Mary's crowning.

dearly loved by Our Blessed Mother, although no more so than all the other children there. But whenever anyone wants to hear the story of Mary's Special Garden and how her magnificent crown of glory came to be, well, there's just no better source than the two little saints. Perhaps someday you can ask them yourself.

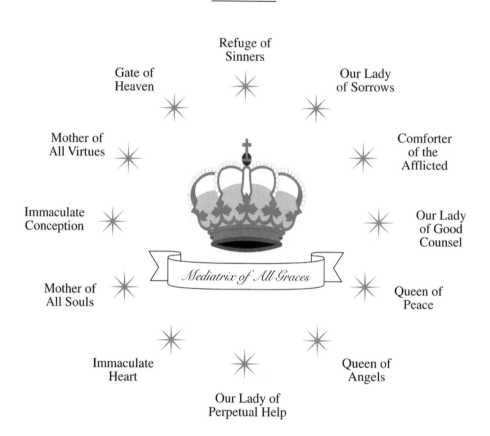

Refuge of
Sinners

Gate of
Heaven

Our Lady
of Sorrows

Mother of
All Virtues

Comforter
of the
Afflicted

Immaculate
Conception

Our Lady
of Good
Counsel

Mediatrix of All Graces

Mother of
All Souls

Queen of
Peace

Immaculate
Heart

Queen of
Angels

Our Lady of
Perpetual Help

CROWN OF MARY

**For she is the refulgence of eternal light,
the spotless mirror of the power of God,
the image of his goodness.**

Wis 7:26

QUESTIONS FOR REFLECTION

(1) What stars would you place in the Mother of God's crown if you were limited to twelve? If not limited?

(2) When you get to heaven, do you think you will be able to see the great coronation ceremony for Mary, or are you afraid Jesus will say, "Gee, I'm sorry, but, unfortunately, VCRs hadn't been invented yet?"

(3) In the light of the way Mary lived her life, and the unequaled honoring of her by God, what message can you find there for your own values and yardsticks of success? What are Mary's virtues, anyway?

(4) Given the clear and repeated lessons of Scripture and the example of hundreds of officially-recognized saints, why do most of us still run first after the things of this world and only secondarily after the virtues of love, humility and self-sacrifice? Why is it so difficult for us to accept the will of God in our lives, seeing that the painful even more than the joyful things will bring us closer to Him if embraced in a spirit of acceptance and voluntary sharing in the sufferings of Jesus Christ?

(5) When you think of the Blessed Virgin Mary, do you think of her as Queen or as Mother? There is a story of a young medieval nun on her deathbed who exclaimed to her Mother Superior, "Oh, Mother, soon I will see Our Blessed Mother!" The Superior replied, "Yes, but don't forget that she is a queen!" What, if anything, is wrong with the Mother Superior's advice? What does it mean to be the Queen of Heaven?

(6) Protestants often question why Catholics pray to Mary. Can you answer them correctly? The *Catechism of the Catholic Church* tells us about Mary:
> "In a wholly singular way she cooperated by her obedience, faith, hope, and burning charity in the Savior's work of restoring supernatural life to souls. For this reason she is a mother to us in the order of grace."

The *Catechism* goes on to note that Mary, taken up to heaven:
> "by her manifold intercession continues to bring us the gifts of eternal salvation . . . Therefore the Blessed Virgin is invoked in the Church under the titles of Advocate, Helper, Benefactress, and Mediatrix."[4]

---

[4] ¶s 968-969

What words would you use to explain why you pray to Mary, being careful, of course, to always note that Mary does not help of her own authority nor dispense grace of her own making?

(7) There is another story told, a joke actually, that Jesus was walking around heaven one day and noticed a few souls who seemed scruffier than the souls in heaven are supposed to be. So He asked St. Peter why he let those people in before they were ready. St. Peter replied, "I told them they could not come in, but they went around to the back gate and your mother let them in." Does this funny little story fit your image of the Blessed Virgin Mary? Why or why not?

(8) When you get to heaven do you think you will be friends with the Blessed Virgin Mary? Close friends? Merely an awe-struck fan? Something in between?

(9) For 2,000 years, Mary has been Christ's emissary on earth. What do you know about her Church-sanctioned appearances and signs/wonders? Have you yourself had any miraculous, or at least inexplicable, experiences related to Mary?

(10) What images and hopes for heaven do you have?

COMMENTARIES ON THE MYSTERIES

THE JOYFUL MYSTERIES

First Joyful Mystery, the Annunciation

This mystery finds Mary in Nazareth in the loving home of her parents, Anne and Joachim. Joseph is portrayed as a man of 25-30 rather than the elderly widower of some traditions. The story includes a version of the tradition regarding the birth of Mary as reported in *Butler's Lives of the Saints*, vol. 3, pp. 189-90.

Mary as a Child

Almost all of the stories that purport to describe Mary's parents and early childhood are derived from the apocryphal work, *The Protoevangelium of James.*[1] This is more-or-less the version presented by the mystics. There are several elements in these stories that are inherently improbable and almost no established scholar today accepts them as historically valid. Nonetheless, *Mystery Stories: A Journey Through the Rosary* is not intended to be a scholarly analysis of the various contending arguments. Nor is it intended to disturb anyone's preferred version of events for their own meditations. Given no reliable historical or archaeological data, I have presented Anne, Joachim and Mary's childhood in ways that attempt to capture Mary's unique character as a person conceived without Original Sin and her divinely ordained role to be the Mother of God, but, at the same time, retaining their character as a family living in the ordinary circumstances of a small Jewish village in ancient Palestine.

The fictional incidents are intended to give personality to Joseph and Mary. I imagine them to be people most of us would like to have as friends, blessed with a sense of humor, behaving as normal members of their society and time.

Some may question whether Mary, a Middle Eastern woman of Semitic origins, could have had blue eyes. Those who prefer to visualize Mary with brown or dark eyes are certainly free to do so. But Saint Bernadette Soubirous, of Lourdes, France, reported in her description of the Blessed Virgin Mary when she appeared to the young Bernadette in the Lourdes grotto that Mary's eyes were blue.[2]

---

[1] Porter, *Jesus Christ: The Jesus of History, the Christ of Faith*, 58.

[2] See Francis Trochu, *Saint Bernadette Soubirous, 1844-1879*, trans. John Joyce, S.J. (New York: Pantheon Books, 1957), 43.

The Virginity of Mary

Possibly the most frequently used title referring to Mary is "Blessed Virgin Mary." Mary's perpetual virginity has always been a central tenet of Catholic dogma.[3] There have been numerous writings on the subject, some of which are cited in the bibliography to this book. The Gospel of Luke refers to Mary as a virgin (Lk 1:27). Her reply to the Angel Gabriel at the Annunciation also indicates that she is a virgin.[4] Many scholars, theologians and even some saints have interpreted this language to *require* a vow of perpetual virginity by Mary, for otherwise her response, goes the reasoning, should have addressed the question of timing, and not what appears to be a permanent obstacle to what the angel has just told her is to take place. Making Joseph an elderly widower, with children from an earlier marriage, then explains subsequent scriptural references to the "brothers and sisters" of Jesus.[5] It also makes an agreement to honor a young fiancee's vow of virginity more palatable in the scheme of normal human relationships.

Joseph: Elderly Widower or Mary's Suitor?

But there are aspects of this particular tradition that are disturbing to me. Personally, I would rather imagine Mary being married to someone nearer her own age than one old enough to be her father, maybe even her grandfather. I am convinced that Joseph would have been a dear friend and close companion to her, that they would have shared similar outlooks, identical values, a sense of humor and joy, an exuberance for living. Surely these are the elements that the Lord wishes all of us to find in our own marriages. It seems unlikely that he would not have arranged them for his own family on earth.

Further, I see Joseph as a heroic figure, a man with great character, faith, understanding, courage and devotion. What better way to manifest that than to have him understand and accept the implications of Mary's miraculous conception of Jesus by the Holy Spirit? From that moment on, the spiritual bond between two people, which is established by the act that brings new life into the world, existed between Mary and the Holy Spirit. Only by being unfaithful to her true Spouse could Mary have had a normal sexual relationship with Joseph after that. In an age when sex is deemed the supreme good, and denial of it the supreme injustice, this sacrifice required of Joseph may seem to be harsh and cruel. But sex has value only to the extent that it advances our growth in the love of God and one another. In some circumstances, such as when religious persons have taken vows of chastity

---

[3]The First Lateran Council declared in 649 that Mary was "ever virgin and immaculate." Father William Saunders, "Brothers and Sisters of Jesus: A Misunderstanding of Word Meaning," *Arlington Catholic Herald*, January 16, 1997.

[4]Lk 1:34: "Mary said to the angel, 'How can this be since I do not know man?'"

[5]See, e.g., Mark 3:31-32, 6:3.

in order to acknowledge their dedication to a higher good, sex is antithetical to a growth in love and holiness. Certainly, the household of the Holy Family must have been a veritable fountain of charity and holiness. In such an environment, it seems reasonable to assume that God provided all the graces necessary to live joyfully without experiencing any sense of loss from the lack of a sexual relationship.

Prenuptial Vows of Virginity?

The foregoing explanation for Mary and Joseph's decision to remain virgins throughout their married life also avoids the incongruity of having two people take prenuptial vows of virginity in a society which not only placed no value on such an action but, rather, perceived barrenness as a sign of disfavor from God. The Jewish people accepted as their personal mandate, within the institution of marriage, God's command in Genesis: **"Be fertile and multiply and fill the earth."**[6] Children were the great blessing of families in ancient times. Not only were they needed to contribute labor and resources to the livelihood and protection of the family, but they were also the "social security system" for aging parents.

There is also the element of purpose involved in entering into a marriage contract with the deliberate intention of remaining chaste and childless. Such an intention on the part of one party to a marriage has long been considered as invalidating the union and affording a right to annulment by the Church, since one of the most fundamental purposes of marriage, procreation, would be frustrated and denied. When both parties agree to live chastely, of course, the element of deception is removed, but the fundamental purpose of marriage remains unfulfilled in such situations. Why would Mary and Joseph be attracted to such an arrangement before the Annunciation? The traditional response has been that Mary needed someone to look out for her and provide for her economic needs. With numerous children of his own already, Joseph is portrayed as disinterested in having more children and willing to honor the request for chastity by Mary. In return, of course, he gets the cleaning, cooking and household maintenance services of a wife. It is hard not to be a little disappointed in the practicality of it all. I prefer to think of Mary and Joseph as being very much in love with each other. I see them as wonderfully noble and true heroes in their willingness to respond completely to God's call to change the rules somewhat in order to accomplish His plan of salvation for mankind.

But what about Mary's response to Gabriel? If she had not taken a vow of virginity, why didn't she just say, "When?" instead of pointing out her lack of a carnal relationship? To answer this question, I think we need to remember that we are trying to interpret words on paper. Mary heard the words from an angel, probably speaking as Mary herself has done to privileged souls who have seen her

---

[6]Gn 9:1

in apparitions down through the ages; i.e., not with words that travel on air currents to anyone within earshot, but in communications that are heard in the mind and heart only of the person intended to receive them.[7] In these cases, there seems never to be a problem understanding what is intended to be understood. In other words, these heavenly messengers know how to say what they mean. In this light, Mary would have understood Gabriel's reference to her conception of the Son of God as being intended to take place immediately. Thus her response would also have referred to her present situation and not to a permanent obstacle.

But What About the "Brothers and Sisters" of Jesus?

But there are still those brothers and sisters of Jesus referenced in the Gospels. How can this be reconciled with Mary's permanent virginity? As I have noted, one answer has been to assert that they were half-brothers and half-sisters of Jesus, children by Joseph in an earlier marriage. Again, this may be true. But an equally plausible explanation is that they were cousins of Jesus, children of siblings of Joseph or Mary. Hebrew and Aramaic, the languages of ancient Palestine, used the same word for cousins as it did for siblings. Extended families routinely lived in close geographical proximity with one another and their members tended to regard themselves as parts of a single family rather than the separate nuclear families which are the norm in modern society. When the Gospels were written in Greek, the word *adelphos* was used for these family relationships. That word, too, includes extended family, not merely blood brothers and sisters.[8]

Thus the words of Scripture do not tell us whether Mary had other children. However, it is significant that no one, except Jesus, is ever referred to explicitly as a child of Mary. Mark's reference to James and Joses as the brothers of Jesus (see Mark 6:3) must be read in the light of Mark 15:40, where we learn that James and Joses are the sons of Mary of Clopas. For both statements to be correct, Mary of Clopas must have been Mary's sister-in-law or her sibling. Sister-in-law seems more likely, if for no other reason than that the two women have the same first name.

Furthermore, because of the recognized mutuality of family obligations, and the Jewish custom of assigning responsibility for the care of a widowed mother to the eldest son, it would have been insulting for Jesus on the cross to designate John to care for Mary if she had other children to perform that function. It would at the very least have indicated that Mary's family was dysfunctional, which seems highly unlikely. This is additional scriptural evidence that Jesus was an only child. Moreover, it lends weight to the cousin theory, rather than the half-

---

[7]For example, during the apparitions at Fatima, the young boy, Francisco, could not hear what the Blessed Virgin Mary was saying to Lucia and Jacinta, who were kneeling right beside him. He could only see her. *Fatima in Lucia's Own Words*, 130, 162.

[8]I am indebted to Father William Saunders for his excellent article on this subject, referenced in note 3 above.

brother theory, because the family support obligation would presumably have applied to the oldest stepson, as well. Only if Mary has no immediate family members living does Jesus' instruction from the cross really make sense.[9]

Mary Was Unique

Finally, while remembering that Mary once lived on earth as a normal member of her society and time, the same way everyone has lived throughout the history of the human race, we must also acknowledge that she was the only person ever to be conceived by two human parents without the stain of Original Sin. In this sense, she was fundamentally different from you and me in that she would not have been subject to confusion and compromise in her attraction for and love of God. Would such a nature have made her adverse to a sexual relationship with her husband?[10] Certainly the bond between her and our Creator would have been much stronger and much more pure. But we know that she had a normal human body in most respects. She herself was conceived and born in the normal way. She grew up. Although some speculate that she was immune from disease and physical suffering (even aging), pain is actually a blessing from God given to man to warn of dangers to survival and well-being in a physical world.

It seems unlikely that we will have a definitive answer in this life as to the effect Mary's immaculate conception had on her physical make-up. Perhaps it did propel her to an early determination to remain a virgin, leading to such a vow as a young girl even in a society that looked upon childlessness as a curse. But since the Gospels give us a picture of Jesus and Mary as being like us in all ways except sin, and because sex within marriage is not sinful, I tend to believe that Mary was probably normal in this sense even if her mystical relationship with God was also dominant.[11] What this means is that I would expect Mary to have entered into the marriage contract with Joseph expecting to live as a normal wife and mother, perhaps feeling torn by a desire to give her life to God, but committed to living as

---

[9]*The New Catholic Encyclopedia* states: "There is no probability to the theory of the *Protoevangelium Jacobi*, Origen, and Ambrosiaster (PL 17:344-345) that 'the brothers of Jesus' were the children of Joseph by an earlier marriage." Ed. Catholic University of America (New York: McGraw Hill, 1967), v. 2, 822.

[10]It is also worth noting the words of Genesis 3:16, where God tells Eve after she and Adam have sinned that she will bring forth children in pain "[y]et your urge shall be for your husband." Because Mary was conceived without original sin, the Church has taught for centuries that her delivery of Jesus would have been free of pain since she would not have fallen under the curse imposed by God. Similarly, all her desire may have flowed toward God and none for a sexual relationship with a man.

[11]The issue comes down to whether Mary's freedom from sin would have released her from all the ills that plague human beings as a result of the Fall of Man; or, whether she would have borne those infirmities as part of her sharing in the redemptive actions of Christ. During her earthly life, was Mary on a pedestal as the Queen she was to become, or was she in the trenches with Jesus, experiencing life the same way everyone else did?

her Jewish faith and society advocated. As we know, the Angel Gabriel's visit changed all that forever.

Second Joyful Mystery, the Visitation

Some traditions have Mary remaining with Elizabeth until after the birth of John the Baptist. But Luke states that Mary stayed with Elizabeth about three months and then returned home.[12] The birth and naming of John are described after this verse, which suggests that Mary left before they took place. Further, Elizabeth and Zechariah would have been concerned about Mary's own growing pregnancy and the fact that Joseph was unaware of it.

John the Baptist in the Desert

There is a tradition that John the Baptist grew up in the desert, released by his parents at an early age into the service of God. Luke's Gospel seems to say as much in 1:80. There is also a tradition that Herod the Great attempted to kill the child. This is quite plausible. Herod the Great was notoriously paranoid, to the point of killing many of his own family, including his beloved wife, Mariamne. After the visit of the Wise Men following Jesus' birth, it seems very likely that Herod would have decided that perhaps John the Baptist, born just a few months before Jesus and heralded by an angel, was part of God's conspiracy against him. To save the child's life, Zechariah and Elizabeth may well have hidden John in a local Essene community, the ascetic Jewish equivalent of a Christian monastery. The Dead Sea Scrolls have been attributed to one or more of these communities.

Third Joyful Mystery, the Nativity

Are the Infancy Narratives of Luke and Matthew Contradictory?

This story reconciles the two nativity narratives of Matthew and Luke. A distressing characteristic of modern Bible scholarship is to suggest that the Gospel writers invented facts to convey spiritual truths. The multifaith Jesus Seminar[13] has taken this approach to such an extreme as to practically eliminate the reality of Jesus Christ himself. Such inconsistencies as exist in the Gospels seem more likely to have been the result of variable witness perspective, alternative versions of events from people who experienced them at different times and under different

---

[12] Lk 1:56

[13] See "The Gospel Truth," *Time*, April 8, 1996, 52-59. According to this article, the members of the Jesus Seminar conclude that it is probable that Christ did not rise from the dead at all and that most of what is in the Gospels was fabricated.

conditions, narrative details that the author thought were accurate enough, editorial adjustments of language and phrasing, or an intent by the Gospel writers to emphasize certain aspects for a specific audience. It seems entirely unnecessary, and disturbing, to suggest that Luke, who ends his nativity story with the Holy Family returning to Nazareth, is incompatible with Matthew, who sends them to Egypt. On the contrary, Herod's inquiry of the time of the star's appearance and the use of that date by both him and the Magi to fix the birth date of Jesus is strong internal evidence that the Wise Men did not arrive in Bethlehem until well after that first momentous night.[14]

Herod's slaughter of male babies two years old and younger also suggests that the Holy Infant was not a literal newborn.[15] Although he was a brutal and insecure man, Herod was also a politically skilled ruler who established a long period of peace and prosperity for his expanded kingdom. He would probably not have ordered the slaughter of any more children than he deemed necessary to include the Messiah in his nefarious net. A newborn baby is easily distinguished even from babies one year old.

There would have been a natural incentive for Mary and Joseph to return to Nazareth after Jesus was born. This was their home. In a society in which the members of extended families routinely lived near one another, the normal and expected decision would have been to return to Nazareth to live. At the very least, there would have been a strong, natural desire within the family to see their newest member, especially if one or both of Mary's parents were still alive and knew that this baby was the Messiah.

Having returned to Nazareth for awhile, it is equally plausible that Mary and Joseph might have decided to go back to Bethlehem. They would have been considering not only the prophecy concerning the origin of the Messiah, but also Herod's grand building schemes and Jerusalem's economic prosperity. These were generating substantial employment for thousands of craftsmen like Joseph. Further, Mary's pregnancy before she was actually wed to Joseph was probably a source of gossip as a minor scandal in Nazareth, so the social environment there may have been uncomfortable for the Holy Family.

Once the round trip is completed, any inconsistencies between Matthew and Luke dwindle to wondering why they did not both report the same things. The use of selective facts is entirely understandable, however, if the authors had different objectives in mind when writing their Gospels. Nearly all Scripture scholars recognize that the Gospel writers did, indeed, have specific and varying objectives and audiences in mind when they wrote their lives of Christ. For example, Luke wrote his Gospel primarily for the Gentiles. Matthew's, on the other hand, is clearly directed to his own people, the Jews in Palestine. The trip to Egypt

---

[14]See Mt 2:7.

[15]See Porter, *Jesus Christ*, 71.

and the calling out of the Son from Egypt had prophetic resonances for the Jews. It would have had no such meaning for the Gentiles. This alone may account for the story's inclusion in Matthew and exclusion in Luke.

Note, also, that Luke does not include in his Passion Narrative the scourging of Jesus and his crowning with thorns. Yet no serious scholar has suggested that this presents a significant conflict with the Gospel writers who do include the incidents.

The fact is that authors writing about the same subject often make editorial decisions to include or exclude something based upon whether it has been addressed adequately by another author. Some common ground is necessary, of course, when the subject matter is the same. But only the Gospel authors could tell us exactly why they wrote their Gospels the way they did.

Who Were the Magi?

There is no consensus about exactly who the three Magi were. Psalm 72:10 refers to tribute to the Messiah from the **"kings of Tarshish and the Isles . . . the kings of Arabia and Seba . . ."** Isaiah 60:6 says: **"All from Sheba shall come/ bearing gold and frankincense . . ."** A sixth century Syriac work, *Cave of Treasures*, describes the Magi as kings of Persia, Saba and Sheba. By the sixth century, they had been named Melchior, Gaspar and Balthasar. The *Armenian Infancy Gospel* identified Melchior as being from Persia, Gaspar from India and Balthasar from Arabia. Melchior has traditionally been regarded as an elderly man, who brought the gold to signify Christ's kingship. Gaspar has been a much younger man, who brought the frankincense to signify Christ's divinity. Balthasar was, according to these traditions, black-skinned and bearded, who brought the myrrh to signify Christ's redemptive suffering and death.

What Was the Star of Bethlehem?

There has been a great deal of scholarly speculation about the Christmas Star. Attempts have been made to identify it with exploding supernovas, or unusual conjunctions of planets and stars, or a comet. Such a natural celestial occurrence would have attracted the attention of ancient astronomers (who were actually more like astrologers). These men might then, as illustrated in the story, have determined that the sign presaged a dramatic event in Israel. They would naturally have traveled to Israel's capital, Jerusalem, to inquire, as we are told in Matthew's narrative, making the assumption that the nation would be rejoicing over such a great gift. But one thing an astronomical event could not do is identify a specific place on earth where Jesus could be found, which is exactly what this star did. Furthermore, apparently no one else, including the Jewish skywatchers, noted the star that the Magi found so significant.

All in all, the simplest explanation is the most likely: God wanted to attract these men to pay homage to His Son, probably mostly for the symbolism of the Gentile world's recognition of Jesus earlier than the Chosen People to whom He was sent, and maybe partly for other reasons. Therefore, He made sure they saw the kind of "sign" that would draw them to seek out the newly born Jesus. There may have been natural "signs in the heavens," too, at the time Jesus was born. God may have wanted to serve this kind of notice on the ancient world. But it seems most likely that the Christmas Star that led the Magi to the house of the Holy Family in Bethlehem must have been like the "miracle of the sun" reported at Fatima and Medjugorje. This phenomenon is one that seems absolutely real to those viewing it, but is not always seen by others in the same vicinity. Usually there is no reported meteorological effect. So obviously there is a spiritual dimension to these signs that is controlled by God. Equally obvious, the birth of His Son was the most appropriate occasion in history for God to employ a similar device to lead a small group of worshipers to the residence of Jesus in Bethlehem.

In 7 B.C. there were, in fact, remarkable astronomical signs in the heavens, as described in the Nativity story. It is also a plausible year for the birth of Jesus because it accords with other historical data placing the death of Herod the Great in 4 B.C. Thus, Jesus would be born in 7 B.C., depart for Egypt six or seven months later, and return to Israel sometime in or after 4 B.C. This timing also places his visit to the Temple of Jerusalem at age 12 (see the fifth joyful mystery) during a time, or not long after, of Jewish rebellion against the heavy-handed rule of Herod Archelaus. Protests from the Jewish people led to Herod's banishment by Caesar Augustus and the imposition of direct Roman rule by procurator in the province of Judea.[16]

How did Jesus end up being born six or so years before himself? The modern calendar was determined by a monk named Dionysius Exiguus (Denis the Short) who in 533 proposed measuring time from the birth of Christ rather than the foundation of Rome. Unfortunately, his calculations were off by several years.[17]

Rachel's Lamentations

The quotation in Mt 2:18 about Rachel mourning her lost children is from Jeremiah 31:15 and most likely refers to the forced deportation of the tribes of the Northern Kingdom of Israel by the Assyrians in 722-721 B.C. It may also refer to the conquest and deportation of the tribe of Judah and residents of Jerusalem by the Babylonians in 597 and 587 B.C. Matthew borrows the vivid imagery and extends it to the oppression of those who will be associated with the New Covenant established through God's Son.[18]

---

[16]However, such an early birth year for Jesus raises questions on the other end in reconciling the Passover dates, Good Friday, and Jesus' age at the time of his crucifixion of around 33.

[17]Raymond Brown, S.S., *The Birth of the Messiah* (Garden City, NY: Doubleday, 1977), 167.

[18]See, ibid., n. 18, 205-206.

Normal or Miraculous Birth?

One important question concerning the birth of Jesus remains: was it a normal birth, or a miraculous delivery akin to Jesus' materializing through walls (and apparently his tomb at the Resurrection)? The Church's teaching is clear and of ancient derivation, so for Catholics that must be the answer. The *Catechism of the Catholic Church* tells us in ¶499:

> The deepening of faith in the virginal motherhood led the Church to confess Mary's real and perpetual virginity even in the act of giving birth to the Son of God made man.

But this does not prevent us from examining the matter to see what the issues are and what arguments can be made to support the Church's position (in the absence of historical evidence or Scriptural testimony, which, of course, would be the best of all).

Let us acknowledge a First Principle: as a person free from original sin, Mary was also entitled to be free from the consequences of original sin, which includes painful childbirth and, presumably, all of the other aches and hardships of life on earth. But, then, so was Jesus, even more so. But Jesus came into the world to share our common humanity (other than sin, of course) so that we would be able to find hope and consolation in him and strength and courage in his example of humility, hard work and patient suffering. Most of all, in Jesus we have an almost incomprehensible example of love. Wouldn't God want the mother of His Son to have the same value for sinful humanity? It is not for her privileges that we love Mary. We love her because of her courage, faithfulness, humility, generosity and selfless suffering in support of the divine redemptive mission of her Son. We love her because she was unhesitatingly obedient to the will of God in the face of what seem like terrifying uncertainties. The more these qualities existed in her life, the more heroic her life was and the more inspiring Mary is for us as we struggle through our own "vale of tears." In this sense, a normal childbirth after the long, difficult trip from Nazareth, borne in love and perfect submission to the will of God, would be powerful testimony to us to accept our crosses and follow the example of Mary despite circumstances that seem to be unfair or even cruel.

Yet there are convincing reasons to believe that the birth of Jesus was, indeed, miraculous. Mary's journey from Nazareth in winter on a donkey near the end of term in her pregnancy would have been extremely difficult for her. She almost certainly made this trip voluntarily. It would be surprising if she did not feel some anxiety in Bethlehem while Joseph searched unsuccessfully for a place for her to deliver her baby. And a stable is obviously not an ideal place for such an event. She most likely felt some initial labor pains, or at least the discomfort of carrying a full-term baby, because this is the means by which women's bodies tell them what is going on and warn them to get prepared for further developments. So, in this sense, Mary was like Abraham when God asked him to sacrifice his son,

Isaac. God let him make all the preparations and suffer the anguish of the process but stopped him from actually carrying out the act, even though God could have let Abraham do it and then resurrected Isaac. God chose in His love not to require of the founder of the Chosen People the sacrifice He would impose upon Himself and His Son. Similarly, it seems likely that God would have, in His goodness and kindness, willed to spare Mary the pain that we explicitly associate with Eve's original sin.

Two other reasons for believing that Jesus' birth was miraculous relate to Mary's virginity. Although virginity has to do with sex, and not with birth, the fact is that Mary was the only woman in history for whom birth of a child was not connected with a human father. Since God had decreed that His Son would be born of a virgin through the power of the Holy Spirit, logic suggests that He would have preserved Mary from this particular consequence of the loss of virginity, a consequence which necessarily implies such a loss. In other words, the miraculous birth complements and reinforces the miraculous conception.

From another perspective, God asked Mary to embrace the Holy Spirit as her divine Spouse. The conception from that union was supernatural. The life which Mary would lead thereafter would involve a mystical union and not the physical union which is normal between husband and wife. Again, it seems likely that God would have granted Mary the benefits of virginity since she was asked to give up what most people regard, at least initially, as the chief benefit of marriage.

Finally, the entrance of Jesus into the world was both humble and spectacular. Humble in its physical circumstances but spectacular in the announcement by the multitude of angels to the shepherds in the fields and the celestial summoning of the Magi from the East. Just as Jesus combined the normal aspects of human life with occasional astonishing displays of his divine power, so his birth seems like the perfect occasion to combine the onerous circumstances of birth in a cave stable with the awesome power of a supernatural delivery. One might think of it as God putting His personal imprint on this most momentous of occasions.

Fourth Joyful Mystery, the Presentation in the Temple

The Law of Moses

Under Jewish law, the first-born male child had to be redeemed from God by the payment of five shekels. This commemorated the sparing by God of the Israelites' first-born at the time of the first "passover" in Egypt. In addition, women were ritually unclean for seven days following childbirth and not permitted to participate in religious ceremonies for forty days (eighty days if the child was female). Ritual purification for the mother was accomplished by the sacrifice of animals, a minimum of two doves or pigeons if the family could not afford a lamb or sheep.

The Temple Treasury

The Temple contained several treasury chambers earmarked for certain funds and purposes. For example, there was the Shekel Chamber, which received the annual half-shekel tax imposed upon all Jewish men. There were chambers for the storage of gold and silver utensils used in the worship rituals, for the assistance of needy members of good families, and even for private safekeeping, much like safe deposit boxes today. In addition, the Court of the Women contained thirteen chests with funnel-shaped *shofars* (hollow rams' horns) on their tops to receive individual, voluntary contributions. These were used to defray the costs of sacrifice and Temple maintenance. It was into one of these that the widow deposited her "mite," leading Jesus to point out that God measures gifts by the size of the sacrifice, not the size of the gift.[19]

Romans in Palestine; Simeon and Anna

The encounter between Mary and Joseph and the Roman soldiers is imaginative, although quite plausible since Roman law gave soldiers the right to demand that civilians carry their baggage for up to one Roman mile. This fictional episode illustrates a facet of life in Palestine in that time and suggests reflections upon the possible effects of the Holy Spirit upon Mary in an everyday situation.

The story also presents a probable relationship between Simeon and Anna, two holy persons gifted with unique insights and expectations regarding the arrival of Israel's Messiah.

Fifth Joyful Mystery, the Finding in the Temple

The Search for the Child Jesus

There is a great deal of drama implied in Luke's fairly short description of this event in the life of the Holy Family. From Mary's words when she and Joseph finally found Jesus after three days, it seems that the emotions experienced by the two parents during this time were very much like you or I would feel in similar circumstances with our own children. The incidents included in this mystery are imaginative but plausible for the times and circumstances. They thus serve to develop our appreciation for just how stressful the search for Jesus probably was.

---

[19]Mk 12:41-44, Lk 21:1-4

What Were Jesus and the Elders Saying to One Another?

We also do not know what it was that Jesus was saying and asking which so impressed the teachers in the Temple. But given his response to his mother's question, and his fundamental mission on earth, it seems likely that he would have been discussing various aspects of Israel's expectations regarding the Messiah. This was a common and fertile topic for discussion at the time. We can be certain that the verbal exchanges dealt with some aspect of the relationship of Israel to God. The educational system for Jewish males considered practically nothing else.

Questions Scripture Does Not Answer

In the context of these stories, the hypothetical dialogue and situations serve to highlight certain points of reflection, which constitute the heart of the mystery. For example, why did Jesus remain behind? Was it accidental or did he plan it? Why didn't God send an angel to tell Mary and Joseph that Jesus was okay and where and when to find him? Where did Jesus spend the two nights he was separated from his parents? Why were Mary and Joseph so anxious? What did they say to each other in discussing what had happened? How did they interpret Simeon's prophecy? What did they think Jesus meant in his response to them since Luke expressly notes they did not understand? Or was it only later that Mary realized that Jesus' answer was more complex than the apparent query about why she and Joseph had not realized that Jesus would wait for them in the Temple? What was Jesus like as a 12-year old boy?

THE SORROWFUL MYSTERIES

Reflection upon the mysteries of the rosary may be narrowly focused upon the specific event mentioned or broadly focused to include the context and surrounding events which are relevant to the specific mystery element. I believe the broad focus is much more meaningful for meditation upon the profound spiritual issues represented by the mysteries of the rosary.

When considering the five sorrowful mysteries, a full understanding of what was transpiring and how all the events came together to produce Christ's Passion requires an awareness of the full drama of Holy Week. Certainly, it makes the story more understandable and more interesting. Consequently, I have included most of the major points mentioned by the four Gospel writers in these stories. As before, I have used imaginative dialogue, characterizations, minor events and some characters to create a coherent and seamless narrative. All of these additions are plausible, however, and could have happened the way I have described them. Therefore, they are appropriate for reflection. As I have noted already, however, readers who imagine other versions of these events, so long as they are compatible with the words of Scripture, are doing exactly what the mysteries of the rosary invite us to do: delve into their facts and circumstances and determine from those what their meaning is for us today.

First Sorrowful Mystery, the Agony in the Garden

This is the first mystery of Christ's Passion. Holy Week begins with Jesus' triumphal entry into Jerusalem and that is about where I begin the story for this mystery.

The Enigma of Judas

One of the enduring fascinations about these events concerns the motivation of Judas. Was he a black-hearted evil man, almost diabolical? Or did he convince himself that what he was doing was harmless, or even beneficial? Was his primary motivation the thirty pieces of silver? Why was he not influenced by Jesus' miracles? Or was he? Was his betrayal entirely at his own initiative, or did one or more of the Jewish authorities approach him first? Franco Zeffirelli's great television production, *Jesus of Nazareth,* portrayed Judas as well-meaning but dense, betraying Jesus under the impression that he was doing what Jesus wanted him to do and not considering that it would be the means for the condemnation of the Lord. This is the benign view of Judas. The harsh view is represented possibly by the Gospel of John who says of Judas that "**Satan entered his heart,**"[20] and that he had been induced by the devil to hand Jesus over. Whatever characterization is selected, it must be consistent with the known facts: Judas, who was a member of Jesus' inner circle and had witnessed up to three years' worth of incredible miracles, betrayed Jesus for the relatively paltry sum of thirty silver coins, then regretted his action and committed suicide within hours after Jesus was condemned to death.

Possible Answers to Some Interesting Questions

Other interesting issues raised in the Gospel accounts of these events include the mysterious arrangements (man carrying a water jar) for the Upper Room (the Cenacle) where Jesus and the apostles would celebrate the Last Supper, and the young man in the linen cloth who runs away naked after Jesus is captured. This latter incident is reported only in Mark's Gospel. In his book, *The Day Christ Died*, Jim Bishop identified the young man as Mark himself.[21] I think this is plausible, especially if we place Mark in the house where the Upper Room was located. Since this was very near to the palace of the High Priest Caiaphas, Bishop's suggestion that Mark has run out in his "pajamas" to warn Jesus makes

---

[20]Jn 13:27

[21]New York: Harper & Row, 1957, 208, 219.

sense. It would also explain the "disciple who was known to the high priest"[22] because Mark would have been a neighbor of Caiaphas and Annas. His own family must have had wealth and position given the neighborhood in which they lived. This also resolves a problem with the tradition that John himself was the disciple known to the high priest. How could a fisherman from the province of Galilee be known to the high priest in Jerusalem? It is not impossible, of course. It might have been through his father, Zebedee, who was by tradition a prosperous businessman with a fleet of fishing boats. But, if so, where was James, John's brother? All in all, the Mark connection seems more plausible.

However, there is the problem that only John describes the interrogation before Annas. He also gives more details about Peter's entrance into the courtyard of the high priest. If Mark were the one present, one would think these things would have been reported by him. But, then again, Mark's Gospel is the most spare and may reflect a deliberate decision by Mark to focus upon the essential elements of Christ's ministry and omit extraneous details, even those that involved him personally. His inclusion of the apparently irrelevant report of the young man nearly apprehended while following Jesus[23] may have been intended simply to establish his bona fides as a reporter.

Should All These New Testament Events Be Taken Literally?

The weakest suggestion is that there was no real person in a linen cloth who ran away naked, that he was just a literary device to represent the separation of Jesus from divine assistance for the duration of his Passion. Until the scholars can produce solid proof that the Gospel writers invented facts, I believe we have to accept their factual reporting as representing real situations. There is nothing in the four Gospels to suggest that their authors were trying to do anything other than lay out the facts of Christ's life as best they could, so that people would see that these events identified him as the Messiah sent by God. Luke says this explicitly (1:1-4). This does not mean that they did not synthesize dialogue and situations to present the meaning which they conveyed. Even a rudimentary study of the Gospels reveals that the four authors do not consistently report events in the same words, or the same sequence, with the same emphasis or with the same elements. They do not all report the same events. Of course, they may simply have been relying upon different witnesses whose recollections varied in minor details.

But inventing dialogue to convey the meaning of something said, because the exact words have been lost, or identifying a time sequence which contains important events but not in the same order as another Gospel, is a far cry from making up the events themselves. It is a slippery slope, indeed, to suggest that the Gospel writers invented facts to convey spiritual truths. What truth is conveyed

---

[22]Jn 18:15

[23]See Mk 14:51-52

by a falsehood? It is one thing to find literary devices in the Psalms, or the Book of Job, which may be a fictional story used to examine the profound mystery of suffering and evil in the world.[24] It is quite another to assert that the Gospel writers mixed fact and fiction without any effort to distinguish them.[25] Jesus used parables and metaphors. We have no trouble recognizing them as such. But we also have no problem seeing that his resurrection of Lazarus and the daughter of Jairus, his multiplication of the loaves and fishes, his calming of the storm on the Sea of Galilee, his walking on the water, and his cure of the blind, crippled and sick are reported as facts, not symbols.

But what about the real inconsistencies in the Gospels? There are numerous questions of this kind throughout the New Testament, and they become particularly pronounced in the Resurrection accounts. The divergencies demonstrate at least one comforting fact: the Gospels were not written to present a synchronized story of Jesus' life. If the story of Jesus' life, miracles and resurrection were just a conspiracy cooked up by a bunch of Galileans out to hoodwink the people, they would have concocted a unified story featuring those elements that the Jewish people would find the most convincing. These elements would certainly have limited or excluded the extraordinarily important role that women play in the Gospels because in the Jewish culture their testimony was considered to be unreliable.[26]

What does come through clearly in the Gospels is their character of eyewitness testimony. The Gospel writers themselves may not have been the eyewitnesses, at least not to all events, but they have obviously garnered the stories of people who were witnesses. Any trial attorney, investigator, judge, or even a reasonably observant adult, knows that witness perspectives vary depending upon a wide range of circumstances and influences. We also know that memory fades on the small details but that major events remain crystal clear in our minds. Thus there is a clear consensus on the basic facts that Jesus was anointed

---

[24]The facts in Job's case are relevant to the lesson only as props to set the scope of the author's thesis. Similar stories of misfortune and apparent injustice are legion in the experience of mankind. The Book of Job would have exactly the same instructional value if it were introduced by, "Imagine that in the land of Uz. . . ." The Gospels, however, depend upon their facts to establish the identity of Jesus as the Messiah sent from God.

[25]A critic might hasten to say at this point: "Ah, ha! But that is what this book does!" But the stories in this book do not modify Scripture in any way. Those words are presented in bold type and the reader is strongly encouraged to read the Bible directly to get the unadorned account. There are many facts in this book derived from my research into the historical, archaeological and medical issues raised by the life of Christ that are not footnoted as to source. Generally, those are reasonably obvious or the footnotes and commentaries identify them. But the bottom line is that these stories simply flesh out the Gospel stories for the purpose of meditation. The intent is to identify *plausible* explanations and situations so that the reader will have a richer visual image of the events that are merely outlined in the New Testament, sometimes in inconsistent ways.

[26]See *A New Catholic Commentary on Holy Scripture,* ed. R.O.C. Fuller (London: Reginald C. Nelson, 1969), 952.

in Bethany shortly (but how shortly?) before his death, that he drove the money changers and animal sellers in the Jerusalem Temple away with whips (but when?), that he was condemned to death by both the Jewish leaders (in what procedure exactly and who participated?) and the Roman governor (where?), that he was crucified on or just before (which?) the day of Passover, and, most important, that he rose bodily from the dead. Only the details of speech, participants and sequence vary somewhat on these vital issues.

As minor as those differences are, even they might be harmonized in many instances if each Gospel writer had attempted to report everything known about the circumstances of each event. Obviously, they did not. Their objective was to communicate all the details needed to make their reports coherent and convincing to a populace that communicated primarily by the spoken word.

The Gospels have a single purpose: to bring all people to faith in Jesus Christ. But the means by which that was to be accomplished include at least two: one, to report a dramatically different way of understanding our lives and our relationships with God and our fellow human beings; and, two, to validate that message by showing God's endorsement through miraculous happenings from the time of Christ's conception until after his resurrection.[27] To confuse symbols with facts in these reports would severely compromise the second objective because it would cast doubt upon the truth of everything else. That our fertile imaginations can find symbolic meaning in many of the events does not undermine their objective truth. God understands symbolism better than we do. He gifted us with minds that can pursue truth beneath the surface of our experiences. But if the experience is not true, then the symbolism is set afloat with no anchor in reality.

Second Sorrowful Mystery, the Scourging at the Pillar

Annas and Caiaphas

Only John reports on the inquiry by Annas. His inclusion raises some logistical problems with Peter's denial of Jesus; i.e., the other Gospels place Peter in the courtyard of Caiaphas when these take place. John's Gospel seems to suggest that he was in the courtyard of Annas. One way to resolve the problem is to place Annas in the palace of Caiaphas. That way their courtyard is the same. But archaeologists associated with Hebrew University in Jerusalem say that Annas had his own palace, which was located close to the Hasmonean palace where Herod Antipas stayed when he was in Jerusalem. I resolve this dilemma by having Peter remain at the palace of Caiaphas while Jesus is taken to the short interview by Annas.

---

[27]See Jn 5:36, 10:37-38 and 10:25, where Jesus tells the Jews: "The works I do in my Father's name give witness in my favor . . ."

Where Was Pilate's Praetorium?

Both Mark and John report that Jesus was brought before Pilate in the *"praetorium."*[28] Praetorium is a Latin word meaning the place where the *"praetor,"* or *"one who goes before,"* resided in a Roman army camp. After praetors became governors as well as generals, the term was applied to their residence in the main city. Often this was the former ruler's palace.

There are two good candidates for the "praetorium" of Pilate during the trial of Jesus. The first is the Fortress Antonia, which was built along the north wall at the west corner of the Temple Mount, facing west and east. Doors opened directly from the fortress onto the Court of Gentiles and onto the rampart atop the colonnaded portico at the north end of the Court. Tradition since at least the time of the Crusaders in the 12th century has identified the fortress as Pilate's praetorium for the trial of Jesus. According to John 19:13, Pilate took his judge's seat on a bench *"at the place called the Stone Pavement—'Gabbatha' in Hebrew."* The Greek word used for "Stone Pavement" is *Lithostrotos*. Oddly, *gabbatha* does not mean stone pavement; it means a high place, ridge, or hill.

The difficulty in placing Pilate's praetorium in Fortress Antonia derives from the fact that the Jews refused to enter it when they took Jesus to be condemned by Pilate (John 18:28) because to do so would have caused them to become ritually impure and prevented their eating the Passover supper. Throughout the description in John of the trial before Pilate, the governor is constantly coming out to meet with the chief priests and then going back in to talk to Jesus. Later, when Pilate tries to get the crowd to choose Jesus instead of Barabbas, he seems to be dealing with a pretty good-sized group of people.[29] But the entrance to the Fortress Antonia on both its eastern and western ends was, according to the latest Jerusalem archaeology, preceded by great, long stairways. In other words, there would have been no place for a crowd to stand outside the Fortress Antonia. If the Jews were unwilling to go inside, where was this "Stone Pavement" located?

Conceivably, Pilate could have gone in and out of the doorway to the Court of Gentiles on the Temple Mount, and even have taken Jesus up onto the rampart atop the colonnaded portico to present him to the crowd below. But the Gospels make it clear that the Jewish authorities were afraid of Jesus' popularity with the people, so it seems unlikely that they would have wanted him anywhere near the huge Passover crowd on the Temple Mount. Nor, it seems, would Pilate have been so imprudent as to run the risk of precipitating a major riot.

Speaking of riots, that raises another question about the location of the *Lithostrotos*. Many authors place the *"Stone Pavement"* inside the Fortress Antonia. But besides the problem with ritual impurity which such a location would cause

---

[28] Mk 15:16, Jn 18:28

[29] Matthew and Luke both speak of *"crowds"* (Mt 27:20, Lk 23:4). Mark says the *"crowd came up"* which suggests a large number of people from the city (15:8).

for Pilate's confrontation with the chief priests, scribes, elders and the "crowds," it would also be an intimidating environment for the Jews. Matthew says a riot started to break out when Pilate hesitated to have Christ crucified (27:24). Mark reports that Pilate was anxious to satisfy the crowd (15:15). Luke tells us the crowds' shouts *"increased in violence"* (23:23), which induced Pilate to order the crucifixion. Inside the Antonia was certainly not a setting conducive to such bold protests. Conversely, it is a little hard to imagine a Roman governor, inside his own fortress, surrounded by his own troops, being so intimidated by an unarmed Jewish gathering, especially since Pilate knew that jealousy was the real basis for the charges against Jesus. Philo of Alexandria, an ancient historian, described Pilate as a particularly brutal governor. If the *Lithostrotos* was actually inside his fortress, he seems to have been remarkably pusillanimous on this occasion.

Father Raymond Brown argues in his two-volume work, *The Death of the Messiah*, that the "Stone Pavement" does not necessarily mean the stones were massive.[30] They might have just been unusually valuable, laid out in a distinctive pattern, or otherwise distinguishable. However, the belief that Jesus was brought to the Fortress Antonia seemed to get a big boost in 1870 when massive stone slabs were discovered in the basement of the Sisters of Sion convent, in the Antonia area. These stone slabs also contain graffiti suggesting the "king game" which may have inspired the crown of thorns placed upon Jesus' head. On the other hand, recent archaeology has suggested that the stone slabs date from the second century A.D. and so would not have been there during the time of Christ.

The other candidate for the praetorium is Herod's palace. Directly across from the palace was a large square called the *Upper Agora* (Upper Market). It was a public square with colonnades, shops, and an open area in the center. It would have been a kind of ancient equivalent to an upscale shopping mall/city center, not the place expected to attract a lot of the followers of Jesus, and big enough to accommodate a large crowd. It was in the Upper City, located on land which was the highest in the city. The Model of Ancient Jerusalem at the Holyland Hotel in Jerusalem portrays the square paved with stone in an attractive and distinctive pattern. Between the square and the palace was a turreted wall with a short flight of steps on either side beneath a curved arch. The square, therefore, would have lent itself very well to the *"Gabbatha,"* or high place, and seemingly to the *"Lithostrotos"* mentioned by John.

As for where Pilate, *the military leader*, would have chosen to be during the time of the Passover festival, a case can be made for either Antonia or the Herodian palace.

More telling, perhaps, is where Pilate *the husband* would have been. It seems self-evident that Claudia Procula, his wife, would have greatly preferred Herod's luxurious palace to the Spartan surroundings of a military fort. It is unlikely that she left her beautiful seaside home in Caesarea cheerfully even if the

---

[30]Brown, *Death of the Messiah*, 709.

visit to Jerusalem was brief. So it is easy to imagine Pilate mollifying her with accommodations in the palace, well away from the noisy throngs of Passover pilgrims.

Father Brown concludes in his book that the palace of Herod is the most likely place to have been the praetorium described by Mark and John.[31] For purposes of these stories, I have tried to be as true to biblical and archaeological scholarship as I could be. Consequently, I have placed the trial of Jesus by Pilate in Herod's old palace.

The Nature of Jesus' Scourging

English maritime law limited the whip lashes for miscreant sailors to forty less one. The number forty has an ancient derivation[32] and was the limit for Roman citizens also. There was no limit, however, for Roman lashings of persons who were not Roman citizens. It is also likely that the flagrum could not be used on Roman citizens. The reason for the limit was that experience had taught the authorities that death occurs at a rapidly increasing rate as the number of lashes exceeds forty.

The Roman flagrum came in several varieties, tipped with round balls, balls with small spikes, bits of bone and other devilish versions. These weapons were easily fatal if used without restraint. They could literally strip a man's flesh off, down to his skeleton. It was not unusual to whip prisoners to death. Jesus was not a Roman citizen and would not have been protected by a legal limit. However, he was a high visibility prisoner for both the Jews and Pontius Pilate. Pilate, according to the Gospel of John, was still trying at this stage to avoid executing Jesus. The Jews wanted him crucified for several reasons. And prisoners sentenced to crucifixion were to die that way and not from an overzealous scourging. It seems likely, therefore, that the soldiers were well aware that they were to avoid scourging Jesus to death.

Persons who have studied the *Shroud of Turin* have reported that the number of scourge marks, indicated by the little dumbbell impressions, is somewhere between 100-120.[33] However, when one counts what seem clearly to be scourging impressions on the photographs of the shroud, the number of marks is more like 100-130 *on each side*. Even Wilson's artist's drawing has this many. With three-strip flagra, each blow would have been tripled. Thus, forty blows would have produced 120 impressions.

---

[31]Ibid., 710. See 706-710 for most of the discussion that I have summarized here.

[32]See Dt 25:3.

[33]See Ian Wilson, *The Shroud of Turin* (Garden City, NY: Doubleday, 1978), 124; Zugibe, *Cross and the Shroud*, 18. Wilson's book includes an artist's rendering in Figure 12.

Some authors have suggested that Jesus was struck literally thousands of times. It would have been impossible for him to survive such a beating. In fact, his flesh would have been flayed from his body long before that number was reached.

Third Sorrowful Mystery, the Crowning with Thorns

This mystery presents two primary elements in the suffering of Christ: the extreme humiliation endured by the Son of God in letting himself be mocked and spit upon and the pain of having sharp thorns repeatedly jammed into his head.

Dr. Frederick Zugibe points out in his book, *The Cross and the Shroud*,[34] that the network of nerves which cover the face and head can be extremely pain sensitive, to the point of immobilizing a person.

As for the mocking of Jesus, this was the third session of this kind of mistreatment (the chief priests and their guards, Herod and his guards, and now the Roman soldiers). Certainly, the Lord has provided us an astonishing example of patience, endurance and humility. We should all try to remember this during those times when we become enraged because our own dignity and public image have been impugned by someone, whether maliciously or simply out of insensitivity. There is a great tendency in modern society to be conscious of and to assert our individual rights. The model that Jesus gives us is to stop thinking about ourselves (*our* rights) and concentrate on loving and serving others (upholding *their* rights).

Before or After Jesus' Condemnation?

Only John presents the scourging and crowning of thorns as part of Pilate's maneuvering to convince the Jews to let Jesus go. Luke does not describe the scourging and crowning with thorns. Matthew and Mark place them after Pilate has ordered Jesus' crucifixion. The crowning of thorns appears to have been a punishment devised uniquely for Jesus. There is no record of it having been done to any other Roman prisoner in Palestine.

The Shroud of Turin

The Shroud of Turin is a 14-foot long piece of linen with the faint image of a man who appears to have been crucified. This image is the most famous Christian relic in the world. It has been studied by numerous scientists, artists, and religious authorities since it first became widely known in the mid-14th century. Many people, including this author, believe it is, in fact, the burial cloth of Jesus Christ. Even if not, however, the image corresponds exactly to the description of Christ's crucifixion as contained in the Gospels. Therefore, it is well worth contemplating whenever one meditates on the Passion of Christ.

---

[34]Pp. 24-27

The images that you see in the pictures on the next three pages are photographic negatives. On May 28, 1898, a photographer named Secondo Pia took what is arguably now the most famous picture in the world. The Shroud was being shown by its then owner, the House of Savoy in Turin, Italy, at a special exposition to honor the 50th anniversary of the Italian constitution.

The image on the cloth looks like a very faint scorch mark. There are no brush strokes of any kind and scientists have yet to determine how the image was formed. But, when viewed, it is very hard to make out more than the faint outline of a male face and body, although the blood stains are more prominent. It was not until Pia was developing his pictures that the world discovered that the "scorched" image is actually a photographic negative. A negative of that negative produces the positive images shown above.

It would require a second book, and a long one, to discuss the Shroud in detail. But there is an extremely comprehensive and current Web site (www.shroud.com) that has a wealth of the latest information, both pro and con, concerning the debate over the authenticity of the Shroud of Turin. And, of course, there are numerous books on the subject, including Ian Wilson's work listed in the bibliography.

Fourth Sorrowful Mystery, the Carrying of the Cross

The Path of the "Via Dolorosa"

Although it is more likely that the praetorium of Pilate was Herod's palace rather than the Fortress Antonia, it seems equally likely that the other prisoners would have been kept in the Roman prison at the fortress. The ritual of criminals carrying their crossbeams through the streets of Jerusalem was an established practice intended to add to the deterrent effect of the punishment.[35] This purpose would have been best served by following the same path each time so that the citizens of Jerusalem would know where to wait to see the latest victims. This journey, the Via Dolorosa, or Way of Sorrows, wound through the city streets for a distance of about ⅓ of a mile (600 yards or so). Rarely did an accused criminal get the kind of high level attention and public trial that Jesus received from the chief priests and Pilate. So it makes sense that Jesus would have been taken from the praetorium, where he was condemned, to the Antonia, where he would pick up his crossbeam and join the other "lower profile" crucifixion victims on their melancholy parade to death.

Golgotha

"*Golgotha*" is the Aramaic word for "place of the skull." It was a limestone quarry just outside the walls of Jerusalem. At this time, the quarry may have been

---

[35]Porter, *Jesus Christ*, 123.

inactive and in a process of reclamation. Evidently, a knoll in the center of the quarry had been preserved for some reason and was used by the Romans as the site for crucifixions. Two roads passed nearby, including the main north-south "Way of the Patriarchs" so the location was ideal for public visibility. It is not certain how high the Golgotha knoll was. Estimates have ranged from at least 15 feet to 40 feet. The knoll had to be large enough to accommodate the soldiers and other witnesses who congregated for these executions.

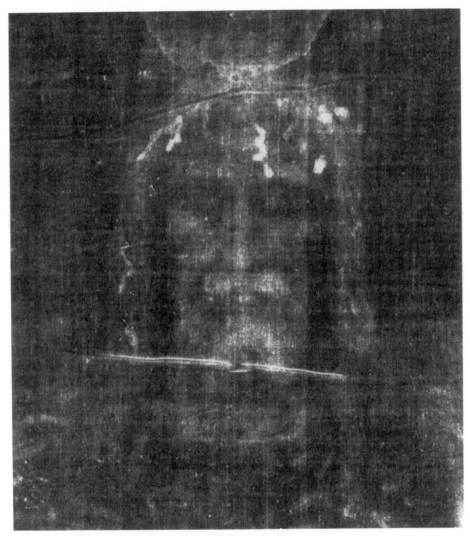

Shroud image of the face of Jesus.

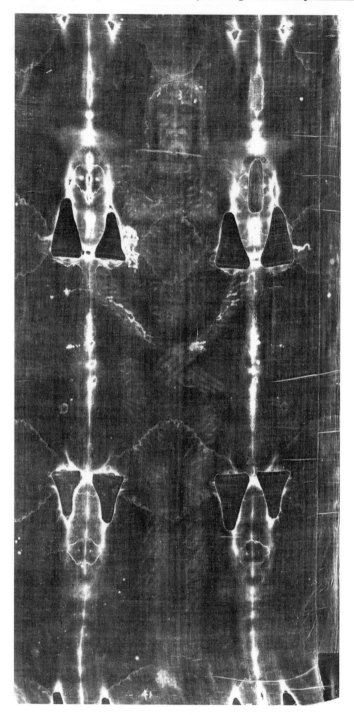

Front view of the Shroud image.

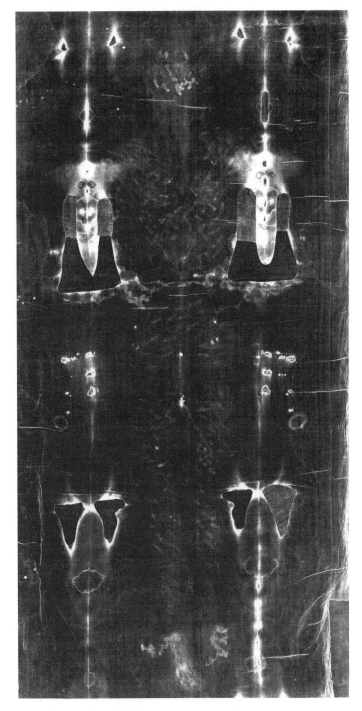

Back view of the Shroud image.

Also located in the quarry, perhaps on one side, or even in the base of the knoll, were carved out openings used as tombs. Joseph of Arimathea owned one of these. The reclamation process seems to have involved development of small cemetery gardens.

The term, "place of the skull," has most often led to speculation that some part of the quarry resembled a human skull. This is the version presented in this book. However, it is also possible that the term was simply a reference to the fact that crucified bodies were at least sometimes left unburied, or to the fate of men taken there.

What Cross Did Jesus Carry?

It is an almost unanimous opinion among biblical scholars today that Jesus did not carry his entire cross to Calvary (derived from *"calvaria,"* the Latin word for skull). Criminals condemned to death by crucifixion carried only the crossbeam, or *patibulum,* to the place of execution. The upright portion of the cross, or *stipes*, was left in place at the site. Estimates of the weight of the crossbeam which Jesus carried vary according to the type of wood believed to have been used as well as the dimensions of the piece. Suggested weights have run from 30 to 125 pounds. The cypress tree was common throughout Palestine and grew straight and tall. It would have been good material for crucifixions, but perhaps it was too good to use for this purpose. Micropaleobotanical studies of pieces of the alleged true cross indicate it was made of pine. A similar study of the piece of wood embedded with a crucifixion victim's bone that was found in an archaeological dig in the Old City of Jerusalem tentatively identified it as olive wood. That crucifixion was dated to about 7 A.D.

Who was "Veronica" and Where Is Her Veil?

The woman who wiped the face of Jesus on the Via Dolorosa has come down to us as "Veronica."[36] The name is probably a corruption of the Greco-Roman term, *vera ikon,* meaning "true image." The incident is not mentioned in Scripture and many scholars regard it as pure legend. It is a tradition of long standing, however. In his book, *The Shroud of Turin,* Ian Wilson concludes that the Veronica story was mixed up with historical facts about the Shroud of Turin.[37] Thus he believes the story is legend but not an out-and-out fabrication.

In Saint Peter's Basilica in Rome today, the Veronica veil is purportedly kept in one of the Bernini columns which surround the great central altar. It seems safe to assume that if there were any recognizable cloth image to be seen, it would

---

[36]In the fourth sorrowful mystery, the name of the woman who wipes the face of Jesus on his way to Calvary is named "Seraphia." Her name and identity as the wife of a Temple councillor are taken from the visions of the Venerable Anne Catherine Emmerich as reported in *The Life of Jesus Christ and Biblical Revelations,* v. 4, 254-259.

[37]Pp. 86-92

have been brought out from time to time. According to Wilson, the last historical record of the veil was of its capture by drunken soldiers of Charles V, who sacked Rome in 1527. He also quotes a report by an art expert, Monsignor Joseph Wilpert, who in 1907 opened the silver reliquary which purportedly contained the veil. All that he saw therein was a light-colored square piece of material bearing two faint, irregular rust-brown stains, connected to each other.[38]

I believe the incident still has value for rosary reflection purposes, even if it is not historically accurate. Veronica's courage and love are challenges to all of us to consider whether we would be willing to extend ourselves under similar circumstances. In fact, of course, we do not have to replicate the details of a death march to an impending crucifixion. Most of us are afraid to speak up for Christ or to appear to be "too religious" in our daily lives simply from fear of social embarrassment, much less in the face of a tangible threat like losing a promotion or job. For example, when was the last time you said grace in a restaurant? Prayed in a public place other than a church? Suggested a moment of prayer to your friends? All of these very minor acts require spiritual conviction and the courage to be "different."

Veronica's act, of course, was much more than confidence in her faith. She might have been motivated purely by altruism. Again, we should ask ourselves when was the last time we were willing to take an unpopular stand to defend an oppressed minority, or to challenge the dishonesty of some unethical action or tactic in our workplace environment? The character of Veronica put her good name and her personal safety on the line for Jesus. Such heroism is worth remembering. Many have done it. Veronica represents all of them for us here.

Weeping Women and the Destruction of Jerusalem

If the weeping women could have foreseen the future the way Jesus did, they would have, indeed, stopped wailing for him and begun crying and beseeching God for mercy for themselves and their children. Beginning in the mid-60s A.D., Palestine was wracked with revolutionary violence. At first it was internal and generational, with the young against the old, the poor against the wealthy, the Upper City versus the Lower City in Jerusalem. The two factions ultimately fought a pitched battle that resulted in the deaths of 12,000 Jews and nearly all of the rich.

By 66, the revolutionary forces in Palestine controlled Jerusalem and most of the countryside. Roman/Gentile retaliation was swift. Vespasian and his son, Titus, commanded the Roman legions. For five months in 70 A.D., the Roman army besieged Jerusalem, which Tacitus estimated to harbor 600,000 Jews at the time. The city quickly consumed its food supplies and starvation took hold. Thousands of Jews, on desperate forays outside the city walls to obtain food, were captured and crucified. Toward the end of the siege, the streets were clogged with corpses;

---

[38]Ibid., 87.

116,000 bodies were thrown over the city walls. After the Jews rejected Titus' terms of surrender, offered when he had captured half of Jerusalem, the Romans launched their final assault without mercy or quarter. The Temple was burned to the ground despite its heroic defense by the Jewish rebels. Nearly 100,000 fugitives were captured and sold into slavery, many of them later dying as involuntary gladiators. Estimates of the total number of Jews killed in the siege and mop-up operations range from 600,000 to 1.2 million. When it was all over in 73, the Jewish state was no more. In fact, there were almost no Jews left in Judea. Those few who remained were impoverished and forced to pay a pagan temple tax. The Sanhedrin and high-priesthood were abolished. The Sadducees disappeared and the Pharisees and rabbis became the leaders of a people that had little remaining but their religion and their hope.[39]

Fifth Sorrowful Mystery, the Crucifixion

When Was Jesus Crucified?

When did the crucifixion take place? This question is obviously related to when Jesus was born. From the Gospels, we know that Jesus was born during the reign of Herod the Great, who died in 4 B.C. If God did, indeed, time his birth to coincide with some very unusual astronomical events (see the third joyful mystery story and commentary), he would likely have been born in 7 or 6 B.C. It is generally accepted that Jesus began his ministry around the age of 30[40] and was crucified around the age of 33; at least, these are the most popular opinions. Therefore, if he was born in December, 7 B.C., to die in March/April[41] at the age of 33, he would have to have been executed in the year 27A.D.[42]

We also know that Jesus was crucified on a Friday just before a major feast day (Passover and the Feast of Unleavened Bread, which were celebrated concurrently and for about a week in ancient times). According to Father Raymond

---

[39]Will Durant, *Caesar and Christ* (New York: Simon and Schuster, 1944), 543-545.

[40]Luke says so explicitly in his Gospel at 3:23.

[41]March 25 is often adopted in pious tradition, perhaps because of its coincidence with the anniversary of the Annunciation.

[42]The arithmetic may seem at first glance to be in error, but the explanation is that there is no year zero. The year before Christ was born was 1 B.C. The next year was 1 A.D. from its beginning, even if he was born near its end, possibly on the date we now celebrate, December 25. The year which began one week after that, in the Gregorian calendar which we use today, was 2 A.D. Under this scenario, if Jesus was born in December, 7 B.C., he would have turned 33 in December, 26 A.D. However, if the year Jesus was born is counted as 1 B.C. because it was so near its end (the monk responsible for calculating the Gregorian calendar assumed Jesus was born on December 25), then Jesus would have been only 32 years old in 27 A.D.

Brown, this narrows the candidate years down to three: 27, 30 and 33 A.D. He and most scholars opt for the year 30, specifically April 7.[43] None of the dates is without significant problems, but I lean toward the earlier date of A.D. 27 which fits better with what seems to be the likely birth year of Jesus. Since Pontius Pilate's rule was from 26-37 A.D., placing the crucifixion in 27 would put it early in his governorship, a time when he was probably still becoming adjusted to his new position. He had already offended Herod Antipas in some way, probably by executing some Galileans in Jerusalem without the concurrence of the tetrarch,[44] so Pilate might have been more susceptible at this early stage to the kind of psychological pressure the Jewish authorities brought to bear upon him in pushing him to crucify Jesus.

The Experience of Crucifixion

Although there are many historical references to crucifixion, and even some archaeological evidence, many of the details of the process remain obscure. Determining the procedure used in a particular crucifixion is even more difficult because there was such a wide variety of practices and no newspapers to report the details of individual cases. For purposes of these *Mystery Stories*, I accept the Shroud of Turin as an historically accurate portrayal of Christ's passion.

In October 1988, however, the Shroud failed a triple laboratory carbon-14 dating test that was expected to definitively establish its age at about 2,000 years. Instead, the test dated the shroud's origin between 1260 and 1390 A.D. This was astonishing to those of us who have studied the other scientific analyses as well as the internal credibility of this remarkable relic. Recently, however, a team from the University of Texas Health Science Center reported that a microscopic layer of bacteria and fungi may throw off the carbon dating of all ancient textiles by hundreds or thousands of years.[45]

My portrayal of the crucifixion wounds in the hands of Christ is based upon the location of the exit wound of the nail as shown on the Shroud of Turin and as explained by Dr. Zugibe in *The Cross and the Shroud*, pp. 47-71. Zugibe takes issue with another famous Shroud analyst, Dr. Pierre Barbet, over the location of the nails in the hands and the cause of death. He shows that Barbet's theory that the nail passed through a gap in the palm bones known as "Destot's Space" is very unlikely because that gap is located much nearer to the little finger side, away

---

[43]The issue of dating Christ's crucifixion is discussed in detail in Appendix II of Brown, *The Death of the Messiah*, 1350-78; see particularly 1373-1376.

[44]See Lk 13:1-3. Some scholars hypothesize this explanation for the enmity of Pilate and Antipas mentioned by Luke in 23:12. See, e.g., Brown, *Death of the Messiah*, 701.

[45]See *The Washington Post*, "Shroud of Turin from 1st Century, Scientists Say," May 21, 1996.

from the median nerve, and would not conform to the Shroud of Turin location of the exit wound.

Ever since Dr. Barbet published his book, *A Doctor at Calvary,* in France in 1950, it has been generally accepted that Jesus and the two men crucified with him probably died of asphyxiation caused by their eventual inability to raise themselves on their crosses to continue breathing. This theory, not tested on living subjects, proposed that the *cruciarius* would not be able to exhale when suspended from his hand/wrist nails. Doctor Zugibe, however, did test the hypothesis on living volunteers by means of a structure which simulated the bodily stresses from crucifixion without actually impaling the hands and feet. He discovered that breathing is not significantly impaired when the arms are outstretched in the traditional T-shape. Only when the arms are pulled up nearly vertical above the body are the diaphragm and lungs compressed to the point where breathing becomes very difficult.[46]

A Personal Experiment

As part of my research for this book, I constructed a simple simulation of what Dr. Zugibe did with his test subjects. I placed two large gate handles at arms' length on a wall and then nailed an old pair of shoes below them at a point where my feet would stand flat against the wall as if they had been nailed. What I found is that this position does, indeed, not impede breathing, at least so long as the legs are still functioning. If one hangs entirely by the hands, breathing is not cut off but the pressure on the chest area is substantially increased. It is also frighteningly unpleasant.

After several tries, I managed to hold myself in place against the powerful pull of gravity for more than three minutes only once! The pull of my 178 pounds on my hands and feet was enormous. I can only shudder at the pain which would ensue from hanging by nails through the bones of the hands/wrists and feet. The thigh muscles quickly began to "burn" from the strain of supporting the body. Before two minutes passed, my body was trembling from the muscle strain.

When I placed the left foot over the right foot, as Jesus probably had his feet nailed, most of the body weight was borne by the right leg alone, which seemed to exponentially increase the strain on those muscles. I could manage this for only a few seconds. To get a further idea of what the Lord suffered, place your left foot on top of your right and shift your weight to the left foot. It is quite painful in itself without having a nail binding the two together. Attempting to relax and hang from the hands put a terrible strain on the elbows and shoulders, not to mention the pull on the hands.

After my very brief but highly uncomfortable experience, I am amazed that men who were crucified did not simply scream with pain until they passed out. It has given me a new appreciation for the terror which Jesus experienced in

---

[46]See Zugibe, *Cross and the Shroud,* 80-81, 86-101.

the garden of Gethsemane and how the vision of what lay in his immediate future could quite understandably have produced the bloody sweat described by Luke, even without the unfathomable weight of all of mankind's sins. To get just a very slight flavor of what it must have been like to be crucified, hold your arms straight out from the sides of your body during the fifth sorrowful mystery the next time you pray the rosary. If this is not too difficult for you, try holding the position from earlier in the rosary, from the Carrying of the Cross, for example. You will probably feel self-conscious if you try this while praying in a group, so consider reserving it to those times when you pray alone.

Getting the Victim onto the Cross

There has also been much speculation about how the cruciarius was mounted on his cross. Because it is much easier to nail both the crossbeam and the victim when they are lying on the ground, I think it highly likely that this is what the Romans did. Therefore, I discount portrayals which have Christ nailed only to the crossbeam and then have that patibulum affixed to the upright stipes with the feet nailed last. I do not question whether the uprights were left in place at the place of execution. I think they probably were. But this does not exclude the very practical approach of pulling them out of the ground, fastening the crossbeams to them, nailing the victims' hands and feet, and then reinserting the stipes in their holes with wedges to anchor them. This is what is described by Venerable Anne Catherine Emmerich and Venerable Mary of Agreda, two mystics who reported visions of the life and passion of Jesus Christ.[47] More important, it conforms with what would have been the easiest and most efficient procedure for the executioners.

Most crucifixes portray the feet of Jesus resting upon a foot support attached to the cross. This support, known as the *suppedaneum*, would have had the effect of reducing the short-term agony and increasing the survival (and display) time of the cruciarius. Given that Pilate did not perceive Jesus as a threat to the empire, and had no interest, therefore, in prolonging his display as an object lesson, and that the Jewish authorities wanted all three men dead and removed by the end of the day, it is almost certain that a suppedaneum was not used.

Was Jesus' Body Washed?

The crucifixion story has Jesus' body washed before he is placed in the tomb. People who believe in the authenticity of the Shroud of Turin may protest that the blood stains and wound markings on the linen cloth indicate the body was not washed. But Zugibe notes that the sharp impressions present on the shroud would be possible only if Jesus' body was washed before being placed in the tomb. Otherwise, the clots, smears and dried sheets of blood would have left very

---

[47]*Life of Jesus Christ and Biblical Revelations*, v. 4, 276; Venerable Mary of Agreda, *Mystical City of God*, trans. Fiscar Marison (Washington, NJ: Ave Maria Institute, 1971), v. 3, 653.

indistinct impressions. The small amount of blood which defined the wounds, and formed the backward "3" on Jesus' forehead, would, according to Zugibe, have oozed out from the pressure of washing Jesus' body.[48]

Who Were the Women at the Foot of the Cross?

Another issue of scholarly concern is determining who were the women at the foot of Christ's cross. The Gospel writers appear not to agree. At least, they are not consistent in their naming. All three agree on the presence of Mary Magdalene. Luke names no one, so he is not a "player" in this controversy. Matthew and Mark list *"Mary, the mother of James and Joseph"* (or *"Joses"* as Mark calls him).[49] John, however, lists *"his* [meaning Jesus'] *mother, his mother's sister, Mary the wife of Clopas, and Mary Magdalene."*[50] If John used "Mary the wife of Clopas" in apposition to "his mother's sister," then all three Gospel writers place three named women in the vicinity of the cross. That result, though, would mean that Mary the wife of Clopas is also the mother of James and Joseph. This seems likely. But that, in turn, would make Clopas and Alphaeus the same person because the Apostle James the Less is identified in the Gospels as the son of Alphaeus.[51] There is plenty of precedent for this double name situation in the New Testament; e.g., Judas/Thaddaeus (even "Lebbeus" in some manuscripts); Levi/Matthew; Simon/Cephas/Peter; Nathanael/Bartholomew (likely); Saul/Paul; and Joseph/Barsabbas/Justus (Acts 1:23).[52]

There appears to be an irreconcilable difference about the third woman present. Matthew describes her as *"the mother of Zebedee's sons"* and Mark calls her *"Salome."*[53] But if Salome is the name of the mother of Zebedee's sons (the Apostles James the Greater and John), that small discrepancy is resolved. The bigger issue is that John does not mention his own mother being present. He mentions, instead, the Virgin Mary, the mother of Jesus, and is the only one of the Gospel writers to do so. It is probably stretching things, but one way to resolve even this conflict is to remember that, of the Gospel authors, only John was actually present at the crucifixion and that Jesus told him from the cross that, henceforth, Mary was to be his mother. It is possible that John is the source of the

---

[48]See Frederick T. Zugibe, M.D., Ph.D., "The Man of the Shroud Was Washed," *Sindon N.S.*, Quad. No. 1, June 1989.

[49]Mt 27:56, Mk 15:40

[50]Jn 19:25

[51]Mt 10:3, Mk 3:18, Lk 6:15

[52]This is also discussed in the *New Catholic Encyclopedia*, v. 7, 805, where Alphaeus and Clopas are suggested as equivalents of the same Aramaic name.

[53]Mt 27:56, Mk 15:40

information about which women were at the foot of the cross and that his reference to his "mother" meant the Blessed Virgin Mary when he said it but was mistakenly understood by the sources for Matthew and Mark to be a reference to his birth mother. In any case, it is not important so long as the Blessed Mother and John were both present. We are told explicitly in John's Gospel that they were.

Longinus

St. Longinus is recognized in the official Roman Martyrology calendar. His feast day is March 15. Like Veronica, his name may be a rendering of the item for which he is remembered, in his case the Greek word for lance. There are legendary traditions identified with him, such as his torture and martyrdom in Caesarea Cappadocia, but no independent documentation to support them. According to this story, Longinus' eyesight had been failing him at the time he supervised the execution of Jesus. When he speared him in the side, blood ran down the lance and touched Longinus' eyes, and his sight was perfectly restored. Another legend has him suffering martyrdom in Mantua, northern Italy, where he allegedly went with a vial of the precious blood shed upon the cross. The Mantuans claim to still possess this relic as well as the body of the saint himself.[54] Still, while the details of his sanctity may have been invented or exaggerated, the existence of the tradition and his apparent faith experience at the time of Christ's death argue that he did, indeed, become a follower of Christ.

THE GLORIOUS MYSTERIES

First Glorious Mystery, the Resurrection

Gospel "Contradictions?"

I cannot say it better than the following quote from *A New Catholic Commentary on Holy Scripture:* "The problem of the divergencies between the accounts of the resurrection appearances in the four evangelists is notorious."[55] According to Matthew and Mark, Jesus wants the apostles and disciples to leave immediately for Galilee where they will see him. Luke and John keep them in Jerusalem. Matthew has one angel outside the tomb to announce the resurrection to two women. Mark has one young man (presumably, but not necessarily, an angel) inside the tomb announcing to three women. Luke has two men in dazzling garments (presumably angels also) inside the tomb announcing to at least three

---

[54]*Butler's Lives of the Saints*, ed. Thurston & Attwater (Westminster, MD: Christian Classics, 1956), 594-595.

[55]Ibid., 952. See also Porter, *Jesus Christ*, 128.

and maybe several women. John has two angels inside the tomb but they say nothing. Instead, he has Jesus himself announce his resurrection when he appears to one woman.

In Matthew, the first appearance by Jesus is to the two women and is described. In Mark, the first appearance is to Mary Magdalene, but is not described. Luke has the first appearance to Peter, but does not describe it. His first detailed description is of Jesus' appearance to the disciples on the way to Emmaus. John has Jesus first appear to Mary Magdalene and describes it in detail. The first appearance to the apostles in Matthew is in Galilee; in all the other Gospels, it is in Jerusalem, although Jesus scolds the apostles in Mark for their failure to believe his resurrection and, by implication, to go to Galilee as they had been directed.

Finally, both Mark and Luke make reference to Jesus' appearance to the two disciples on the way to Emmaus, but only Luke describes it in detail. In Mark, the apostles refuse to believe the report of these two men and are not convinced of Jesus' resurrection until he himself appears to them in the Upper Room. In Luke, they already believe in the resurrection because of an undescribed earlier appearance to Peter and do themselves report their belief before the two disciples from Emmaus can speak.

As in all the mysteries previously, I have attempted to reconcile the Gospel versions as much as a plausible narrative would permit. Not every discrepancy could be accounted for, however. Biblical literalists may have some trouble here, but what comes through the Gospels to me is an attitude by the evangelists that these scene-setting details are not very important. They all seem to have accepted a particular version and not bothered to reconcile other, divergent accounts. It is as if they were so focused upon the great validating event of the Christian faith that the details seemed unimportant to them. This is understandable. People who witness horrendous accidents or history-making events often remember only the core occurrence vividly. Nothing else seems very important. Extraneous details are either forgotten or are reconstructed with the aid of other accounts and a natural human tendency to create missing details by "filling in the blanks" from assumptions, rumors, biases and personal preferences whenever the story is re-told. The four evangelists all agree that Jesus rose bodily from the dead, that his resurrection was announced or acknowledged by one or more heavenly messengers, that it was reported first to one or more of his women followers, and that the apostles as a group saw the risen Lord fairly soon afterwards. Truly, the other details, especially the few which cannot be accounted for by differences in timing, are extraneous and unimportant.

Some may question the plausibility in the consolidated narrative I present here of Mary Magdalene hearing from an angel that Jesus is risen and then within an hour asking a man she mistakes for the gardener where Jesus' body has been taken.[56] But in emotionally-charged circumstances where extraordinary events are

---

[56]Compare Mt 28:1-8 with Jn 20:14-15.

discounted or derided by others, it is easy to doubt one's own perception and to decide that an earlier experience may not have been real. I saw, and to some extent experienced, some of that same reaction in my parish in Lake Ridge, Virginia in 1992-93.[57]

Did John See the Shroud of Turin in the Tomb?

According to John's Gospel, he was the first of the apostles to believe that Jesus had been resurrected. What caused him to accept this fact before seeing Jesus, or even an angel, is not clear. There is some suggestion that it might have been connected with Jesus' burial cloths. If the Shroud of Turin is genuine, John may have been the first to recognize Jesus' image upon the cloth. This is the version included in the story presented here. Or, perhaps there was something else miraculous about the burial cloths, such as being tied and uncut with no body inside. Or, maybe John was simply more disposed to accept Jesus' prediction of his resurrection.

Second Glorious Mystery, the Ascension

More Gospel Inconsistencies?

As with the resurrection accounts, there is a lot of seemingly irreconcilable reporting by the four Gospel authors. There appear to have been several "ascensions" by Jesus with the first one to his Father on the day of his resurrection, and others taking place in both Galilee and Jerusalem. That may be of great interest to the theologians, but the purpose of these mystery stories is simply to capture all of the happenings reported in the New Testament and to tie them together in a narrative that is reasonable and understandable. You, the reader, can then reflect upon them in the same way that you reflect upon your own life: by remembering experiences and evaluating them for their significance in the light of what you have learned since.

There is, of course, nothing inherently contradictory about Jesus returning to his Father numerous times privately but only once in a dramatic, visible, aerial ascension skyward. Still, the most likely explanation is that the Gospel writers just were not terribly concerned about establishing an ironclad chronology. Even Luke's own Gospel reference to Jesus leading the apostles out to Bethany from where he ascends to heaven (Lk 24:50-51) seems inconsistent as to timing with his reporting of the ascension in Acts (40 days after the resurrection according to Acts 1:3).

---

[57]For a comprehensive account of what is apparently the most extensive occurrence of weeping statues and related physical phenomena in the history of the Church, see James L. Carney, *The Seton Miracles: Weeping Statues and Other Wonders* (Woodbridge, VA: Marian Foundation, 1998).

The Kingdom of God

Christ's final ascension to heaven left unanswered the great question that hovered around his life and mission. When would God transform the world into His personal kingdom under the leadership of the Messiah? The apostles and their contemporaries expected this new world to be established under the aegis of Israel. The failure of Jesus to address this expectation was the primary reason for his rejection by the political/religious authorities of the nation. His very last public comment[58] on earth included a specific refusal to answer this question. His ministry had repeatedly emphasized the importance and necessity of faith. Now, as he left the earth, he made the point once again.

The Importance of Faith

Next to the problem of suffering and evil in the world, perhaps the greatest mystery in the relationship of God to man is *why* He puts such a premium on faith. Why not be more explicit, more demonstrative with miracles and divine power? This is not the place for a full discussion of this basic issue, but it may be fruitful to consider both a negative and a positive aspect of the question. From a negative perspective, our ignorance may protect us. Being somewhat in the dark about God may shield us from immediate and irreversible consequences of our sin. If we were fully aware of Whom we offended and did it anyway, perhaps, like Satan and his fallen angels, our wills would be locked in perpetual enmity of God and there could be no forgiveness.

On a positive note, faith is the one thing we can give to God which He does not already have. Our love, which is what He really wants, may be ineffective spiritually if it is not carried on the wings of our faith. When times are hardest and our faith is most challenged, then is the gift we give, and the reward by grace, the greatest. Without faith, everything we do is solely for the rewards and pleasures of earth. God calls us all to a far more significant existence. Our passport to enter there seems to be labeled *FAITH*. How do we know when we have it? When we live the commands Christ gave us: love God with our whole heart, soul, mind and strength; and love our neighbors as we love ourselves. We certainly cannot love what we do not believe in.

Another word for faith is trust. It seems safe to say that most people regard being trusted as one of their highest compliments and are most grievously hurt by a lack of trust from those they love. In this sense, we are very much made in the image and likeness of God. We should not wonder, then, why faith is the

---

[58]"Public" as opposed to private revelation. The Church teaches us that revelation of God's plan for the world was completed with the death of the last apostle. In other words, all that we need to know is to be found in Scripture, particularly the New Testament. Disclosures which come to us through mystical revelations, or apparitions and locutions, or the brilliant insights of holy persons may be helpful to us in understanding our faith and conforming our lives to what Jesus commanded, but they do not add to the deposit of truth which is complete in the Holy Bible.

centerpiece of our relationship with Him. Faith/trust is the centerpiece of our most valued human relationships as well.

Third Glorious Mystery, the Descent of the Holy Spirit

Effect on the Disciples

The heart of this mystery is the transformation of the apostles and other disciples from Jews to Christians. Oh, they did not realize immediately that this transformation had taken place. But they were the "new wine" Jesus spoke of and he had already told them that this new wine could not be contained within the old wineskin of Judaism.[59] The difference that the Holy Spirit accomplished was to make them totally consumed with the need and importance of sharing the truths taught by Christ. This was Zeal with a capital Z.

The Paraclete whom Jesus sent does not come empty-handed. The gifts of the Holy Spirit are wisdom, understanding, counsel, fortitude, knowledge, piety and fear of the Lord.[60] All of these were manifested immediately in the apostles.

The Greatest Miracle

Less dramatic but no less profound was the effect the apostles and the Holy Spirit had on the crowd of Jews who gathered near the Upper Room. Their acceptance of the crucified Jesus as the Messiah without seeing his resurrected body themselves and strictly on the testimony of the apostles seems miraculous, indeed; especially since the Christ presented to them was one who came to lead Israel to God's kingdom, and not to earthly power for the Jews. The miracle of tongues would have been pretty impressive and obviously served well to get the people's attention. But greater miracles than this have been ignored by hearts and minds which are closed to God's grace. Otherwise, Jesus could not have been delivered up to crucifixion by his own people. Only the Holy Spirit acting interiorly could have effected the conversion of 3,000 Jews this first day. The ability to communicate across the language barrier was miraculous and awesome. But the greatest miracle of communication took place in the souls of these converts. There the Holy Spirit's gift of understanding was not so visible as his vocal gift of counsel to the apostles, but it was even more powerful.

But we also see from the Scriptural description of this event that not everyone in the crowd comprehended the words of the Holy Spirit. What must one do to one's soul to absolutely block the message of God? At what point does a life of selfishness and sin cause permanent spiritual blindness? All things are possible with God, of course, including the restoration of sight in these hard-hearted

---

[59]See Lk 5:37-38.

[60]*Catechism of the Catholic Church*, ¶1831.

cases.[61] But who will intercede for them, who will pray for them, who will help them? If no one does, there is, indeed, little hope for their salvation. Fortunately, all of us have some help from the prayers and intercessions of the Blessed Virgin Mary and the other residents of heaven.

It is difficult to imagine where thousands of people assembled outside the house where the Upper Room was located. It is possible that the apostles adjourned to the nearby Upper Market. But the way the scene is described in Acts seems to keep them in the immediate vicinity of the house. According to the Model of Ancient Jerusalem at the Holyland Hotel in modern-day Jerusalem, it may be that the house with the Upper Room fronted on open space containing King David's monument. Thus, there might have been more room there than we imagine.

Fourth Glorious Mystery, the Assumption of Mary

About the assumption of Mary body and soul into heaven, we know only one thing for sure: it did happen. In one of the rare declarations by the Pope of his *ex cathedra* ("from the chair" of St. Peter) authority to declare infallibly as a matter of Catholic dogma, Pope Pius XII declared in 1950:

> We pronounce, declare, and define it to be a divinely revealed dogma: that the Immaculate Mother of God, the ever Virgin Mary, having completed the course of her earthly life, was assumed body and soul into heavenly glory.[62]

But there is no historical record of the event, nor Scriptural description, so the details are unknown.

Assumption Site

There are, however, several traditions that describe the assumption of Mary. The three main ones have her assumed into heaven from Ephesus (located in modern Turkey) after having lived there several years, or from Jerusalem after a period of residence in Ephesus, or from Jerusalem after residing there continuously following the crucifixion of Christ. Within Jerusalem, two sites compete for the honor: one is a location near the Cenacle of the Last Supper, marked now by the crypt of the Dormition Abbey, which is managed by the Benedictine Order. The other is a tomb very close to the Garden of Gethsemane,

---

[61]Cf. Mt 19:24-26 where Jesus assesses a rich (worldly) man's chances of getting into heaven as about the same as passing a camel through a needle's eye but then reassures the apostles that all things are possible with God.

[62]*Munificentissimus Deus*, November 1, 1950.

called the Church of the Assumption and Tomb of the Virgin Mary. It is run jointly by the Greek Orthodox and Armenian Churches.

The Character of Mary

With no Scriptural core, the story presented here is highly imaginative. The fictional events presented are designed to illustrate points of reflection about the character and holiness of the Blessed Virgin Mary as well as the nature of heaven. These include her absolute devotion to the Son of God, of whom she is mother, and her sharing in his redemptive sacrifice by her own empathetic sufferings, much like what we today would call a "victim soul." They can reasonably include scenes that reveal Mary's compassion and love, especially for children in need. Surely there must have been excitement in heaven when it was time for Mary to come home, so a story line that captures some of this element is also appropriate for reflection. Surely, too, the happiness of heaven includes laughter, the joy of celebration and the playfulness of children. The adventures of Benjamin and Natali are intended to convey this aspect of life there. Hopefully, their story may help children to reflect on this mystery. Finally, Marian apparitions down through the centuries have left us with a sense of how Mary often leaves her "calling card" by means of a miraculous spring, or transformed rosary, or other physical sign of her presence.[63] Her garland of flowers serves that purpose here.

Other Questions

There is a tradition in the Church that Luke derived his information about the annunciations and births of Jesus and John the Baptist directly from Mary. I think this is likely to be true, so I have included an episode to capture that experience. It is not *per se* a part of Mary's assumption, but it relates to her life between the descent of the Holy Spirit and her departure from this earth.

A final issue which is also still unresolved theologically, and, of course, historically, is whether Mary actually died or merely went into a deep sleep, a coma basically, before she was assumed into heaven. Actually, even the coma scenario is hypothesis since it is possible that Mary was simply taken "home" without any sign of failing health. Most of the existing legends seem to lean toward dying, so I followed them. This is also more consistent with what I have said elsewhere about the inspirational value of Mary's experiencing life the same way we must.

---

[63]The most astonishing of these "mementos," of course, is the inexplicable image on the cactus fiber *tilma* (poncho) of Juan Diego, known today as the Image of Our Lady of Guadalupe. It dates to 1531.

Fifth Glorious Mystery, the Coronation of Mary

To describe the glorious coronation of Mary as Queen of Heaven and Earth, or Queen of the Universe as some prefer, is to embark upon uncharted waters, indeed. As St. Paul tells us:

**Eye has not seen, ear has not heard,
nor has it so much as dawned on man
what God has prepared for
those who love him.**[64]

The descriptions and metaphors I have chosen for this meditation are not intended to break new theological ground. Specifically, my concept of the residents of heaven "borrowing" holiness from one another in order to approach nearer to the Throne of God is strictly a literary device to illustrate the fact that some persons in heaven are holier than others and that all persons there find their greatest delight in giving love and sharing blessings.[65] This is very sound theology. The notion that all the residents of heaven would be joined in a common enterprise by God for the periodic benefit of selected individuals also seems quite sound and rather appealing.

There are numerous other aspects of Our Blessed Mother that could be substituted for the stars which I have chosen to place in her crown. I am certain that the Queen of Heaven will be delighted if you, as you meditate upon this mystery, find and consider other insights that increase your understanding and appreciation for the infinite goodness, love and generosity of the God who created us. Nothing could make her happier than to know that what God has done for her and through her helps us to draw closer to her Son, our Lord Jesus Christ.

---

[64]1 Cor 2:9. Apparently Saint Paul was speaking with personal knowledge because he speaks in 2 Cor 12:1-4 about "a man" (almost universally considered to be St. Paul himself) who was "snatched up to the third heaven" (12:2) and heard "words which cannot be uttered, words which no man may speak." (12:4).

[65]"Holier" in this sense means greater in capacity. Everyone in heaven is 100% holy but, presumably, those whose earthly lives were most filled with the love of God and neighbor will have a greater capacity for God's love in the life hereafter.

APPENDIX I
How to Pray the Rosary

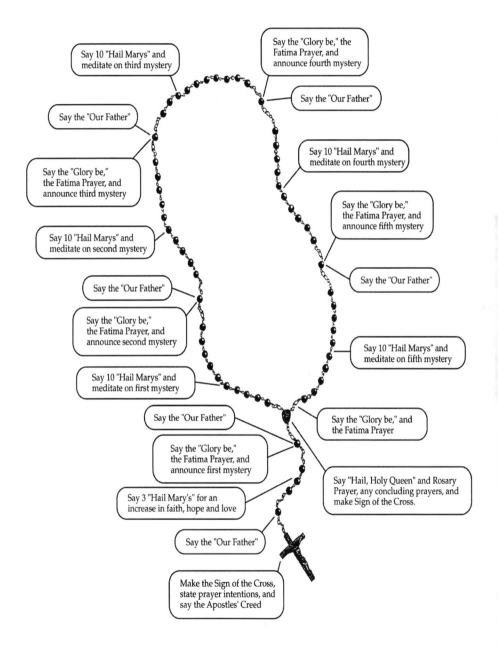

Say the "Glory be," the Fatima Prayer, and announce fourth mystery

Say 10 "Hail Marys" and meditate on third mystery

Say the "Our Father"

Say the "Our Father"

Say 10 "Hail Marys" and meditate on fourth mystery

Say the "Glory be," the Fatima Prayer, and announce third mystery

Say the "Glory be," the Fatima Prayer, and announce fifth mystery

Say 10 "Hail Marys" and meditate on second mystery

Say the "Our Father"

Say the "Our Father"

Say the "Glory be," the Fatima Prayer, and announce second mystery

Say 10 "Hail Marys" and meditate on fifth mystery

Say 10 "Hail Marys" and meditate on first mystery

Say the "Our Father"

Say the "Glory be," and the Fatima Prayer

Say the "Glory be," the Fatima Prayer, and announce first mystery

Say "Hail, Holy Queen" and Rosary Prayer, any concluding prayers, and make Sign of the Cross.

Say 3 "Hail Mary's" for an increase in faith, hope and love

Say the "Our Father"

Make the Sign of the Cross, state prayer intentions, and say the Apostles' Creed

The word "rosary" is from the Latin *rosarium*, which means a rose garden. This rose theme has been developed for centuries to encourage those who pray the rosary to think of it as offering to the Mother of God a beautiful bouquet of 50 spiritual roses, one for each *Hail Mary* said in meditation upon events in the life of Jesus and Mary.

The complete rosary consists of the 15 mysteries presented in this book, which form the basis for reflection and meditation, while the prayers shown on the previous page are recited vocally or mentally. Normally, only five of the mysteries, or five decades of the rosary, are prayed at one time. It has been said that the vocal prayers of the rosary constitute its *body* while the reflection upon the mysteries constitutes its *soul*. Both together engage the whole individual in a form of prayer that is undoubtedly the best outside of attending Mass. Pope John Paul II has declared: "The rosary is my favorite prayer."[1] Pope John XXIII prayed the 15-decade rosary every day. Nearly all of the popes for the past 400 years have had a strong devotion to the rosary.

There are numerous variations on the method of praying the rosary. Some are very minor, consisting of slight changes in wording for the various prayers. For example, the archaic form of the second person pronoun is "thee, thou, thy, and thine," and is commonly used in the Hail Mary, Our Father and other rosary prayers. It is the official liturgical form for these prayers and will, therefore, always be the form used in formal liturgies. Some people prefer to use "you, your and yours," however, since these words are the ones we use in speech today. When praying by yourself or with your family and friends, you should use the version that will be most effective in making these prayers come from your heart. In church gatherings or larger groups, however, it is better to use the official liturgical version because otherwise even such a slight change may be distracting to others.

Not everyone says the Fatima Prayer and those who do may not use exactly the same words. The Legion of Mary does not include it at all because it has never been adopted by that organization and variations from the prescribed format when Legion members pray as a group are forbidden. Some prefer to change the "rosary prayer" which follows the Hail, Holy Queen and say a different prayer; for example, the *Angelus* prayer. The important thing is to pray the basic prayers and reflect upon the great spiritual events that are presented in the mysteries of the rosary. If you do this faithfully, we are assured by St. Louis de Montfort, despite "the gravity of your sins, 'you shall receive a never fading crown of glory.'"[2] (See Appendix III for further discussion about the advantages of praying the rosary.)

---

[1] From the Holy Father's Angelus message of October 28, 1978: "The Rosary: So Rich, So Simple." Reported in *The Holy Rosary: Papal Teachings*, 281.

[2] St. Louis de Montfort, *The Secret of the Rosary*, trans. Mary Barbour, T.O.P. (Bay Shore, NY: Montfort Publications, 1954), 12.

How often is "faithfully?" The Blessed Virgin Mother told the children of Fatima to pray the rosary daily. But, "faithfully," is a matter for your individual conscience and obviously will depend upon your ability to do so. Certainly, fifteen minutes a day does not seem like a great burden, especially in light of the benefits and blessings that will shower down upon you.

There are also other ways of praying the rosary than the standard version presented here. Some of these will be explained below.

ROSARY PRAYERS

Sign of the Cross
In the name of the Father, and of the Son, and of the Holy Spirit. Amen.

Prayer Intentions
Announce (if praying in a group) or think about (if praying alone) the specific requests and intentions you have for this particular rosary; e.g., an end to abortion, or for the grace to know and accept God's will, or for healing, or for the conversion of unbelievers and world peace; or for priests and religious; or for anything else that will help you, others and the world to become holier and healthier. It is common, and excellent, to always include the intentions of the Holy Father.

Apostles' Creed
I believe in God, the Father almighty, creator of heaven and earth. I believe in Jesus Christ, his only Son, our Lord. He was conceived by the power of the Holy Spirit and born of the Virgin Mary. He suffered under Pontius Pilate, was crucified, died, and was buried. He descended into hell. On the third day he rose again. He ascended into heaven and is seated at the right hand of the Father. He will come again to judge the living and the dead. I believe in the Holy Spirit, the holy catholic Church, the communion of saints, the forgiveness of sins, the resurrection of the body, and the life everlasting. Amen.

Our Father
Our Father who art in heaven, hallowed be thy name. Thy kingdom come. Thy will be done on earth, as it is in heaven. Give us this day our daily bread, and forgive us our trespasses, as we forgive those who trespass against us, and lead us not into temptation, but deliver us from evil. Amen.

Hail Mary
Hail Mary, full of grace, the Lord is with thee. Blessed art thou among women, and blessed is the fruit of thy womb, Jesus. Holy Mary, Mother of God, pray for us sinners, now and at the hour of our death. Amen.

Prayer of Praise (Doxology)

Glory be to the Father, and to the Son, and to the Holy Spirit, as it was in the beginning, is now, and ever shall be, world without end. Amen.

Fatima Prayer

O my Jesus, forgive us our sins, save us from the fires of hell. Lead all souls to heaven, especially those who are most in need of thy mercy.

Hail, Holy Queen (Salve Regina)

Hail, holy queen, mother of mercy, our life, our sweetness and our hope. To thee do we cry, poor, banished children of Eve; to thee do we send up our sighs, mourning and weeping in this valley of tears. Turn then, most gracious advocate, thine eyes of mercy toward us; and after this, our exile, show unto us the blessed fruit of thy womb, Jesus.

O clement! O loving! O sweet Virgin Mary!

V. Pray for us, O holy Mother of God.

R. That we may be made worthy of the promises of Christ.

Let us pray (Rosary Prayer).

O God, whose only-begotten Son by his life, death and resurrection has purchased for us the rewards of eternal life, grant, we beseech you, that meditating upon these mysteries of the most holy rosary of the Blessed Virgin Mary, we may imitate what they contain and obtain what they promise. Through the same Christ, Our Lord. Amen.

The joyful mysteries of the rosary are said on Mondays and Thursdays. The sorrowful are said on Tuesdays and Fridays. The glorious mysteries are said on Wednesdays and Saturdays. Sundays are variable. From Easter to Advent, the glorious mysteries are said on this day; some say the glorious on all Sundays in Ordinary time on the liturgical calendar. During Advent, and some will include all the Sundays between Advent and Lent as well, the joyful mysteries are said. During Lent, the sorrowful mysteries are said on Sundays.

ROSARY VARIATIONS

Other versions of the rosary include the Scriptural Rosary. This form of prayer is particularly suited for groups. The rosary starts off the same, but when the decades begin, each one is preceded by a meditation, which is read, and a separate prayer intention. Then before each Hail Mary a one- or two-sentence passage from Scripture, which is appropriate for that mystery, is given. Often, the Scriptural passages are cumulative so that they tell the Bible's story of the events presented in the mystery. A portion of a hymn or chorus may conclude each decade.[3]

Another way of praying the rosary that includes an aid to meditation is to say only the first half of the Hail Mary and immediately after the name "Jesus" is spoken to add a descriptive phrase, or *clausulae*. For example:

> Hail Mary, full of grace, the Lord is with thee.
> Blessed art thou among women and blessed is the
> fruit of thy womb, Jesus, *who has freed us from*
> *the sin of Adam.*

In this way of praying the rosary, the second part of the Hail Mary, which begins with "Holy Mary, Mother of God, . . .," is said only after the 10th Hail Mary and just before the Glory Be. This type of rosary is similar to the way it was prayed hundreds of years ago when it was called the "Psalter of Our Lady." Usually, it will require booklets or prayer sheets with the add-on phrases for each person praying since these will rarely be memorized.[4]

Yet another version of the rosary is called the Rosary of Jesus. Strictly-speaking, this is not a rosary but a chaplet, or corona. It commemorates the 33 years of Jesus' life on earth. The prayers consist of the *Apostles' Creed*, 33 *Our Fathers*, and 7 *Glory Be's*. It is divided into 7 mysteries, each focused upon some aspect of the life of Christ. Each mystery is given its own prayer intention and is followed by a spoken meditation or spontaneous prayer. Each mystery concludes with the prayer affirmation, "O Jesus, be our strength and protection," and a verse or refrain from a hymn. The first six mysteries are each followed by five Our Fathers; the seventh by three Our Fathers. The rosary concludes with a meditation on the Holy Spirit followed by seven Glory Be's.

The Seven Sorrows of Mary is also a chaplet type of rosary with ancient roots. It contemplates the major sorrows of Mary's life, which are the *Prophecy of Simeon, the Flight into Egypt, the Loss of Jesus in the Temple, the Meeting with Jesus on His way to Calvary, the Death of Jesus, Receiving the Body of Jesus from the Cross*, and *Laying Jesus in the Tomb*. The rosary begins with an Act of Contrition and includes a meditation for each mystery which is followed by one or seven Hail Marys and

---

[3]Two good resources for praying the scriptural rosary are: Christine Haapala, *From Genesis to Revelation: Seven Scriptural Rosaries* and David Rosage, *Praying the Scriptural Rosary*.

[4]A charming little booklet for praying the rosary in this fashion is *Through the Rosary With Fra Angelico* by Domenico Marcucci. This book includes some lovely art work by the Renaissance painter, Fra Angelico.

one Glory Be. This type of rosary concludes with a prayer oriented toward Mary's sorrows.[5]

ROSARY DIFFICULTIES

Despite the spiritual power and beauty of the rosary, many Catholics either do not pray the rosary at all, or do so very seldom. This is very unfortunate (see Appendix III) for all of us since Our Lady has told us that we can bring peace to the world through the rosary and the scapular. It may be worthwhile, therefore, to take a moment and examine some of the objections.

(1) **It is difficult to recite vocal prayer and meditate at the same time.** If this is your problem, you may not be saying the rosary correctly. The object is to meditate upon the mysteries, not the words of the prayers. The prayers are said almost as a mantra, to provide background and context to our thoughts. If you are leading a decade in public, of course, you may be nervous and self-conscious, which makes it difficult to think about anything else. But these occasions are usually rare, or are diminished by frequency. If your problem is, *I can't hear myself think,* this, too, will diminish as you become adjusted to the experience from repetition.

"Why say the prayers at all?" you might ask. The vocal prayers remind us that we are communicating with God and also define the scope and time length of the prayer.

(2) **My mind wanders.** Some of this is normal, especially for people leading busy lives. If it happens, just keep going. Don't go back and repeat the prayers. St. Francis de Sales wrote that if one did nothing for the whole time but a continuous cycle of trying to meditate, becoming distracted, and bringing the mind back to focus again it would still be a lovely prayer which the Lord would appreciate very much.[6] A good way to minimize the problem is to pray at times when your mind is relatively relaxed. For example, some people like to pray the rosary while driving, especially if the driving is tedious. Right after dinner is a good time for the family rosary. A wandering, distracted mind is frequently an indication of stress. Praying the rosary is a wonderful antidote for this problem. If your mind wanders excessively during the rosary, you may find it much more focused after you have finished.

---

[5]The information summarized here and additional details about these and other forms of rosary prayer may be found in *The Gold Book of Prayers,* Milford, OH: Riehle Foundation, 1989.

[6]See Father Paul A. Duffner, O.P., "Some Objections Against the Rosary," *The Rosary Light & Life,* Sep-Oct, 1985, 3.

(3) **Repetition is monotonous.** Because of the variation in the meditation series from joyful, through sorrowful, to glorious, you should not find praying the rosary painfully monotonous. But, if you do, it is probably because you are not meditating correctly. As already noted, you should not be listening to the words of the prayers but reflecting upon the events included in the rosary mystery and considering how they apply to your own life. Unlike some cult or pagan incantations, the prayers of the rosary are not considered to be "magic words" to unlock the secrets of the divine. They merely set the stage for the action that takes place in your mind and heart.

You should be considering as many of the details as you can of each of the mysteries, because often a previously-overlooked detail may open up a whole new insight for you. Occasionally, you may experience a real flash of understanding of some spiritual point which will provide you food for thought for a long time.

It takes only about two minutes to say a decade of the rosary. As you can see from the stories in this book, two minutes is nowhere near enough time to consider even a few of the details included. If you build upon what is given to you here and let your own imagination consider other aspects or points of view, you will find that it is not only not monotonous but, rather, difficult to complete your meditation before the decade ends.

The more you read and study Scripture and books relating to these mysteries, the more you will find to reflect upon. So, rather than quitting the rosary, open up your horizons and let more knowledge in!

(4) **I get bored with the meditations**. Some of what was just said applies here. The more you learn, the easier it will be to find new aspects of the mysteries to consider when you pray. Hardly anyone gets bored thinking about their own life experiences, no matter how many times they have remembered them. This is because these memories bring back a whole set of emotions and issues relating to what happened, the persons involved, events since then, and the consequences of the earlier emotions, actions and decisions. In a nutshell, it all remains real to us.

If you think of the rosary mysteries in the same way, you will find it much easier to reconsider them. Let the characters come to life in your mind. Give them words to say, things to do, reactions to show, choices to make. All this must be faithful to what we are given in Scripture and to our Catholic faith, of course. But, as the stories in this book show, that leaves plenty of room for imaginative reflection.

Expand your meditation. For example, the sorrowful mysteries take place in the context of a swirl of dramatic tension, conflict and climax which we call Holy Week. It is certainly relevant to the sufferings of Jesus to reflect upon the mystery of the Eucharist which He gave us at the Last Supper, or the tragedy of Judas, or the weakness of the apostles, or the stubborn blindness of the Jewish authorities, etc., etc. In fact, consideration of such other related elements frequently heightens our appreciation of just what a sacrifice Jesus made for us and how incredible His love must have been to endure what He did in the face of the failings of those He came to save.

Another good suggestion is to "look" at the scene in your mind's eye. Don't deal in abstractions. Approach your meditation the way you approach a movie or television. Sit back and relax and watch what is going on. Don't work so hard to discover or appreciate theological profundities. When you find these, it is usually because they sneak up on you when you least expect them.

ONE LAST THOUGHT: it is a nearly universal human experience that what is worth having takes work to get and to keep. If it comes too easily, we do not value it. Just as we admire people who overcome adversity to achieve something, so God, too, appreciates our prayer even more when it is difficult for us, if we continue to try. Most of us do not like quitters. Neither does the Lord,[7] although he is infinitely patient and merciful and always ready to help us start up again.

Athletes, writers and foreign language students often experience dry spells or plateaus when they seem unable to progress further. Such "staleness" frequently affects human relationships as well. But, in every case, perseverance can not only overcome the block but usually leads to advancement in the particular endeavor. The same thing will happen to your prayer life if you do not give up. Work through the dry periods. Pray when it seems like a terrible chore. Thank God for the opportunity He is giving you to show Him that you love Him even when the going is tough.

---

[7]See Lk 9:62: "Whoever puts his hand to the plow but keeps looking back is unfit for the reign of God," says Jesus to the would-be follower who wants to say goodbye to his family first.

APPENDIX II

History of the Rosary

The history of the rosary is the story of the development of a powerful religious devotion shepherded by the Blessed Virgin Mary herself. It is not a story without controversy and disagreement. But these arguments over who did and said what and when are fundamentally irrelevant to the truth that the Holy Mother of God has personally endorsed this method of prayer and promised that it would be God's instrument for overcoming the evil in the present age.[1]

What follows below is an outline of the evolution of this great prayer.

YEAR	MILESTONE
±900 B.C. - Present	Stones, knots on a cord, beads on a chain, etc., are used as a simple, effective means in many religions, including Buddhism, Hinduism, Islam, and Christianity, of keeping count of the number of prayers said.
±300-400 A.D.	Christian hermits (anchorites) use heaps of pebbles to count their daily prayer requirement.
750	Irish monks begin to assign Our Fathers *(Paternosters)* as penance instead of psalms or meditations.
800	Irish monks divide the 150 psalms (the Psalter) into three groups of 50 each.[2]

---

[1]The Blessed Virgin Mary not only exhorted the three children of Fatima several times to pray the rosary to obtain peace for the world and an end to World War I, which was then raging, but she identified herself in the October 13, 1917, apparition as "Our Lady of the Rosary." (See *Fatima in Lucia's Own Words*, 168). She also appeared in the same apparition as Our Lady of Carmel (p. 170), which many interpret as a call to wear the cloth Brown Scapular as a visible sign of devotion to her Immaculate Heart.

[2]"The 150 psalms of the Hebrew Scriptures have comprised, since the earliest of Christian times, the most important part of the canonical hours." Richard Gribble, C.S.C., *History and Devotion of the Rosary* (Huntington, IN: Our Sunday Visitor, 1992), 19. During the early to late Middle Ages, the Psalter (entire 150 psalms) was arranged within the Divine Office, which members of the clergy pray, so that the 150 psalms would be recited weekly.

YEAR	**MILESTONE**
±900 A.D.	The laity begin saying 150 popular prayers as their version of the Psalter since they were mostly illiterate and could neither read nor gain easy access to the written psalms.
950	Practice of saying psalms in three groups of 50's appears in northern Italy.
1000	"Little Psalter" of 3 x 50 Our Fathers is widespread in Europe for the laity and religious incapable in Latin.
±1000	Use of beads to count Our Fathers.
±1100-1200	Development of Marian Psalters consisting of 150 short verses of praise for the Blessed Virgin Mary; evolved into recitation of 150 shortened versions of the Hail Mary.[3] The rose garden becomes a symbol of the Virgin Mary and *Aves* (Hail Marys) are compared to spiritual roses.
1200-1300	Marian Psalter, using knotted cords or beads, becomes standard form of repetitive prayer for clergy, religious and laity alike.
1208-1214	Date uncertain: Saint Dominic reportedly has a vision of the Blessed Virgin Mary who tells him to use the Marian Psalter to combat the Albigensian heresy.
1259	Confraternity of Prayer founded by Dominicans in Piacenza; members

---

[3]At this time, the Hail Mary consisted of the Archangel Gabriel salutation: "Hail Mary, full of grace, the Lord is with thee" plus increasingly throughout the period, the Elizabeth salutation: "Blessed art thou among women and blessed is the fruit of thy womb." The 1970 edition of the New American Bible also included "Blessed art thou among women" in the greeting of Gabriel but removed it in the 1986 edition.

YEAR	MILESTONE
1259 A.D. (cont'd)	required to pray the Marian Psalter daily. "Militia of Jesus Christ," founded earlier by St. Dominic, had a similar requirement.
1261	Pope Urban IV adds word "Jesus" following "womb" at end of Elizabeth salutation. Grants indulgence for saying it. However, the practice does not take hold until about 200 years later.
±1400	Adolph of Essen, Carthusian monk at the Trier Charterhouse, combines meditation upon the life of Jesus with saying of 50 Hail Marys. Earliest version of modern rosary.
1409	Dominic of Prussia, a sickly Carthusian monk also at the Trier Charterhouse, devises 50 separate themes from the Life of Jesus to say with each of the Hail Marys. These *clausulae* are added at the end of each Hail Mary following the word "Jesus." Henry of Kalbar develops rosary with five decades of Hail Marys and 50 *clausulae*, preceded by an Our Father for each decade.
1400s	Mystery themes (*clausulae*) are developed for all 150 Hail Marys in the Marian Psalter.
1470	Blessed Alanus de Rupe (also known as Alan de la Roche) founds Confraternity of the Psalter of Jesus and Mary. This Dominican priest was a tireless promoter of the rosary devotion and has been called the "Father of the Rosary." Confraternities lead to group praying of the rosary and thereby its standardization.

YEAR	MILESTONE
1489 A.D.	*Unser Lieben Frauen Psalter* is published with 15 mysteries, one for each decade, virtually the same as the modern set.
1495	The Apostles' Creed appears as an addition to the rosary.
1500-1600	The doxology (Glory Be) is added by common usage after each decade of Hail Marys.
1521	Alberto da Castello, O.P., is first to use word "mystery" in connection with the rosary; organizes 150 *clausulae* into 15 groups of 10 and publishes rosary picture book.
1568	Modern version of the Hail Mary is officially adopted in the Roman Breviary following earlier acceptance by Council of Trent (1545-1563).
1573	Pope Gregory XIII establishes, for churches with a rosary altar, first Sunday in October as Feast of the Most Holy Rosary in recognition of rosary-aided defeat of Turks at 1571 Battle of Lepanto.
1573	Book *Rosario della Sacratissima* by A. Giametti, O.P., sets modern 15 rosary mysteries in three sets of joyful, sorrowful and glorious.
1600	By this time, the Hail, Holy Queen *(Salve Regina)* is part of the rosary.
1612	Pendant of the rosary, consisting of crucifix and initial three beads plus Our Father bead, added by this date.
1680	Rosary as we know it today, except for Fatima Prayer, in use. Not long after,

YEAR	MILESTONE
1680 A.D. (cont'd)	St. Louis Marie de Montfort writes his enormously influential book: *The Secret of the Rosary*.
1716	Pope Clement XI extends Feast of the Holy Rosary to universal church.
1858	During 18 appearances to St. Bernadette, the Blessed Virgin Mary, "Our Lady of Lourdes," carries a rosary and encourages Bernadette to pray it.
1878-1903	The "Rosary Pope," Pope Leo XIII, makes devotion to Mary through the rosary a focus of his pontificate; establishes October as the month to be especially devoted to praying of the rosary; reestablishes Confraternity of the Rosary.
1917	Blessed Virgin Mary gives Fatima Prayer to Lucia, Jacinta and Francisco of Fatima, Portugal. She requests everyone to pray the rosary for world peace and refers to herself as the "Lady of the Rosary."
1942-1992	Father Patrick Peyton, C.S.C., launches family rosary crusade which produces slogan: "The family that prays together, stays together;" founds Family Theater Productions and becomes internationally known as "the Rosary Priest."
1978-Present	Pope John Paul II reinvigorates devotion to the rosary by his personal example and exhortations.

APPENDIX III
Why You Should Pray the Rosary

The rosary is an intimidating prayer for most people. It may seem old-fashioned. It requires 15 to 20 minutes. If you kneel, you may feel embarrassingly pious. In a group, you may end up being asked to lead one of the decades, which makes some people nervous. In an age when families often cannot meet even to share dinner, coming together to say the rosary seems impossible. For persons whose religious education was limited and who are relatively unfamiliar with the New Testament, the mysteries of the rosary may be as mysterious in their historical facts as they are in their theological and salvific meaning. For those who know what the mysteries are describing, there is still the problem of monotony or shallow comprehension. It frequently seems way too much like work and conflicts with other activities that appear to offer more in the way of relaxation or productivity.

If any of these attitudes fit you, this appendix is especially important for you to ponder because you are being left out of the richest spiritual investment program known to man. As St. Louis de Montfort tells us: "For never will anyone who says his Rosary every day become a formal heretic or be led astray by the devil. This is a statement that I would gladly sign with my blood."[1]

It is not an exaggeration to say that as long as you pray the rosary sincerely every day and make an effort to reflect on its mysteries, you cannot lead the kind of life that will forfeit your soul! This is because praying the rosary affects the sinner in the same way as aversion therapy. It causes a powerful adverse reaction to the harmful addiction. You cannot do both at the same time. You do not have to account to anyone for how or when you say it. It does not cost a penny. You do not have to kneel. You do have to stay awake, though. And you do have to make a sincere effort to reflect on the mysteries of the rosary and what they mean for you and the world. Not so burdensome, really. For this little effort, you will open a veritable treasure chest of graces that will lead to eternal salvation for yourself. If you can find a better deal than this anywhere in the universe, you should definitely grab it. Best of all, you do not have to take this assurance on faith. As soon as you put it into practice in your own life, you will start to see the spiritual benefits. If you persevere, those benefits will steadily increase. You will grow in holiness.

Don't get me wrong here. This transformation does not come about because of some new and improved attitude, like a self-help course in positive motivation. Nor does it establish even the slightest obligation on the part of God.

---

[1]Montfort, *The Secret of the Rosary*, 62.

What it does is put you into a stream of grace generously and lovingly offered to all by Jesus Christ. That stream WILL transform your life.

Still hesitating? Okay, read on.

No less an authority than the Holy Mother of God, the Blessed Virgin Mary herself, has called upon all of us to pray the rosary for world peace. In 1917 at Fatima, Portugal, she said it would prevent future wars. Well, it seems to have kept Portugal out of the two world wars this century, but there was no international response to our Blessed Lady's request and so the "worse war" she predicted (World War II) came along in fairly short order.

Since 1981 in Medjugorje, she has been asking us to pray 15 decades of the rosary, to attend Mass every day, and to fast on bread and water on Wednesdays and Fridays. It seems the ante has been raised for saving the world. What are the odds that mankind will respond to this new, much more stringent request? That's what I think, too. But God is so merciful that if we would just take a single step, it would dramatically improve our situation. It has been estimated that if only 10% of Catholics would pray the rosary for only one hour per week, it would be sufficient to defeat Satan completely.[2]

In any event, your soul is *your* responsibility. No matter what happens to the world, you, and everyone else, are going to be here for a comparatively very short time. The rosary is not only a lifeline from you to heaven, but it will enormously enhance the quality of your life while you are here on earth. It puts you in touch with the cross of Jesus, which is a very sobering antidote to any tendency you may have to become proud, complacent or self-indulgent.

According to a long tradition dating back at least 400 years to Blessed Alan de la Roche (aka Alanus de Rupe), the Blessed Virgin Mary has promised the following 15 benefits for those who pray the rosary:

1. To those who recite my Rosary devoutly, I promise my special protection.
2. Those who shall persevere in the recitation of my Rosary will receive some very special grace.
3. The Rosary will be a powerful armor against hell; it will destroy vice, deliver from sin and dispel heresy.
4. The Rosary will make virtue and good works flourish, and will obtain for souls the most abundant divine mercies; it will

---

[2]See Rev. Albert J.M. Shamon, *The Power of the Rosary* (Milford, OH: Riehle Foundation, 1990), 40. Compare Gn 18:22-32 where the Lord agrees to spare Sodom and Gomorrah if Abraham can find but ten innocent people in the city.

Note, also, that the Church has not declared the reported apparitions at Medjugorje worthy of belief. The matter is still under investigation and review. My comments here are in no way intended to anticipate the judgment of the Church, to which I wholeheartedly submit, whatever the outcome.

substitute in hearts a love of God for love of the world and lead them to seek the things of heaven.

5. Those who trust themselves to me through the Rosary will not perish.

6. Those who recite my Rosary piously, meditating upon its mysteries, will not be overwhelmed by misfortune; nor die a bad death. The sinner will be converted and the just shall grow in grace.

7. Those truly devoted to my Rosary will not die without the consolations of the Church.

8. Those who shall recite my Rosary will find the light of God during their life and, at their death, the fullness of His grace, and will share in the merits of the blessed.

9. I will deliver promptly from Purgatory those souls who were devoted to my Rosary.

10. The true children of my Rosary will enjoy great glory in heaven.

11. What you shall ask through my Rosary you shall obtain.

12. Those who spread devotion to my Rosary will obtain through me aid in all their needs.

13. I have obtained from my Son that all advocates of the Rosary shall have the saints of heaven as their friends in life and in death.

14. Those who recite my Rosary faithfully are all my beloved children, the brothers and sisters of my Son, Jesus Christ.

15. Devotion to my Rosary is a great sign of one's eternal destination.[3]

Historically, the power of the rosary has been demonstrated in dramatic fashion on several occasions. Probably the most famous of these, and the one which prompted the Church to establish the Feast of the Holy Rosary (October 7), is the Battle of Lepanto. In that naval engagement in 1571, Don Juan of Austria led the Christian naval forces against the Moslem Turk invaders. He was outnumbered 3 to 1. Pope Pius V initiated a rosary crusade, including processions in Rome, to ask the Blessed Virgin Mary's help. At a key point in the battle, the winds suddenly shifted, the Turks were thrown into confusion, and the Austrian forces defeated them.

In 1683, the rosary was again credited with assisting the Christian West to defeat the land forces of the Turks near Vienna, Austria. In that case, King John Sobieski of Poland led the outnumbered and weary Christian populace and

---

[3]The 15 promises of the Blessed Virgin Mary are reported in numerous places, including the World Apostolate of Fatima, Washington, NJ; Johnson, *The Rosary in Action*, 33; and Bob and Penny Lord, *The Rosary: The Life of Jesus and Mary* (Fair Oaks, CA: Journeys of Faith, 1993), 188-189.

soldiers in first appealing to Our Blessed Mother for help and then, with a much smaller force, in defeating 200,000 Turkish soldiers.

Another remarkable testimony to the miraculous protection of Our Lady of the Rosary is the story of the four Jesuit priests located nearly at ground zero in Hiroshima, Japan, on August 6, 1945, when the first atomic bomb was dropped on a populated city. The city was essentially levelled to the ground since 99 percent of it was composed of flimsy Japanese housing. The Jesuits' Church of our Lady's Assumption, 1,200 meters from the center of the blast, was also destroyed but their rectory, right next to it, survived. The four priests, none of whom ever developed cancer or suffered any of the ill effects of radiation, attributed their survival to their praying of the rosary daily and "living the message of Fatima."[4]

Following World War II, Austria was occupied by Russian troops. It began to look like they might remain a permanent occupation force, as in East Germany, until they suddenly agreed to leave in a treaty signed May 15, 1955. This followed a huge rosary prayer gathering two days earlier on May 13 to commemorate the first Fatima apparition on May 13, 1917. In 1946, a Franciscan priest, Father Peter Pavlicek, had organized a national rosary crusade in the nation, seeking a "tithe" of the population to pledge to pray the rosary. By 1953, the Federal Chancellor and the Foreign Minister of Austria were participating in a candlelight rosary procession on the eve of the feast of the Name of Mary. A year later, the Rosary Crusade had nearly a half million active members. At a time when the West seemed to have little leverage over them, the Soviets nonetheless abandoned Austria without any significant *quid pro quo*. Many attribute this to Mary's divine influence.

In 1962, Brazil appeared to be on the verge of a major Communist Party victory at the polls. The women of Brazil, under the leadership of Dona Amelia Bastos who formed a group called "Campaign of Women for Democracy," rose up in a gigantic rosary crusade. On March 19, 1962, 600,000 women marched through the streets of São Paulo praying the rosary for three hours. Within two weeks, President Goulart fled the country and the communist threat collapsed.

Some attribute the collapse of the leftist Allende government in Chile in the early 1970's to a three-year rosary and scapular crusade which preceded it.

A great outpouring of the Portuguese people in 1975 turned to Our Lady of Fatima, reaching a climax on October 13, a Fatima anniversary date, to try to head off what appeared to be a certain Communist take-over of the country. A few weeks later, the communist threat collapsed. Portugal had already managed to avoid entanglement in either of the two World Wars this century. To many, the elimination of the Communist threat seemed to be additional evidence of the Mother of God's protection.

---

[4]Francis Johnston, *Fatima: The Great Sign* (Rockford, IL: TAN Books, 1980), 139.

Still others believe that prayer to the Blessed Mother resulted in catastrophes to the Soviet Union's missile program on Fatima anniversary dates in 1960 and 1984.

In late February 1986, the supporters of Corazon Aquino marched against the tanks and troops of the corrupt Philippines dictator, Ferdinand Marcos. They were outnumbered by at least 10:1. Their weapons were rosaries and flowers. But no shots were fired that day. Instead, many of the soldiers embraced the marchers, crawling out of their tanks and joining the civilians in celebrating the victory of Corazon and her champion, the Blessed Mother. Some soldiers would later report seeing an apparition of the Blessed Virgin Mary in the sky imploring them not to fire on her people.

Corazon Aquino's devotion to the rosary and the Lady whom it honors was well known during the six years of her presidency of the Philippines (1986-1992). During that period, this political novice, thrust unexpectedly and totally unprepared onto the political stage by the 1983 assassination of her husband, Benigno S. Aquino, Jr., survived several threatened coup attempts. Whether or not you believe there were miraculous apparitions of the Mother of God in support of Corazon Aquino, the facts in her case make a persuasive argument for praying the rosary.

Since June 24, 1981, when the Blessed Virgin Mary reportedly began appearing on a daily basis to six young people in Medjugorje, Bosnia, that little village has been completely spared the devastation that has produced valid charges of genocide against the Serbs and even the Croations in other parts of Yugoslavia. Tales of planes unable to find their targets in the little village and troops who mysteriously abandoned offensive operations float around. These things are often hard to pin down and credibility becomes strained in the presence of unsubstantiated claims of miraculous interventions. But one fact is starkly clear and uncontroverted: Medjugorje remained an island of peace and tranquility only 20 miles from Mostar, which was largely destroyed.

Captain Scott O'Grady, an American F-16 pilot, was shot down over Bosnia in June 1995. He survived six days on the ground in the midst of hostile Serbian troops and came away from the experience convinced that he had seen "something" that substantiated the claims that the Blessed Mother has been appearing in Medjugorje. To my knowledge, he has not publicly elaborated on this statement to provide more details..

Ultimately, however, the rosary is not about political power and world peace and tranquility. God loves us and He cares deeply about our welfare in this life. But this world is merely a battleground. The *war* is won or lost in eternity. It is our souls which are at stake. In this struggle, what happens to us on earth is insignificant, indeed, except in the consequences for our eternal salvation. What can the rosary do for us in this truly dangerous struggle with Satan?

The rosary takes us directly into Scripture, into the life of the Son of God, who is our hope and our salvation. The joyful mysteries tell us about the early life of Jesus Christ. They also provide us a beautiful model of family life which, if followed in our own lives, would put an end to all the intrafamily conflict and misery that currently afflicts modern society.

The sorrowful mysteries confront us with the inescapable reality that suffering is necessary and has meaning. It is the means by which the doors of heaven were finally opened to us. It is the means by which we may do penance for our own sins and contribute the merits of our acceptance of suffering toward atonement for the sins of others. No one with an open mind and heart can pray the sorrowful mysteries of the rosary for long without understanding the great truth that suffering has value. It may seem paradoxical that we are also called by the Gospels to do everything we can to ameliorate suffering in the lives of others. But it is not. By helping others overcome and cope with their problems, we share in their crosses. Our suffering becomes a means of healing for others. In this, we are Christ in miniature. As already noted, just praying the rosary may involve some minor suffering because it often seems tedious, inconvenient and uncomfortable. The sorrowful mysteries invite us to realize the grace value of accepting our hardships and offering them to God as signs of our unselfish love for Him.

The glorious mysteries are a beautiful reminder to us that our eternal destination lies beyond this world. That should be a wonderful comfort to us no matter what afflictions we may suffer in our temporal lives. Great suffering leads to great glory. We can see that with crystal clarity in the glorious mysteries. How else can we demonstrate our love for God unselfishly than by accepting our crosses cheerfully and even gratefully? So few seem able to do it, but the principle of its value is obvious. In an age of euthanasia and the right to die to avoid any and all pain, even the emotional pain of depression, the glorious mysteries remind us that suffering has its reward, not only for the individuals concerned but also for all of us who receive grace because of *their* willingness to join their sorrows with those of Jesus Christ.

By taking us into the Gospels and, from there, into the inspired writings of Saint Paul and the other authors of the New Testament epistles, the mysteries of the rosary teach us about our faith. Thus, the rosary has been called the "Little Summa" because it embodies all of the doctrines of our Christian beliefs.[5] Each time you meditate seriously upon these events from the lives of Jesus and Mary, you are learning about your faith and giving the Holy Spirit an opportunity to deepen your understanding of the profound truths contained in them.

The rosary is a powerful antidote to the rampant materialism that has infected our society. One cannot reflect upon the mysteries of the rosary without realizing that the spiritual world is not only of infinitely greater importance than the material world in which we temporarily live, but the temptations and

---

[5]See Pope Leo XIII's encyclical, *Magnae Dei Matris*, Sep. 7, 1892, ¶97; Pope Paul VI, Apostolic Exhortation, *Marialis Cultus*, Feb. 2, 1974, ¶439; Robert Feeney, *The Rosary*, "The Little Summa" (San Francisco: Ignatius Press, 1997);" and Fr. Thomas A. Feucht, O.P., "The Riches of the Rosary," *The Rosary, Light and Life*, Sep-Oct, 1976.

corruptions of material success directly threaten our eternal welfare. In this sense, the rosary is wonderfully sobering.

Even the very act of praying the rosary, involving the fingering of beads, is a tension-relieving exercise. It is comparable to the therapeutic benefits of knitting, which was used after World War I to help calm shell-shocked soldiers.[6]

In an address on April 25, 1987, to a group of 5,000 children who were participating in a "Living Rosary," Pope John Paul II said:

> The mysteries of the Rosary have rightly been compared to windows through which you can thrust and immerse your glance in the 'world of God.' It is only from that world, from 'the example that Jesus has left us' (1 Pet. 2:21) that you learn to be courageous in time of difficulty, patient in adversity, secure in temptation.[7]

On October 13, 1972, an Italian priest, Fr. Stefano Gobbi, founded the Marian Movement of Priests in response to what he believed to be a direct call from the Mother of God while he was praying at Fatima. Since 1973, Father Gobbi has reported the words of the Blessed Virgin Mary, which come to him in the form of interior "locutions;" i.e., communications that are received from an outside source but without an external apparition or voice. Here are some of the things he has reported hearing from the Blessed Virgin Mary:

> "Your entire rosary, which you recite in the cenacle [prayer group formed specifically to pray the rosary and consider the Blessed Mother's messages through Father Gobbi] in accordance with the urgent request of your Mother, is like an immense chain of love and salvation with which you are able to encircle persons and situations, and even to influence all the events of your time.
>
> "The rosary is the prayer which I myself came down from heaven to ask of you.
>
> "By it you are able to lay bare the plots of my Adversary; you escape from many of his deceits; you defend yourselves from many dangers which he puts in your way; it preserves you from evil and brings you ever closer to me, because I am able to be truly your guide and your protection." [No. 184, "Your Rosary," October 7, 1979].

---

[6]See Father Basil Cole, O.P., "Understanding the Rosary," *The Rosary, Light and Life,* Sep-Oct 1983, 2.

[7]Reported in *The Rosary, Light and Life,* Sep-Oct, 1987, 1. A "Living Rosary" is one in which the members each pledge to say one decade of the rosary each day.

"While this prayer is despised by the great and the proud, it is recited with so much love and so much joy by my little ones, by the poor, by children, by the humble, the suffering, by the many, many faithful souls who have welcomed my invitation.

"It is a prayer you say together with me.

"By contemplating its mysteries, you are led to understand the plan of Jesus, as spelled out in all of his life, from

the Incarnation to the consummation of his glorious Pasch, and

thus you penetrate ever more profoundly into the mystery of the redemption." [No. 275, "The Dragon Will Be Shackled," October 7, 1983].

"I am the Queen of the Holy Rosary.

"Pray above all with the prayer of the holy rosary. Let the rosary be, for everyone, the powerful weapon to be made use of in these times.

"The rosary brings you to peace. With this prayer, you are able to obtain from the Lord the great grace of a change of hearts, of the conversion of souls, and of the return of all humanity to God, along the road of repentance, of love, of divine grace and of holiness." [No. 336,"The Rosary Brings You to Peace," October 7, 1986].[8]

Finally, there is the very practical benefit of indulgences granted by the Church for praying the rosary under certain circumstances. These indulgences, although abused in the past, nonetheless are offered with the solemn assurance of the Popes, whom Jesus empowered to speak for Him,[9] that they will reduce in whole or in part the temporal punishment of purgatory due for the commission of sins that are forgiven.

These indulgences are earned under specific circumstances, and are offered with relative frequency to members of the Confraternity of the Rosary. It thus behooves all devotees of the rosary to join the Confraternity. Membership requires praying the 15 decades of the rosary at least once in the course of a week

---

[8]These selections are taken from the compilation of the Marian locutions to Father Gobbi in *To The Priests, Our Lady's Beloved Sons* (St. Francis, Me: Marian Movement of Priests, 1993) and are reprinted by permission. Readers interested in knowing more about Father Gobbi's locutions and the Marian Movement of Priests should write to The Marian Movement of Priests, P.O. Box 8, St. Francis, Maine 04774-008, or call (207) 398-3375.

[9]"I will entrust to you the keys of the kingdom of heaven. Whatever you declare bound on earth shall be bound in heaven; whatever you declare loosed on earth shall be loosed in heaven." Mt 16:19.

and having one's name recorded in the register of the Confraternity. Failure to honor one's commitment is **NOT** a sin, not even a very minor one. But, of course, the indulgences would not be available, and Our Blessed Mother might wonder about your faithfulness.

Perhaps even more important, members of the Confraternity share in the value of the rosaries said by all other members, which is an incredible way of multiplying the benefits of praying the rosary.[10] Members are special spiritual concerns of the entire Dominican Order. There are no meetings and no dues. Those who desire it will receive *The Rosary, Light and Life*. Finally, members receive the special protection of the Mother of God. So what are you waiting for? Send your name and address and a request to be enrolled to:

The Rosary Center
P.O. Box 3617
Portland, OR 97208

Do yourself a huge favor. BE HAPPY! Pray the rosary every day. Take 15 minutes from your daily efforts to maintain your mental and physical health and appearance and improve the health and appearance of your *soul*. You can even pray it on your way to and from the gym or library. Then when you complete your individual "marathon of life," the Holy Mother of God will be standing at the finish line to personally place upon your brow the wreath of eternal joy.

---

[10]This is another reason why praying the rosary as a family is superior to praying it alone. Not only do you get the love and bonding which comes from the grace of God given to all of the participating family members, but you get the multiplier effect as well. See Montfort, *The Secret of the Rosary*, 97.

Selected Bibliography

17 Papal Documents on the Rosary, Boston: Daughters of St. Paul, 1980.

Agreda, Venerable Mary of. *Mystical City of God.* 4 vols. Translated by Fiscar Marison. Washington, NJ: Ave Maria Institute, 1971.

Barbet, Pierre. *A Doctor at Calvary.* Translated by the Earl of Wicklow. Garden City, NY: Doubleday Image Books, 1963.

Batey, Richard A. *Jesus & the Forgotten City.* Grand Rapids, MI: Baker Book House, 1991.

Bishop, Jim. *The Day Christ Died.* New York: Harper & Row, 1957.

Brown, Michael H. *The Day Will Come.* Ann Arbor, MI: Servant Publications, 1996.

———. *After Life, What It's Like in Heaven, Hell, and Purgatory.* Milford, OH: Faith Publishing Co., 1997.

Brown, Raymond E., S.S. *The Birth of the Messiah.* Garden City, NY: Doubleday, 1977.

———. *The Death of the Messiah.* New York: Doubleday, 1994.

Butler's Lives of the Saints. Edited by Thurston and Attwater. Westminster, MD: Christian Classics, 4 vols., 1956.

Bryson, David Burton, *A Western Way of Meditation, the Rosary Revisited.* Chicago: Loyola University Press, 1991.

Burnside, Eleanor T. *Bible Rosary: the Life of Jesus.* Edited by Rev. Philip Gage, S.M. Birmingham, MI: Rosary Thirty-Five, 1979.

Calkins, Arthur B., Rev. *Our Lady's Vow of Virginity.* Washington, NJ: AMI Press, 1993.

Callan, Charles J. and McConnell, John F. *Spiritual Riches of the Rosary Mysteries.* New York: Joseph F. Wagner, 1957.

Carney, James L. *The Seton Miracles, Weeping Statues and Other Wonders.* Woodbridge, VA: Marian Foundation, 1998.

Catechism of the Catholic Church. Libreria Editrice Vaticana. St. Paul Books & Media, 1994.

Catholic Study Bible. Edited by Donald Senior. New York: Oxford University Press, 1990.

Chittister, Joan, OSB. *Mary, Wellspring of Peace.* Erie, PA: Pax Christi USA, 1987.

Connell, Janice T. *Meetings with Mary, Visions of the Blessed Mother.* New York: Ballantine Books, 1995.

Cruz, Joan Carroll. *Miraculous Images of Our Lord.* Rockford, IL: TAN Books, 1995.

———. *Relics.* Huntington, IN: Our Sunday Visitor, 1984.

Cunneen, Sally. *In Search of Mary: the Woman and the Symbol.* New York: Ballantine Books, 1996.

Dante, Alighieri. *The Divine Comedy.* Translated by Lawrence G. White. New York: Pantheon Books, 1963.

Dollen, Charles, Msgr. *My Rosary, Its Power and Mystery.* New York: Alba House, 1988.

Durant, Will. *Caesar and Christ.* New York: Simon and Schuster, 1944.

Durham, Michael S. *Miracles of Mary: Apparitions, Legends and Miraculous Works of the Blessed Virgin Mary.* Harper San Francisco: New York, 1995.

Edwards, William D., M.D., *et. al.* "On the Physical Death of Jesus Christ," *Journal of the American Medical Association,* 255, No. 11 (Mar. 21, 1986): 1455-1463.

Eicher, Peter. *Visions of Mary.* New York: Avon Books, 1996.

Encyclopedic Dictionary of Religion. Washington: Corpus Publications, 1979.

Feeney, Robert. *The Rosary, "The Little Summa."* San Francisco: Ignatius Press, 1997.

Ferraro, John Rev. *Ten Series of Meditations on the Mysteries of the Rosary.* Boston: St. Paul Books & Media, 1981.

Fuerst, Anthony N., S.T.D. *This Rosary.* Milwaukee, WI: Bruce Publishing, 1942.

Gaffney, J. Patrick, S.M.M. *The Rosary, A Gospel Prayer.* Bay Shore, NY: Montfort Publications, 1991.

Gobbi, Don Stefano. *To the Priests, Our Lady's Beloved Sons.* 14th ed. St. Francis, ME: Marian Movement of Priests, 1993.

Gold Book of Prayers. Milford, OH: Riehle Foundation, 1989.

Gonen, Rivka. *Biblical Holy Places, an Illustrated Guide.* New York: Macmillan Publishing, 1987.

Gower, Ralph. *The New Manners and Customs of Bible Times.* Chicago: Moody Press, 1987.

Gribble, Richard, C.S.C. *The History and Devotion of the Rosary.* Huntington, IN: Our Sunday Visitor, 1992.

Guardini, Romano. *The Rosary of Our Lady.* Manchester, NH: Sophia Institute Press, 1994.

Haapala, Christine. *From Genesis to Revelation: Seven Scriptural Rosaries.* Front Royal, VA: Christendom Press, 1996.

Harper Atlas of the Bible. Edited by James B. Pritchard. New York: Harper & Row, 1987.

Hastings, Arthur F. *In His Honor, a Pictorial Journey Through the Early Years of the Christian Church.* Muskego, WI: H.H.P. Publishing, 1994.

Hebert, Albert J., S.M. *Mary and Her Hidden Life.* P.O. Box 309, Paulina, LA, 1986.

Heller, John H. *Report on the Shroud of Turin.* Boston: Houghton Mifflin, 1983.

Holy Rosary, Papal Teachings. Translated by Rev. Paul J. Oligny, O.F.M. Boston: Daughters of St. Paul, 1980.

Hophan, Otto, O.F.M. (Cap.). *The Apostles.* Translated by L. Edward Wasserman, Westminster, MD: Newman Press, 1962.

House, H. Wayne. *Chronological and Background Charts of the New Testament.* Grand Rapids, MI: Zondervan Publishing, 1981.

Houselander, Caryll. *The Essential Rosary*. Manchester, NH: Sophia Institute Press, 1996.

Hutchinson, Gloria. *Praying the Rosary, New Reflections on the Mysteries*. Cincinnati: St. Anthony Messenger Press, 1991.

Jelly, Frederick M., O.P. *Madonna, Mary in the Catholic Tradition*. Huntington, IN: Our Sunday Visitor, 1986.

Jepsen, Dee. *Jesus Called Her Mother*. Minneapolis: MN, Bethany House, 1992.

Jerome Biblical Commentary. Edited by Raymond Brown, S.S. Englewood, NJ: Prentice-Hall, 1968.

Jesus and His Times. Edited by Kaari Ward. Pleasantville, NY: Reader's Digest Assn, 1987.

Johnson, John S. *The Rosary in Action*. Rockford, IL: TAN Books, 1954.

Johnson, Kevin Orlin. *Rosary: Mysteries, Meditations, and the Telling of the Beads*. Dallas, TX: Pangaeus Press, 1996.

Johnston, Francis W. *Fatima, the Great Sign*. Rockford, IL: TAN Books, 1980.

Keller, Werner. *The Bible as History*. Translated by William Neil and B.H. Rasmussen. New York: Bantam Books, 1980.

Kevane, Eugene, Msgr. *Mary of Nazareth and the Hidden Life of Jesus*. Washington, NJ: AMI Press, 1989.

Klinkhammer, Karl J., S.J. *Where Did the Rosary Come From?* Translated by Rev. A.R. Peile, S.A.C. Melbourne: A.C.T.S. Publications, 1974.

Latourelle, René. *The Miracles of Jesus and the Theology of Miracles*. Translated by Matthew J. O'Connell, Mahwah, NJ: Paulist Press, 1988.

Life of Jesus Christ and Biblical Revelations. From the Visions of Venerable Anne Catherine Emmerich. Recorded by Clemens Brentano. 4 vols. Rockford, IL: TAN Books, 1979.

Life of Mary as Seen by the Mystics. Compiled by Raphael Brown. Rockford, IL: TAN Books, 1991.

Liguori, Saint Alphonsus de. *Glories of Mary*. Brooklyn, NY: Redemptorist Fathers, 1931.

Lord, Bob and Penny. *The Rosary, The Life of Jesus and Mary*. Fair Oaks, CA: Journeys of Faith, 1993.

Lucia, Sr. Mary of the Immaculate Heart. *Fatima in Lucia's Own Words*. Edited by Fr. Louis Kondor, SVD. Postulation Centre: Fatima, Portugal, 1976.

Marcucci, Domenico. *Through the Rosary with Fra Angelico*. New York: Alba House, 1989.

Meditations on Mary. Edited by Viking Studio. Essays by Kathleen Norris. New York: Penguin Group, 1999.

Monk, A Trappist. *Father Peyton's Rosary Prayer Book*. Dublin: Veritas Publications, 1991.

Montfort, Saint Louis de. *Secret of the Rosary*. Translated by Mary Barbour. Bay Shore, NY: Montfort Publications, 1954.

————, *True Devotion to Mary*. Translated by Fr. Frederick Faber. Rockford, IL: TAN Books, 1941.

Morison, Frank. *Who Moved the Stone?* London: Faber and Faber, 1966.

Most, William G. *Vatican II Marian Council.* Athlone, Ireland: St. Paul Publications, 1972.

National Conference of Catholic Bishops. *Behold Your Mother, Woman of Faith: A Pastoral Letter on the Blessed Virgin Mary.* Washington, DC: U.S. Catholic Conference, November 21, 1973.

Nelson's Complete Book of Bible Maps and Charts. Nashville, TN: Thomas Nelson, 1993.

Nelson's Illustrated Encyclopedia of Bible Facts. Edited by James I. Packer, *et al.* Nashville, TN: Thomas Nelson, 1995.

New American Bible. Translated by Catholic Biblical Association of America, Washington, DC: The Catholic Press, 1970.

New Catholic Commentary on Holy Scripture. Edited by R.O.C. Fuller. London: Thomas Nelson and Sons, 1969.

New Catholic Encyclopedia. Edited by Catholic University of America. New York: McGraw Hill, 1967.

Norris, Kathleen. *Meditations on Mary.*

O'Brien, Isidore, O.F.M. *The Drama of the Rosary.* Paterson, NJ: St. Anthony Guild, 1948.

O'Brien, Michael. *The Mysteries of the Most Holy Rosary.* Ottawa, Canada: White Horse Press, 1992, 1994.

O'Carroll, Michael, C.S.Sp. *Theotokos: A Theological Encyclopedia of the Blessed Virgin Mary.* Wilmington, DE: Liturgical Press, 1982.

O'Malley, William J. *Matthew, Mark, Luke & You.* Allen, TX: Thomas More, 1996.

Oxford Bible Atlas. Edited by Herbert G. May. New York: Oxford University Press, 1984.

Paul VI (Pope). *Dogmatic Constitution on the Church (Lumen Gentium)*, 1964.

Pennington, M. Basil, O.C.S.O. *The Fifteen Mysteries in Image and Word.* Huntington, IN: Our Sunday Visitor, 1993.

——, *Praying by Hand, Rediscovering the Rosary as a Way of Prayer.* New York: Harper San Francisco, 1991.

Pius XII (Pope). *Munificentissimus Deus.* Apostolic Constitution, 1950.

Plato. *The Republic.* Jowett translation. New York: Vintage Books, 1991.

Porter, J.R.. *Jesus Christ: The Jesus of History, the Christ of Faith.* New York: Oxford University Press, 1999.

Proctor, J. Very Rev., S.T.L. *The Rosary Guide.* New York: Benziger Bros., 1901.

Rasmussen, Carl G. *Zondervan NIV Atlas of the Bible.* Grand Rapids, MI: Zondervan Publishing, 1989.

Reader's Digest Atlas of the Bible. Edited by Joseph L. Gardner. Pleasantville, NY: Reader's Digest Assn, 1981.

Rosage, David E. *Praying the Scriptural Rosary.* Ann Arbor, MI: Servant Publications, 1989.

Schwertner, Thomas. *The Rosary, A Social Remedy.* Milwaukee: Bruce Publishing, 1952.

Shamon, Albert J.M., Rev. *A Graphic Life of Jesus the Christ*. Milford, OH: Riehle Foundation, 1996.

———, *The Power of the Rosary*. Milford, OH: Riehle Foundation, 1990.

Shaw, J.G. *The Story of the Rosary*. Milwaukee: Bruce Publishing, 1954.

Sheed, F.J. *To Know Christ Jesus*. New York: Sheed and Ward, 1962.

Sheen, Fulton J. *Life of Christ*. New York: McGraw-Hill, 1958.

Sheler, Jeffery L. *Is the Bible True?* New York: HarperCollins, 1999.

Suarez, Federico. *The Afterlife, Death, Judgment, Heaven, and Hell*. Manila: Sinag-Tala Publishers, 1986.

Tazewell, Charles. *The Littlest Angel*. Nashville, TN: Ideals Children's Books, 1946.

Thornton, Francis B., Rev. *This is the Rosary*. New York: Hawthorn Books, 1961.

Trochu, Francis. *Saint Bernadette Soubirous*. Translated by John Joyce, S.J. New York: Pantheon Books, 1957.

Unger, Merrill F. *The New Unger's Bible Handbook*. Chicago: Moody Press, 1984.

Walker, Winifred. *All the Plants of the Bible*. Garden City, NY: Doubleday & Co., 1979.

Walls, Roland, Father. *The Royal Mysteries of the Rosary, Scriptural Meditations on the Life of Jesus from Jordan to Jerusalem*. Ann Arbor, MI: Servant Publications, 1993.

Ward, Maisie. *The Splendor of the Rosary*. New York: Sheed and Ward, 1945.

Who's Who in the Bible. Edited by Gardner Associates. Pleasantville, NY: Reader's Digest Assn, 1994.

Willam, Franz M., Rev. *The Rosary in Daily Life*. New York: Benziger Bros., 1953.

———, *The Rosary: Its History and Meaning*. Translated by Edwin Kaiser, C.PP.S., New York: Benziger Bros., 1952.

Wilson, Ian. *The Shroud of Turin*. Garden City, NY: Doubleday & Co., 1978.

Yamauchi, Edwin M. *Persia and the Bible*. Grand Rapids, MI: Baker Book House, 1990.

Zugibe, Frederick T. *The Cross and the Shroud*. New York: Paragon House, 1988.

VIDEOS

A.D. Vincenzo Labella. Muskegon, MI: Gospel Films, Inc., 1985. 3 cassettes.

The Gospel According to Luke. Washington, DC: The Genesis Project, 4 cassettes. 1977, 79.

How Jesus Died: the final 18 hours. Trinity Pictures, 1994.

In Pursuit of the Shroud. The Learning Channel (Discovery Communications), 1998.

Jesus and His Times. Pleasantville, NY: The Reader's Digest Association, 1991. 3 cassettes.

Jesus of Nazareth. Zeffirelli, Franco. Livonia, MI: CBS/FOX Video, 1986. 3 cassettes.

The Life of Christ. Hollywood, CA: Family Theater Productions, 1963. 3 cassettes.

VIDEOS (cont'd)

Mysterious Man of the Shroud. CBS Video, 1996.

The Passion According to Saint Luke. Beaverton, OR: Saint Luke Productions, 1987.

Passion in Jerusalem: The Easter Story. Worcester, PA: Gateway Films/Vision Video, 1987.

The Silent Witness. Rolfe, David W. Santa Monica, CA: Pyramid Home Video, 1992.

The Temple at Jerusalem. Chosen People Ministries. New York: Doko Communications, 1988.

This Land of God. Danville, CA: Holy Land Video Tours, 1986.

About the Author

James L. Carney is an honors graduate of Spring Hill College, a Jesuit college in Mobile, Alabama, and a graduate of Harvard Law School. He was an assistant professor of law at the University of Oregon School of Law and, prior to that, taught law at Northwestern School of Law at Lewis and Clark College in Portland, Oregon.

He has taught high school religious education and Confirmation classes, as well as adult religious education, for many years. He was invited to present his award-winning essay, "Just War Traditions in the Nuclear Age,"[1] to the U.S. Army Chaplains School.

Other Books by James L. Carney

The Seton Miracles, Weeping Statues and Other Wonders. This is an account of the most extensive and dramatic episode of weeping statues and similar supernatural phenomena in the history of the Church.

It began on Thanksgiving Day in 1991 at the home of the parents of a humble young priest, Father James Bruse, in Stafford, Virginia. A month later, Father Bruse received stigmata wounds in his wrists, feet and side. At the time, Father Bruse was Associate Pastor at Saint Elizabeth Ann Seton Catholic Church in Lake Ridge, Virginia, a suburb of Washington, DC.

Before it effectively ended in 1993, hundreds of statues, crucifixes, and pictures had wept tears, sometimes of blood, in the presence of thousands of witnesses. Some statues of the Blessed Virgin Mary added or rotated colors. Statues were reported to be animated in some instances and numerous rosaries changed color after Father Bruse had blessed them. Other people reported the "miracle of the sun" or the inexplicable and powerful fragrance of roses. Miraculous healings were claimed.

With 14 beautiful, full-color photos, mostly 8" x 10", this is a book to challenge those who say that there is no evidence for the existence of God and that reports of such divine intervention cannot withstand scientific scrutiny.

The book is available from the Marian Foundation, P.O. Box 2589, Woodbridge, Virginia 22193-2589 (Telephone: 703-491-1563) for $14.95 plus applicable sales tax and $3.00 for shipping. See the Foundation's Website at www.pwcweb.com/marian for further information. It may also be ordered from www.Amazon.com.

---

[1]Published under the title, "Is It Ever Moral to Push the Button?" in *The Parameters of Military Ethics*, ed. Matthews & Brown (Washington: Pergamon-Brassey's, 1989), 39.

ORDER FORM

Additional copies of *Mystery Stories: A Journey Through the Rosary* may be obtained directly from the publisher. Send your order to:

Crown of Mary Publishing Company,
ATTN: Books,
P.O. Box 259237,
Madison, WI 53725-9237
Tel: 608-270-1266   FAX: 608-270-1267

Number of books: _____

Times: ____$24.95

TOTAL: _____

Plus sales tax ($1.35 per book)
if Wisconsin shipping address: _____

Plus shipping (U.S. only) @ $4.00 for one book
plus $1.00 for each additional book in the
same order: _____

TOTAL: _____

Name: _____

Address:_____

City:_____State:_____ Zip:_____

Telephone:_____

E-mail address:_____

Payment: ❒   Check

❒   Credit Card: ❒   Visa   ❒   MasterCard

Card Number: _____

Name on Card:_____ Exp. Date: _____/_____